Frommer's 96

Bermuda

**by Darwin Porter
& Danforth Prince**

D0109922

Macmillan • USA

ABOUT THE AUTHORS

A native of North Carolina, **Darwin Porter** was a bureau chief for the *Miami Herald* when he was 21, and later worked in television advertising. A veteran travel writer, he is the author of numerous bestselling Frommer guides, notably to England, France, Germany, Italy, and the Caribbean. When not traveling (which is rare), he lives in Georgia. Working with Darwin is **Danforth Prince,** formerly of the Paris bureau of the *New York Times.*

MACMILLAN TRAVEL

A Simon & Schuster Macmillan Company
1633 Broadway
New York, NY 10019

Copyright © 1995 by Simon & Schuster, Inc.

ISBN 0-02-860650-7
ISSN 1069-3572

Editor: Yvonne Honigsberg
Map Editor: Douglas Stallings
Design by Michele Laseau
Digital Cartography by Ortelius Design

SPECIAL SALES

Bulk Purchases (10+ copies) of Frommer's travel guides are available to corporations at special discounts. The Special Sales Department can produce custom editions to be used as premiums and/or for sales promotion to suit individual needs. Existing editions can be produced with custom cover imprints such as corporate logos. For more information write to: Special Sales, Simon & Schuster, 1230 Avenue of the Americas, New York, NY 10020.

Manufactured in the United States of America

Contents

1 The Best of Bermuda 1

1 The Best Beaches 1

2 The Best Dive Sites 2

3 The Best Outdoor Activities 3

4 The Best Views 4

5 The Best Places to Discover Old Bermuda 4

6 The Best Honeymoon Resorts 5

7 The Best Restaurants 6

2 Getting to Know Bermuda 8

1 The Lay of the Land 8

★ *What's Special About Bermuda* 9

2 The Natural Environment 11

3 Bermuda Today 14

★ *Bermuda Shorts* 15

4 A Look at the Past 17

★ *Dateline* 17

★ *The Bermuda Triangle* 18

5 Local Art 21

6 Bermuda Style 22

7 The Music of the Islands 24

8 Bermudian Cuisine 25

3 Before You Go 29

1 Visitor Information, Entry Requirements & Money 29

★ *What Things Cost in Bermuda* 35

2 When to Go 36

★ *Bermuda Calendar of Events* 37

3 Weddings & Honeymoons in Bermuda 39

★ *Wedding-Cake Traditions* 40

4 Spa Vacations 40

5 Home Exchanges 41

6 Health & Insurance 41

7 Tips for Travelers with Disabilities, Seniors,
Singles & Families 43

4 Arriving in Bermuda 46

1 Getting There 46

2 Orientation 53

3 Getting Around 57

★ *Island Hopping on Your Own* 59

4 Tips on Accommodations 61

5 Tips on Dining 62

6 Tips on Shopping 62

★ *Fast Facts: Bermuda* 63

5 Accommodations 70

1 Resort Hotels 71

★ *Family-Friendly Hotels* 76

★ *Hotels of Bermuda at a Glance* 78

2 Small Hotels 84

3 Cottage Colonies 89

4 Housekeeping Units 92

5 Guesthouses 97

6 Dining 101

1 City of Hamilton 101

2 Paget Parish 112

★ *Family-Friendly Restaurants* 114

3 Warwick Parish 114

4 Southampton Parish 115

5 Sandys Parish 118

6 St. George's Parish 121

7 Hamilton Parish 125

8 Smith's Parish 126

9 Afternoon Tea & Sunday Brunch 127

10 Fast Food & Picnic Fare 127

7 What to See & Do 130

★ *Did You Know?* 131

★ *Suggested Itineraries* 132

1 The Top Attractions 133

2 St. George's Parish 134

3 Hamilton Parish 141

4 Smith's Parish 142

★ *For Spelunkers* 143

5 Devonshire Parish 144

★ *Nature Reserves* 144

6 Pembroke Parish (City of Hamilton) 145

7 Paget Parish 149

8 Warwick Parish 150

9 Southampton Parish 150

10 Sandys Parish 151

11 Ireland Island 152

★ *Bermuda's Luckiest Treasure Hunter* 153

12 Especially for Kids 154

13 Special-Interest Sightseeing 155

★ *Frommer's Favorite Bermuda Experiences* 156

14 Organized Tours 157

8   Walking Tours   159

1 City of Hamilton 159

2 Historic St. George's Town 163

★ *The Bermuda Railway Trail* 167

3 Sandys Parish 167

9   Beaches, Water Sports & Other Outdoor Activities   171

1 Spectator Sports 171

2 Beaches & Outdoor Activities 173

★ *Bird-Watching* 177

★ *Helmet Diving* 186

10   Shopping   188

1 The Shopping Scene 188

2 Hamilton Shopping A to Z 189

3 Shops Around the Island 199

11   Bermuda After Dark   202

1 Cultural Entertainment 202

★ *The Hollywood Connection* 203

2 The Club & Music Scene 203

3 The Bar Scene 205

Index   208

List of Maps

Bermuda Accommodations   74–75

Hamilton Accommodations &
   Dining   81

Bermuda Dining   104–105

St. George's Dining   123

Bermuda Attractions   138–139

Bermuda Walking Tours
   City of Hamilton   161
   Historic St. George's Town   165
   Sandys Parish   169

Ten Best Public Beaches   174–175

Hamilton Shops   191

INVITATION TO THE READER

In researching this book, we discovered many wonderful places—hotels, restaurants, shops, and more. We're sure you'll find others. Please tell us about them, so we can share the information with your fellow travelers in upcoming editions. If you were disappointed with a recommendation, we'd love to know that, too. Please write to:

Darwin Porter/Danforth Prince
Frommer's Bermuda '96
Macmillan Travel
1633 Broadway
New York, NY 10019

AN ADDITIONAL NOTE

Please be advised that travel information is subject to change at any time—and this is especially true of prices. We therefore suggest that you write or call ahead for confirmation when making your travel plans. The authors, editors, and publisher cannot be held responsible for the experiences of readers while traveling. Your safety is important to us, however, so we encourage you to stay alert and be aware of your surroundings. Keep a close eye on cameras, purses, and wallets, all favorite targets of thieves and pickpockets.

WHAT THE SYMBOLS MEAN

✪ Frommer's Favorites

Hotels, restaurants, attractions, and entertainment you should not miss.

⑤ Super-Special Values

Hotels and restaurants that offer great value for your money.

The following abbreviations are used for credit cards:

AE	American Express	EU	Eurocard
CB	Carte Blanche	JCB	Japan Credit Bank
DC	Diners Club	MC	MasterCard
DISC	Discover	V	Visa

The Best of Bermuda

You've come to Bermuda to relax—not to exhaust yourself searching for the best deals and most eclectic experiences. With this guide in hand, you can spend your vacation in peace and let us do the work. Below you'll find our carefully compiled lists of the islands' superlative beaches, dive sites, restaurants, sports, sightseeing, and nearly anything else your heart might desire.

1 The Best Beaches

One of your first priorities on your Bermuda vacation will be to lounge on the beach. But which beach to choose? Hotels often have their own private beaches, which we've described in each accommodation review to help you choose a place to stay. There are many fine public beaches as well. Here are our picks for the top 10, arranged clockwise around the island, beginning with the south shore beaches closest to the city of Hamilton.

- **Elbow Beach.** Pale pink sand stretches almost a mile at Paget Parish's Elbow Beach, one of the most consistently popular beaches in Bermuda. At least three hotels have swimming facilities along the beach's perimeter. There's usually a $3 fee imposed for visitors who are not guests of one of these hotels. The beach, because of the protective coral reefs that surround it, is one of the safest on the island. It's packed with college students vacationing on Bermuda during Easter break. The Elbow Beach Hotel/ A Wyndham Resort (☎ 441/236-3535) offers facilities and rentals.
- **Astwood Cove.** In Warwick Parish, at the bottom of a steep and winding road that intersects with South Shore Road, this beach is so remote that it's rarely overcrowded. The trees and shrubbery of Astwood Park provide a verdant backdrop.
- **Warwick Long Bay.** This popular beach features a half-mile stretch of sand, one of the longest on the island. Against a backdrop of scrubland and low grasses, the beach lies on the southern side of South Shore Park, in Warwick Parish. Despite the frequent winds, the waves are surprisingly small because of an offshore reef. Less than 200 feet offshore a jagged coral island appears to float above the water.

- **Chaplin Bay.** At the southern extremity of South Shore Park, straddling the boundary between Warwick and Southampton Parish, this small but secluded beach almost completely disappears during storms or particularly high tides. An open-air coral barrier partially separates one half of the beach from the other.
- **Horseshoe Bay Beach.** This is Bermuda's most famous beach. It's at Horseshoe Bay, South Shore Road, Southampton Parish, where the Beach House (☎ 441/ 238-2651) offers complete facilities, including rental equipment, for beachgoers.
- **Church Bay.** If you like to snorkel, this is the beach for you. The relatively calm waters, sheltered by offshore reefs, harbor a variety of marine life. Sunbathers love to nestle within the beach's unusually deep pink sands.
- **Somerset Long Bay.** The waters off this beach are often unsafe for swimming, but its isolation will appeal to anyone looking to escape from the madding crowd. The undeveloped parkland of Sandys Parish shelters it from the rest of the island, and the beach's long length—about a quarter-mile of crescent-shaped sand—is unusual by Bermudian standards. It's ideal for beach-walking.
- **Shelly Bay Beach.** On the north shore of Hamilton Parish, you'll discover calm waters and soft pink sand.
- **Tobacco Bay Beach.** A popular stretch of pale pink sand, this is the most popular beach on St. George's Island, offering lots of facilities.
- **John Smith's Bay.** The only public beach within Smith's Parish. Long, flat, and boasting the pale pink sand for which the south shore is famous, this beach usually has a warm-weather lifeguard—a plus for boating families with children. Toilet and changing facilities are on site.

2 The Best Dive Sites

The following are some of the most exciting shipwreck and coral reef dives.

- **The *Marie Celeste*.** A Paddlewheeler that sank in 1964. Its 15-foot diameter paddlewheel, located off the southern portion of the island, is overgrown with coral standing about 55 feet off the ocean floor.
- **The *North Carolina*.** One of Bermuda's most colorful wrecks, this English sailing barque shipwrecked in 1879 and today lies in about 40 feet of water off the western portion of the island.
- **Tarpon Hole.** A coral reef dive located near Elbow Beach off the south shore.
- **South West Breaker.** A coral reef dive located off the south shore about 1 1/2 miles off Church Bay. Hard and soft coral decorate these sheet walls in depths of 20 to 30 feet.
- **L'Hermanie.** This first-class 60-gun French frigate was 17 days out of its Cuban port and heading back when it sank in 1838. The ship lies in 20 to 30 feet of water off the western portion of the island with 25 cannons still visible.
- **The *Hermes*.** This 165-foot steamer ship about one mile off Warwick Long Bay on the South Shore, shipwrecked in 1985, lies in about 80 feet of water.
- **The *Rita Zovetta*.** A 360-foot Italian cargo ship, located in about 20 to 70 feet of water off the southern portion of the island, ran aground off St. David's Island in 1924.
- **The *Tauton*.** This British Royal Mail steamer sank in 1914 and lies in 10 to 40 feet of water off the northern end of the island.
- **The *Constellation*.** Off the northwestern portion of the island, about eight miles west of Dockyard, this 200-foot, four-masted shipwrecked schooner lies

in 30 feet of water. It never reached Venezuela in 1943 and later became the inspiration for Peter Benchley's book *The Deep*.

- **The *Cristóbal Colón*.** This 480-foot Spanish luxury liner is the largest known shipwreck in Bermuda, having run aground in 1936 on a northern reef between North Rock and North Breaker. It lies in 30 to 55 feet of water.

3 The Best Outdoor Activities

Sports, fitness, and beaches are what Bermuda is all about. Any one of the activities below would be reason enough to visit.

- **Golfing.** Known for its outstanding golf courses, Bermuda attracts the world's leading golfers and those who'd like to be. In the past these have included such luminaries as President Eisenhower, President Truman, and the Duke of Windsor. Rolling, hummocky fairways characterize the greens. Many avid golfers come to Bermuda to play all the courses; they call this "collecting courses." Some holes are from hell, as golfers say. That includes Port Royal's notorious 16th hole. Both the tee and the hole are placed high on cliff edges with the rich blue water looming a dizzying 100 feet below.

- **Boating and Sailing.** As yachties around the world agree, Bermuda is in the premier class for this pastime. With the fresh wind of the Atlantic blowing in your hair, you can set out upon your own voyage of discovery, perhaps sailing Great Sound with its tiny islets that take in Long Island and Hawkins Island. Tiny secluded beaches beckon frequently. Many people forget that Bermuda is not just one island, but a series of islands—an archipelago, really—waiting to be discovered. A novice at sailing? Try Mangrove Bay; it's protected and safer than some of the more turbulent seas.

- **Bicycling.** Since island law forbids you to rent a car, you might as well take up bicycling, even if you haven't been on two wheels since you were a kid. Let's be honest: Bermuda isn't the world's greatest cycling terrain. If you don't want to face narrow roads and heavy traffic, opt instead for the Railway Trail, the island's premier cycling route. The paved trail runs the route of the long-deserted railway line, almost the entire length of Bermuda. It's a paradise for cyclists.

- **Horseback Riding.** Because this sport is so restricted and limited it's all the more memorable. Taking a horse through the dune grass and oleander of the island, especially at South Shore Park, is an experience you won't want to miss. As you ride along beaches looking out over coral bluffs, you and your fellow riders may agree it isn't Kentucky, but what it is, isn't bad. Horseback riding centers will guide you on trail rides through not only the best of the Bermudian countryside, but also to beautiful hidden spots along the north coast.

- **Diving.** Whatever is demanded on the scuba calendar, Bermuda has it. That means wreckage of countless ships that went aground in storm-tossed seas, underwater caves, coral and marine life almost unequaled in its part of the world, more reefs than most divers will ever see, and, for most of the year, warm, gin-clear waters. Many scuba experts cite Bermuda as one of the safest and best places to learn this sport. One scuba expert over a period of time explored the wrecks of nearly 40 ships, all of which were said to be in "good condition," although there may be more than 300 wreck sites in all. Depths begin at 25 feet or less, but can go up to 80 feet or more. Some wrecks are in about 30 feet of water, which would even put them within the range of snorkelers.

4 The Best Views

There is a 1950s play called *I Am a Camera,* and that is how you'll feel as you stroll about Bermuda: It's a shutterbug's delight, with panoramas and vistas unfolding at nearly every turn. But some views are more spectacular than others.

- **Warwick Long Bay.** The longest stretch of pristine pink sand in Bermuda—stretching for half a mile or so—makes this a dream beach of the picture-postcard variety. This much-photographed beach is set against a backdrop of towering cliffs and hills studded with Spanish bayonet and oleander. A 20-foot coral outcrop, rising some 200 feet offshore, resembles a sculpted boulder, and adds even more variety to this beachscape.
- **Fort Scaur.** From Somerset Bridge in Sandys Parish, head for this fort atop the highest hill in the parish. Walk the fort's ramparts, enjoying the vistas across Great Sound to Spanish Point. You can also gaze south to the dockyard to take in the fine view of Somerset Island. On a clear day, a look through the telescope will reveal St. David's Lighthouse, some 14 miles away on the northeastern tip of the island. After taking in the fantastic view from the fort, stroll through the 22 acres of beautiful gardens.
- **The Queen's View.** At Gibb's Hill Lighthouse in Southampton Parish, a plaque designates the spot where Queen Elizabeth II paused on November of 1953 to take in the view of Little Sound. The same view that impressed Her Majesty so long ago is still there to admire today. You can look out at Riddell's Bay Golf Course and Perot's Island. (Although Ross Perot has a home in Bermuda, the island is *not* named for him, but for the father of William Bennett Perot, Bermuda's first postmaster.)
- **Gibb's Hill Lighthouse.** For an even greater view than that which greeted Queen Elizabeth II, climb the 185 spiral steps of the lighthouse itself, one of the oldest cast-iron lighthouses in the world, dating from 1846. At the top you can take in what islanders regard as the single finest view in all of Bermuda. You can, that is, if the wind doesn't blow you away. Hang on to the railing. In heavy winds, the tower actually sways in space and you may retreat on certain days regardless of the view.

5 The Best Places to Discover Old Bermuda

Much of Bermuda is modern, but its history dates back to the arrival of its first settlers in 1609. The following places provide insights—often maritime—into the old way of life, now largely gone with the wind.

- **The Back Streets of St. George's.** The 17th-century stocks on Kings Square in historic St. George's have been photographed by virtually every tourist who's been to the island. But it is in the narrow cobblestoned lanes such as Shinbone Alley and the back streets and alleyways that you can recapture the old spirit of this town. Arm yourself with a good map and wander at leisure through such places as Silk Alley (also called Petticoat Lane); Barber's Lane Alley (named for a former slave from South Carolina); Printer's Alley (where Bermuda's first newspaper was published); and Nea's Alley (former stomping ground of the Irish poet, Tom Moore). Finally, walk through Somers Garden and head up the steps to Blockade Alley. On the hill lies the so-called Unfinished Church.

- **The Royal Dockyard.** Nothing recaptures the maritime spirit of this little island nation more than this sprawling complex of several attractions on Ireland Island. Beginning in 1809, Britain began constructing this dockyard, perhaps fearing attacks on its fleet from warmongering Napoleón or from pirates. Convicts and slaves, many of whom died in the construction, created a shipyard for the Royal Navy that was to last for almost 150 years. It closed in 1951. The Royal Navy is mostly gone today, but in the Maritime Museum and other exhibits, a largely vanished era comes back again.
- **St. David's Island.** Much of Bermuda looks pristine and proper, its old way of life largely replaced with pretty pink cottages and tourist hotels. If there's any rustic maritime life still left that's not in a museum, it's on St. David's. Some islanders never bother to even visit neighboring St. George's. To some locals, the west end of Bermuda would be like a walk on the moon. St. David's Lighthouse is a local landmark from 1879. To see how people used to really eat and cook, you can drop in at Dennis's Hideaway. Dennis Lamb personifies the eccentric nature of St. David islanders, and his grubby place, with its mussel stew, conch steak, conch fritters, and shark hash, will let you know how Bermudians used to eat before all that New York strip steak started arriving by plane.
- **Verdmont.** Bermuda is filled with historic homes, but none finer or more historic than Verdmont, dating from 1710. It was built by John Dickinson, a prosperous shipowner of his day. At the end of the Revolutionary War, it also sheltered the American Loyalist, John Green, who fled to Bermuda from Philadelphia. This place is a virtual treasure trove of Bermudiana. Many of the furnishings were crafted from the rare Bermuda cedar by cabinetmakers of the day. The last occupant was considered eccentric: she lived there for three quarters of a century, refusing electricity or "any other modern gadgets."

6 The Best Honeymoon Resorts

Bermuda has long been one of the world's favorite destinations for honeymooners, offering peace, solitude, and seclusion. Apparently all those honeymoon packages offered by hotels, ranging from deluxe resorts to guest houses, seem to work, as Bermuda is also a favorite vacation spot for couples on their second honeymoon.

Although some couples on their honeymoon prefer to seek out the small housekeeping cottages and guest houses, most honeymooners prefer one of the packages offered by the splashy resort hotels. A travel agent will help you secure the best deal (so you'll have a shot at having some money left when you return home). The following resorts are not only the best choices in Bermuda for a honeymoon, but they feature some of the best inclusive deals as well.

- **Elbow Beach Hotel/A Wyndham Resort.** This hotel promises "marriages made in heaven." Its "Romance Packages" include daily breakfasts and a romantic candlelit dinner for two in your room on the first night. The staff even offers the Elbow Beach Cookbook for the new bride (or groom, as the case may be) when the loving couples return home. Contact the hotel at ☎ 441/236-3535 or 800/882-4200 in the U.S.
- **Marriott's Castle Harbour Resort.** The island's largest beach resort might be an oasis for a perfect honeymoon, as it offers plenty of seclusion for couples when they want it, while providing a range of activities and tours when they tire of the bedroom. The staff here offers five honeymoon packages with an array

of offerings that include a champagne breakfast in your room the first day, parasailing rides, gourmet dinners for two, and moped rentals. Call ☎ 441/293-2040 or 800/223-6388 in the U.S. and Canada.

- **Grotto Bay Beach.** This resort aggressively pursues the honeymoon market, featuring everything from midnight swims at a private beach to rooms that are cozy lovers' nests, with private balconies overlooking the ocean. Champagne, fruit, and flowers are just some of the extras featured in its honeymoon packages, including romantic dinners, with lots of cruises and walking tours arranged. Call ☎ 441/293-8333 or 800/582-3190 in the U.S.

- **Sonesta Beach Hotel & Spa.** The champagne's in your room chilling and awaiting your arrival. To make it even more romantic, the staff will include a horse and buggy ride in the old Bermuda style, although the next day they'll give you a motorized scooter. The sports director will also offer one free tennis or scuba lesson. Countless couples prefer the location of this hotel, right on the beach. There's also a fully equipped, professionally staffed health spa. Honeymooners dance to live entertainment at the Boat Bay Club and Lounge, with its views of moonlit Boat Bay. For reservations, call ☎ 441/238-8122 or 800/766-3782 in the U.S.

- **Southampton Princess Hotel.** The Southampton Princess does everything it can to entice honeymooners seeking seclusion. Its honeymoon packages, which start at four days and three nights, include breakfast and dinner on a MAP "dine around plan," a bottle of champagne, a basket of fruit, even a special occasion cake, plus a souvenir photo and watercolor print by a local artist, and admission to the exercise club. For details, call ☎ 441/238-8000, 800/223-1818 in the U.S., or 800/268-7176 in Canada.

7 The Best Restaurants

Admittedly, cuisine is not the reason you came to Bermuda in the first place, but there are some places where you'll have a memorable meal.

- **Once Upon a Table** (city of Hamiliton; ☎ 441/295-8585). Savvy Bermudians, including one critic who has dined "at every single place on the island, even the dives," claim this is the best restaurant on Bermuda. Even if you don't agree, you'll like the atmosphere: a romantic setting of Victorian memorabilia softened with flamboyant flowers.

- **Plantation** (Hamilton Parish; ☎ 441/293-1188). In-the-know locals always refer to this place as "real" Bermudian or "truly" Bermudian. Freshly caught seafood, including the famed Bermuda lobster, dominates the fare. On the site of Leamington Caves, guests are seated at tables with flickering candles inside or in good weather, al fresco in the tropical garden.

- **Waterlot Inn** (Southampton Parish; ☎ 441/238-8000). Housed in a historic inn and warehouse on the grounds of the Southampton Princess, this place is the most famous venue for Sunday brunch on the island, but it's also an ideal choice for dinner. Everybody from Eleanor Roosevelt to Mark Twain has praised the French cuisine here, sampling such dishes as poached chicken breast stuffed with foie gras.

- **Newport Room** (Southampton Parish; ☎ 441/238-8000). Also part of the Southampton Princess complex, this nautically decorated restaurant attracts the elite, especially yachties. The glistening teak makes it the most expensively decorated restaurant in Bermuda. Its French cuisine lives up to the decor. The rack of lamb with a mixed nut crust is the stuff of which memories are made.

- **Tom Moore's Tavern** (Hamilton Parish; ☎ 441/293-8020). In a home dating from 1652, this restaurant overlooks Bailey's Bay. The Irish poet Tom Moore was said to be a frequent visitor. The menu, however, is not a relic from the past—it's quite innovative. Duck is a specialty, as is Bermuda lobster, but who can forget the quail in puff pastry stuffed with foie gras?
- **Fourways Inn** (Paget Parish; ☎ 441/236-6517). In this 1700s Georgian house of cedar and coral stone, you'll dine as they did back in the days of plantation owners with their crystal, silver, and china. While listening to the best piano music on the island, introduce yourself to a bowl of Bermudian fish chowder, followed by a choice of French or Bermudian dishes.
- **Henry VIII** (Southampton Parish; ☎ 441/238-1977). Its mock Tudor decor is a bit corny, but sometimes you want some fun with dinner, and you'll find it here. In spite of the decor the food is really good, as you get your fill of mussel pie (available sometimes) and such old pub favorites as steak-and-kidney pie. Some diners actually manage to "tuck in" desserts like bananas flambé in dark mellow rum.
- **Lantana Colony Club Restaurant** (Sandys Parish ☎ 441/234-0141). At the western tip of the island, this enclave of elegance and grace fusses over its guests and presents them with a frequently changing continental menu. French classical cuisine is impeccably served, and there's a wine cellar worthy of the menu. Wahoo with orange peppercorn sauce is something to write home about.
- **Lobster Pot and Boat House Bar** (city of Hamilton; ☎ 441/292-6898). If you don't find the most food-savvy islanders at the places above, they'll surely be at this local favorite. Against the backdrop of a nautical decor, the island's best regional dishes will delight you here. Black rum and sherry peppers might be the secret ingredients of their fish chowder, and they keep tempting tastebuds with their baked fish and lobster.
- **Black Horse Tavern** (St. David's Island; ☎ 441/293-9742). When you crave hearty food that's good and plentiful, and an atmosphere that's casual, you go here. Islanders fill up most of the tables at night ordering their favorite dishes—everything from shark hash to curried conch.

2 Getting to Know Bermuda

Only about two hours from the southeastern coastline of the United States, another, quite different world comes into view as you approach it from the air. It is a world of natural beauty, with lush green hills, crystalline blue waters, and pink-hued sandy beaches. It is also a world of striking incongruities, where the modern coexists in harmony with the traditional and even the antiquated. That world is the British crown colony of Bermuda, an island in the Atlantic Ocean about 570 miles ESE of Cape Hatteras, N.C.

In Hamilton, the capital, you'll see colorful horse-drawn carriages ambling through tree-lined streets, indifferent to the sleek foreign cars that pass by. You'll see "bobbies" and businessmen walking around in shorts and knee-high socks—normal attire in this semitropical island where the annual average temperature is 70°F. You'll even see judges still wearing their customary powdered wigs as they head to Sessions House (the Parliament Building), where the Supreme Court meets.

Such a blend of contrasts—evident also in the island's architecture, music, and cuisine—gives Bermuda its character and makes it an enchanting place to visit. With its large luxury hotels, fashionable shops, and evening entertainment—as well as its beaches and historical sites—Bermuda is one of the world's most popular resorts.

1 The Lay of the Land

"Bermuda" is actually a group of some 300 islands, islets, and coral rocks, clustered in a fishhook-shaped chain about 22 miles long and 2 miles wide at the broadest point. Together, they're known as the Bermudas and form a landmass of about 21 square miles. Only 20 or so of the islands are inhabited. The largest one, called the "mainland," is Great Bermuda; about 14 miles long, it's linked to the other major islands near it by a series of bridges and causeways. The capital of this archipelago, Hamilton, is situated on the mainland.

The other islands bear such names as Somerset, Watford, Boaz, and Ireland in the west, and St. George's and St. David's in the east. This chain of islands encloses the archipelago's major bodies of water, which include Castle Harbour, St. George's Harbour, Harrington Sound, and Great Sound. Most of the other smaller islands, or islets, lie within these bodies of water.

What's Special About Bermuda

Beaches
- Elbow Beach, Paget, which some say made Bermuda a vacation legend—it's tops for fun in the sun.
- Horseshoe Bay, Southampton, one-quarter mile of pink sands—this is the beach that often appears in those Sunday travel supplements.
- Warwick Long Bay, the pinkest of the pink sandy beaches, and also the sun strip containing the longest stretch of sands.

Great Towns/Villages
- Hamilton, the colony's capital, in pretty pastels and whites and the center for shopping.
- St. George's, Bermuda's first capital, founded in 1612—a town filled with historical sights.

Places to Explore
- Ireland Island, a cruise-ship dock and tourist village, site of the Royal Naval Dockyard and the Bermuda Maritime Museum.
- Bermuda Railway Trail, stretching along the old train right-of-way for 21 miles and crossing three islands that make up the Bermuda archipelago.
- Fort St. Catherine, at St.George's—now a museum—towers over the beach where the shipwrecked *Sea Venture* crew first landed in 1609.
- Verdmont, Smith's Parish, an 18th-century mansion built on land once owned by the founder of South Carolina.
- Fort Hamilton, a massive Victorian fortification overlooking the city of Hamilton and its harbor.

Natural Spectacles
- Crystal Caves, Bailey's Bay, translucent formations of stalagmites and stalactites, including a crystal-clear lake.
- Leamington Caves, also at Bailey's Bay, with a grotto with crystal formations and underground lakes—first discovered in 1908.

Events and Festivals
- Bermuda Festival, a six-week winter International Festival of the Performing Arts—drama, dance, jazz, classical and popular music, and more.
- Bermuda College Weeks during the spring break, a ritual that draws some 10,000 students from the United States.

Bermuda lies far north of the Tropic of Cancer, which cuts through the Bahamian archipelago—about 775 miles SE of New York City, some 1,030 miles NE of Miami, and nearly 3,450 miles away from London. It has a balmy climate year-round, with sunshine prevailing almost every day. The chief source of Bermuda's mild weather is the Gulf Stream, a broad belt of warm water formed by equatorial currents, whose northern reaches separate the Bermuda islands from North America and, with the prevailing northeast winds, temper the wintry blasts that sweep across the Atlantic from west and north.

Bermuda is based on the upper parts of an extinct volcano, which may date back 100 million years. Through the millennia, wind and water have brought limestone deposits and formed the islands far from any continental landmass—the closest is Cape Hatteras.

The first, recorded discovery of the islands was made by the Spanish in the early 1500s (see "A Look at the Past," below). The uncharted islands were a navigational menace to ships that followed the trade routes of the Atlantic, as Spanish vessels did on voyages from the New World. Bermuda's location is at a point where galleons from New Spain could easily run into trouble in stormy weather, and the eroded wreckage of many ships, scattered on the ocean floor amid reefs and shoals, bears mute testimony to such tragedies.

Until the mid-17th century or so, the Bermudas were known to seafarers as the "Isles of Devils." They probably had contributed to the popular pre-Columbian belief that ships sailing too far west from Europe fell over the edge of the earth into a monster-filled pit. Many ships sailing too close to these remote and uninhabited islands came to ruin on the treacherous reefs close to the surface of the Atlantic. Even Shakespeare was familiar with the reputation of the Isles of Devils, making "the still-vex't Bermoothes" the setting for *The Tempest*.

THE PARISHES

The islands of Bermuda are divided, for administrative purposes, into several parishes. They are:

SANDYS PARISH In the far-western part of the archipelago, Sandys Parish is centered around Somerset Village. This parish (pronounced *Sands*) takes in the islands of Ireland, Boaz, and Somerset and is named for Sir Edwin Sandys, a major shareholder of the 1610 Bermuda Company. Somerset Long Bay is the biggest and best public beach in Bermuda's west end.

SOUTHAMPTON PARISH Going east, Southampton Parish (named for the third earl of Southampton) stretches from Riddells Bay to Tucker's Island, site of the U.S. Naval Air Station Annex. This parish is split by Middle Road and is known for its public beach stretching along Horseshoe Bay. The parish is the site of such famed resorts as the Southampton Princess.

WARWICK PARISH Named in honor of another shareholder in the Bermuda Company, the second earl of Warwick, this parish lies between Southampton and Paget parishes. Known for its golf courses and hotels, it offers Warwick Long Bay, along the South Shore, one of Bermuda's best public beaches.

PAGET PARISH East of Warwick Parish, Paget Parish begins at Hamilton Harbour in the east and lies directly south of the capital city of Hamilton. Named after the fourth Lord Paget, it has many residences and historic homes. It is also the site of the 36-acre Botanical Gardens.

PEMBROKE PARISH This parish contains the capital city of Hamilton (the only full-fledged city in Bermuda), which is most often viewed as passengers arrive aboard a cruise ship in Hamilton Harbour. Named after the third earl of Pembroke, the parish shelters one-quarter of Bermuda's population.

DEVONSHIRE PARISH Lying east of both Paget and Pembroke parishes, near the geographic center of the archipelago, Devonshire Parish is green and hilly. It has some housekeeping apartments, a cottage colony, and one of Bermuda's oldest churches, the Old Devonshire Parish Church, which dates from 1716. Named for the first earl of Devonshire, the parish can be traversed by three of the major roads of Bermuda—the aptly named South Road, Middle Road, and North Road.

SMITH'S PARISH   Directly east of Devonshire Parish, Smith's Parish opens onto Harrington Sound along its eastern flank. Its northern and southern coasts face the Atlantic. Named after Sir Thomas Smith, another member of the Bermuda Company, the parish takes in Flatts Village, along with two bird sanctuaries.

HAMILTON PARISH   Not to be confused with the city of Hamilton (which is in Pembroke Parish), Hamilton Parish lies directly north of Harrington Sound, opening onto the Atlantic. Named for the second marquis of Hamilton, the parish ropes itself around Harrington Sound, a saltwater lake stretching some six miles. On its eastern periphery, it opens onto Castle Harbour.

ST. GEORGE'S PARISH   In Bermuda's extreme eastern end, this historic parish is composed of several different islands, the largest of which are St. George's Island and St. David's Island. St. George's Island was the site of the *Sea Venture's* wreck in 1609. Its major settlement, St. George's, was founded in 1612 and was once the capital of Bermuda. Filled with historic buildings, it contains St. Peter's Church, the oldest continuously used Protestant house of worship in the Western Hemisphere. The parish is flanked by Castle Harbour on the western and southern edges and divided into two halves by St. George's Harbour. St. David's Island is linked to the rest of Bermuda by the Severn Bridge, which lies near the U.S. Naval Air Station and the country's international airport. The people who inhabit this most easterly part of Bermuda are long-time sailors and fishers. St. George's Parish also includes Tucker's Town, founded in 1616 by Governor Daniel Tucker on the opposite shore of Castle Harbour.

2 The Natural Environment

FLORA

Bermuda's temperate climate, frequent sunshine, and adequate moisture account for some of the most verdant gardens in the Atlantic. Coupled with its fertile soil are the effects of the Gulf Stream, which brings warm air currents to a climate that would otherwise be colder. Bermudian gardeners, in fact, pride themselves on the mixture of temperate-zone and subtropical plants that thrive on the island, despite the salty air.

Bermuda's once proud cedar forests succumbed to the effects of commercialization (many trees were felled for their copper-colored wood, used in boatbuilding) and a disastrous blight that struck in the late 1930s. The loss of the cedar forests is said to have removed valuable nesting sites for birds, as well as some of the island's most effective windbreaks.

Today, those native stands have been replaced on a large scale with casuarinas (Australian pines) and an array of deciduous and evergreen trees and shrubs (an estimated 500 species) imported from the far corners of the British Empire. Recent attempts at reforesting Bermuda with scale-resistant hybrids of the native cedar have proved moderately successful.

Impressions

You go to heaven if you want to—I'd rather stay here in Bermuda.
                    —Mark Twain, in letter to Elizabeth Wallace, 1910

Even soils not noted for their clemency to plants manage to produce gratifying covers of foliage. Examples include the indigenous sea grape, which flourishes along the island's sandy coastlines, preferring sand and salt water to more arable soil, and the cassava plant, whose roots resemble the tubers of sweet potatoes. When ground into flour and soaked to remove a mild poison, these roots comprise the main ingredient for Bermuda's traditional Christmas pies. Also growing wild and abundant are prickly pears, aromatic fennel, yucca, and a spiked-leaf plant bearing, in season, a single white flower, known as a Spanish bayonet.

To the early colonial settlers Bermuda's only native palm, the palmetto, proved particularly useful. Its leaves were used to thatch colonial roofs. When crushed and fermented, the leaves provided a strong alcoholic drink called *bibby*, whose effects were condemned by the early Puritans. Its leaves were also fashioned into women's hats during a brief period in the 1600s, when they represented the height of fashion in London.

The banana, which flourishes today in Bermuda and constitutes one of its most dependable sources of fresh fruit, was introduced to the island in the early 1600s. Bermudian bananas, in fact, are said to have been the first ever brought back to London from the New World. They immediately created a sensation, leading to the cultivation of bananas in many other British colonies.

The plant that probably contributed most to the renown of Bermuda was the Bermuda onion (*Allium cepa*). Imported from England in 1616, and later grown from seed brought from the Spanish and Portuguese islands of Tenerife and Madeira, the Bermuda onion became so famous along the eastern coast of the United States that Bermudians themselves became known as "Onions." Sadly, however, during the 1930s Bermuda's flourishing export trade in onions declined because of high tariffs, increased competition from similar species grown in Texas, among other places, and the lack of arable land on the island.

Today, what you'll see decorating Bermuda's gently rolling landscapes are oleander, hibiscus, royal poinciana, poinsetta, bougainvillea, and dozens of other flowering shrubs and vines. Of the island's dozen or so species of morning glory, three are indigenous; they tend to grow rampant and overwhelm everything else in a garden.

Popular trees include pine, paw-paw (used in olden days for treating warts and fungal diseases of the skin), the indigenous olivewood bark, palm, casuarina, fiddlewood, the ubiquitous bay grape, and a luxuriant fruit tree known as loquat, which was introduced to the island by one of its governors in 1850. Indigenous flowers include the Bermudiana (sometimes known as the Bermuda iris), Darrell's fleabane (a member of the daisy family), and the maidenhair fern. Today, nearly all the important plants of the Bermudian islands are sheltered in the government's Botanical Gardens in Paget Parish.

Impressions

They be so terrible to all that ever touched on them, and such tempests, thunders, and other fearefull objects are seene and heard about them, that they be called commonly, the Devils Ilands, and are feared and avoyded of all sea travellers alive, above any other place in the world.

—William Strachy, *A True Reportory of the Wracke and Redemption of Sir Thomas Gates* (1610), in *Purchas His Pilgrimes* (1625)

FAUNA

Because of the almost total lack of natural freshwater ponds and lakes, Bermuda's amphibians have adapted to seawater or to slightly brackish water. Amphibians include the tree frog (*Eleutherodactylus Johnstonei* and *Eleutherodactylus Gossei*), whose nighttime chirping is sometimes mistaken by newcomers for the song of birds. Small and camouflaged by the leafy matter of the forest floor, the tree frog may be spotted in the warm months between April and November.

More visible are Bermuda's giant toads, or road toads (*Bufo marinus*), which sometimes reach the size of an adult human's palm. Imported from Guyana in the 1870s in the hope of controlling the island's cockroach population, they search out the nighttime warmth of the asphalt roads, and are often crushed by cars in the process; they are especially prevalent after a soaking rain. The road toads are not venomous—and, contrary to legend, they do not cause warts.

Island reptiles include colonies of harmless lizards, often seen sunning themselves on rocks until the approach of humans or predators sends them away. The best-known species is the Bermuda rock lizard (*Eumeces longirostris*), also known as a skink, which is said to have been the only nonmarine, nonflying vertebrate in Bermuda before the arrival of European colonists. Imported reptiles include the Somerset lizard (*Anolis Roquet*), whose black-eye patches give it the look of a bashful bandit, and the Jamaican anole (*Anolis Grahami*), a kind of color-changing chameleon.

Bermuda, partly because of its ample food sources, is home to abundant bird life, many species of which nest upon the island's terrain during annual migration patterns. Most of these birds arrive during the colder winter months, usually between Christmas and Eastertime. The island has recorded almost 40 different species of eastern warblers, which peacefully coexist alongside species of martin, doves, egrets, South American terns, herons, fork-tailed flycatchers, and even some species from as far away as the Arctic Circle. Two of the most visible imported species are the cardinal, probably introduced during the 1700s, and the kiskadee. Imported from Trinidad in 1957 to control lizards and flies, the kiskadee has instead wreaked havoc on the island's commercial fruit crops.

The once-abundant eastern bluebird has been greatly reduced in number since the depletion of the cedar trees, its preferred habitat. Another bird native to Bermuda is the gray and white petrel, known locally as a cahow, which burrows for most of the year in the sands of the isolated eastern islands; the rest of the year it feeds at sea, floating for hours in the warm waters of the Gulf Stream. One of the most rarely sighted birds in the world, and once regarded as extinct, it is now protected by the Bermudian government.

Also native to Bermuda is the cliff-dwelling tropic bird, recognized by the elongated plumage of its white tail. Resembling a swallow, it is considered the island's harbinger of spring because of its annual appearance in March.

Although the gardens and golf courses of many of the country's hotels attract dozens of birds, some of the finest bird-watching sites are maintained either by the Bermuda Audubon Society or the National Trust. Isolated sites known for sheltering thousands of native and migrating birds include Paget Marsh, just south of Hamilton, the Walsingham Trust in Hamilton Parish, and Spittal Pond in Smith's Parish.

In the deep waters off the shores of Bermuda, photographers have recorded some of the finest game fish in the world, including blackfin tuna, marlin, swordfish, wahoo, dolphin, sailfish, and barracuda. Also prevalent are bonefish and pompano, both of which prefer sun-flooded shallow waters closer to shore. Any beachcomber is likely to come across hundreds of oval-shaped chitons (*Chiton tuberculatus*), a mollusk that adheres tenaciously to rocks within tidal flats (locally, this mollusk is known as "suck-rock").

Beware of the Portuguese man-o'-war (*Physalia physalis*), a floating colony of jellyfish whose stinging tentacles sometimes reach 50 feet in length. Washed up on Bermuda beaches, usually between March and July, it can sting even though it may appear dead. Give this dangerous and venomous marine creature a wide berth: severe stings may require hospitalization.

The most prevalent marine animal in Bermuda is responsible for the formation of the island's greatest tourist attraction, its miles of pale-pink sands. Much of the sand is composed of broken shells, pieces of coral, and the calcium carbonate remains of other marine invertebrates. The pinkest pieces are shards of crushed shell from a single-celled animal called foraminifer. Its vivid pink skeleton is pierced with holes, through which the animal extends its rootlike feet (pseudopodia), which cling to the underside of the island's reefs during the animal's brief life and are then washed ashore.

3 Bermuda Today

Bermuda's social life is imbued with British traditions. A profound sense of decorum is probably the most noticeable social feature on the island; it accounts for its somewhat formal dress code, which requires that even in ordinary social gatherings men should wear jackets and neckties and women should wear casually elegant clothes. Such attire is common during afternoon tea, a ritual observed as punctiliously on the manicured lawns of Pembroke Parish as in the finest hotels of London. Adherence to ritual is evident also during family events, such as weddings and funerals, when one is careful to do things precisely as they are done back in Britain, in accordance with the rites and traditions of the Church of England.

Politeness and formality are the norm, even on occasions when, confronted by life's petty problems, one would be more inclined, at least elsewhere, to raise one's voice in anger or exasperation. Such formality manifests itself physically in the islanders' clean-cut style, as well as in the many well-kept cottages and carefully tended gardens, which serve to enhance the natural setting of Bermuda and give it an unmistakable stamp of civilized orderliness. It even extends to a love of animals, which is here regarded as a peculiarly English virtue.

Cultural life in Bermuda attains a high point during the midwinter Bermuda Festival, held over a six- or seven-week period in January and February. The festival offers an opportunity to put on dramatic works from Britain, the United States, and Canada, as well as from other English-speaking Atlantic islands, with Bermudian and visiting theater troupes. An especially important feature of the festival is the volunteer efforts of many local residents, who administer to the transportation and hospitality-related needs of the festival's visiting artists.

THE PEOPLE

Some Bermudians can trace their ancestry back to the first settlers and some to successful privateers and to slaves. Today's 58,000 residents—mostly of African, British, and Portuguese descent—have a high standard of living, with no personal income tax and virtually no unemployment. The population density, one of the highest in the world, is about 3,210 per square mile. About 61 percent of the population is black, and 39 percent is white. Many other minority groups are represented, the largest and most established being the Portuguese. The color bar, which continued even after slavery was abolished, has almost disappeared, and African-Bermudians have assumed a prominent place in the island's civic and government affairs. There is no illiteracy, and you won't see any slums or poverty.

As mentioned, the British influence is prevalent in Bermuda, what with predominantly English accents, police wearing helmets like those of London bobbies, and cars driving on the left. Schools also are run along the lines of the British system and provide a high standard of preparatory education. Children 5 to 16 years of age must attend school. The Bermuda College offers academic and technical studies and boasts a renowned hotel and catering program.

POLITICS

Bermuda was accorded the right of self-government in 1968. It is therefore a self-governing dependency of Great Britain, with a governor appointed by the queen of England and representing Her Majesty's government in the areas of external affairs, defense, and internal security. The 12-member cabinet is headed by a premier. The elected legislature, referred to as the Legislative Council, consists of a 40-member House of Assembly and an 11-member Senate. Bermuda's oldest political party is the Progressive Labor Party, formed in 1963. In 1964 the United Bermuda Party was established and is the party currently in power. Bermuda's legal system is founded on common law. Judicial responsibility falls to the Supreme Court, headed by a chief justice. English law is the fundamental guide, and in court English customs prevail, as in the tradition of having judges don wigs and robes.

The nine parishes into which the island is divided are each managed by an advisory council. The capital, Hamilton, is located in Pembroke Parish.

THE ECONOMY

Bermuda's political stability has proved beneficial to the economy, which relies heavily on tourism and foreign investment.

For much of the island's early history, the major industry was ship building, made possible by the abundant cedar forests. But when, in the second half of the 19th century, wooden ships gave way to steel ones, the island turned to tourism. Today, tourism, with annual revenues estimated at $450 million, is the leading industry. Approximately 550,000 tourists visit Bermuda each year. An estimated 86% arrive from the United States, 4% from Britain, and 7% from Canada. Bermuda enjoys a 42% repeat-visitor rate.

Bermuda Shorts

Bermuda shorts originated with the British Army in India. Later, when British troops were stationed in Bermuda, they were issued shorts as part of the military's tropical kit gear.

Bermuda shorts are now considered suitable attire for the Bermuda businessman and are worn with a blazer, collared shirt, tie, and knee socks. They should not be more than three inches above the knee and must have a three-inch hem.

Because of favorable economic legislation incentives, several international companies are registered in Bermuda, representing the island's second-largest source of employment. More than 6,000 companies are registered—engaged mostly in investment holding, insurance, commercial trading, consultancy services, and shipping—but fewer than 275 companies are actually located on the island. No corporate or income tax exists in Bermuda.

The island's leading exported goods are pharmaceuticals, concentrates, essences, and beverages. Leading imports include foodstuffs, alcoholic beverages, clothing, furniture, fuel, electrical appliances, and motor vehicles. Bermuda's major trading partners are the United States, Canada, Great Britain, the Netherlands, and the Caribbean states.

RELIGION

About a third of Bermuda's population adheres to the Church of England, which has been historically dominant in the colony. Indeed, the division of Bermuda into nine parishes dates from 1618, when each parish was required by law to have its own Anglican church, to the exclusion of any other. That division still exists today, but more for administrative than religious purposes.

Religious tolerance is now guaranteed by law. There are some 10,000 Catholics, many of them from the Portuguese Azores. There are also many members of Protestant sects whose roots lie within what were originally slave churches, among them the African Methodist Episcopal Church. Established in 1816 by African Americans, the sect was transported to Bermuda from Canada around 1870. Today the church has about 7,000 members.

Also found in Bermuda are Seventh-Day Adventists, Presbyterians, Baptists, Lutherans, and Mormons. Less prevalent are a handful of Jews, Muslims, Rastafarians, and Jehovah's Witnesses.

Bermuda today boasts more than 110 churches, an average of five per square mile. They range from the moss-encrusted parish churches established in the earliest days of the colony to modest structures with only a handful of members.

FOLKLORE

Much of the folklore of Bermuda has its origins in the myths and legends of West Africa that the slaves brought to the island. Some of it, however, is homegrown.

Many tales are told about the fate of persons condemned for witchcraft during the 1600s. Anyone suspected of collusion with the devil was thrown into St. George's Harbour; whoever did not sink was adjudged guilty. Many women floated because of their skirts and petticoats; they were then fished out of the water and burned at the stake. The first woman to be found floating after her trial was Jeanne Gardiner, in 1651. Since her failure to plunge to the depths "proved" that she was a witch, the court ordered her removed from the water and hanged; she was then burned at the stake. Not only women, however, were tried for witchcraft; in 1652 a man was condemned to death for having cast a spell over his neighbor's turkeys. Justice in those Puritan times was stern, in Bermuda no less than in the American colonies.

Other kinds of tales abound, having to do with the island's maritime traditions. Many are ghost stories about colonial shipwrecks—stories about the tortured souls of sailors and passengers still roaming the coastlines of Bermuda on dark, stormy nights, searching for the wreckage of their sunken ships.

4 A Look at the Past

THE EARLY YEARS The discovery of the Bermuda islands is attributed to the Spanish, probably the navigator Juan Bermúdez, sometime before 1511, for in that year a map was published in the *Legatio Babylonica* that included "La Bermuda" among the Atlantic islands. A little more than a century later, the British staked a claim and began colonization.

In 1609 the flagship of Admiral Sir George Somers, the *Sea Venture,* while en route to Jamestown, Virginia, was wrecked on Bermuda's reefs. The dauntless crew built two pinnaces (small sailing ships) and headed on to the American colony, but three sailors hid out and remained on the island. They were the first settlers of Bermuda.

Just three years after the wreck of the *Sea Venture,* the Bermuda islands were included in the charter of the Virginia Company; 60 colonists were sent there from England, and St. George's Town was founded soon after.

Bermuda's status as a colony dates from 1620, when the first parliament convened (it is thus the oldest parliament in continuous existence in the British Empire, now Commonwealth). In 1684, Bermuda became a crown colony, under King Charles II. Sir Robert Robinson was appointed the crown's first governor.

Slavery became a part of life in Bermuda shortly after the official settlement. The majority of slaves were from Africa, but a few were Native Americans. Later, Scots imprisoned for fighting against Cromwell were transported to the islands, followed, in 1651, by Irish slaves. The lot of these bond servants, however, was not as cruel as that of plantation slaves in America and the West Indies. All slaves were freed by the British Emancipation Act of 1834.

DEALINGS WITH AMERICA Bermuda established close links with the American colonies. The islanders set up a thriving mercantile trade on the eastern seaboard, especially with southern ports. The major commodity sold by Bermuda's merchant ships was salt from Turks Island.

During the American Revolution, trade with loyalist Bermuda was cut off by the rebellious colonies, despite the network of family connections and close friendships that bound them. The cutoff in trade proved a great hardship for the islanders, who, having chosen seafaring to farming, depended

Dateline

- **c. 1511** Juan Bermúdez discovers Bermuda while sailing aboard the Spanish ship *La Garza.*
- **1609** The British ship *Sea Venture* is wrecked upon the reefs of Bermuda; all on board make it to shore safely and the settlement of Bermuda begins.
- **1612** The Virginia Company dispatches the *Plough* to Bermuda with 60 colonists on board. Richard Moore is appointed governor of Bermuda.
- **1620** The first Bermuda parliament session is held in St. Peter's Church, St. George's.
- **1684** The Bermuda Company's charter is taken over by the British crown. Sir Robert Robinson is appointed the crown's first governor of Bermuda.
- **1775** Gunpowder is stolen in St. George's and is shipped to the American colonies for use against the British.
- **1861** Bermuda becomes involved in the American Civil War when it runs supplies to the South to undermine the Union's blockade.
- **1919-33** Bermudians profit from Prohibition in the United States by engaging in rum running.
- **1940-45** Bermuda plays an important role in World War II counterespionage for the Allies.

continues

The Bermuda Triangle

The area known as the Bermuda Triangle encompasses a 1.5-million-square-mile expanse of open sea between Bermuda, Puerto Rico, and the southeastern shoreline of the United States. It is the source of the most famous—and certainly the most baffling—legend associated with Bermuda.

The legend of the Bermuda Triangle persists in many guises, some less credible than others, despite attempts by skeptics to dismiss them as fanciful tales. Can some of them be true? Here are three.

In 1881 a British-registered ship, the *Ellen Austin*, encountered an unnamed vessel in good condition sailing aimlessly without a crew. The *Austin*'s captain ordered a handful of his best seamen to board the mysterious vessel and sail it to Newfoundland. A few days later, the two ships encountered each other again on the high seas—but to everyone's alarm, the crewmen who had transferred from the *Austin* were nowhere to be found on the other ship!

Another often-told tale concerns the later disappearance of a merchant ship called *Marine Sulphur Queen*. It disappeared suddenly and without warning, and why no one could say. The weather was calm when the ship set sail from Bermuda, and apparently everything on board was fine, too, for no distress signal had been received from the crew. In looking for explanations, some have held that the ship probably had a weakened hull, which gave way, causing it to descend quickly to the bottom. Others attribute its loss to the mysterious forces that are behind all the Bermuda Triangle stories.

The most famous of all the Bermuda Triangle legends occurred in 1945. On December 5, five U.S. Navy bombers departed from Fort Lauderdale, Fla., on a routine mission. The weather was fine; no storm of any kind threatened. A while into the flight, however, the leader of the squadron suddenly radioed that they were lost—and then the radio went silent; all efforts by the ground to establish further communication proved fruitless. A rescue plane was quickly dispatched to search for the squadron—but it, too, disappeared. The Navy ordered a search, which lasted five days; but it found no evidence of a wreckage of any kind. To this day, the disappearance of the squadron and of the rescue plane remains a mystery as deep as the waters of the region.

How do believers of the Bermuda Triangle myth explain these phenomena? Some contend that the area is a time warp to another universe; others, that the waters off Bermuda are the site of the lost kingdom of Atlantis, whose power sources still function deep beneath the surface of the waves. Still others believe that there exists a perpetual focusing of laser rays upon the region from outer space, or that underwater signaling devices are guiding invaders from other planets, who have chosen the site for the systematic collection of human beings for scientific observation and experimentation.

Some, drawing upon the Book of Revelation, are fully persuaded that the Bermuda Triangle is really one of the gates to Hell, the other lying midway between Japan and the Philippines, in the Devil's Sea.

No matter what your views on the Bermuda Triangle may be, you're bound to provoke an excited response by asking local residents their opinion of it. For no one is immune to the power of myths and legends, and on Bermuda almost everyone has an opinion of some kind about the biggest and most fascinating legend of all.

heavily on America for their supply of food. Many of them, now deprived of profitable trade routes, turned to privateering, piracy, and "wrecking" (salvaging goods from wrecked or foundered ships).

Britain's loss of its important American colonial ports led to a naval buildup in Bermuda. It was from there that ships and troops sailed in 1814 to burn Washington, D.C., and the White House.

Bermuda got a new lease on economic life during the American Civil War. The island was sympathetic to the Confederacy and, with approval of the British government, ran the blockade that the Union had placed on exports, especially of cotton, by the southern states. St. George's Harbour was a principal Atlantic base for the lucrative business of smuggling manufactured goods into Confederate ports and bringing out cotton and turpentine cargoes.

When the Confederacy fell, so did Bermuda's economy. Seeing no immediate source of money from the Atlantic, the islanders turned their attention to agriculture and found that the colony's fertile soil and salubrious climate produced excellent vegetables. Portuguese immigrants were brought in as farmers, and soon celery, potatoes, tomatoes, and especially onions were being shipped to the New York market (indeed, so brisk was the onion trade that Hamilton became known as "Onion Town").

During the Prohibition era, Bermudians again profited by developments in the United States as they engaged in the lucrative business of rum running. Although the distance from the islands to the mainland was too great to allow for quick crossings in small booze-laden boats, as could be done from the Bahamas and Cuba, Bermuda nevertheless accounted for a good part of the alcoholic beverages transported illegally to the United States before the repeal of Prohibition in 1933.

- **1946** The automobile is introduced into Bermuda.
- **1957** Great Britain withdraws militarily after two centuries of rule.
- **1963** Voter registration becomes open to all citizens.
- **1973** The governor, Sir Richard Sharples, and an aide are assassinated.
- **1979** Bermudians celebrate their own Gina Swainson as winner of Miss World contest.
- **1987** Hurricane Emily causes millions of dollars damage, some 70 people injured.
- **1990** Prime Minister Margaret Thatcher confers with President Bush.
- **1991** Prime Minister John Major meets with President Bush.

WORLD WAR II ESPIONAGE   Bermuda played a key role in World War II counterespionage for the Allies. The story is dramatically told in *A Man Called Intrepid*, by William Stevenson, about the "secret war" with Nazi Germany.

Under the Hamilton Princess Hotel, a carefully trained staff worked to decode radio signals to and from German submarines and other vessels operating in the Atlantic, close to the United States and the islands offshore. Unknown to the Germans, the British, early in the war, had broken the Nazi code through use of a captured German coding machine called "Enigma." The British also intercepted and examined mail between Europe and the United States.

Bermuda served as a refueling stop for airplanes flying between the two continents. While pilots were being entertained at the Yacht Club, the mail would be taken off the carriers and examined by experts. An innocent-appearing series of letters from Lisbon, for example, often had messages written in invisible ink. These letters were part of a vast German spy network. The British became skilled at opening sealed envelopes, examining their written contents, and then carefully resealing them.

These surreptitious letter readers were called "trappers." Many of them were young women without any previous experience in counterespionage work, yet some performed very well. As Stevenson writes, it was soon discovered that, "by some quirk in the law of averages, the girls who shone in this work had well-turned ankles." A medical officer involved with the project even reported it as "fairly certain that a girl with unshapely legs would make a bad trapper." So, amazingly, the word went out that women seeking recruitment as trappers would have to display their "gams," as the expression was then.

These women—and their colleagues, to be sure—in the course of their work discovered one of the methods by which the Germans were transmitting secret messages: They would shrink a whole page of regularly typed text down to the size of a tiny dot and then conceal the dot under an innocuously looking punctuation mark, such as a comma or period! The staff likened these messages with their secret-bearing dots to a plum duff, a popular English dessert. For these "punctuation dots [were] scattered through a letter like raisins in the suet puddings." The term "duff method" then came to be applied to the manner in which the Germans were sending military and other messages through the mail.

When the United States entered the war, it assigned agents of the Federal Bureau of Investigation to Bermuda. There, they joined the British in their intelligence operations.

POSTWAR CHANGES   In 1953, British Prime Minister Winston Churchill chose Bermuda, which he had visited during the war, as the site for a conference with U.S. President Dwight D. Eisenhower and the premier of France. Several such high-level gatherings have followed in the decades since, the most recent, between British Prime Minister John Major and U.S. President George Bush, taking place in 1991.

Bermuda's increasing prominence led to changes in its relationship with Great Britain and the United States and also resulted in significant developments on the island itself. In 1957, after nearly two centuries of occupation, Britain withdrew its military forces, having decided to grant self-government to its oldest colony. The United States, however, under the Lend-Lease Agreement signed in 1941 and due to expire in 2040, continues to maintain a naval air station at Kindley Field, in St. George's Parish. Nearby, on Cooper's Island, the U.S. National Aeronautics and Space Administration operates a space-tracking system.

As Bermudians assumed greater control over their own affairs, they began to adopt significant social changes, but at a pace that did not satisfy some critics. Although racial segregation in hotels and restaurants ceased in 1959, it wasn't until 1971 that schools were integrated. Women received the right to vote in 1944, but the law still restricted suffrage only to property holders. However, this was rescinded in 1963, when voter registration became open to all citizens.

During the rocky road to self-government, Bermuda was not without its share of problems. Rioting broke out in 1968, so serious that British troops had to be called back to restore order. Then, in 1973, Sir Richard Sharples, the governor, was assassinated; in 1977 those believed to have been the assassins were themselves executed. These events, which occurred at a time when several of the islands in the region as well as in the Caribbean were experiencing domestic difficulties, proved to be the exception rather than the rule. For in the years since, the social and political climate in Bermuda has been markedly calm, which is better for the island's economic well-being, as it encourages the industries on which Bermuda depends—tourism among them.

In 1970, Bermuda was "expelled" from the sterling currency area, and Bermudians hitched their currency to the U.S. dollar.

The 1990s have brought talk about what role Bermuda will play in the future. Some advocate complete independence from Britain, while others want to retain connections to the crown.

5 Local Art

Bermuda's earliest artworks involved portraits painted by itinerant artists for the local gentry. The bulk of these were painted by the English-born Joseph Blackburn, whose brief visit to Bermuda in the mid-1700s resulted in requests from local landowners to have their portraits painted. Many of these hang today in the Tucker House Museum in St. George's. A handful of portraits from the same period were done by the American-born artist John Green.

Also prized are a series of paintings, from the mid-19th century, depicting sailing ships. They're signed "Edward James," but the artist's real identity remains unknown.

During the 19th century also, the traditions of the English landscape painters, particularly the Romantics, came into vogue in Bermuda. Constable, with his lush and evocative landscapes, became the model for many.

Other than a few naïve artists, however, whose works showed great vitality but little sense of perspective, most of Bermuda's landscape paintings were executed by British military officers and their wives. Their body of work includes a blend of true-to-life landscapes with an occasionally stylized rendering of the picturesque or Romantic tradition then in vogue in England. Among the most famous of the uniformed artists was Lt. E. G. Hallewell, a member of the Royal Engineers, whose illustrations of the island's topography were used in the planning of naval installations.

Another celebrated landscapist was Thomas Driver, who arrived as a member of the Royal Engineers in 1814 and remained on the island until 1836. Trained to reproduce detailed landscape observations as a means of assisting military and naval strategists, he later adapted his style into a more elegant and evocative one. He soon abandoned the military and became a full-time painter of the scenes of Bermuda. Because of their attention to detail, Driver's works are frequently reproduced by scholars and art historians hoping to recapture the aesthetic and architectural elements of the island's earliest constructions.

Later in the 19th century, other artists spent hours depicting the botany and floral life of Bermuda. Lady Lefroy, whose husband was governor of the island

Impressions

Bermuda, despite her small size, her isolation and her position among evil reefs and evil Atlantic [hurricane] weather, was [once for imperial Britain] and is [now for superpower America] of considerable military importance.

—Simon Winchester, *The Sun Never Sets: Travels to the Remaining Outposts of the British Empire* (1985)

between 1871 and 1877, painted the trees, shrubs, fish, flowers, and animals of the island in much-imitated detail. Later, at scattered intervals of careers, such internationally known artists as Winslow Homer, Andrew Wyeth, George Ault, and French-born impressionist and cubist Albert Gleizes have all painted Bermudian scenes.

Among today's prominent Bermuda-born artists is Alfred Birdsey. His watercolors represent some of the most elegiac visual odes to Bermuda ever produced. Birdsey's paintings, as well as the paintings of the other artists mentioned, may be viewed in galleries around the island. Protecting these works, however, so that they might continue to be exhibited in the future, is a constant problem in Bermuda because of the island's semitropical climate. As the administrator for a major art gallery explains, "Bermuda's climate is unquestionably the worst in the world for the toll it takes on works of art, with three elements—humidity, salt, and ultraviolet light all playing their part." The U.S. Navy uses Bermuda to test the durability of paint; if paint can stand up in Bermuda, it can stand up anywhere. The island's humidity can cause serious harm to a painting. It can be absorbed by the canvas, where you will see it later as mildew coming through the oils. Some very valuable prints have been totally destroyed. As a result, more and more galleries and exhibition rooms on the island have been air-conditioned.

In addition to painters, Bermuda also boasts several noted sculptors, among them Chelsey Trott, who produces cedarwood carvings, and Desmond Hale Fountain, who creates works in bronze. Fountain's life-size statues often show children in the act of reading or snoozing in the shade.

6 Bermuda Style

The architecture of Bermuda is sometimes considered its only truly indigenous art form—a collection of idiosyncratic building techniques dictated by climate and the types of building supplies available on the island. Early settlers quickly recognized the virtues of the island's most visible building material, coral stone. A conglomerate of primeval sand packed beside crushed bits of coral and shells, this stone has been quarried for generations on Bermuda. Cut into oblong building blocks, it is strong but porous, rendering it unuseable in any climate where cycles of freezing and thawing would cause it to crack. Mortared together with imported cements, the blocks provide solid and durable foundations and walls.

Bermuda's colonial architects ingeniously found a way to deal with a serious problem on the island—the lack of an abundant supply of fresh water. During the construction of a house or any other sort of building, workers excavated a water tank (cistern) first, either as a separate underground cavity away from the house or as a foundation for the building. These cisterns served to collect rainwater funneled from rooftops via specially designed channels and gutters.

The design of these roof-to-cellar water conduits led to the development of what is considered Bermuda's most distinct architectural feature, the gleaming rooftops of its houses. Gently sloping, and invariably painted a dazzling white, they are constructed of quarried limestone slabs sawed into "slates" about an inch thick and between 12 and 18 inches square. Roofs are installed over a framework of cedarwood beams (or, more recently, pitch pine or pressure-treated wood beams), which are interconnected with a series of cedar lathes. The slates are joined together with cement-based mortar in overlapping rows, then covered with a cement wash and one or several coats of whitewash or synthetic paint. This process corrects the porosity of the coral limestone slates, rendering them watertight. The result is a layered effect, as each course of limestone appears in high relief atop its neighbor. The angular, step-shaped geometry of Bermudian roofs have inspired watercolorists and painters to emphasize the rhythmically graceful shadows that trace the path of the sun across the rooflines.

Bermudian houses—unlike houses in the Caribbean, which they in many respects resemble—are designed without amply proportioned hanging eaves. Large eaves are desired because of the shade they afford, but smaller ones have proved to be structurally sounder during tropical storms. Wind gathers more lifting power from an overhanging eave than from any other part of a roofline.

No discussion of Bermudian architecture can fail to mention a garden feature that many visitors consider distinctive to Bermuda—the moon gate. A rounded span of coral blocks arranged in a circular arch above a wooden gate, the moon gate was introduced to Bermuda around 1920 by the duke of Westminster's landscape architect; the inspiration came from China and Japan.

The interiors of Bermudian houses are usually graced with large windows, ample doors, and, in the older buildings, floors and moldings crafted from copper-colored planks of the almost extinct Bermuda cedar. Also common is a feature found in colonial buildings in Caribbean and other western Atlantic islands as well—tray ceilings, so named because of their resemblance to an inverted serving tray. Their shape allows them to follow the lines of the inside roof construction into what would otherwise have been unused space. The effect of these ceilings, whether sheathed in plaster or planking, gives Bermudian interiors unusual height and airiness even if the building has relatively low eaves.

Despite the distinctively individualistic nature of Bermuda's architecture, the island's interior decors remain faithfully (some say rigidly) British, and rather more formal than you might have expected. Interiors seem designed as a felicitous cross between what you'd expect in a New England seaside cottage and what a nautically minded society hostess might add to her drawing room in London. Bermuda interiors usually contain an ample use of Chippendale or Queen Anne furniture (sometimes authentic, sometimes reproduction), and decorators love to include—whenever possible—any piece of antique furniture crafted from almost-extinct, copper-colored Bermuda cedar. Mingle these aspects with the open windows, gentle climate, and carefully tended gardens of a fertile, Mid-Atlantic setting, and you get some charming and soothing decors indeed.

All of the above-mentioned tenets, however, are being challenged as old Bermuda families intermarry with less conservative newcomers from Europe or the east coast of the United States, and as the guidelines expressed in such publications as *Architectural Digest* become more widespread. According to one of Bermuda's leading decorators, Richard Klein of Hamma Galleries, 1 Lane Hill, Front Street, Hamilton (☎ 809/292-8500), color palettes have become more clear and more bright in recent years, thanks to the direct influence of the American market, and furniture (especially in second, rather than primary homes) tends to be more contemporary. Despite that, at presstime there were, in his estimation, only about five hi-tech homes on Bermuda, most of them owned as second or third homes by full-time residents of America's east coast. And even those hi-tech houses are restricted, because of local building codes, to maintaining conservative, time-tested exteriors that don't depart too radically from those of their neighbors.

7 The Music of the Islands

Modern Bermudian music is a mixture of native traditions and outside influences, chiefly from the islands to the south—Jamaica, Trinidad, and Puerto Rico—and from the United States and Britain. As elsewhere, American and British rock, modified by local rhythms, has proved the strongest and most lasting influence.

Yet, despite the popular new musical forms, Bermuda retains great pride in its original musical idioms. *Gombey* dancing, an art form whose roots lie deep within West Africa, is the island's premier folk art. Gombey dancers are almost always male; in accordance with tradition, men from the same family pass on the rhythms and dance techniques from generation to generation. Gombey is a combination of Africa's tribal heritage, mingled with the Native American and British colonial influences of the New World. Dancers outfit themselves in masquerade costumes, whose outlandish lines and glittering colors evoke the brilliant plumage of tropical birds. The most strenuous dances are usually presented during the Christmas season.

Gombey (spelled goombay in some other places, such as the Bahamas) signifies a specific type of African drum, as well as the Bantu word for "rhythm." These rhythms escalate into an ever faster and more hypnotic beat as the movements of the dancers become more and more uninhibited and the response of the spectators grows more and more fervent.

Although gombey dancing, with its local rituals and ceremonies, may be considered a major cultural contribution of Bermuda, it is not unique to the island. Variations of it may be found elsewhere in the western Atlantic, as well as in the Caribbean. Indeed, during its development, it was significantly influenced by some of these other versions. In colonial times, for example, when African-Caribbeans were transported to Bermuda as slaves or convicts to help build the British military installations on the island, they brought with them their own gombey traditions, which they mingled with those of Bermuda. What is unique about the Bermudian version of gombey, however, is its use of the British snare drum, played with wooden sticks, as accompaniment to the dancing.

A handful of gombey recordings are available from which you can get a fair idea of what this African-based music sounds like, with its rhythmic chanting and rapid drumbeat. Among them, the album *Strictly Gombey Music* (Edmar 1165), performed by four members of the Pickles Spencer Gombey Group, offers a good selection of gombey dances.

Aficionados of the art form, however, will argue that gombey's allure lies not so much in the music as in the feverish, almost trancelike dancing that accompanies it, as well as in the colorful costumes of the dancers. For that reason, they say, audio recordings cannot convey the full mesmerizing power of a gombey dance the way a videotape can. So, while you're in Bermuda, consider taping a gombey dance to show when you get back home and perhaps remind yourself of some of the enchanting sounds and sights of the island.

Bermuda also has a surviving balladeer tradition. Although its exponents are fewer than they used to be, they continue to enjoy considerable popularity, among islanders and visitors alike. Reflecting the wry, self-deprecating humor that has always distinguished their compositions, they can strum on their guitar a song for any occasion. Many of their songs nowadays have to do with Bermuda's changing way of life.

In the past few years, calypso and reggae, the popular sounds of the Caribbean, have indeed become famous in Bermuda. A more recent import to listen for is *soca*, a rock-influenced calypso, and *zouk*, which is a fusion of the various Caribbean rhythms, with French melodies thrown in.

Visitors are often pleased to discover that the island's best-known singers and musicians can be heard at many of the hotels and nightclubs. Inquire what group is performing during the cocktail hour at your hotel; chances are it may be one of the most popular.

By virtually everyone's estimate, the musical patriarch of Bermuda is Hubert Smith, the island's official greeter in song. A balladeer of formidable talent and originality, Smith has composed and performed songs for the visits of nearly all the foreign heads of state who have graced Bermuda's shores in recent memory. His performances for members of the British royal family include one of the most famous songs ever written about the island, "Bermuda Is Another World." The song is now the island's unofficial national anthem; it's included in the best-selling album *Bermuda Is Another World* (Edmar 1025).

Almost as popular is a five-member calypso band, the Bermuda Strollers, whose lively rhythms can be heard on gala nights at Bermuda's larger hotels. Look for their album *The Best Of* (Edmar 2005) and also a collection of musical odes to the island's natural beauty, *South Shore Bermuda* (Edmar 1156).

One of the island's youngest and most promising talents is Gene Steede, a balladeer and comic who frequently performs at the Southampton Princess. His most popular album is *Bermuda's Natural Resource* (Edmar 2003).

Bermuda ballads, songs of love, and calypsos are also performed by Stan Seymour, a popular soloist who has been compared to Harry Belafonte. Look for *Our Man in Bermuda* (Edmar 1070).

The lively calypsos of Trinidad and the pulsating rhythms of Jamaica have had their influence on musical tastes in Bermuda. Youth Creation, a dreadlock-sporting local reggae group, adopts the Rastafarian style in *Ja's on Our Side* (Edmar 2002).

Dance aficionados will appreciate the five-member Trinidad-born Clay House Steel Band. They can usually be seen at the New Clay House Inn; three months a year they perform aboard various cruise ships. Their most popular album is *The Real Thing* (Edmar 1111).

A Bermuda-born trio, Steel Groove, performs only instrumentals in the Trinidadian style. Their trademark adaptations use the calypso-derived steel pan combined with a keyboard, an electric guitar, and occasionally a bass guitar. Their most popular album is *Calypso Hits* (produced by Danny Garcia).

A slightly older calypso group (one of the first on the island) is the Esso Steel Band. Their popular albums, among them *The Esso Steel Band* (Sunshine 1003) and *It's a Beautiful World* (produced by Rudy Commissiong), are widely hummed and whistled throughout the islands.

8 Bermudian Cuisine

For years Bermuda was not considered an island of grand cuisine; food was too often bland, lacking in flavor. However, since the 1970s there has been a change. Bermuda has shared the revived interest in fine cuisine that has swept across America. Chefs seem better trained than ever, and many top-notch, albeit expensive, restaurants dot the archipelago, from Sandys Parish in the west to St. George's Parish in the east.

Italian food currently enjoys much vogue. The Chinese have also landed. And fast food is available, including Kentucky Fried Chicken.

In recent years, some Bermudians have shown an increased interest in their heritage, and many of the old-time dishes and recipes have been revived and published in books devoted to Bermudian cookery (not a bad idea for a souvenir).

Today, Bermuda imports most of its foodstuffs from the United States. Because of the high population density, much farmland has now given way to the construction of private homes. Nevertheless, private gardens are still cultivated, and at one Bermudian home I was amazed at the variety of vegetables grown on just a small plot of land. These plants included sorrel, from which a good-tasting soup was made, along with oyster plants and Jerusalem artichokes.

As related in any history of Bermuda, Admiral Sir George Somers and his 150 castaways arrived on the shores of Bermuda from their ill-fated *Sea Venture.* Within 30 minutes they set about fishing for food. They named the fish they caught "rockfish," and later wrote about how sweet and fat it was.

These early settlers also found wild hogs roaming the island. The swine were believed to have swum to shore when some ship or ships were wrecked off the coast of Bermuda. The settlers captured the boars and fed them cedarberries. Thus, when they didn't want to go fishing or the weather was too choppy, they could roast a pig.

DINING CUSTOMS

Perhaps the most delightful custom on Bermuda is the English ritual of afternoon tea. Many local homes and hotels have maintained the tradition, and visitors to Bermuda quickly take it up.

The typical afternoon tea is served in hotels daily from 3 to 4pm. Adding a modern touch, it is often served around a swimming pool, the guests partaking of the ritual in their bathing suits—a tolerated lapse from the code of formality that otherwise governs social functions on the island.

In its more formal observance, the tea is served at a table well-laid with silver, crisp white linen napery, and fine china, often imported from Britain. Finger sandwiches made with thinly sliced cucumber or watercress, or scones and strawberry jam, usually accompany the tea.

Again like the British, Bermudians enjoy a good sociable pub lunch. Several pubs are found in Hamilton and elsewhere on the island, especially St. George's. For further information, however, see Chapter 6, "Dining." For the visitor a pub lunch—consisting of a healthy serving of fish and chips or some other "pub grub," a pint or two of ale (preferably English), and much animated discussion about politics, sports, or the most recent royal visit—is an experience to be cherished, here as much as in any city or town in Britain.

In many resort hotels, guests are booked in high season (April through November) on the modified American plan (MAP) or half-board arrangement. To escape the routine of eating in the same dining room every night, some hotels offer a "dine around" program, allowing you to dine at other hotels either on your MAP plan or else at somewhat reduced prices. You should inquire about such arrangements when booking a room.

Most of the upmarket restaurants of Bermuda request that men wear a jacket and tie for dinner; some restaurants dispense with the tie but require a jacket. When making reservations, it is always wise to ask what the dress code is before showing up.

Perhaps the favorite meal of the typical Bermudian is Sunday brunch. Your hotel is likely to feature a big buffet at that time, or else you may take the opportunity to dine at another establishment. "Casual but elegant" dress is preferred at most Sunday buffets.

Nearly all the major restaurants, except fast-food places, prefer that you make a reservation; many establishments require that you do so as far in advance as possible. Weekends in summer can be especially crowded. At certain popular restaurants, some travel-wise vacationers make their reservations even before coming to Bermuda.

The food of Bermuda is better than ever. When in doubt, however, order seafood. Nearly all meat is imported and may have arrived on the island considerably earlier than you have.

THE CUISINE

SEAFOOD   Around the coastline of Bermuda more species of both shore and ocean fish are found than in any other place—that is, if you can believe what any local fisher is likely to tell you. The fish include grunt, angel fish, yellowtail, gray snapper, and the ubiquitous rockfish.

Rockfish is similar to the Bahamian grouper, and it appears on nearly every menu. It weighs anywhere from 15 to 135 pounds (or even more). Steamed, broiled, baked, fried, or grilled, rockfish is a challenge to any chef. There's even a dish known as "rockfish maw," which I understand only the most old-fashioned cooks—a handful still left on St. David's Island—know how to prepare. It's the maw, or stomach, of a rockfish that has been stuffed with a dressing of forcemeat and simmered slowly on the stove. You may want to try it, if you view dining as an adventure.

The most popular dish on the island is Bermuda fish chowder. Waiters usually pass around a bottle of sherry peppers and some black rum with which you lace your own soup. This adds a distinctive Bermudian flavor.

Shark is not as popular as it used to be. Many traditional dishes, though, are still made from shark, including hash. Some still use shark liver oil to tell the weather. It's said to be more reliable than the weatherperson. The oil is extracted at a specific time, then poured into a small bottle and left in the sun. If the oil lies still, then fair weather can be predicted; if, however, droplets form on the sides of the bottle, then foul weather can be expected.

The Bermuda lobster—or "guinea chick," as it is known locally—has been called a first cousin of the Maine lobster and is in season only from September to March. Its high price tag has led to overfishing, forcing the government at times to issue a ban on its harvesting. Lobster then is likely to be imported instead of caught in local waters.

You can occasionally still get a good conch stew in Bermuda at one of the local restaurants. Sea scallops, while still available, have become increasingly rare. Mussels are cherished in Bermuda. One of the most popular and most traditional mussel dishes is mussel pie Bermuda style.

FRUITS & VEGETABLES   In both restaurants and private homes Portuguese red-bean soup, the culinary contribution of the farmers brought to the island to till the land, precedes many a meal.

The Bermuda onion (once so common on the island that the people of Bermuda were called "onions") figures in a lot of Bermudian recipes, including onion pie.

Bermuda-onion soup, an island favorite, is most often flavored with Outerbridge's Original Sherry Peppers.

Bermudians grow more potatoes than any other vegetable, chiefly the Pontiac red and the Kennebec white potato. At some homes, the traditional Sunday breakfast of codfish and banana cooked with potatoes is still served.

"Peas and plenty" is a Bermudian tradition. Black-eyed peas are cooked in onions and salt pork, to which rice is sometimes added. Dumplings or boiled sweet potatoes can also be added at the last minute. Another peas-and-rice dish, called Hoppin' John, is eaten either as a main dish or as a side dish with meat or poultry.

Bermudians and Bahamians share the tradition of Johnny Bread, or johnnycake, a simple pan-cooked cornmeal bread. Fishers would make it over a fire in a box filled with sand to keep the flames from spreading to the craft itself.

The cassava, once very important in Bermuda, is now used chiefly at Christmas to make the traditional cassava pie. Another dish that has a festive holiday connection is sweet-potato pudding, traditionally eaten on Guy Fawkes Day.

Bermuda grows many fresh fruits, including strawberries, Surinam cherries, guavas, avocados, and, of course, bananas. Guavas are made into jelly, which in turn is often used to make the famous Bermuda syllabub, traditionally accompanied by johnnycake.

DRINKS

All the name-brand alcoholic beverages are sold in Bermuda, but prices on such a typical drink as a scotch and soda can run as high as $5. You have to watch where you drink or else you can run up some huge bar tabs.

For some 300 years rum has been considered the national drink of Bermuda. Especially popular is Bacardi rum (they have headquarters in Bermuda) and Demerara rum (also known as black rum). The rum swizzle is perhaps the most famous alcoholic drink in Bermuda.

An interesting drink is loquat liqueur, now exported. It can be made with loquats, rock candy, and gin, or more elaborately, with brandy instead of gin and the addition of such spices as cinnamon, nutmeg, cloves, and allspice.

Before bottled drinks, ginger beer—made with green ginger and lemons—was an island favorite.

Before You Go 3

Getting to Bermuda has now become easier than ever, thanks to more frequent flights, often direct ones, from such gateway cities as New York, Boston, and Washington, D.C., among others. For those who'd like to relive the glamorous days of "cruising down to Bermuda," several cruise lines sail there from spring until late autumn.

In this chapter you'll find everything you need to plan your trip — from when to go to what things cost.

1 Visitor Information, Entry Requirements & Money

VISITOR INFORMATION

To obtain information about Bermuda before your trip, write to the **Bermuda Department of Tourism** at the office nearest you. In the **United States,** the Bermuda Department of Tourism has offices in: *New York,* Suite 201, 310 Madison Ave., New York, NY 10017 (☎ **212/818-9800** or **800/223-6106**); *Boston,* Suite 1010, 44 School St., Boston, MA 02108 (☎ **617/742-0405**); *Chicago,* Suite 1070, Randolph Wacker Building, 150 North Wacker Dr., Chicago, IL 60606 (☎ **312/782-5486**); and *Atlanta,* Suite 803, 245 Peachtree Center, NE, Atlanta, GA 30303 (☎ **404/524-1541**). In **Canada,** write to Bermuda Department of Tourism, Suite 1004, 1200 Bay St., Toronto, Ontario, Canada M5R 2A5 (☎ **416/923-9600**). In the **United Kingdom,** write to Bermuda Department of Tourism, 1 Battersea Church Road, London SW11 3LY (☎ **071/734-8813**).

Other useful sources are, of course, newspapers and magazines. To find the latest articles on Bermuda, check the *Reader's Guide to Periodical Literature* at your local library.

You may also want to contact the U.S. State Department for background information; write to Superintendent of Documents, **U.S. Government Printing Office,** Washington, DC 20402 (☎ **202/783-3238**).

A good travel agent can be a valuable source of information. Make sure he or she is a member of the American Society of Travel Agents (ASTA), though. If you get poor service from an agent, you can write to the ASTA **Consumer Affairs,** 1101 King St., Alexandria, VA 22314 (☎ **703/739-2851**).

And, the best source of all—friends and other travelers who have just returned from Bermuda.

ENTRY REQUIREMENTS

A U.S. or Canadian citizen does not need a passport to enter Bermuda, although one would be useful as your required identification. Visitors from Great Britain and Europe do need a passport.

Bermuda Immigration authorities require U.S. visitors to have in their possession any one of the following items: a birth certificate or a certified copy of it, a U.S. naturalization certificate, a U.S. Alien Registration card, a U.S. reentry permit, or a U.S. voter registration card bearing the signature of the holder.

Visitors from Canada must have either a birth certificate (or a certified copy of it), a Canadian certificate of citizenship, or a valid passport plus proof of their Landed Immigrant status.

If you stay longer than three weeks, you must apply to the Chief Immigration Officer for an extended stay. You must have a return or onward ticket.

All travelers must pay a passenger tax under the Passenger Tax Act of 1972; see "Taxes" under "Fast Facts" in Chapter 4, "Arriving in Bermuda."

It is a good policy before leaving home to make copies of your most valuable documents, including the inside page of your passport that has your photograph. You should also make copies of your driver's license, an airline ticket, strategic hotel vouchers, and any other sort of identity card that might be pertinent. You should also make copies of any prescriptions you take. Place one copy in your luggage and carry the original with you. Leave the other copy at your home. The information on these documents will be extremely valuable should you encounter loss or theft abroad.

PASSPORTS

In the **United States,** citizens 18 and older who meet the requirements are granted a 10-year passport. For an application, go to a U.S. post office or federal court office. In addition, there are federal passport agencies in 13 cities that you can visit in person. These include New York, Washington, D.C., Stamford, Conn., Seattle, Philadelphia, San Francisco, New Orleans, Boston, Honolulu, Chicago, Los Angeles, Miami, and Houston. Youths under 18 are granted a five-year passport. Children under 13 must have their parents apply for their passport, and teenagers 13 to 16 must also have a parent's permission before applying for a passport. If your passport is 12 years old or older, or was granted to you before your 16th year, you must apply in person at a passport agency, post office, or federal or state court office. You can also write Passport Service, Office of Correspondence, Department of State, Suite 510, 1111 19th St., NW, Washington, DC 20522-1075; ask for form DSP-11 for a new passport or DSP-82 for a renewal by mail. You can also call **202/647-0518** 24 hours a day for data about agency locations and hours.

First-time applicants for passports pay $65, $40 if under 18 years of age. Persons with expired passports can renew by mail for $55.

To apply for a passport, you must complete a government passport application form and provide proof of U.S. citizenship—a birth certificate or naturalization papers. An old passport (providing it's less than 12 years old) is also accepted. You should also have identification with your signature and photograph, such as a driver's license. You'll also need two identical passport-size photographs. You'll wait the longest to receive your passport between mid-March and mid-September; in winter it usually takes only about two weeks by mail. Passports can sometimes be issued quickly in an emergency, providing you present a plane ticket with a confirmed seat.

In **Canada,** citizens seeking a passport may go to one of the nearly two dozen regional offices in such cities as Ottawa and Montréal. Alternatively, you can mail an application to the Passport Office, Section of External Affairs, Ottawa 1, K1A 0G3.

Post offices have applications forms. Passports, valid for 5 years, cost $35 Canadian, and proof of Canadian citizenship is required, along with two signed identical photographs. For 24-hour information within Canada only, call **800/ 567-6868.** In Toronto call **416/973-3251;** in Montréal call **514/283-2152.**

In the **United Kingdom,** citizens may apply at one of the regional offices in Liverpool, Newport, Glasgow, Peterborough, and Belfast, or in London if they reside there. You can also apply in person at a main post office. The fee is £18, and the passport is good for 10 years. Documents required include a birth certificate or a marriage certificate. Two photos must accompany the application.

In **Australia,** citizens can apply for a passport, valid for 10 years, at a post office. Residents of the following cities can apply at passport offices in Adelaide, Brisbane, Canberra, Darwin, Hobart, Melbourne, Newcastle, Perth, and Sydney. Passport fees are adjusted every three months.

In **New Zealand,** application forms for passports are available at travel agents or local Link Centres. Mail them to the New Zealand Passport Office, Documents of National Identity Division, Department of Internal Affairs, P.O. Box 10-526, Wellington (☎ **04/478-8100**). The application fee is NZ$80.

In **Ireland,** write in advance for requirements or procedures to the Passport Office, Setanta Centre, Molesworth Street, Dublin 2, Ireland (☎ **01/67-11-005**). The cost is IR£45. Irish citizens living in North America can contact the Irish Embassy, 2234 Massachusetts Ave. NW, Washington, DC 20008 (☎ **202/ 462-3939**). The embassy can issue a new passport or direct you to one of four North American consulates that have jurisdiction over a particular region. If arranged by mail through Irish consulates, an Irish Passport costs U.S. $80.

CUSTOMS

U.S. CUSTOMS You may take out of Bermuda $400 worth of merchandise duty free if you've been outside the United States for 48 hours or more and have not claimed a similar exemption within the past 30 days. Articles valued above the $400 duty free limit but not over $1,000 will be assessed at a flat duty rate of 10%. Gifts for your personal use, not for business purposes, may be included in the $400 exemption, and unsolicited gifts totaling $50 a day may be sent home duty free. You are limited to one liter of wine, liqueur, or liquor, and five cartons of cigarettes. U.S. Customs preclearance is available for all scheduled flights. Passengers leaving for the United States must fill out written declaration forms before clearing U.S. Customs in Bermuda. The forms are available at Bermuda hotels, travel agencies, and airlines.

Collect receipts for all purchases made. If a merchant suggests giving you a false receipt, misstating the value of the goods, *beware:* the merchant may be a Customs informer. You must also declare all gifts received during your stay abroad.

Compile a list of expensive carry-on items, and ask a U.S. Customs agent to stamp your list at the airport before your departure. For additional information, write to the **U.S. Customs Service,** 1301 Constitution Avenue, P.O. Box 7407, Washington, DC 20229, for the free pamphlet, *Know Before You Go.*

CANADIAN CUSTOMS   For more information, write for the booklet *I Declare,* issued by Revenue Canada, 875 Heron Rd., Ottawa, ON K1A 0L5. Canada allows its citizens a $300 exemption, and they are allowed to bring back duty free 200 cigarettes, 2.2 pounds of tobacco, 40 imperial ounces of liquor, and 50 cigars. In addition, they are allowed to mail gifts to Canada from abroad at the rate of Can$60 a day, provided they are unsolicited and aren't alcohol or tobacco (write on the package: "Unsolicited gift, under $60 value"). All valuables should be declared on the Y-38 Form before departure from Canada, including serial numbers, as in the case of, for example, expensive foreign cameras that you already own. *Note:* The $300 exemption can be used only once a year and only after an absence of seven days.

BRITISH CUSTOMS   Citizens can bring in goods valued up to £136; and one must be 17 or older to import liquor or tobacco. Britons are allowed 200 cigarettes or 100 cigarillos, 50 cigars, or 250 grams of tobacco. Two liters of table wine, one liter of alcohol greater than 22% by volume, and two liters of alcohol equal to or less than 22% by volume may also be brought in. British Customs tends to be strict and complicated in its requirements. For details get in touch with Her Majesty's Customs and Excise Office, New King's Beam House, 22 Upper Ground, London SE1 9PJ (☎ 071/382-5468 for more information).

AUSTRALIAN CUSTOMS   The duty-free allowance in Australia is Aus$400 or, for those under 18, Aus$200 for goods that physically accompany anyone entering Australia, including Australian citizens. Used personal property mailed back from the United States or Bermuda should be marked "Australian goods returned," to avoid payment of duty. Upon returning to Australia, citizens can bring in 200 cigarettes or 250 grams of tobacco and one liter of alcohol. If you will be returning with valuable goods you already own, such as expensive foreign-made cameras, you should file form B263. A helpful brochure available from Australian consulates or Customs offices is called *Customs Information for Travellers.*

NEW ZEALAND CUSTOMS   The duty-free allowance is NZ$700. Citizens over 17 years of age can bring in 200 cigarettes or 50 cigars or 250 grams of tobacco (or a mixture of all three if their combined weight doesn't exceed 250 grams), plus 4.5 liters of wine or beer or 1.125 liters of liquor. New Zealand currency does not carry import or export restrictions. A Certificate of Export listing already-owned valuables taken out of the country allows you to bring them back in without paying duty. Most questions are answered in a free pamphlet available

---

Impressions

. . . Bermuda is, without doubt, a success. It is, generally speaking, a peaceful place—more so than many Caribbean islands nearby. [Still, there are critics, from whom] you hear complaints about the Americanization of the place, the suggestion that Bermudianism is merely an anomalous cultural hybrid, a mule of a culture, attractive in its own way but of no lasting value or use. And yet it does seem to work; it is rich, it is as content as any place I know, and it is stable.
—Simon Winchester, *The Sun Never Sets: Travels to the Remaining Outposts of the British Empire* (1985)

at New Zealand consulates and Customs offices called *New Zealand Customs Guide for Travellers*, Notice No. 4.

IRISH CUSTOMS   Irish citizens may bring in 200 cigarettes or 100 cigarillos or 50 cigars or 250 grams (approximately nine ounces) of tobacco; one liter of liquor exceeding 22% volume (such as whisky, brandy, gin, rum, or vodka), or two liters of distilled beverages and spirits with a wine or alcohol base of an alcoholic strength not exceeding 22% volume, plus two liters of other wine; and 50 grams of perfume. Other allowances include duty-free goods to a value of IR£34 per person or IR£17 per person for travelers under 15 years of age.

MONEY

CASH/CURRENCY

Legal tender is the Bermuda dollar (BD$), which is divided into 100 cents. Prior to 1972, the Bermuda dollar was pegged to the pound sterling; now it is pegged through gold to the U.S. dollar on an equal basis—BD$1 equals to U.S. $1. U.S. currency is generally accepted at par in shops, restaurants, and hotels. Currencies from the United Kingdom and all other foreign countries are not accepted. They can easily be exchanged for Bermuda dollars at banks. Banking and credit-card transactions in all foreign currencies involving currency exchange are subject to exchange rates.

TRAVELER'S CHECKS

Before leaving home, purchase traveler's checks and arrange to carry some ready cash (usually about $250, depending on your habits and needs). In the event of theft, if the checks are properly documented, the value of your checks will be refunded. Most large banks sell travelers checks, charging fees that average between 1% and 2% of the value of the checks you buy, although some out-of-the-way banks, in rare instances, have charged as much as 7%. If your bank wants more than a 2% commission, it sometimes pays to call the traveler's check issuers directly for the address of outlets where this commission will cost less.

American Express (☎ 800/221-7282 in the U.S. and Canada) is one of the largest and most immediately recognized issuers of traveler's checks. No commission is charged to members of the American Automobile Agency, and to holders of certain types of American Express credit cards. The company issues checks denominated in U.S. dollars, Canadian dollars, British pounds sterling, Swiss francs, French francs, German marks, Japanese yen, and Dutch guilders. Checks are also sold in Saudi riyals, although these are negotiable only within Saudi Arabia. The vast majority of checks sold in North America are denominated in U.S. dollars. For questions or problems that arise outside the U.S. or Canada, contact any of the company's many regional representatives.

Citicorp (☎ 800/645-6556 in the U.S. and Canada, or 813/623-1709 collect from anywhere else in the world) issues checks in U.S. dollars, British pounds, German marks, Japanese yen, and Australian dollars.

Thomas Cook (☎ 800/223-7373 in the U.S. and Canada, otherwise call **609/987-7300** collect from other parts of the world) issues MasterCard traveler's checks denominated in U.S. dollars, Canadian dollars, French francs, British pounds, German marks, Dutch guilders, Spanish pesetas, Australian dollars, and Japanese yen. Depending on individual banking laws in each of the various states, some of the above-mentioned currencies might not be available at every outlet.

The British Pound & the U.S. Dollar

Here is how British pounds sterling break down into U.S. dollars. At this writing £1 = approximately $1.58 U.S. (or $1 = approximately 63 pence), although these ratios can and will change according to complicated political and economic factors worldwide. This table should be used, therefore, only as a general guide.

The Bermudian dollar—no longer pegged to pound sterling—has the same value as the U.S. dollar.

US$	UK£	US$	UK£
1	.63	75	47.25
2	1.26	100	63.00
3	1.89	125	78.75
4	2.52	150	94.50
5	3.15	175	110.25
6	3.78	200	126.00
7	4.41	225	141.75
8	5.04	250	157.50
9	5.67	300	189.00
10	6.30	350	220.50
15	9.45	400	252.00
25	15.75	450	283.50
50	31.50	500	315.00

Interpayment Services (☎ **800/221-2426** in the U.S. or Canada, call **212/858-8500** collect from other parts of the world) sells VISA checks that are issued by a consortium of member banks and the Thomas Cook organization. Travelers checks are denominated in U.S. or Canadian dollars, British pounds, and German marks.

CREDIT CARDS

Credit cards are accepted in many shops and restaurants, but not all hotels. Check first. VISA and MasterCard are the major cards used, although American Express and, to a lesser extent, Diners Club are also popular.

WHAT WILL IT COST?

Time is money, and since Bermuda is less than a two-hour flight from most cities on the East Coast, the savings begin even before visitors land on the island. A four-day, three-night vacation in Bermuda really does include four days of vacation for the price of only three nights' accommodation. An 8:30am flight from New York gets travelers to Bermuda in time for lunch, with the whole afternoon to play.

The variety of accommodations allows travelers to indulge their preferences and tastes while keeping budgets under control. There are luxury resort hotels, small hotels, intimate guesthouses, and cottage colonies. Most large resorts offer money-saving package plans that include meals. If a stay of a week or more is planned, a housekeeping unit or cottage with kitchenette might be a good choice.

What Things Cost in Bermuda	U.S. $
15-minute taxi ride	15.00
One-way ride on a bus	1.25
Local telephone call	.20
Double room at Belmont Hotel (deluxe)	225.00
Double at Rosedown (moderate)	166.00
Double at Salt Kettle House (budget)	84.00
Lunch for one at Tio Pepe (moderate)*	17.00
Lunch for one at Bombay Bicycle Club (budget)*	11.95
Dinner for one at Romanoff Restaurant (deluxe)*	66.00
Dinner for one at Chancery Wine Bar (moderate)*	32.50
Dinner for one at Chopsticks Restaurant (budget)*	21.00
Bottle of beer in a bar	3.75
Coca-Cola in a café	1.50
Cup of coffee in a café	1.75
Glass of planter's punch in a restaurant	4.50
Roll of ASA 100 color film, 36 exposures	7.85
Admission to Elbow Beach	3.00
Movie ticket	7.00
*Includes tax and tip but not wine.	

No rental cars are available, but Bermuda's local transportation is efficient, and inexpensive, saving visitors up to $250 over the cost of one week's car rental. Options include the simple and comprehensive bus system, ferries, and bicycle or moped rentals.

Golfers will find that greens fees are comparable to or below fees at other destinations. For example, Ocean View Golf & Country Club and St. George's Golf Club charge only $28 and $35, respectively, for 18 holes of golf. There are eight world-class golf courses with varying fees.

Athletic and cultural activities, such as tennis, riding, guided tours, museums, and attractions are good values in Bermuda.

Hotel costs will depend on when you arrive. If you're seeking reductions, perhaps 20% to 40% per person, go in the off-season. In Bermuda, unlike the Caribbean, this is from November through March.

On the half-board plan (MAP), many hotels ask $125 to $275 per person per day based on double occupancy, with some of the smaller properties charging from $100 to $180 per person per day, double occupancy. A hotel without meals (EP), charges from about $100 to $150 per person daily.

To combat these high tabs, travel agents offer special package deals, which can represent a substantial savings over regular hotel tariffs, for families, golfers, tennis players, or honeymooners and some others.

To cut costs even more, families can rent housekeeping efficiencies, apartments, cottages, or even condominiums (some condos are rented like time-share units when the owners aren't in residence).

In figuring your budget, think about transportation. Getting around the island isn't always easy since visitors aren't allowed to rent cars. You'll therefore have to rely on public transportation or the very expensive taxis. The more agile can rent bicycles or mopeds. (See Getting Around, in Chapter 4, "Arriving in Bermuda," for more information.) Fortunately, once you reach a particular parish, many attractions can be covered on foot, and Bermuda becomes almost one vast walking tour.

Dining out is an expensive undertaking in Bermuda. If you patronize the very expensive establishments, you can end up spending as much as $100 per person, including wine. Even moderate to expensive restaurants charge $25 to $50 per person. Any dinner under $25 per person is considered inexpensive. To cut dining costs, have a picnic lunch or else enjoy pub grub at noon.

If all these hidden or extra costs are intimidating, consider a package tour in which everything will be arranged for you. You'll know the bottom-line vacation cost before you embark on your journey.

2 When to Go

Bermuda enjoys a mild climate, and the term "Bermuda high" has come to mean sunny days and clear skies. Bermuda, being farther north in the Atlantic than the Bahamas, is much cooler in winter. Its off-season begins in December and lasts until around the first of March. Many hotels, therefore, quote their low-season rates—discounts of from 20% to 60%—in winter. During autumn and winter, many hotels also quote some discounted package deals. Other hotels shut down for a week to a month or two in winter.

The off-season rates, which are also listed in this guide, are a bonanza for cost-conscious travelers who are free to travel to Bermuda from November to March.

CLIMATE

Bermuda is a semitropical island, and the Gulf Stream, flowing between it and North America, keeps the climate temperate. There is no rainy season, and no typical month of excess rain. Showers may be heavy at times, but the skies clear quickly. In summer temperatures rarely rise above 85° Fahrenheit. There's nearly always a cool breeze in the evening, and accommodations that require it are air-conditioned. Springlike temperatures prevail from mid-December to late March, with the average ranging from the low 60s to 70°F. From mid-November to mid-December and from late March through April, be prepared for either spring or summer weather.

A look at the official chart on temperature and rainfall will show you what to expect during your visit to Bermuda.

Bermuda's Average Daytime Temperatures & Rainfall

	Jan	Feb	Mar	Apr	May	June	July	Aug	Sept	Oct	Nov	Dec
Temp.°F	65	64	64	65	70	75	79	80	79	75	69	65
Temp.°C	19	18	18	19	21	24	30	27	30	24	21	19
Rainfall (in.)	4	5	4.6	3	3.9	5.2	4	5.3	5.3	6	4.5	3.9

THE HURRICANE SEASON

The hurricane season—the curse of the Caribbean and Bermuda—officially lasts from June through November. But don't panic. More tropical cyclones pound the U.S. mainland than hurricanes devastate Bermuda. And Bermuda isn't as likely to be pounded by a hurricane as is a Caribbean island. Satellite forecasts generally give adequate warning of any really bad weather so that precautions can be taken in time.

If you're really concerned, you can call the nearest branch of the National Weather Service. It's listed under the U.S. Department of Commerce. Radio and TV weather reports from the **National Hurricane Center** in Coral Gables, Florida, can also keep you posted.

HOLIDAYS

The following public holidays are observed in Bermuda (the ones without a date change from year to year): New Year's Day (January 1), Good Friday, Easter, Bermuda Day (May 24), the Queen's Birthday (first or second Monday in June), Cup Match Days (cricket; Thursday and Friday preceding first Monday in August), Labour Day (first Monday in September), Christmas Day (December 25), and Boxing Day (December 26). Public holidays that fall on a Saturday or Sunday are usually celebrated on the following Monday.

BERMUDA CALENDAR OF EVENTS

January

❂ **Bermuda Festival** During the winter months, the Bermuda calendar is jam-packed with such events as golf and tennis invitationals, an international marathon race, a dog show, open house and garden tours, and, of course, the **Bermuda Festival,** the six-week International Festival of the Performing Arts, held in Hamilton, featuring drama, dance, jazz, classical and popular music, and other entertainment by the best international artists.

> **Where:** Islandwide. **When:** January and February. **How:** Some tickets are reserved until 48 hours before curtain time for visitors. For details, write the Bermuda Festival, Box HM 297, Hamilton HM AX, Bermuda (☎ 441/295-1291).

- **The Bermuda International Marathon,** with international and local runners, takes place January 13–15. For further information and entry forms, contact the International Race Weekend Committee, Bermuda Track and Field Association, P.O. Box DV 397, Devonshire, Bermuda DV BX. (☎ 809/238-2333).

March

❂ **Bermuda College Weeks** This is an annual spring odyssey for at least 10,000 students who flock here every year. These weeks began as Rugby Weeks in 1933.

Impressions

[Above all the attributes of Bermuda is] that uninterrupted health and alacrity of spirit, which is the result of the finest weather and gentlest climate in the world.
—George Berkeley, in letter to Lord Percival (1722)

Rugby teams from Ivy League schools came to compete against British or Bermudian teams. "Where the boys are," to borrow the popular song title, led to "where the girls are." A tradition was born. The Department of Tourism issues a College Week Courtesy Card to those who have a valid college identification card. This becomes a passport to a week of free—courtesy of the Bermudian government—beach parties, lunches, boat cruises, dances, and entertainment.

Where: Islandwide. **When:** Dates arranged to coincide with U.S. college spring vacations. **How:** Obtain a list of events from the tourist office.

- **Home & Garden Tours.** Each spring the **Garden Club of Bermuda** lays out the welcome mat at a number of private homes and gardens that are open to view. A different set of houses, all conveniently located in the same parish, is open every Wednesday during this springtime viewing. Normally a total of 20 homes participate in the program, many of them dating back to the 17th and 18th centuries.

Where: Islandwide. **When:** End of March to mid-May. **How:** The tourist office provides a complete list of schedules.

April

- **Beat Retreat Ceremony.** Ceremony of the Bermuda regiment and massed pipes and drums, on Front Street in Hamilton at 9pm. Held on the last Wednesday in every month from April through October, except August. (Periodically held in Somerset and St. George's.)
- **Peppercorn Ceremony.** His Excellency the governor collects the annual rent of one peppercorn for use of the island's Old State house in St. George's. April 21 (dates may vary).
- **An agriculture show.** A three-day exhibit of Bermuda's best fruits, flowers, vegetables, and livestock; and equestrian and other ring events. Dates vary.
- **Invitational International Week.** Yachtspeople from the United States, the United Kingdom, Canada, and other countries compete with Bermudians. (Other boat-racing events take place in alternate years.)

May

- **Bermuda Game Fishing Tournament.** Special prizes for top catches of 17 species of game fish. All amateur anglers are eligible. Held from May 1 to November 30.
- **Bermuda Heritage Month.** Culminates in **Bermuda Day,** May 24, a public holiday.

June

- **Queen's Birthday** (first or second Monday in June) is celebrated by a parade on Front Street in Hamilton.
- **The Blue Water Cruising Race.** Race from Marion, Massachusetts, to Bermuda is held in June in odd-numbered years, as is the **MultiHull Ocean Yacht Race** from Newport, Rhode Island, to Bermuda. In June of even-numbered years, some 180 of the world's finest yachts compete in the **Bermuda Race,** from Newport to Bermuda.

July

- **Marine Science Day.** Lectures, hands-on demonstrations, and displays for adults and children, by Bermuda Biological Station. Call **441/297-1880** for more information. Different date each year, usually mid-month.

August

- **Cup Match and Somers Days.** This spectacular cricket match pits the east against the west end of the island. Held on Thursday and Friday before first Monday in August.

September

- **Labor Day.** This public holiday features a host of activities (ideal time for a picnic). Climax of the day is a parade from Union Square in Hamilton Bernard Park. Held first Monday in September.

October

- **Omega Gold Cup International Match Race Tournament.** Top-ranking Match Racing skippers compete with Bermudians. Hosted by the Royal Bermuda Yacht Club. October 18–25.

November

- **The Opening of Parliament.** Traditional ceremony and military guard of honor connected with the **Opening of Parliament** by His Excellency the governor as the queen's personal representative. November 6.
- **World Rugby Classic.** Former international rugby players compete with Bermudians at Bermuda National Sports Club. November 6–12.
- **Guy Fawkes Day.** Annual celebration with a minifair starts with the traditional burning of the Guy Fawkes effigy at the Keepyard of the Bermuda Maritime Museum, Royal Naval Dockyard, beginning at 4:30pm. November 7.
- **Remembrance Day.** A gala parade is held, with Bermudian police, British and U.S. military units, Bermudians, and veterans' organizations taking part. November 11.
- **Bermuda Equestrian Festival.** International Show Jumping Competition at the Botanical Gardens. November 28 and 29.
- **Invitation Tennis Weeks.** More than 100 visiting players vie with Bermudians in two weeks of matches.

December

- **Bermuda Goodwill Tournament.** Pro/amateur foursomes from international golf clubs play over 72 holes on four of Bermuda's eight courses during golfing activity. December 5–9.

3 Weddings & Honeymoons in Bermuda

There are good reasons why Bermuda hosts more than 23,000 honeymooners and second honeymooners each year. It offers an ideal environment for couples who prefer active *and* relaxing agendas. While some visitors prefer to fill their days with scuba diving and swimming, others enjoy leisure activities, such as strolling along the beach at sunset or reading poetry to each other while snuggling in a secluded cove. Many of Bermuda's hotels, from luxurious resorts to intimate cottage colonies, have special honeymoon packages. These include airfare, accommodations, meal plans, champagne upon arrival, flowers in the room, and special discounts at local attractions and restaurants. Call **800/BERMUDA (800/237-6832)** for details. Even more specific information can be obtained by calling **800/223-6106.**

Wedding-Cake Traditions

Custom dictates that Bermudians have two wedding cakes—a plain pound cake covered with gold leaf for the groom, and a tiered fruit cake covered with silver leaf and topped off with a mini-cedar tree for the bride. The tiny tree is planted on the day of the wedding to symbolize the hope that the marriage will grow and mature like the tree. The rest of the first tier of the bride's cake is frozen until the christening of the first child.

GETTING MARRIED IN BERMUDA

Couples who wish to get married in Bermuda must file a "Notice of Intended Marriage" with the Register General, accompanied by a fee of $150 (in the form of a bank draft, not a personal check). The draft should be made out to "The Accountant General." The draft should be mailed or delivered personally to the Register General at the Government Administration Building, 30 Parliament St., Hamilton HM 12 (☎ **441/295-5151,** fax 441/292-4568). Notice of Intended Marriage forms can be obtained from the Bermuda Department of Tourism offices in Atlanta, Boston, Chicago, Los Angeles, and New York. Airmail to Bermuda from the United States can take 6 to 10 days, so plan accordingly.

Once the Notice of Intended Marriage is received, it will be published—including names and addresses—once in any two of the island's newspapers. Assuming there is no formal objection, the Registry will issue the license 15 days after receiving notice. It will be valid for three months.

CIVIL CEREMONIES   Weddings are performed at the Registry by appointment only Monday through Friday, 10am to 4pm, and Saturdays between 10am and noon. The fee is $153, which includes the cost of the ceremony and certificate. Copies of the marriage certificate are available for $17 each. If either party of the intended marriage has been married before, they need to attach a photocopy of the final decree to their Notice of Intended Marriage.

WEDDING ARRANGEMENTS   Many hotels can help make wedding arrangements, from reserving the church and clergy, to hiring a horse and buggy, ordering the wedding cake, or securing a photographer. **Bermuda Travel Planners,** 350 5th Ave., Suite 2718, New York, NY 10018 (☎ **212/564-9502** or 800/323-2020), offers popular wedding packages at many of the island's hotels. In addition, the following on-island wedding consultants can assist with these and other details: **The Wedding Salon,** 51 Reid St., P.O. Box HM 2085, Hamilton HM HX, Bermuda, ☎ **441/292-5677,** fax 441/292-2955; and **The Bridal Suite,** 4 St. Anne's Close, Southampton (☎ **441/238-0818**).

4 Spa Vacations

Full-fledged spa facilities are available at the **Sonesta Beach Hotel & Spa,** Southampton (☎ **441/238-8122** or 800/766-3782 in the U.S.), which is recognized by some experts as one of the top 10 health-and-beauty spas of the world. Designed in the European mode, it offers the health-and-fitness regimens so popular at American spas. Many exotic and beneficial treatments are also offered, one being Ionithermie, the inch-reducing treatment from Europe, as well as deluxe facial care from Paris, ancient forms of therapeutic and relaxing massage such as aromatherapy and reflexology, and Swedish massage. Some people check into the hotel on calorie-controlled four-, five-, or seven-day programs. Clients are almost totally occupied from 8:30am to 7pm with the likes of aerobics, skin and body care, supervised indoor and outdoor stretching exercises, massages, facials, and beauty regimens.

The facilities can also be used by hotel guests or outsiders who opt for pin-pointed treatments rather than the full spa treatment. The up-to-date accoutrements include Universal gym equipment, saunas, steambaths, and massage rooms. The staff directs daily exercise classes, which outsiders can join for a fee. Each procedure is priced separately for nonpackage participants. For after-workout pick-me-ups, there's a beauty salon adjacent to the health spa. Half- or full-day packages are sold to nonresidents of the hotel.

5 Home Exchanges

If you don't mind "staying put," you can avail yourself of a "house swap," as it's often called. It certainly keeps costs low if you don't mind a stranger living in your mainland home or apartment. Sometimes the exchange includes use of the family car.

Possibilities for this type of service are a straight house exchange for vacation purposes, or something more complicated. For example, your teenage child might be housed free in exchange for free room and board when the host child visits your hometown. In this day of increased crime, sometimes the deal is for a "house-sitter." Unfortunately, though, there's no guarantee that you'll find a house or an apartment in the area you desire.

The Invented City, 41 Sutter St., Suite 1090, San Francisco, CA 94104 (☎ 415/673-0347), is an international home-exchange agency. Home-exchange listings are published three times a year, in February, May, and November. A membership fee of $50 allows you to list your home, as well as your preferred time to travel, your occupation, and your hobbies.

6 Health & Insurance

STAYING HEALTHY

If you need treatment while in Bermuda, finding a good doctor is no real problem. See Fast Facts, in Chapter 4, "Arriving in Bermuda," for specific locations and addresses.

It's a good idea to carry all your vital medicines and drugs (the legal kind) with you in your carry-on luggage, in case your checked luggage is lost.

If your medical condition is chronic, always talk to your doctor before leaving home. He or she may have specific advice to give you, depending on your problem. For conditions such as epilepsy, a heart condition, or diabetes, wear a Medic

Impressions

I find Bermuda is a place where physicians order their patients when no other air will keep them alive.
——Thomas Moore, in letter to his mother (1803)

Alert identification tag. This tag provides Medic Alert's 24-hour hotline number, so a foreign doctor can obtain medical records for you. For a lifetime membership, the cost is a well-spent $35 for a stainless steel ID bracelet. In addition, there is a $15 annual fee. Contact the **Medic Alert Foundation,** P.O. Box 1009, Turlock, CA 95381 (☎ **800/432-5378**).

At some point in a vacation, most visitors experience some diarrhea, even those who follow the usual precautions. This is often the result of a change in diet and eating habits, rather than bad or contaminated food and water.

Mild forms of diarrhea usually pass quickly without medication. As a precaution, take along some antidiarrhea medicine, moderate your eating habits, and drink only mineral water until you recover. Drink plenty of fluids to prevent dehydration. Consuming more than your usual intake of salt will help your body retain water. Eat only simply prepared foods at such times, such as plain bread (no butter) and boiled vegetables or some broth. Avoid dairy products, except yogurt.

WATER   Although tap water is generally considered safe to drink, if you have a delicate stomach it is better to avoid it and drink mineral water instead. This applies even to iced drinks. Stick to beer, hot tea, or soft drinks.

INSECTS & PESTS   Mosquitoes are a nuisance, but nothing more than that (the malaria-carrying kind are rare). Among the most annoying insects are the no-see-ums; even if you can't see these little gnats, you can sure "feel-um." They appear mainly in the early evening. Because even screens can't keep them out, you'll have to use your favorite bug repellent.

MEDICINES   Take along an adequate supply of any prescription drugs that you need and a written prescription that uses the *generic* name of each drug, not the brand name. Consult your pharmacist about taking such over-the-counter drugs as Colace and Metamucil. Also, if you wear glasses or contact lenses, be sure to take along your prescription (as well as an extra pair).

Other useful items to take along are first-aid cream, insect repellent, aspirin, nose drops, Band-Aids, and hydrogen peroxide. If you're subject to motion sickness, include motion-sickness medicine as well.

INSURANCE

Insurance needs for the traveler abroad fall into three categories: health and accident, trip cancellation, and lost luggage.

First, review your present policies before traveling internationally—you may already have adequate coverage between them and what is offered by credit-card companies if the trip tickets were purchased with their card. Fraternal organizations sometimes can provide policies that protect members in case of sickness or accident abroad.

Many homeowners' insurance policies cover theft of luggage during foreign travel and loss of documents, for instance, your airline ticket, although coverage is usually limited to about $500. To submit a claim on your insurance, remember that you'll need police reports or a statement from a medical authority that you did in fact suffer the loss or experience the illness for which you are seeking compensation. Such claims, by their very nature, can be filed only when you return from Bermuda.

Some policies (and this is the type you should have) provide cash advances or else transferral of funds so that you won't have to dip into your precious travel funds to settle medical bills.

If you've booked a charter fare, you'll probably have to pay a cancellation fee if you cancel a trip suddenly, even if you cancel because of an unforeseen crisis. It's possible to get insurance that will cover such a fee, either through travel agencies or through a credit card company—for example, VISA and American Express—when such insurance is written into tickets paid for by credit cards.

Companies offering special travel insurance policies include the following: **Travel Guard International,** 1145 Clark St., Stevens Point, WI 54481 (☎ **800/ 826-1300** outside Wisconsin, **715/345-0505** in Wisconsin), offers a comprehensive seven-day policy that covers lost luggage, emergency assistance, accidental death, trip cancellation, and medical coverage abroad. The cost of the package is $62, but there are restrictions that you should understand before you accept the coverage.

Travelers Insurance PAK, Travel Insured International, Inc., P.O. Box 280568, East Hartford, CT 06128 (☎ **800/243-3174** or **203/528-7663**), offers illness and accident coverage costing from $10 for 6 to 10 days. For lost or damaged luggage, $500 worth of coverage costs $20 for 6 to 10 days. You can also purchase trip cancellation insurance for $5.50 per $100 of coverage to a limit of $10,000 per person.

Access America, 6600 W. Broad St., P.O. Box 11188, Richmond, VA 23230 (☎ **800/284-8300**), offers travel insurance and 24-hour emergency travel, medical, and legal assistance for the traveler. One call to their hotline center, staffed by multilingual coordinators, connects travelers to a worldwide network of professionals able to offer specialized help in reaching the nearest physician, hospital, or legal advisor, and in obtaining emergency cash or the replacement of lost travel documents. Varying coverage levels are available.

7 Tips for Travelers with Disabilities, Seniors, Singles & Families

FOR TRAVELERS WITH DISABILITIES

Hotels rarely publicize what facilities, if any, they offer the disabled, so it's always better to contact the hotel directly. A number of agencies can also provide information to help you plan your trip. The **Travel Information Service,** MossRehab Hospital, 1200 W. Tabor Rd., Philadelphia, PA 19141-3099, provides information to telephone callers only. Call **215/456-9600** for assistance with your travel needs.

Air Transportation of Handicapped Persons, published by the U.S. Department of Transportation, is free. Write to Distribution Unit, U.S. Department of Transportation, Publications Division, M-4332, Washington, DC 20590, and ask for Free Advisory Circular No. AC12032.

You may also want to consider joining a tour specifically designed for disabled visitors. Write (and enclose a stamped, self-addressed envelope) to the **Society for the Advancement of Travel for the Handicapped,** 347 Fifth Ave., Suite 610, New York, NY 10016 (☎ **212/447-7284**), for a list of such tour operators. Yearly membership dues are $45 for senior citizens or $25 for students.

You might also consider the **Federation of the Handicapped** (FEDCAP), 154 W. 14th St., New York, NY 10011 (☎ **212/727-4200**), which offers summer tours for its members, who pay a yearly membership fee of $4.

The **Information Center for Individuals with Disabilities,** Fort Point Place, 27–43 Wormwood Street, Boston, MA 02210 (☎ 617/727-5540), is another good source. It has lists of travel agents who specialize in tours for the disabled.

For the blind or visually impaired, the best source is the **American Foundation for the Blind,** 15 W. 16th St., New York, NY 10011 (☎ 800/232-5463 or 212/620-2147 for ordering of information kits and supplies). It offers information on travel and various requirements for the transport and border formalities for seeing-eye dogs. It also issues identification cards to those who are legally blind.

For a $20 annual fee, consider joining **Mobility International USA,** P.O. Box 10767, Eugene, OR 97440 (☎ 503/343-1284). It answers questions on various destinations and also offers discounts on videos, publications, and programs it sponsors.

Finally, a bimonthly publication, *Handicapped Travel Newsletter,* keeps you current on accessible sights worldwide for the disabled. To order an annual subscription for $15 call **903/677-1260.**

FOR SENIORS

Many discounts are available for seniors, but be advised that you have to be a member of an association to obtain some of them.

Write for a free booklet called *101 Tips for the Mature Traveler,* available from Grand Circle Travel, 347 Congress St., Boston, MA 02210 (☎ 617/350-7500 or 800/221-2610). This tour operator offers extended vacations, escorted programs, and cruises that feature unique learning experiences for seniors at competitive prices.

Mature Outlook, 6001 N. Clark St., Chicago, IL 60660 (☎ 800/336-6330), is a travel organization for people over 50 years of age. Members are offered discounts at ITC-member hotels and will receive a bi-monthly magazine. Annual membership is $9.95, which entitles its members to discounts and in some cases free coupons for discounted merchandise from Sears Roebuck Co. Savings are also offered on selected auto rentals and restaurants.

SAGA International Holidays is well known for its all-inclusive tours for seniors, preferably those 60 years old or older. Both medical and trip cancellation insurance are included in the net price of any of their tours except for cruises. Contact SAGA International Holidays, 222 Berkeley St., Boston, MA 02115 (☎ 800/343-0273).

Information is also available from the **National Council of Senior Citizens,** 1331 F St., N.W., Washington, D.C. 20004 (☎ 202/347-8800). A nonprofit organization, the council charges $12 per person or couple, for which you receive a monthly newsletter that is devoted partly to travel tips. Benefits of membership include discounts on hotels, motels, and auto rentals, and also includes supplemental medical insurance for members.

FOR SINGLES

One company that has made heroic efforts to match single travelers with like-minded companions is now the largest and best-known such company in the United States. Jens Jurgen, the German-born founder, charges $99 for a six-month listing in his well-publicized records. New applicants fill out a form stating their preferences and needs. They then receive a minilisting of potentially suitable travel partners. Companions of the same or opposite sex can be requested.

A 46-page bimonthly newsletter also gives numerous money-saving travel tips of special interest to solo travelers. A sample issue is available for $5. For an application and more information, write to **Jens Jurgen,** Travel Companion, P.O. Box P-833, Amityville, NY 11701 (☎ **516/454-0880**).

Singleworld, 401 Theodore Fremd Ave., Rye, NY 10580 (☎ **914/967-3334** or **800/223-6490**), offers a selection of cruises and tours for single travelers. Tours and cruises fall into three categories: 20s to 30s, 40s plus, and "all ages." Annual dues are $25.

Grand Circle Travel, mentioned above, also offers escorted tours and cruises for singles. Once you book one of their trips, membership is included; in addition, you get vouchers providing discounts for future trips.

FOR FAMILIES

Bermuda contends for top position on the world list of places for vacations for the entire family. The smallest toddlers can spend blissful hours in shallow seawater or pools constructed with them in mind, while older children can enjoy boat rides, horseback riding, hiking, discoing, or even snorkeling.

Most resort hotels will advise you what there is in the way of fun for all, and many have play directors and supervised activities for various age groups. However, there are some tips for making the trip a success that parents should attend to in advance.

Take along a "security blanket" for your child. This might be a pacifier or a favorite toy or book.

Arrange ahead for necessities such as a crib and a bottle warmer, as well as for cots in your room for larger children. If the place you're staying at doesn't stock baby food, bring your own.

Draw up guidelines on bedtime, eating, keeping tidy, being in the sun, even shopping and spending. It will make everybody's vacation more enjoyable.

Take protection from the sun. For tiny tots, this should include a sun umbrella, while the whole family will need sunscreen (a factor of 15 is a good idea) and sunglasses. Also take along anti-insect lotions and sprays. You'll probably need both to repel such unwanted island denizens as mosquitoes and sand fleas, as well as to ease the itching and other possible aftereffects of insect bites.

Don't forget the thermometer, basic first-aid supplies, any medications your doctor may suggest, swimsuits, beach and pool toys, waterwings for tiny mites, beach sandals for everybody, and terrycloth robes.

Family Travel Times is published quarterly by Travel With Your Children (TWYCH), and includes a weekly call-in service for subscribers. Subscriptions cost $55 a year and can be ordered by writing to TWYCH, 45 W. 18th St., 7th Floor, New York, NY 10011 (☎ **212/206-0688**).

TWYCH also publishes two nitty-gritty information guides, *Skiing with Children* and *Cruising with Children*, which sell for $29 and $22, respectively, and are discounted to newsletter subscribers. An information packet, which describes TWYCH's publications and includes a recent sample issue, can be purchased by sending $3.50 to the above address.

Most hotels will help you find a babysitter.

4

Arriving in Bermuda

This chapter explores the different options for getting to Bermuda, treating not only the most obvious choices, but some alternatives you may not have considered. Also suggested are several itineraries to help you get the most out of your vacation time. You'll find tips, too, on determining where to stay and dine and what to buy.

1 Getting There

BY PLANE

From North America's East Coast, you can be in Bermuda in approximately two hours by plane.

THE MAJOR AIRLINES

American Airlines (☎ 800/433-7300) flies into Bermuda every day nonstop from New York's JFK Airport. Its departure is timed to co-incide with dozens of connecting flights from throughout the rest of North America. Although they'd been discontinued just before presstime, watch during the lifetime of this edition for a re-initiation of American's nonstop flights to Bermuda from Raleigh-Durham, North Carolina.

Delta (☎ 800/241-4141) offers daily nonstop service to Bermuda every day of the year from both Boston and Atlanta. The Boston flight departs early every morning (around 9:05am), whereas the Atlanta flight departs around noon, late enough to allow connections from most of the other cities within Delta's vast network.

Northwest Airlines (☎ 800/447-4747) flies to Bermuda every day throughout most of the year (between March and October) from Boston's Logan Airport. Departures are late enough in the morning (9:50am) to allow easy and convenient connections from other points on Northwest's network, including flights from the airline's massive hubs in Minneapolis and Detroit.

Continental Airlines (☎ 800/231-0856) offers daily nonstop service to Bermuda from New Jersey's Newark Airport during spring, summer, and fall, and nonstop service to Bermuda about five times a week between mid-December and mid-March.

From Toronto, **Air Canada** (☎ 800/776-3000) offers nonstop flights between six and seven days a week into Bermuda, with frequent connections into Toronto to virtually every other city in

Canada. The flight departs around 9:30am, late enough to permit convenient connections from both Montréal and Québec City. The airline also offers once-per-week nonstop flights into Bermuda from Halifax, Nova Scotia, either on Friday or Saturday, depending on the season.

The final contender in the high-stakes routes between North America and Bermuda is **USAir** (☎ 800/428-4322), which flies nonstop throughout the year to Bermuda from Philadelphia (daily), Boston (daily), Baltimore–Washington (six days a week), and New York's La Guardia Airport (daily).

The airline of choice for the thousands of annual visitors from the United Kingdom is usually **British Airways** (☎ 800/247-9297), which flies between London's Gatwick Airport and Bermuda around three times a week throughout the year. One offbeat but attractive option offered by this airline are packages that combine a visit to Bermuda with an ongoing excursion to London, and then a nonstop flight from London back to the United States. British Airways offers schedules and discounted APEX fares well-suited for midwinter pilgrimages to London's West End theater district and the city's countless shops and museums.

REGULAR FARES

The best strategy for securing the lowest airfare is to keep calling the airlines, keeping in mind the bonus miles and frequent flyer programs that many of them offer. Most airlines give the best deals on tickets ordered at least 14 days before a traveler's anticipated departure and that include stopovers in Bermuda of at least three days. Airfares fluctuate with the season, but tend to remain competitive among the companies vying for shares of the lucrative Bermuda run.

Peak season—summer in Bermuda—is the most expensive time to go; low season—usually mid-September or early November until mid-March—offers less expensive fares. Few if any of the airlines designate spring and autumn as shoulder (intermediate) seasons, dividing their calendar year into only two instead of three seasons.

Most airlines flying from North America to Bermuda offer only two classes of service: first class and economy. (Because most aircraft flying to Bermuda are medium-sized, there is no allowance for business class.) Economy class is the lowest-priced regular airfare carrying no special restrictions or requirements.

OTHER GOOD-VALUE CHOICES

Bear in mind that in the airline industry what constitutes good value is always changing. What was the lowest possible fare one day may not be lowest the next day when a new promotional fare is offered.

BUCKET SHOPS   A bucket shop (or consolidator) acts as a clearinghouse for blocks of tickets that airlines discount and consign during normally slow periods

---

Impressions

[As you approach Bermuda by air, you'll notice] dozens of small houses, their roofs pyramid-shaped, and whitewashed, their walls picked out in a variety of soft pastels— lemon, bluebell, lilac, primrose. It all looks very prim and ordered: the lawns look neat, the swimming pools glitter in the late morning sun, the sea is the palest of greens and splashes softly against low cliffs of pink and well-washed orange.
—Simon Winchester, *The Sun Never Sets: Travels to the Remaining Outposts of the British Empire* (1985)

of air travel. For Bermuda, that usually means November through March. Charter operators (see below) and bucket shops used to perform separate functions, but the line has become blurred lately and many outfits now perform both functions.

Tickets are sometimes discounted up to 35%. Time of payment can vary from 45 days prior to departure to the last minute. Such discount tickets may be purchased through regular travel agents, who, however, usually mark them up at least 8% to 10%, reducing your discount.

Many users of consolidators complain that since they do not qualify for advance seat assignment, they are likely to be assigned a "poor seat" on the plane at the last minute. And in a recent survey many passengers reported no savings at all, since airlines sometimes match the consolidator ticket when they announce a promotional fare. So, carefully investigate all options to make sure you are really saving.

Bucket shops abound. Look for their ads in your local newspaper's travel section. It's much easier to get a bucket shop fare to Europe than to Bermuda, though. Getting a low-cost ticket by this route sometimes pays off, if you're willing to expend a lot of time and effort. In New York, try **TFI Tours International,** 34 W. 32nd St., 12th Floor, New York, NY 10001 (☎ **212/736-1140** in New York State or **800/745-8000** elsewhere in the United States).

CHARTER FLIGHTS Charter flights to Bermuda are severely limited, but not as strictly as they once were. In general, they are not allowed from "gateway" cities such as New York or other points where major international carriers service Bermuda. It is a complicated situation that changes yearly or even monthly, and it's best to go to a good travel agent, who should know the least expensive and most direct route for you.

Essentially, charter flights allow visitors to Bermuda to fly at a less expensive fare than on a regularly scheduled flight, in some cases at 30% or more less than a regular airfare. But this can vary considerably from flight to flight.

Charter flights do have several drawbacks, however. One is the long advance booking often required. For example, many require that you make reservations and purchase your ticket at least 45 days or more before your actual trip. Should you be forced by unforeseen circumstances to cancel your flight, you could lose most of the cash you've advanced. To avoid such a disaster, take out cancellation insurance; ask your travel agent about it.

The charter flight always requires that you go to Bermuda and come back on certain dates. Again, this allows for no flexibility in your scheduling. Some also require that you prebook hotel rooms and pay for certain "ground arrangements."

For a charter flight, work through a travel agent, who will be aware of the business reputation of a packager. If you're a do-it-yourselfer, you can always check the Sunday travel section of your local or a big-city newspaper, looking for the announcements of any charter operators advertising flights to Bermuda.

STANDBY FARES Since courier services no longer operate to Bermuda, there is another cheap alternative. **Air-Tech Ltd.,** 584 Broadway, Suite 1007, New York, NY 10012 (☎ **212/219-7000**), is a "space-available" travel service, offering standby fares mainly to the Caribbean, Mexico, and Europe. You'll stand a far better chance of getting a standby fare to some point in the Caribbean, perhaps Jamaica or Puerto Rico, than you will to Bermuda, but why not give it a try anyway?

Space-available travel with Air-Tech is easy. All travelers need do is: register with Air-Tech, specify their preferred destination, give a two-to-five day travel window (when they wish to fly), and call Air-Tech the Wednesday before their travel window begins. Travelers are then informed of flights and seating availability for their specified window period. After that, it is simply a matter of going to the airport to catch your flight. It's that easy.

Passengers unable to get a flight within their chosen travel window are offered the opportunity to reschedule or get a full refund. Air-Tech's guarantee is to get you on board a flight within your designated travel window or they will refund your money.

TRAVEL CLUBS Yet another possibility for low-cost air travel is the travel club, with Bermuda heavily featured in the discounted offerings. A club supplies an unsold inventory of tickets discounted in the usual 20%–60% range. Some deals involve cruise ships and complete tour packages.

After you pay an annual fee to join, you are given a hot line number to call when you're planning a trip. Many discounts become available several days in advance of an actual departure; many give you at least a week and sometimes as much as a month of notice. Because you're limited to what's available, however, you have to be fairly flexible. Some of the best of these clubs include the following:

Moment's Notice, 425 Madison Ave., New York, NY 10017 (☎ 212/ 486-0500), charges $25 per year for membership that allows spur-of-the-moment participation in dozens of tours to sunny climes. Each is geared for impulse purchases and last-minute getaways, and each offers air and land packages that sometimes represent substantial savings over what you'd have paid through more conventional channels. Although membership is required for participation in the tours, anyone can call the company's hot line (☎ 212/750-9111) to learn what options are available. Most of the company's best-valued tours depart from New Jersey's Newark Airport.

Sears Discount Travel Club, 3033 S. Parker Rd., Suite 900, Aurora, CO 80014 (☎ in the U.S. **800/255-1487**), offers members, for $50, a catalog (issued four times a year), maps, discounts at select hotels, and a limited guarantee that equivalent packages will not be undersold by any other travel organization. It also offers a 5% rebate on the value of all airline tickets, tours, and hotel and car rentals that are purchased through them. (To collect this rebate, participants are required to fill out some forms and photocopy their receipts and itineraries.)

Vacations to Go, 2411 Fountain View, Houston, TX 77057 (☎ 800/ 338-4962), established in 1984, specializes in making contacts between cruise lines and cruise participants and discounted prices. Annual membership costs $19.95 per family, and provides access to catalogs and newsbriefs about cost-conscious cruises through the Atlantic, the Caribbean, and the Mediterranean.

BY CRUISE SHIP

Conditions have improved remarkably since that "innocent abroad," Mark Twain, made his rough sea trips to Bermuda. He considered the place "hell to get to," but thought the charms of Bermuda worth the tough sea voyage. He would surely be amazed at the luxurious way today's seagoing passengers travel to sunny Bermuda.

Cruise ships aren't for everyone, but if you'd like to try this method of travel, Bermuda is a good choice for a first-timer. Since you can sail from the east coast of the United States to Bermuda and back in just a few days, you aren't locked into a long time at sea (as you might be on a Caribbean cruise).

Unfortunately, cruise-ship trips to Bermuda are limited, mostly because of the lack of facilities there for big cruise ships. Cruise ships tie up at three harbors in Bermuda: St. George's in the East End, the Royal Naval Dockyard in the West

End, and the most visited port of call on the island, Hamilton Harbour (the city of Hamilton).

The cruise-ship season is from April to November. Once only the wealthy could afford such a trip, but package deals and other cost-saving arrangements devised by the travel industry have opened up the decks of the cruise ship to today's middle-income voyager.

Once you've decided to go by cruise ship, it's time to select your cruise line. Some lines want their passengers to have a total vacation—one filled with activities from "sunup to sundown." Others see time at sea as a period of tranquillity and relaxation, with less emphasis on "fun, fun," organized activities (which tend to get a little corny anyway).

To keep costs down, ask for inside cabins, which are usually very small and thus less desirable and cheaper. If you plan to be active during most of the day, you won't be spending much time in your cabin, anyway. Most cabins have a private shower and toilet, so you won't be sharing facilities. Many readers also report that in a midship cabin you are less likely to experience severe rolling and pitching. Cabins on older vessels come in widely different sizes, beginning with deluxe state-room suites, a throwback to the old days of transatlantic voyages. Modern vessels have more standardized accommodations.

Although "white tie and tails" are no longer de rigueur, it's still a good idea for men to take along a dark suit, and for women to bring at least one cocktail dress. Most of the time more casual wear is appropriate for evening: sports coats, slacks, and open shirts for men and sports dresses and pants suits for women.

Unfortunately (considering the investment), one of the most important ingredients for a successful cruise is the hardest thing to know in advance—your fellow passengers. The right crowd can be a lot of fun, an incompatible one can leave you sulking in your cabin.

Economy tip: You get considerable savings on seven-day cruises by booking early. See a travel agent or call the cruise line.

Celebrity Cruises 5200 Blue Lagoon Dr., Miami, Fl 33126 (☎ **305/262-8322** or **800/437-3111**), offers cruises to Bermuda from New York and other East Coast cities in spring and summer. Seven-night cruises usually leave New York on Saturday, heading for Bermuda, with two nights each at St. George's and Hamilton. The 30,400-ton, 553-cabin SS *Meridian*, dating from 1967, carries 1,106 passengers, with an international crew of 580, with mainly Greek officers. More than half of its cabins are outside. This is a family favorite, with a children's program offered. Older people seem to like it too, but singles and young couples might seek other vessels.

Celebrity Cruises also sails the MV *Horizon* to Bermuda. A 46,811-ton vessel with 677 cabins, about 85% of which are outside, this 1990 ship carries 1,354 passengers with an international crew of 642. The passenger/crew ratio is two to one. The ship offers nine passenger decks, filled with entertainment lounges, bars, and other facilities. Cabins are up to date and quite spacious for the most part.

Cunard Line, 555 Fifth Ave., New York, NY 10017 (☎ **212/880-7500** or **800/221-4770**), sails RMS *Queen Elizabeth 2* to Bermuda on a five-day cruise July 2 through July 7, costing from $1,560 to $5,105 per person round trip. Another five-day sailing is scheduled from August 16 through 21, costing $1,510 to $4,890 per person round trip.

Built in 1969, this 67,139-ton vessel is the most famous cruise ship in the world, carrying 1,864 passengers, with a crew of 1,025 men and women. In November and December of 1994, the ship underwent a $45 million refurbishment. The flagship of the Cunard fleet, the QE2 sails the British flag to every corner of the globe.

The Golden Lion Pub, in the traditional British style, is the social point. On the Upper Deck near the theatre and the casino, it offers a variety of draft beers and other drinks, even pub games, an upright piano, and a karaoke center. The Grand Lounge is the venue for big name entertainment, with a new dance floor. The Lido is an informal buffet-style restaurant, offering breakfast, lunch, and a traditional midnight buffet. The atmosphere is that of an informal winter garden. The Mauretania Restaurant on the Quarter Deck has been completely refurbished, and the Caronia Restaurant on the Upper Deck was renamed to honor the Cunard ship of legendary opulence. All of the restaurants have been refurbished, including the Queens Grill, which has been compared to the top dining choices of Paris, London, and New York. The Princess Grill and the Britannia Grill are other dining choices.

You can get lost on the QE2, as it rises 13 stories high and is three football fields long. The vessel features the QE2 Spa, the most luxurious spa afloat, with rejuvenating sea-water massage jet and whirlpool treatments, three French hydrotherapy baths, and saunas for men and women. Beauty therapists are also on hand. Some of its many other features include a sports center, a jogging track, a library, a club casino, and a shopping promenade with a branch of Harrod's.

Majesty Cruise Line, 901 South America Way, Miami, FL 33132 (☎ 305/530-8900 or 800/532-7788), formed in 1991 as a companion company to the Dolphin Cruise Line, offers the $220 million MV *Royal Majesty*, sailing to Bermuda. With a tonnage of 32,400, it carries 1,056 passengers overseen by a crew of 500. It features 343 outside staterooms and 185 inside staterooms. It's the first ship to offer a totally smoke-free dining room, and 25% of its cabins are smoke-free. Built in 1992, it offers more amenities and refinement than most vessels used on three- to four-day cruises, such as those to Bermuda. Bountiful buffets and first-class meals are provided by the line, and meal service is virtually non-stop. The Royal Majesty kitchen staff also caters to special diets. You can stay in shape at the Bodywaves Spa, with computerized weight machines and aerobics. The average daily rate is $185 per passenger.

The **Norwegian Cruise Line,** 95 Merrick Way, Coral Gables, FL 33134 (☎ 305/460-4760 or 800/327-7030), offers the 1,242-passenger MS *Dreamward* weighing 41,000 tons. Built in 1992, it sails the high seas with a crew of 483. The passenger/crew ratio is 2.5 to 1. With 10 passenger decks, the vessel has 623 cabins, 85% of which are outside.

On Saturdays from April through October (dates subject to change), the *Dreamward* makes seven-day, round-trip cruises from New York to St. George's or the port of Hamilton. Prices range from $1,599 to $3,729 per person, double occupancy, including air fare from major North American gateways. Some holiday and special cruise fares may be slightly higher.

Instead of the large dining room of yore, the cruise line has developed a series of four, formal dining rooms. On the International Deck, the Four Seasons Dining Room has two seatings nightly, accommodating 256. The Sun Terrace Dining Room, also with two seatings and accommodating 190, is located on the Sun Deck. The largest dining room of all, The Terraces Dining Room, also on the

International Deck, has two nightly seatings, accommodating 282. This dining room on several levels offers panoramic-view windows on three sides. The smallest of all, Le Bistro, a South Beach–style bistro with a menu featuring light Italian and continental dishes, is also on the International Deck, accommodating 76. All dining rooms feature children's menus. Hot dogs and hamburgers, and similar fare, are served at the Sports Bar and Grill on the Sports Deck.

Eight bars and lounges are available, including the Stardust Lounge on the Star Deck, a two-story main show lounge with a proscenium stage that can accommodate as many as 635. Full-length Broadway-type revues can be presented here. At the end of the show, the lounge becomes a late-night disco. The Casino Royale lies on two levels, both the Star and Sun Decks, offering seven blackjack tables, one roulette, one dice, two Caribbean stud poker games, and 99 slot machines.

On the Sports Deck, the Fitness Center and Spa features the usual exercise equipment, aerobics area, Lifecycles, and Lifesteps. A range of other features includes a jogging track on the Promenade Deck, a children's playground, a medical center, a duty-free shop in The Galleria, and a Video Arcade on the Sports Deck touting video games and a 45-foot TV broadcasting a series of sports events. A third or fourth passenger in a double cabin is granted substantial discounts. Two swimming pools, one on the Sun Deck, another on the International Deck, are offered, along with twin Jacuzzis on the Sports Deck. Except for the Sky Deck, all decks and activities are wheelchair accessible.

Royal Caribbean Cruises Ltd., 1050 Caribbean Way, Miami, FL 33132 (☎ **800/327-6700**), offers MS *Song of America*, weighing 37,584 tons and carrying 1,402 passengers with an international crew, but with Norwegian officers. Built in 1982, the vessel offers 702 cabins, more than half of which are outside. In spite of its size, the *Song of America* is most often compared to an ocean-going yacht. From May 7 through October 22, it makes seven-night cruises to Bermuda from New York. Suites lie on the Promenade Deck, but all cabins are above the waterline.

Single passengers pay 150% of the double rate, but if you're a flexible single and are prepared to wait until embarkation time for your room assignment, you can get discounts.

Half a dozen bars, including the Schooner and the Viking Crown Lounge, see that you have plenty to drink, and, later, there is the Casino Royale for gambling, a disco, and a piano bar. Entertainment is provided, with activities ranging from a masquerade parade to a country and western jamboree. In all, four lounges are devoted to entertainment. The kitchen aboard serves bountiful meals and is open to special requests.

After all the wining and dining, both the Sun Deck and Promenade Deck offer "trails" to work it off. In addition, the health club features massages, saunas, treadmills, stationary bicycles, and rowing machines. During holidays and in summer special programs for children are offered. For the disabled, wheelchair access is limited.

BY PACKAGE TOUR

Economy and convenience are the chief advantages of a package tour: the costs of transportation (usually airplane fare), hotel, food (sometimes), and sightseeing (sometimes) are combined in one package, neatly tied up with a single price tag.

If you booked your flight or hotel separately, you would pay more than a package tour—hence their immense and increasing appeal. Also, because tour operators can mass-book hotels and make volume purchases, transfers between your hotel and the airport are often included. Of course, there are disadvantages: you may find yourself in a hotel you dislike immensely, yet you are virtually trapped there because you've already paid for it. The single traveler, regrettably, usually suffers too, since nearly all tour packages are based on double occupancy.

Choosing the right package tour can be a problem, but your travel agent might offer one, and certainly all the major airline carriers will. There are also companies that specialize in package tours.

One company that has specialized in marketing travel to Bermuda since 1978 is the **Bermuda Travel Planners,** 350 5th Ave., Suite 2718, New York, NY 10018 (☎ **212/564-9502** or **800/323-2020**). It represents almost 50 of the island's hotels, ranging from modest and out-of-the-way guesthouses to deluxe hotels. Particularly popular are the company's wedding packages. Bermuda Travel Planners also arranges vacation packages for horseback riders, scuba enthusiasts, golf and tennis players, and honeymooners. Hours are 9am to 6pm Monday through Friday.

Other well-recommended tour operators include outfits endorsed and approved by two of North America's largest airlines. These include **Delta Dream Vacations,** 110 E. Broward Blvd., Fort Lauderdale, FL 33301 (☎ **205/522-1440** or **800/ 872-7786**), and **American Airlines Flyaway Vacations** (☎ **800/433-7300**). Both outfits factor inexpensive airfare into land (i.e. hotel) packages that can save substantial amounts of money over what you'd have paid if you'd booked the arrangements yourself.

As a final participant in the organized tour sweepstakes, consider contacting one of the world's largest travel organizers, **American Express.** Favored treatment and special discounts are sometimes offered to holders of gold or platinum American Express cards (if you have one of these, call **800/525-3355**); but a wide array of interesting and unusual tours are offered to members of the general public as well. (Dial ☎ **800/937-2639** and your call will be routed to the regional American Express representative closest to the source of your call.)

Shopping around for the right package can be time-consuming and a bore. To speed up the process, call **Tourscan Inc.,** P.O. Box 2367, Darien, CT 06820 (☎ **203/655-8091** or **800/962-2080**). Its computerized list provides both hotel and air package deals not only to Bermuda, but also to the Bahamas and the Caribbean. It usually has the whole range of offerings so you can pick and choose from what's out there. Its *Island Vacation Catalog,* which costs $4, is issued twice yearly and contains complete details. Your $4 is refunded if you book a tour. Once you decide on a tour, you can either book it directly through Tourscan, or use any travel agent.

2 Orientation

ARRIVING
BY PLANE

Chances are, you'll arrive by air, as most visitors do. Arrivals are at the Civil Air Terminal at Kindley Field Rd., St. George's, 9 miles east of Hamilton and about 17 miles east of Somerset at the far western end of Bermuda.

The flight from most East Coast destinations, including New York, Raleigh/ Durham, Baltimore, and Boston takes only about two hours, so you won't have jet lag upon arrival. Even flights from more remote Atlanta take only $2^{1}/_{2}$ hours, or nearly 3 hours from Toronto.

After clearing Customs, you can pick up tourist information at the airport before heading out to your hotel. Since you aren't allowed to rent a car in Bermuda, you must rely on a bus, taxi, or limousine to reach your hotel.

More than 600 taxis are available in Bermuda, and cabbies meet all arriving flights. Taxis are metered and are allowed to carry a maximum of four passengers. If you and your companion/spouse have a lot of luggage, you will need the taxi all to yourself, of course. Including a tip of 10% to 15%, it costs about $25 to reach a destination in Hamilton. Since you're already near St. George's, the fare there is about $11, or $14 to Tucker's Town. To the south shore hotels, the charge is likely to be $30 or more.

To the West End, site of many more resorts, the charge is likely to be more than $40. Fares go up 25% between 10pm and 6am and all day on Sundays and holidays. Luggage placed on the roof or trunk carries a surcharge of 25¢ per piece. Expect to pay about $4 for the first mile and $1.40 for each additional mile. A rise in fares, perhaps 5% to 10%, is anticipated some time in 1996. The number for calling a radio cab is **441/295-4141**. The taxi company's head office is at **441/295-0041**.

A party of four will do better financially to call a minivan and split the cost between them. This can be done before you arrive in Bermuda by contacting **Bermuda Hosts Ltd.** at **441/293-1334.** This outfit can arrange to have a minivan waiting for your flight. Even if you're a couple and not four passengers you can always ask a waiting minivan at the airport if it has room to take on two extra passengers. That way, you can shave the cost you'd incur by having a taxi all to yourself. Bermuda Hosts can provide transportation for golfers and can also arrange sightseeing tours.

BY CRUISE SHIP

This is perhaps the easiest way to arrive in Bermuda. The cruise ship staff presents you with a list of tour options long before your arrival in port; everything is virtually done for you, unless you opt to take an independent taxi tour, which is far more expensive, of course, than an organized tour. Most passengers book shore excursions at the same time they reserve the cruise.

Seven-day cruises out of New York spend four days in the Atlantic, with three days in port. Most cruise ships arrive in the traditional port of Hamilton, which is the capital of Bermuda and its chief commercial and shopping center. If shopping is more important than sightseeing to you, select a cruise that docks here.

If you're more interested in history, arrange to go on a ship that anchors at St. George's, at the eastern tip of the island. With its narrow lanes and old buildings and streets, St. George's has been called the island's equivalent of Colonial Williamsburg in Virginia. It has some shops and boutiques, although not nearly as many as Hamilton does.

It is much more unlikely (because of volume of arrivals) that you'll disembark at Somerset, which is the western end of the island and the farthest cruise port from Bermuda's major attractions. The West End is not without its own charm and sightseeing allure, though. It is, after all, home to the Royal Naval Dockyard, one of the major sightseeing targets of Bermuda. In a shopping mall at the dockyard, craft stores and museums exist side by side.

During your stay in port, you can avail yourself of the waiting taxis outside your vessel, or else you can rent mopeds and bicycles (see "Getting Around," below) and do some touring and shopping on your own.

VISITOR INFORMATION

You can get answers to most of your questions at the **Visitors Service Bureau** at the Ferry Terminal, Hamilton (☎ **441/295-1480**); King's Square, St. George's (☎ **441/297-1642**); or in Somerset (☎ **441/234-1388**). The Visitors Service Bureau is open Monday through Saturday from 9am to 4:45pm.

ISLAND LAYOUT

THE CITY OF HAMILTON AND ENVIRONS   With Hamilton at the center, Bermuda can be divided into the West End and the East End, the latter the site of the previously mentioned airport. As you leave the Ferry Terminal at Hamilton Harbour, you'll come upon the Visitors Service Bureau and the birdcage police officer.

To your east lies the main shopping artery of Hamilton, Front Street, and to your west is Pitts Bay Road leading to the Princess, Hamilton's leading hotel.

Front Street follows the line of the harbor and boasts many of the stores for which Bermuda is famous, including Trimingham's, established in 1844, and Smith's, established in 1889.

Moving inland and on a parallel line with Front Street are the other many shopping streets of Hamilton, including Reid Street, Church Street, and Victoria Street.

Par-La-Ville Park, lying directly north of the Ferry Terminal, is the city's largest and most central public garden.

North Hamilton is in Pembroke Parish, the name of the parish in which the city of Hamilton is located. The parish of Hamilton is a largely residential area beginning at Victoria Park; it is mainly a working-class district. Unlike a Caribbean island, where it would likely be a slum, it is an area of relatively neat small houses.

East of Hamilton, Fort Hamilton is one of originally 55 forts that once guarded Bermuda. Sitting alone in the Atlantic, Bermuda was easy to attack before the installation of these forts. Nearby is the 20-acre Arboretum.

THE EAST END   Continuing east from Hamilton, the parish of Devonshire is named after the famous shire in England's West Country, with its rolling hills and "green lungs." The parish's newer name of Devonshire is quite an improvement on its former label: Brackish Pond. One of its major landmarks is Old Devonshire Church, lying to the south of Middle Road.

From Hamilton you can take Middle Road all the way to Flatts Village, which opens onto the landlocked Harrington Sound. It's also possible to go along South Shore Road (also called South Road), which will eventually lead to Tucker's Town, an exclusive residential area of multimillion-dollar properties.

The just-mentioned Harrington Sound is filled with attractions, and if you're in Bermuda for a few days, you'll probably spend much of your time here, seeing the Bermuda Aquarium, the Bermuda Glass Blowing Studio, Crystal Caves, Leamington Caves, Bermuda Perfumery, Spittal Pond, and Verdmont, to name only some of the sights.

Continuing west, follow Blue Hole Hill until you reach the causeway, which takes you east to St. George's, the historic old city of Bermuda and its former capital. St. George's is on an island, also known as St. George's. To explore the town, it's best to take a walking tour (see Chapter 8, "Walking Tours").

The eastern end of Bermuda was forever changed when the United States created a sprawling landfill during World War II and used it as a military base. The present-day Bermuda airport grew out of that base. The remaining part of the American base is used mainly for routine antisubmarine surveillance flights and as a tracking station of the National Aeronautics and Space Administration. (American rights to the base—part of a 99-year lend-lease agreement between the United States and Britain signed in 1941, under which the British received American submarines and other needed war matériel in exchange for use of the base—terminate in the year 2040.) Bermuda's only McDonald's is on the base, but it can be visited only on Wednesdays, when the base is open to the public.

The base is on St. David's Island, the most rustic spot in Bermuda. The island lighthouse, dating from 1879, occupies the loftiest point on Bermuda's East End. Some St. David's islanders, the most provincial of whom are said to have never visited Hamilton, refused to be relocated when the naval base was built, stubbornly staying on their homeland. In a section called "Texas," the government built cottages for these islanders, and they and their families remain there today.

THE WEST END   To the west of Hamilton, a different world unfolds, as visitors explore, in this order, the parishes of Paget, Warwick, Southampton, and Sandys, the last-named lying in the far western corner. The landmass of Sandys along Great Sound juts eastward as if it were trying to reconnect with the city of Hamilton.

South of Hamilton heading west is Harbour Road, which borders the harbor of Hamilton for several miles until it reaches the vicinity of Darrell Island, a tiny green islet that was the site of Bermuda's first airport. You can take ferries from the city of Hamilton to this southern peninsula, which borders the north coast of Paget and Warwick parishes.

Alternatively, you can take Middle Road, which goes through Paget and Warwick parishes. Continue west through Southampton until you reach Somerset Bridge, which you use to cross into Sandys Parish.

Many of the best hotels and beaches, including the Elbow Beach Hotel and Warwick Long Bay along with Horseshoe Bay, lie along the southern coast of the western peninsula, reached by going along South Shore Road (also called South Road). If you continue west far enough, South Shore Road runs into Middle Road for its final push through the parish of Southampton.

Middle Road continues to Somerset Bridge, which leads into the parish of Sandys. This parish consists of Somerset Island, the Royal Naval Dockyard, and Ireland, Watford, and Boaz islands. Although facing the Atlantic on their northern shorelines, these islands and settlements open onto the more protected Great Sound.

Somerset Bridge is best reached by taking the ferry from Hamilton. From the ferry dock at the bridge, you can continue by ferry to Ireland Island and the Dockyard, or you can take the ferry directly from Hamilton to the Dockyard. Sandys Parish is bisected by Somerset Road.

Many visitors come here to visit Mangrove Bay, an idyllic beach strip lying directly east of Somerset Village, the tiny hamlet of the parish dominated by Sandys Boat Club.

Somerset Village is the beginning of Bermuda's Railway Trail, and it's a good place to begin if you wish to take this walk through the island.

FINDING AN ADDRESS

The island chain of Bermuda isn't the center of Manhattan, and, as such, doesn't follow a system of street addresses too rigidly. Most hotels, even in official government listings, don't bother to include street addresses, although they do include post boxes and zip codes. It's just assumed that everybody knows where everything is, which is fine if you've lived in Bermuda all your life. But, if you're a first-time visitor, you should get a good map and some landmark locations before setting out.

Most of the establishments you will be seeking are on some street plan. Some places use numbers in their street addresses; others, perhaps their neighbors, don't! The actual street number is not that important in many cases, since a building such as a resort hotel is likely to be set back so far from the main road you couldn't see its numbers anyway. It's far better to look for signs indicating, for example, the Sonesta Beach Hotel than for a street number. Cross streets will also aid you in finding an address.

Plot your itinerary carefully and ask questions. If you get lost, know that some well-traveled people believe that one of the charms of a visit to Bermuda is getting lost along some unmarked country lane. Many interesting discoveries have been made that way.

MAPS

Bookstores on the island will sell you more detailed maps, but most visitors get by using the free *Bermuda Handy Reference Map* published by the Bermuda Department of Tourism. This tiny pocket map, distributed by the tourist office and available at most hotels, has on one side an overview and orientation map (with key) of Bermuda, highlighting and numbering its major attractions, golf courses, public beaches, and hotels. It does not, however, locate individual restaurants unless they are attached to hotels.

On the flip side of the map is a detailed street plan of the city of Hamilton, indicating all its major landmarks and service facilities, such as the Ferry Terminal and the Post Office.

There is also a detailed map of the Royal Naval Dockyard, the West End, and the East End, plus tips on transportation—ferries, taxis, buses—and other helpful hints, even a depiction of various traffic signs.

3 Getting Around

Driving is on the left, and the national speed limit is 20 mph in the Bermuda countryside, 15 mph in busier areas. Cars are limited to one per family—and none at all for visitors. In such a far-off Eden, the most popular form of transportation is the motorized bicycle, called a "putt-putt," and the most romantic means of transport is the colorful fringe-topped surrey.

BY BUS   You can't have a car. Taxis are expensive. You may not want or be able to ride a bicycle or a motor bike. What's left for getting around Bermuda? Buses,

Impressions

Bermuda is essentially a small town in a glamorous setting.
                    —David Shelley Nicholl, letter to the (London) *Times* (1978)

of course. All major routes are covered by the bus network, but be prepared for waits. There's even a do-it-yourself sightseeing tour by bus and ferry, and regularly scheduled buses go to most of the destinations that tourists find of interest in Bermuda. However, some routes are not operated on Sunday and holidays, so be sure to find out about routes for the trip you want to make.

Bermuda is divided into 14 zones of about two miles each. In cash the regular fare for up to 3 zones is $2.50 or $4 for more than 3 zones. Token fares are $2 for up to 3 zones or $3.50 for more than 3 zones. Children 3 to 13 years pay $1 for all zones. Those 2 and under go free. *Note:* You must have the exact change or tokens ready to deposit in the farebox as you board the bus. Drivers do not make change.

You can also purchase tokens at sub-post offices or at the **Central Bus Terminal** on Washington Street in Hamilton, where all routes begin and end. The terminal is just off Church Street a few steps east of City Hall. You can get there from Front Street or Reid Street by going along Queen Street or through Walker Arcade and Washington Mall. If your plan is to travel a lot around Bermuda, a booklet of 15 14-zone tickets costs $22 or 15 3-zone tickets $13. Children pay a flat fare of $6 regardless of zones. For more information regarding the bus service, telephone **441/292-3854.** Nearly all hotels, guesthouses, and restaurants have bus stops close by.

In the east, **St. George's Mini-Bus Service** (☎ **441/297-8199**) operates a minibus service around St. George's Parish and St. David's Island. The basic fare is $1.50 for adults or 75¢ for children. Senior citizens ride for 85¢. Buses leave from King's Square in the center of St. George's, but they can also be flagged down along the road. Service is daily from 7am to 11pm March through November. Off-season hours are daily from 7am to 10pm.

The **West End Mini-Bus Service** (☎ **441/234-2344**) runs a minibus service leaving from Somerset Bridge and going all the way to the Royal Naval Dockyard on Ireland Island. Fares depend on how far you go, but they're never more than $3.50 for the entire run. Children and senior citizens go for half price. Passengers can be dropped off where they want, providing it is on the regular bus route. With slight variations, hours are Monday from 8:30am to 1pm, Tuesday through Saturday from 8:30am to 5pm, and Saturday and Sunday from 8:30am to 1pm.

BY TAXI   An expensive means of getting around, taxis are necessary at times. The hourly charge for taxis is $20 for 1 to 4 passengers. If you want to use one for a sightseeing tour, the minimum is 3 hours. When a taxi has a blue flag on the hood of the vehicle (the locals refer to it as the "bonnet"), the driver, man or woman, is qualified to serve as tour guide. Because he or she is checked out and tested by the government, this is the type of driver you should use if you're planning to use the expensive method of touring Bermuda by taxi. "Blue-bonnet" drivers charge no more than regular taxi drivers.

For more information, call **Bermuda Taxi Operators, 441/292-5600.** For radio-dispatched cabs, call **Radio Cabs Bermuda** (☎ **441/295-4141**).

BY CYCLE & SCOOTER   If you're looking for a lot of exercise, you may want to try a pedal bicycle, the old Bermudian way to travel around the island, although some of the hills may be a real challenge to your stamina.

Many people prefer a motor-assisted cycle—moped, motor scooter, whatever—that you can rent on an hourly, daily, or weekly arrangement. The operator of such a vehicle must be at least 16 years of age, although younger persons may be

Island Hopping on Your Own

Most first-time visitors think of Bermuda as one island when in fact it is a small archipelago. Many of these islands are uninhabited. If you're a bit of a skipper, you can explore them . With the guidance of the marina from which you've rented a small vessel, and armed with the proper maps, you can discover not only these islands (isles, really), but visit the coral reefs and hidden coves, many evocative of an old Brooke Shields movie.

For this boating adventure, acquire a Boston Whaler with an outboard engine. The romantic-sounding name of these sturdy although small boats reveals their origins, that of the 1990s version of the boats that New Englanders, such as seafarers from Fall River, Mass., used in their pursuit of Moby Dick. Of course, it's important to exercise caution, remembering that Bermuda itself was founded in 1612 only after the *Sea Venture*, en route to the Jamestown Colony, wrecked off the Bermuda coast.

In the East End, go exploring in the protected Castle Harbour, which is almost surrounded by islands forming a protected lake. You can stop somewhere and go fishing. Snapper is your likely catch. Some visitors renting condos or apartments often take their catch of the day home for dinner to prepare in their kitchenette.

To avoid an often powerful swell, drop anchor on the west side of Castle Harbour, which would be directly east of the Castle Harbour Golf Club and Tucker's Town. Then, head across Tucker's Town Bay for Castle Island, with its Castle Islands Nature Reserve. In days of yore, Castle Island was fortified to protect Castle Harbour from enemy attack. Governor Moore in 1612 ordered a fort to be built here, the ruins of which remain today.

In the West End, it's best to begin your water wonderland exploration by going under Somerset Bridge into well-protected Ely's Harbour. To the north you can visit Cathedral Rocks before making a half-circle to Somerset Village, from which you can explore the uninhabited islands off of Mangrove Bay.

Boston Whalers can be rented from the following places: **Mangrove Marina Ltd.,** end of Cambridge Rd., Mangrove Bay, Somerset (☎ **441/234-0914**); **South Side Scuba Water Sports,** at Grotto Bay Beach Hotel, Hamilton Parish (☎ **441/293-2915**), with another location at Marriott's Castle Harbour Resort, also in Hamilton Parish (☎ **441/293-2543**); **Rance's Boatyard,** Crow Lane, in Paget Parish (☎ **441/292-1843**); **Robinson's Charter Boat Marina,** Somerset Bridge, Sandys Parish (☎ **441/234-0709** or **441/238-9408**); and **Salt Kettle Boat Rentals, Ltd.,** Salt Kettle, Paget Parish (☎ **441/236-4863**).

Most Boston Whalers are 13 to 15 feet. For two hours, charges range from $45 to $60 depending on the vessel. Half-day rentals go from $65 to $85; and full-day rentals cost from $100 to $135.

carried as passengers. Some are large enough for two adults. Both driver and passenger are required by law to wear a helmet, which will be furnished by the place from which you rent your machine. Straps must be securely fastened. *Warning:* Visitors on mopeds have a high accident rate. Exercise extreme caution. Also, *you must*, as mentioned, *drive on the left*, as in England.

In the rentals recommended below, there is a tendency toward price-fixing, so it's not possible to shop around for a better deal, as it was in the past.

Mopeds for one rider rent for $31 for the first day, $54 for two days, and $70 for three days. Scooters for two riders cost $39 for one day, $70 for two days, $96 for three days, $118 for four days, and $135 for five days. For the rental of either mopeds or scooters, a fully refundable $20 deposit is required, plus the purchase of a one-time insurance policy priced at $10. The insurance is valid for the entire length of the rental. You can rent bikes at most cycle liveries.

Astwood Cycles Ltd. (☎ 441/292-2245) has shops where you can rent either mopeds or 50-cc scooters: 77 Front St. in Hamilton; at Flatts Village; at the Princess, Sonesta Beach, and Belmont Hotels; Coral Beach Cottages; and at Horizons and Cottages.

Charging comparable prices and renting out either type of vehicle, is **Wheels Ltd.,** Don Donald St., Hamilton (☎ 441/295-0112), or at the Southampton Princess (☎ 441/238-3336).

One of the best rental deals on the island is offered by **Eve's Cycle Livery,** 114 Middle Rd., Paget Parish (☎ 441/236-6247). Named after a now-legendary matriarch who founded it more than 40 years ago, it rents men's and women's pedal bicycles (usually 10- to 12-speed mountain bikes well suited to the island's hilly terrain) for $15 for the first day, $10 for the second day, and $5 for each supplemental day. A $10 deposit is required. The shop lies within a 10-minute drive (or a 20-minute leisurely cycle) west of Hamilton. The company also rents a selection of motorized pedal bikes or scooters for between $20 and $36 for the first day, depending on the model, with a descending tier of prices for each additional day.

At **Oleander Cycles Ltd.,** Valley Road, P.O. Box 114, Paget Parish (☎ 441/236-5235) scooters and mopeds tend to be reliable and well maintained. There is another location on Gorham Road in Hamilton (☎ 441/295-0919). Both locations are open daily from 8am to 5pm. Rentals require a $20 deposit and a supplemental charge of $12 for an insurance policy that lasts for the duration of your rental (a day or a week), or until you cause any damage to your rented moped.

BY FERRY   One of the most interesting methods of transportation is the government-operated ferry service. Ferries crisscross Great Sound between Hamilton and Somerset, charging $3.50 fare one way; they also take the harbor route, going from Hamilton to the parishes of Paget and Warwick, where so many hotels are concentrated. The ride from Hamilton to Paget costs only $2; children pay half fare. Motorcycles are allowed on the Hamilton to Somerset run (you must pay $3.50 for your cycle, however). Bicycles are carried free. For ferry service information, telephone 441/295-4506 in Hamilton. Ferry schedules are posted at each landing. They are also available at the Ferry Terminal or the Central Bus Terminal in Hamilton. Actually, most hotels will give you a timetable if you ask.

BY HORSE-DRAWN CARRIAGE   Being romantics, Bermudians have retained at least some of their horse-drawn carriages. Although once plentiful, there are now only about a dozen left. Drivers congregate on Front Street in Hamilton, adjacent to the No. 1 passenger terminal near the cruise-ship docks. Before 1946 the horse was the principal mode of transport. After that, the first automobiles came to the island. You can book one of these four-wheeled rigs for a chauffeured tour of the island's midriff. A single carriage drawn by one horse costs $20 for 30 minutes and can carry one to four passengers. An additional 30 minutes costs another $20. If you want to take a ride lasting more than three hours, the fee is negotiable. Unless you make special arrangements for a night ride, you aren't likely to find any carriages after 4:30pm. Contact **Bermuda Carriages** at **441/238-2640.**

4 Tips on Accommodations

Accommodations in Bermuda basically fall into six major categories, descriptions of which are given below.

RESORT HOTELS   These often sprawling properties are Bermuda's best, offering many facilities, services, and luxuries—but also charging the highest prices, especially in summer. It's usually cheaper to check into them on MAP rates (breakfast and dinner) than it is to order all your meals à la carte. They charge the lowest rates from mid-November to March, usually about 20% less. Most of the large resorts have their own beaches or beach clubs, along with swimming pools. Some even offer their own golf courses.

COTTAGE COLONIES   A uniquely Bermudian offering, these colonies are usually a series of bungalows constructed around a main clubhouse, which is the center of social life, drinking, and dining. The cottages are usually set scenically on landscaped grounds. Most of them have been built to give guests maximum privacy, and nearly all have their own kitchenettes (used mainly for preparing light meals). Most of the colonies have either their own beaches or swimming pools.

HOUSEKEEPING COTTAGES & APARTMENTS   These accommodation units are usually called efficiencies in the United States. Most of them lie on landscaped estates, have swimming pools, and usually are built around a main clubhouse. All of them offer kitchen facilities, and some are designed as wings or modern apartment-style units surrounding a pool or opening onto a beach. Most of them offer minimal daily maid service.

GUESTHOUSES   These accommodations are the cheapest means of living in Bermuda. Most of the large ones are old Bermuda homes, with garden settings. Generally, they have been modernized, with comfortable guest rooms. Some of them have their own pools. A number of these guesthouses are small, modest places, offering breakfast only; the bath is often shared with other guests. You will usually have to commute to the beach if you stay in one of these places.

RENTAL VILLAS & VACATION HOMES   You might rent a big villa, a good-sized apartment in someone's condo building, or even a small beach cottage (more accurately called a cabaña).

Private apartments are also available with or without maid service. These are more of a no-frills option than the villas and condos. The apartments may not be in buildings with swimming pools, and they may not have a front desk to help you.

Cottages, or cabañas, offer the most freewheeling life-style available in this category of vacation accommodations. Many ideally open onto a beach, although others may be clustered around a communal swimming pool. Most of them are fairly basic, containing no more than a simple bedroom plus a small kitchen and bath. In the peak summer season, reservations should be made at least five or six months in advance.

Several agents throughout the United States and Canada offer these types of rentals. To get you going, try **Rent-a-Home International,** 7200 34th Ave. NW, Seattle, WA 98117 (☎ **206/789-9377**), which specializes in condos and villas. It arranges weekly or longer bookings.

5 Tips on Dining

Whenever possible, it is best to stick to local food; for a main dish, that usually means fish caught in the deep sea. But let me state at the very beginning that food is not one of the reasons people go to Bermuda. So-called "gourmet fare" often isn't, although the prices charged would make you think that you're getting something really special. To find the many dishes that *are* truly worthy, you'll have to pick and choose your way carefully through the menu.

In general, it is unwise to order too many meat dishes. Red meats have probably been flown in, and may have been resting on the island for some time.

Dining in Bermuda also is generally more expensive than it is in the United States and Canada. Because virtually everything except the fish has to be imported, restaurant prices are more in tune with those of Europe than with those of America. Service is automatically added to most restaurant tabs, usually 10% to 15%. Even so, if service has been good, it is customary to leave something extra.

If you're booked into a hotel on MAP rates (half board), which hotels sometimes require in the peak summer season, you can sample some of the local restaurants at lunch. That way, your stomach won't become completely "hotel bound."

In some establishments, men are required to wear jackets. Ties are not usually required—an open-neck shirt usually suffices. If in doubt, check the policy of a restaurant before going there.

At the better places, women usually appear casually chic in the evening. During the day, no matter what the establishment, wearing a coverup is the proper thing to do—do not arrive for lunch decked out in a bikini.

Because of the lack of inexpensive transportation on the island, many travelers on a budget eat at their hotels at night to avoid adding an expensive taxi fare to their already overburdened dinner cost. If you like to dine around, find a hotel in or around Hamilton that has a number of restaurants. That way, you can walk to and from the restaurant.

6 Tips on Shopping

Retailers on less prosperous islands have claimed that the endless popularity of Bermuda is a result of its superb climate and its many years of skilled marketing. Indeed, no one has ever accused the Bermudians of not knowing how to market themselves or their rich inventories of retail goods. Bermuda, perhaps better than any other island in the world, draws richly upon its British antecedents to produce a battery of shops and stores, both large and small, whose charm and desirability is almost breathtaking. Even if your goal is only to window-shop (a highly engrossing art form in its own right), you'll find ample quantities of some of the most realistically priced, elegant merchandise anywhere. Much of it seems to literally beckon through the display windows for the attention of vacationing visitors.

What produces this alluring jumble of saleable goods? Much of it might have to do with the built-in sense of conservative style that permeates much of Bermuda. Most stores take full advantage of their placement within charming cottages or historically important buildings. Shopkeepers are for the most part both polite and discreet, and merchandise is often unusual and well made. Despite the fact that much of it seems to exude a kind of upscale quality and innate tastefulness, most of it is significantly cheaper than you might have expected.

Some frequent visitors to Bermuda take careful stock of their needs for porcelain, crystal, silverware, jewelry, timepieces, and perfume, perhaps anticipating several months in advance a needed wedding gift. The island is filled with merchandisers of fine tableware, the prices of which are between 25% and 50% less than you might have found at home. Famous makers whose goods fill the shops of Bermuda include Royal Copenhagen, Wedgwood, and Royal Crown Derby. Crystal is also an excellent bargain in Bermuda, with many of the finest manufacturers in Europe and North America providing wide selections of glittering merchandise. For a fee, all of these can be shipped, usually in well-wrapped packages that keep breakage to a minimum.

Not all the acquisitional temptations of Bermuda, however, derive from goods imported from abroad. The island produces endless quantities of unusual merchandise of its own. These include watercolors of Bermuda landscapes, etchings of its famous rooflines, oil paintings executed on pieces of aromatic local cedar, and jewelry configured into shapes inspired by the island's nautical traditions. They also include such culinary delights as sherry peppers preserved in herb-laced vinegar, or buttery cakes laced with Bermuda rum.

Antique lovers appreciate the mixture of the British aesthetic with mid-Atlantic charm. And, naturally, anyone interested in carrying home a piece of the island's nautical heritage will find oversized ship's propellers, captain's bells, brass nameplates, scale models of the sailing ships of long ago, or perhaps an old-fashioned ship's steering wheel from a salvaged shipwreck. Then there is the island's wealth of antique engravings, 19th-century furniture, modern artwork, and handmade pottery and crafts, all of which make for richly elegant heirlooms. In fact, the island's material (and saleable) allures are almost endless.

How does Bermuda maintain prices that many visitors consider low and/or at least extremely fair? Many of the merchandisers buy their inventories directly from manufacturers in Europe or North America, thereby avoiding high distribution costs. Duties imposed on goods imported into Bermuda are low, and there is no sales tax. In fact, some prices are low enough, and the merchandise tempting enough, to equalize whatever import duties might be imposed upon them by your government's Customs. (For more information on this, refer to the section on Customs in Chapter 3, "Before You Go.")

FAST FACTS: Bermuda

American Express The representative in Hamilton is **L. P. Gutteridge, Ltd.,** 16 Church St., P.O. Box 2905, Hamilton HM LX (☎ **441/295-4545**). The office provides complete travel service, sightseeing tours, airport transfers, hotel reservations, traveler's checks, and emergency check cashing.

Area Code Beginning in September 1995, Bermuda broke away from the traditional area code for the Caribbean (809) and began using the area code of 441. A grace period will extend to October 1996, so if you accidentally use the 809 area code, your call will still go through.

Banks There are three banks, all with their main offices in Hamilton: The **Bank of Bermuda Ltd.,** 6 Front St., Hamilton (☎ **441/295-4000**), has branches on Church Street, Hamilton; Par-la-Ville Road, Hamilton; King's Square, St. George's; and in Somerset.

The **Bank of N.T. Butterfield & Son, Ltd.,** 65 Front St., Hamilton (☎ 441/295-1111), is one of the major banks of Bermuda, with several branches throughout the island, including one at St. George's and another in the Southampton Princess Hotel.

The **Bermuda Commercial Bank Ltd.** is at 44 Church St., Hamilton (☎ 441/295-5678).

All banks and their branches have the same hours. They are open Monday through Thursday from 9:30am to 3pm, on Friday from 9:30am to 4:30pm. All banks are closed Saturday, Sunday, and on public holidays. Many of the big hotels will cash traveler's checks.

Boosktores Bermuda Book Store (Baxters) Ltd., Queen St. (☎ 441/295-3698), stocks everything that is in print about Bermuda. Some books are available only through this store. There are books on gardening, flowers, local characters, and poets, among other subjects. There are also many English publications not easily obtainable in the United States, as well as a fine selection of children's books. You can also buy maps and prints here.

Business Hours Most businesses are open Monday through Friday from 9am to 5:30pm. Stores are generally open Monday through Saturday from 9am to 5:30pm. Several shops open at 9:15am, closing at 5pm. A few shops are also open in the evening, but usually only when big cruise ships are in port.

Car Rentals There are no car-rental agencies in Bermuda.

Cigarettes Tobacconists and other stores carry a wide array of tobacco products, generally from either the United States or England. Prices vary but tend to be high. At most tobacconists you can buy classic cigars from Havana, but you must enjoy them on the island, since they can't be taken back to the United States because of Customs restrictions. Smoking in public places such as restaurants is generally allowed, but check first before lighting up. Movie theaters set aside a section for nonsmokers.

Climate See "When to Go," in Chapter 3, "Before You Go."

Crime See "Safety" below.

Currency See "Visitor Information, Entry Requirements & Money" in Chapter 3, "Before You Go."

Currency Exchange Because the U.S. dollar and the Bermudian dollar are on par, both currencies can be used and it's not necessary to convert U.S. dollars into Bermudian dollars. It will be necessary to, however, convert Canadian dollars into local currency because of different valuations between the Canadian dollar and the Bermuda dollar.

Customs Visitors going through **Bermudian Customs** may bring into Bermuda duty-free apparel and articles for their personal use, including sports equipment, cameras, 200 cigarettes, one quart of liquor, one quart of wine, and approximately 20 pounds of meat. Other foodstuffs may be dutiable. All imports may be inspected on arrival. Visitors entering Bermuda may claim a duty-free gift allowance.

Dentists For dental emergencies, call the **King Edward VII Hospital,** 7 Point Finger Rd., Paget Parish (☎ 441/236-2345) and ask for the emergency department. They maintain lists of island dentists on call for dental emergencies. One well-recommended dentist you might consider calling directly is Dr. David

Roblin, Outerbridge Building, Pitts Bay Rd., Pembroke Parish (☎ 441/292-7676).

Doctors For an emergency, call the **King Edward VII Hospital,** 7 Point Finger Rd., Paget Parish (☎ 441/236-2345) and ask for the emergency department. A private doctor, Dr. Gordon Campbell, Sea Venture Building, Parliament St., Hamilton (☎ 441/295-8106) handles colds, the flu, and other medical problems.

Documents Required See "Visitor Information, Entry Requirements & Money" in Chapter 3, "Before You Go."

Driving Rules There are no specific automobile-driving requirements for visitors for a very simple reason—there are no car-rental agencies in Bermuda. However, motor-assisted cycles are available (see "Getting Around" earlier in this chapter), but they may not be operated by children under 16. All cycle drivers and passengers are required by law to wear safety helmets that are securely fastened.

Driving is on the left side of the road. The speed limit is 20 mph, 15 mph in busy areas.

Drug Laws Importation of, possession of, or dealing with unlawful drugs, including marijuana, is an offense under Bermuda laws, with heavy penalties levied for infractions. Customs officers, at their discretion, may conduct body searches for drugs or other contraband goods.

Drugstores In Hamilton, try **Bermuda Pharmacy,** Church St. W. (☎ 441/295-5815). It's in the Russell Eve Building and is open Monday through Saturday from 8am to 6pm. Under the same ownership is the **Phoenix Drugstore,** 3 Reid St. (☎ 441/295-3838), open Monday through Saturday from 8am to 6pm.

In Paget Parish, you can go to **Paget Pharmacy,** 130 South Rd. (☎ 441/236-7275), open Monday through Saturday from 8am to 8pm and on Sunday from 2 to 6pm. At 49 Mangrove Bay, the **Somerset Pharmacy** in Somerset Village (☎ 441/234-2484) is open Monday through Saturday from 8am to 6pm.

Electricity Electricity is 110 volts, 60 cycles, AC. American appliances are compatible without converters or adapters.

Embassies and Consulates The **American Consulate General** is at Crown Hill, 16 Middle Rd., Devonshire (☎ 441/295-1342). Hours are Monday through Friday from 8:30am to 4:30pm. Canadians can refer to the **Canadian Consulate General** (Commission to Bermuda) at 1251 Avenue of the Americas, New York, NY 10020-1175 (☎ 212/768-2400). Britain doesn't have an embassy or consulate in Bermuda.

Emergencies To call the police in an emergency, dial **911;** if you need to reach the police, but it's not an emergency, dial **295-0011.** To report a fire, dial **911;** to summon an ambulance, call **911.** For Air-Sea Rescue, dial **297-1010.**

Etiquette Well-tailored Bermuda shorts are acceptable on almost any occasion, and many men wear them with jackets and ties at rather formal gatherings. But aside from that, the people are rather conservative in their attitude toward dress—bikinis, for example, are banned more than 25 feet from the water.

Eyeglass Repair **Argus Optical Company** (Henry Simmons, O.D.), Melbourne House, Parliament St., Hamilton (☎ 441/292-5452), works with both prescription glasses and contact lenses. Hours are 9am to noon and 1pm to 4:45pm Monday through Friday.

Gasoline   Since you aren't able to rent a car, you won't have to worry much about gasoline or "petrol" as some call it here. Mopeds take a mixture of oil and gas, and there's always a separate pump at gasoline stations for these vehicles. Honda scooters take regular unleaded gasoline, and it costs about $4 to fill up a tank. If you tour the distance of most bikers, you'll need only one refill per week. Both Honda scooters and mopeds are rented with full tanks. Gasoline stations are conveniently placed throughout the islands.

Holidays   See "When to Go" in Chapter 3, "Before You Go."

Hospital   **King Edward VII Memorial Hospital,** 7 Point Finger Rd., Paget Parish (☎ **441/236-2345**), has a staff of many nationalities and high qualifications. It has Canadian accreditation. Take bus no. 1 to reach it.

Hotline   Call **441/236-0224** for any consultation on psychiatric problems, but only from 8:45am to 5pm Monday through Friday. After 5pm, call **441/236-3770.** Depending on the hours of your call to this number, you'll be connected to one of two island hospitals, either the Bermuda Psychiatric Hospital's outpatient clinic, or (in the evening) the St. Brendan's Hospital. Either can help with life-threatening problems, personal crises, or can refer you to the proper medical specialist.

Information   For information before you go, refer to "Visitor Information, Entry Requirements & Money" in Chapter 3, "Before You Go." Once on the island, you can also obtain information: see Visitor Information under "Orientation" in this chapter.

Legal Aid   Should you become ill or injured in Bermuda, American citizens may need the services of the U.S. Consulate (see "Embassies and Consulates" above). The staff there can suggest where you might get medical help and will notify close relatives. Should your problem be a legal one, such as a drug arrest, the consulate will inform you of your rights (limited) and offer a list of attorneys. However, the consulate's office cannot interfere with the law-enforcement officers in Bermuda.

A hot line in an emergency—useful for questions about U.S. citizens arrested abroad—is the Citizens' Emergency Center of the Office of Special Consular Services in Washington, DC (☎ **202/647-5225**). They'll also tell you how to get money to U.S. citizens arrested abroad.

Liquor Laws   Bermuda sternly regulates the sale of alcoholic beverages. The legal drinking age is 18, and most bars close at 1am. Sometimes nightclubs and bars in hotels can serve liquor until 3am, depending on the hotel. Many places are closed on Sunday.

Mail   Regular mail can be deposited in red pillar boxes on the streets. You'll recognize them by the monogram of Queen Elizabeth II. The postage rates for airmail letters up to 10 grams and for postcards is 60¢ to the United States and Canada, 75¢ to the United Kingdom. Airmail letters and postcards to the North American mainland can take 5 to 7 days, and perhaps the same time or even longer to reach Britain. Often visitors have returned home before their postcards arrive.

Maps   Visitors wanting a more detailed map than the previously mentioned *Bermuda Handy Reference Map* can pick up a map entitled *Bermuda Tourist Map*, on sale at the Public Works Department, next to the General Post Office on Parliament Street in Hamilton. The yard-wide map is extremely detailed, pin-pointing specific buildings, with a scale of two inches to the mile.

Newspapers/Magazines   One daily newspaper is published in Bermuda, the *Royal Gazette*. Three weekly papers, the *Bermuda Sun*, *The Bermuda Times*, and the *Mid-Ocean News*, are issued on Friday. Major U.S. newspapers, including the *New York Times* and *USA Today*, and magazines (such as *Time* and *Newsweek*) are delivered to Bermuda on the day of publication on the mainland. *This Week in Bermuda* is a weekly guide published for tourists.

Passports   See "Visitor Information, Entry Requirements & Money" in Chapter 3, "Before You Go."

Pets   If you want to take your pet with you to Bermuda, you'll need a special permit issued by the director of the Department of Agriculture, Fisheries & Parks, P.O. Box HM 834, Hamilton HM CX, Bermuda (☎ 441/236-4201). Dogs and cats entering Bermuda from any country other than the United Kingdom, Australia, or New Zealand must have received a vaccination against rabies at least one month and not more than one year before the date of their intended arrival. Some guesthouses and hotels will permit you to bring in small animals, but others will not, so be sure to check into this in advance.

Photographic Needs   If you want to buy a camera or film, or develop either Kodak or Fuji film, try **Stuart's**, 5 Reid St., near the corner of Queen St. (☎ 441/295-0303), Hamilton's leading camera store. Film can be developed in-house in about three hours, and in some cases, within one hour for a surcharge.

Police   In an emergency, call **911**; otherwise, call **295-0011.**

Post Offices   The General Post Office is at 56 Church St., Hamilton (☎ 441/ 295-5151), and is open Monday through Friday from 8am to 5pm, on Saturday from 8am to noon. Post office branches and the Perot Post Office, Queen Street, Hamilton, are open Monday through Friday from 8am to 5pm. Some take a lunch break from 11:30am to 1pm. Airmail service for the United States and Canada closes at 9:30am in Hamilton, leaving daily. Also see "Mail" above.

Radio and TV   News is broadcast on the hour and half hour over AM stations 1340 (ZBM), 1230 (ZFB), and 1450 (VSB). The FM stations are 89 (ZBM) and 95 (ZFB). Tourist-oriented programming, island music, and information on activities and special events are aired over AM station 1160 (VSB) daily from 7am to noon.

The television channel, 10 (ZBM), is affiliated with America's Columbia Broadcasting System (CBS).

Restrooms   Hamilton and St. George's provide public facilities, but only during business hours. In Hamilton, toilets are found at City Hall, in Par-la-Ville Gardens, and at Albouy's Point. In St. George's, they are at Town Hall, Somers Gardens, and Market Wharf. Outside of these towns, you'll find restrooms at the public beaches, the Botanical Gardens, in several of the forts, at the airport, and at service stations; but, often you'll have to use the facilities in hotels, restaurants, and whatever else you can find.

Safety   There is no particular need for a crime alert regarding Bermuda. Bermudians are generally a peaceful people, not given to the expression of violence. To be sure, the island has experienced racial tensions in the past, but now relations between its white and black residents seem to be harmonious, as blacks assume a greater role in Bermuda's affairs.

Crimes, violent or otherwise, against tourists are rare, but don't be lulled into any false sense of security, either. Crime does exist, as in any society—for instance, someone might try to pick your wallet in Hamilton. Protect your valuables, especially when you're at the beach. Lock your moped each time you leave it. Very valuable items should be placed in your hotel safe (if your hotel is big enough to have one) and never left carelessly in your room.

It is usually safe to go anywhere in Bermuda, but, here again, caution should be exercised, particularly late at night and especially if you're a woman traveling alone.

Taxes   Visitors to Bermuda are levied a tax before departing from the island. For those who leave by air, the tax, collected at the airport, is $15 for adults and $5 for children between the ages of 2 and 11 (children under 2 are exempt). For those who leave by ship, the tax, collected in advance from the cruise ship company, is $60 (children under 2 are exempt).

All room rates, regardless of the category of accommodation or the plan under which you stay, are subject to a 6% Bermuda government tax, to be paid when you check out of your hotel.

Taxis   See "Getting Around" earlier in this chapter.

Telegrams/Telexes/Faxes   Worldwide phone and cable service is available, and charges may be reversed. Direct dialing is possible from Bermuda to the United States and Canada. To send telegrams, telexes, or faxes, go to **Cable & Wireless Office,** 20 Church St., Hamilton (opposite the City Hall). Hours are Monday through Saturday from 9am to 5pm. For information, phone **441/297-7000.**

Telephone   Cable & Wireless (see above), in conjunction with the **Bermuda Telephone Co., Ltd.,** provides international direct dialing (IDD) to more than 150 countries. Country codes and calling charges may be found in the current edition of the Bermuda telephone directory. Telephone booths are provided at the Cable & Wireless office, and customers have the choice of prepaying for calls, or purchasing cash cards in $10, $20, and $50 denominations. Cash cards may also be purchased at Visitor's Service Bureaus in Hamilton, St. George's, and the Dockyard. Cash card phone booths are also available at numerous locations on the island. Making international calls using cash cards can be a lot cheaper than using the phone at your hotel, which might impose stiff surcharges. To make a local call, deposit 20¢, either Bermudian or US. Hotels often charge from 20¢ to $1 for local calls.

Special phones are also in place at passenger piers in Hamilton, St. George's, and the Dockyard, connecting directly to AT&T, US Sprint, and MCI operators in the United States, thus permitting collect or calling card calls.

Telephone Directory   All Bermuda telephone numbers appear in one phone book, revised annually. The helpful *Yellow Pages* in the back list all the goods and services you are likely to need.

Time   Standard time in Bermuda is Greenwich mean time minus four hours, which makes it one hour ahead of eastern standard time. Daylight savings time is in effect from the first Sunday in April to the last Sunday in October, as it is in the United States. Thus when it's 6am in New York, it's 7am in Bermuda.

Tipping   In most cases, a service charge is added to your hotel and/or restaurant bill. In hotels, this is in lieu of tipping the various individuals such as the bellman, maids, and restaurant staff (for meals included in a package or in the daily rate). Otherwise, a 15% tip for service is customary.

Tourist Offices   See "Visitor Information" in Section 2 of this chapter.

Transit Information   For information about ferry service, call **441/295-4506.** For bus information, call **441/292-3854.**

Useful Telephone Numbers   For time and temperature, call **977-1.** To learn "What's On in Bermuda," dial **974.** For medical emergencies or the police, dial **911.** If in doubt during any other emergency, dial "**0,**" which, depending on where you are, will connect you with either your hotel's switchboard or the Bermuda telephone operator.

Water   Tap water is generally considered safe to drink.

Weather   This might be an all-important consideration for your Bermuda plans. In addition to the newspaper and the radio, you can call **977** at any time of the day or night for forecast covering the next 24-hour period.

5 Accommodations

Bermuda offers a wide selection of lodgings, ranging from small guesthouses to large luxury hotels. You'll find variations in size and facilities in each category. The Bermuda Hotel Association requires two nights' deposit within 14 days of confirmation of a reservation; full payment 30 days prior to arrival; and cancellation advice 15 days prior to scheduled arrival or your deposit will be lost. Some smaller hotels and other accommodations levy an energy surcharge, so you should ask about this when you make your travel arrangements.

All room rates, regardless of what plan you're staying on, are subject to a 6% Bermuda tax, which is added to your bill. A service charge ranging from 10% to 15% is added to your room rates in lieu of tips. Service charges do not cover bar tabs. Third-person rates are lower for those occupying a room with two other people, and children's tariffs vary according to their ages.

Generally, there are two major seasons in Bermuda, winter and summer. Bermuda has the reverse of the Bahamian or Caribbean high season, with its major season in spring and summer. Most establishments start to charge their high-season tariffs in March (Easter is the peak period) and lower their rates again around mid-November. A few hotels have all-year rates, and others charge in-between, or "shoulder," prices in spring and autumn. If business is slow, many smaller places will shut down in winter.

What follows is only a rough guideline to price ranges. In several large old resorts, because of the wide range of accommodations, prices are not uniform. Thus, while one guest at the Elbow Beach Hotel, for example, might be staying at a "moderate" cost, another guest might be booked in at a "very expensive" rate. It all depends on your room assignment.

In general, "very expensive" hotels in Bermuda offer double rooms for around $275 and up—and we do mean *up*. These rates are on the modified American plan (MAP) or half board.

Hotels considered "expensive" offer MAP doubles for anywhere from $200 to $275. Hotels classified as "moderate" charge from $115 to $200 for a double, but are likely to include only breakfast. Hotels or guesthouses classified as "inexpensive" ask around $100 for a double room, most often including breakfast. Of course, these prices are only rough guidelines. Within the same hotel, you often get widely varying price structures because rooms are not standardized. Therefore, you might be staying at a cottage colony on a "moderate" rate whereas one of your fellow guests in a better accommodation would be booked in on a "very expensive" rate.

In many of the cottage colonies, breakfast is not offered. You can either go out for breakfast or else pick up supplies the night before and prepare your own morning meal.

EMERGENCY ACCOMMODATIONS

If you haven't had time to reserve rooms before going to Bermuda, you may avail yourself of the services offered by the **Visitors Service Bureau** at the airport (☎ 441/292-0030). Located near Customs clearance, it is open from 11am to 4pm. Unless you have a hotel reservation and a return airplane ticket, you will not be allowed to proceed beyond this point. In the event that you do not have prebooked reservations, the bureau will help you make a reservation from the airport.

1 Resort Hotels

The big resort hotels can provide enough amenities to make it unnecessary for their patrons to leave the premises, although most visitors tend to want to see what's on the outside. Most of the large hotels have their own beaches or beach clubs and swimming pools. Some offer their own golf courses. Most hotels in this category boast luxury resort facilities, such as porter and room service, planned activities, sports facilities, shops (including a cycle shop), beauty salons, bars, nightclubs, entertainment, and taxi stands.

Few hotels or guesthouses include taxes and service charges in the prices quoted, so be aware that they will be added to your bill. The hotel tax is 6%, and service charges range from 10% to 15%.

VERY EXPENSIVE

Belmont Hotel Golf & Country Club

Middle Rd., P.O. Box WK 251, Warwick WK BX, Bermuda. ☎ **809/236-1301** or 800/225-5843 in the U.S. and Canada. Fax 809/236-6867. 151 rms (all with bath). A/C MINIBAR TV TEL. Transportation: Government ferry from Hamilton. Rates (MAP): Apr–Oct, $145–$170 single; $225–$250 double; Nov–Mar, $135–$154 single; $210–$235 double. AE, DC, MC, V.

Overlooking Hamilton Harbour with views over Great Sound, this British-inspired, country-club resort is situated on 118 acres of manicured grounds

Impressions

No, ne'er did the wave in its elements steep
 An island of lovelier charms;
It blooms in the giant embrace of the deep,
 Like Hebe in Hercules' arms.
The blush of your bowers is light to the eye,
 And their melody balm to the ear;
But the fiery planet of day is too nigh,
 And the Snow Spirit never comes here.
—Thomas Moore, "The Snow Spirit," in *Poems
Relating to America* (1806)

Various Rate Plans

AP (American Plan)   Includes three meals a day (sometimes called full board or full pension).

BP (Bermuda Plan)   Popularized first in Bermuda, this option includes a full American breakfast (sometimes called an English breakfast).

CP (Continental Plan)   A continental breakfast (that is, bread, jam, and coffee) is included in the room rate.

EP (European Plan)   This rate is always cheapest, as it offers only the room— no meals.

MAP (Modified American Plan)   Sometimes called half board or half pension, this room rate includes breakfast and dinner (or lunch, if you prefer).

---

that include an outstanding golf course. The Forte hotel chain, the managing company, poured millions of dollars into the creation of one of the most desirable properties in Bermuda.

The hotel's exterior is a modern interpretation of a Bermuda colonial building. Wide latticed porches flank the entrance portico, which leads into a formal reception area paneled in Virginia cedar and dotted with Sheraton and Chippendale reproductions. Plushly upholstered English sofas and comfortable wing chairs are illuminated by light streaming through big windows with views of the lawn and the scattered cays of the Bermuda coast. The rooms feature designer decor and Queen Anne–style furniture. Bathrooms tend to be small. The hotel has a garden with a limestone moon gate, plus summer-only outdoor bars.

Dining/Entertainment: Guests enjoy their meals in the main dining room, called the Tree Frogs, with a view of the golf course. The hotel offers continental cuisine and Bermudian specialties. The hotel's newest restaurant, Kiskadee's, features Caribbean food and is named in honor of a local bird. My favorite place for a drink is the Harbour Sights Bar, off the main lobby; it's one of the most elegant modern bars in Bermuda, with finished hardwoods and panoramic views.

Services: Complimentary taxi to Horseshoe Bay Beach in summer, a seven-minute ride; the hotel pier serves as a stopping point for the government ferryboat that travels every 30 minutes to and from Hamilton, but from there it's a long walk up the hill unless you take the hotel shuttle. Also laundry, babysitting, room service (breakfast and dinner only), two gift shops, children's program.

Facilities: A 17-hole championship golf course, designed by Robert Trent Jones; three tennis courts; outdoor swimming pool.

✪ Elbow Beach Hotel/A Wyndham Resort

60 South Shore Rd., P.O. Box HM 455, Hamilton HM BX, Bermuda. ☎ **441/236-3535** or 800/882-4200 in the U.S. Fax 441/236-8043. 220 rms, 80 suites. A/C MINIBAR TV TEL. Bus No. 1, 2, or 7 from Hamilton. Rates (including MAP): Apr 1–Nov 15, $305–$450 double; from $475 suite for two. Off-season, $225–$295 double; from $320 suite for two. Packages available. Children 12 and under stay free and eat free when sharing with adults using existing bedding. AE, DC, MC, V.

This self-contained Wyndham resort, set in 34 acres of gardens some 10 minutes by taxi from the center of Hamilton, has its own quarter-mile pink-sand beach on the South Shore. Originally built in 1908, it has been popular over the decades.

Usually it attracts tradition-minded guests, but during spring College Weeks it draws the largest concentration of young students in Bermuda.

After a $20-million restoration, guests can select from a wide array of air-conditioned hotel rooms or suites, including everything from bedrooms with balconies overlooking the water to duplex cottages. Some lanai rooms overlook the pool and the Atlantic, and others are surfside. During the restoration, the rooms were gutted and rebuilt. Many rooms were given Italian marble baths with up-to-date plumbing, and bedroom walls draped in silk.

Dining/Entertainment: All guests, including those on MAP, may choose dinner at any of the hotel's three restaurants, all with ocean views, or from one outdoor theme party nightly. The main dining room, Ondine's, is the most formal of the restaurants; its pastel pink-and-green decor is reminiscent of a garden gazebo. Here, a breakfast buffet is served daily, as is classic French cuisine at dinner. Spazzizi's on the pool level, the most casual of the three eateries, has been given a rustic tavern look. A wood-burning pizza oven and a selection of pastas complement salads, sandwiches, and snacks at lunch and a range of grilled and sautéed seafood, steaks, chicken, and veal at dinner. At Café Lido, the resort's beachfront restaurant, seafood with a Mediterranean accent is the focus. Lunch is served on the outdoor terrace overlooking the beach, while dinner is served indoors in a greenhouse ambience. Casual poolside dining at Elbow Beach's Pool Terrace Barbecue features steak, chicken, and corn-on-the-cob Monday through Thursday evenings and on Saturday evenings. St. David's Island Buffet on Friday evenings offers dining under the stars, accompanied by mellow music. Bermuda specialties headline the menu: conch chowder, fresh local fish, curried chicken, mussel pie, and more. After dinner the festivities continue with "bamboo dancing," or limbo. Every Sunday a lively Elbow Beach Party and barbecue is held on the resort's pink sand beach, featuring music and entertainment. Some of the island's top musical performers appear nightly in Spazzizi's Bar, and piano music fills the lounge, adjacent to the cozy Library Bar and Orangerie sun room, during the evening.

Services: Room service, babysitting, laundry, beauty salon, moped rental.

Facilities: Private beach, five all-weather tennis courts, large swimming pool with controlled temperatures, game room, health club with exercise room and whirlpool.

Grotto Bay Beach Hotel

11 Blue Hole Hill, Hamilton Parish CR 04, Bermuda. ☎ **441/293-8333** or 800/582-3190 in the U.S. Fax 441/293-2306. 198 rms (all with bath), 3 suites. A/C MINIBAR TV TEL. Bus No. 1, 3, 10, or 11. Rates (EP): Apr–Oct, $180–$198 single or double; Nov–Mar, $110–$130 single or double. Suites from $350 year round. MAP $48 per person extra. AE, MC, V.

The only major complaint any guest could have about this top-notch resort is that it's slightly isolated from the rest of the island, although only a mile from the airport; however, the natural surroundings and other advantages of the hotel make up for any inconvenience.

The resort is named after the subterranean caves that perforate the 21 acres surrounding it. The organizers have turned these caves to their best advantage and conduct tours, communal swimfests, and spelunking expeditions through them, thus creating one of the most unusual hotel attractions in Bermuda. Furthermore, the property is rife with tropical fruit trees, allowing patrons to eat loquats, oranges, papayas, and a local kind of kiwi called "locust and wild honey."

The swimming pool is blasted out of natural rock and ringed with serpentine edges, much like a grotto in its own right. Under a peaked Bermuda roof,

Bermuda Accommodations

Atlantic Ocean

Ireland Island N.

Ireland Island S.

Mangrove Bay

Somerset Village

[1]

SANDYS

Ely's Harbour

[2]

Two Rock Passage

Great Sound

Bay Rd.

PEMBROKE

North Shore Rd.

[37]
[36]
[35] [33] [32]
[34] [31]

Hamilton

Middle Rd.

[3]

Ferry

Hawkins Island

Long Island

Hamilton Harbour

[22]

Botanical Gardens

Ports Island Hinson Island

[18]
[19] [20] [21]

PAGET

Darrell Island

[4]

Little Sound

Harbour Rd.

[15]

[17]

[16]

Middle Rd.

[30]

[28] [29]
[27]
[23]   [25]
[24]

[26]

WARWICK

[11] [13]

[14]

SOUTHAMPTON

[7] [8]

South Shore Rd.

[9] [10] [12]

[5]
[6]

Angel's Grotto [40]
Ariel Sands Beach Club [38]
Astwood Cove [11]
Belmont Hotel
Golf & Country Club [15]
Cambridge Beaches [1]
Edgehill Manor [36]
Elbow Beach Hotel [24]
Fourways Inn [16]
Greenbank Guest House [19]
Greene's Guest House [4]
Grotto Bay Beach Hotel [43]

Harmony Club [30]
Hill Crest Guest House [45]
Horizons and Cottages [23]
Lantana Colony Club [2]
Little Pomander Guest House [22]
Longtail Cliffs [10]
Loughlands [29]
Marley Beach Cottages [12]
Marriott's Castle Harbour Resort [42]
Mermaid Beach Club [9]
Newstead [21]

9726

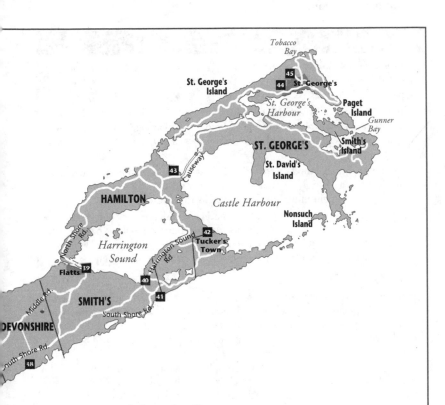

Tobacco
Bay

St. George's
Island

45
44 St. George's

*St. George's
Harbour*

**Paget
Island**

*Gunner
Bay*

ST. GEORGE'S

**Smith's
Island**

**St. David's
Island**

HAMILTON

Causeway

43

Castle Harbour

**Nonsuch
Island**

*Harrington
Sound*

North Shore Rd.

Harrington Sound Rd.

42
**Tucker's
Town**

Flatts **39**

40

41

Middle Rd.

SMITH'S

South Shore Rd.

DEVONSHIRE

South Shore Rd.

18

Atlantic Ocean

0 ————— 2 km
        1.5 m

N

Oxford House **32**
Palm Reef Hotel **18**
Palmetto Hotel & Cottages **39**
Parquet Guest Apartments **27**
Pink Beach Club & Cottages **41**
Pompano Beach Club **3**
Pretty Penny **17**
The Princess **34**
The Reefs **5**
Rosedon **33**
Rosemont **35**
Royal Heights Guest House **7**

Royal Palms Hotel **37**
Salt Kettle House **20**
Sandpiper Apartments **13**
Sky-Top Cottages **28**
Sonesta Beach Hotel & Spa **6**
Southampton Princess **8**
St. George's Club **44**
Stonington Beach Hotel **25**
Surf Side Beach Club **14**
Waterloo House **31**
White Sands Hotel & Cottages **26**

😊 Family-Friendly Hotels

Belmont Hotel Golf & Country Club *(see p. 71)* Its "Kee Kee Club" allows visitors to enroll their kids (ages 2–12) in a package plan that features day-care services and free meals.

Elbow Beach Hotel/A Wyndham Resort *(see p. 72)* Children stay free in parents' room. Ask, however, about the "Family Value Package," which includes accommodations, transfers, daily breakfast buffet, and a host of activities and extras.

Grotto Bay Beach Hotel *(see p. 73)* A long-enduring family favorite, this hotel features a "Family Special" (two adults and two children under 16), requiring a four-night minimum. Rates heavily discounted.

Southampton Princess *(see p. 82)* This pocket of posh offers the best children's program on the island. It includes parties for the kiddies and reliable babysitting services. Not only that, but children 16 and under stay free in a room with one or two adults and receive a complimentary breakfast and dinner daily.

---

swimmers enjoy the swim-up bar, where a handful of underwater chairs permit guests to "sip and dip." A sandy beach nearby offers a view of an unused series of railroad pylons, leading onto forested Coney Island across the bay. A lighthouse there was demolished for one of the explosion scenes in the film *The Deep*.

From the sea side, the airy public areas look like a modernized version of a mogul's palace, with big windows, thick white walls, and a trio of peaked roofs with curved eaves. The hotel's lighthearted decor includes quilted wall hangings and pendulous macramés.

The double accommodations are contained in 11 three-story "lodges" (actually modern buildings with prominent balconies and sea views). These lodges don't have elevators. All rooms were renovated in 1994 and are equipped with safes and hairdryers. Several package rates are available for those who remain more than six nights and for families who stay more than four. Scuba diving, tennis, and golf packages are also available for stays of more than five nights.

Dining/Entertainment: Nightly live entertainment is provided in the Rum House Lounge, and there are a handful of other bars on the property. Guests can also enjoy the afternoon tea and the daily happy hour.

Services: Nature walks, twice-weekly "cave crawls," daily cave swims, complete program for children, frequent tennis clinics, daily "Jazzercise" in the Rum House Lounge before breakfast, scavenger hunts, communal croquet near the bar, fish feeding, bridge competitions, organized activities for teenagers. Also laundry, room service, babysitting.

Facilities: Beach, excursion boat, small health club, scuba diving, snorkeling, putting green, swimming pool with swim-up bar, four tennis courts, and a nearby golf course.

Marriott's Castle Harbour Resort

2 South Rd., St. George's, P.O. Box HM 841, Hamilton HM CX, Bermuda. ☎ **441/ 293-2040** or 800/223-6388 in the U.S. and Canada. Fax 809/293-8288. 405 rms (all with bath), 19 suites. A/C TV TEL. Bus No. 1 from St. George's. Rates (EP): Apr–Oct, $225–$350 single or double; Nov–Mar, $115–$160 single or double. Suites from $450 year round. MAP $45 per person extra. AE, DC, MC, V.

Originally built of coral blocks in the 1920s on a hilltop overlooking Castle Harbour and Harrington Sound, this property had fallen into disrepair before Marriott poured $60 million into one of the most major renovations in Bermuda late in 1986. The renovation added more than 100 bedrooms, landscaped the gardens, and enhanced the public rooms into one of the most strikingly elegant array of interiors of any hotel on the island. The 250 acres of prime real estate surrounding the property are maintained by at least 50 gardeners. From the outside, the place looks almost severe, a bit like a modernized version of a Tuscan fortress with angular outbuildings. One of these is connected to the main building by an elevated concrete catwalk. The most dramatic wing slopes like a modern version of a Mayan pyramid down to the sea.

The '20s-era core was entirely transformed. What might be the most glamorous room in Bermuda is an 18th-century salon, much like what you'd find in an English country house. Filled with copies of Chippendale and Queen Anne furniture, and sheathed with mahogany paneling, it's a showplace for morning coffee, afternoon fish chowder, four o'clock tea, and after-dinner dance music. Adjacent to it is an elegant dining room, where copies of the original Castle Harbour china from the 1920s are part of the meal service. Throughout the property are such touches as stone moon gates and formal garden terraces built around a Bermuda cedar.

Depending on your tastes, your room might be within one of at least three different buildings on the property. The accommodations were last renovated in 1992, and they are invariably furnished with a sense of tradition, usually with good replicas of English furniture. The hotel is often filled with groups and conventions.

Dining/Entertainment: The hotel has a disco and three restaurants: the Windsor Room, the Golf Club Grill, and the Mikado (reviewed separately).

Services: Massages, laundry, babysitting, room service.

Facilities: Well-equipped and upgraded health club free to guests, 18-hole Castle Harbour Golf Course, three pools (one Olympic size), full watersports complex. The hotel has access to two very small beaches, but offers guests access to a private beach on the south shore.

Palm Reef Hotel

1 Harbour Rd., P.O. Box HM 1189, Hamilton HM EX, Bermuda. ☎ **441/236-1000** or 800/ 221-1294 in the U.S. Fax 441/236-6392. 94 rms (all with bath). A/C TEL. Transportation: Bus No. 7 or hotel ferry. Rates (EP): Apr 1–Nov 15, $100–$160 single; $120–$190 double; Nov 16–Mar 31, $75–$90 single; $96–$116 double. Continental breakfast $8 extra; American breakfast $12 extra. AE, MC, V.

Located on Harbour Road and Cobbs Hill Road where Paget and Warwick parishes meet, the Palm Reef Hotel has had a loyal following throughout its long history. Dating back to the 17th century, it is Bermuda's first hotel and has benefitted from a one million dollar massive renovation and refurbishment. The resort overlooks Hamilton Harbour, with Hamilton only a 10-minute ride by the frequent ferries. The main buildings, in Bermuda pink, have a decorative style originally set by Dorothy Draper and are surrounded by landscaped grounds. Many of the well-furnished bedrooms offer refrigerators, and all have sliding glass doors that open onto private terraces or balconies. Golf, honeymoon, and family plans are featured.

Dining/Entertainment: The hotel has a cocktail lounge, a dining room, Le Bistro, and a nightclub called The Gombey Room, where Greg Thompson's *Bermuda Follies* perform May through October. A simple luncheon menu is offered on the

Hotels of Bermuda at a Glance	Access for Disabled	Directly beside the beach	On-site swimming pool	Restaurant on premises	Cable TV in bedroom	Fitness facilities	Nearby access to a golf course	On-site tennis courts	Convention facilities	Welcomes children	Childcare facilities	On-site spa facilities	Access to watersports	Accepts credit cards	Air-conditioned bedrooms	Live on-site entertainment	Wharf or marina facilities
Angel's Grotto	✓				✓		✓			✓			✓	✓	✓		
Ariel Sands Beach Club		✓	✓	✓			✓	✓		✓	✓		✓	✓	✓	✓	
Astwood Cove			✓							✓					✓		
Belmont Hotel Golf & CC	✓		✓	✓			✓	✓	✓	✓	✓		✓	✓	✓	✓	✓
Cambridge Beaches		✓	✓	✓		✓	✓	✓	✓			✓	✓		✓		✓
Edgehill Manor			✓		✓					✓					✓		
Elbow Beach Hotel	✓	✓	✓	✓	✓		✓	✓	✓	✓	✓	✓	✓	✓	✓	✓	
Fourways Inn			✓	✓	✓		✓		✓						✓		
Greenbank Guest House										✓			✓	✓	✓		✓
Greene's Guest House			✓		✓					✓					✓		
Grotto Bay Beach Hotel	✓	✓	✓	✓	✓	✓	✓	✓	✓	✓	✓		✓	✓	✓	✓	✓
Harmony Club			✓	✓	✓		✓	✓						✓	✓	✓	
Hillcrest Guest House							✓			✓					✓		
Horizons and Cottages			✓	✓			✓	✓		✓					✓	✓	
Lantana Colony Club			✓	✓			✓	✓	✓	✓			✓		✓	✓	✓
Little Pomander Guest House	✓				✓		✓			✓			✓	✓	✓		
Longtail Cliffs	✓		✓		✓		✓			✓				✓	✓		
Loughlands			✓				✓			✓					✓		
Marley Beach Cottages		✓	✓		✓		✓			✓			✓	✓	✓		
Marriott's Castle Harbour Resort	✓		✓	✓	✓	✓		✓	✓	✓			✓	✓	✓	✓	
Mermaid Beach Club		✓	✓	✓						✓				✓	✓		
Newstead			✓	✓			✓	✓		✓			✓		✓	✓	✓

Hotels of Bermuda at a Glance	Access for Disabled	Directly beside the beach	On-site swimming pool	Restaurant on premises	Cable TV in bedroom	Fitness facilities	Nearby access to a golf course	On-site tennis courts	Convention facilities	Welcomes children	Childcare facilities	On-site spa facilities	Access to watersports	Accepts credit cards	Air-conditioned bedrooms	Live on-site entertainment	Wharf or marina facilities
Oxford House					✓					✓					✓		
Palm Reef			✓	✓						✓			✓	✓	✓	✓	✓
Palmetto Hotel & Cottages			✓	✓			✓		✓	✓			✓	✓	✓	✓	✓
Paraquet Guest Apartments				✓	✓		✓			✓					✓		
Pink Beach Club & Cottages		✓	✓	✓			✓	✓	✓	✓			✓	✓	✓	✓	
Pompano Beach Club		✓	✓	✓			✓	✓	✓	✓			✓		✓	✓	
Pretty Penny			✓				✓			✓				✓	✓	✓	
Princess (The Hamilton)	✓		✓	✓	✓	✓	✓	✓	✓	✓		✓	✓	✓	✓	✓	✓
Reefs, The	✓	✓	✓	✓		✓	✓	✓	✓	✓			✓	✓		✓	✓
Rosedon			✓		✓					✓							
Rosemont			✓		✓					✓				✓	✓		
Royal Heights Guest House			✓		✓					✓				✓	✓		
Royal Palms Hotel			✓	✓	✓					✓				✓	✓		
Salt Kettle House							✓			✓			✓		✓		✓
Sandpiper Apartments			✓		✓					✓				✓	✓		
Sky-Top Cottages							✓			✓				✓	✓		
Sonesta Beach Hotel & Spa	✓	✓	✓	✓	✓	✓	✓	✓	✓	✓	✓	✓	✓	✓	✓	✓	
Southampton Princess	✓	✓	✓	✓	✓	✓	✓	✓	✓	✓	✓	✓	✓	✓	✓	✓	✓
St. George's Club	✓	✓	✓	✓	✓		✓	✓	✓	✓		✓		✓	✓	✓	
Stonington Beach Hotel		✓	✓	✓			✓	✓	✓				✓	✓	✓	✓	
Surfside Beach Club		✓	✓	✓	✓		✓		✓	✓			✓	✓	✓		
Waterloo House			✓	✓					✓	✓				✓	✓	✓	
White Sands Hotel & Cottages		✓	✓	✓	✓		✓			✓			✓	✓	✓	✓	

Waterside Terrace, and an English afternoon tea is offered daily. The Marine Terrace features outdoor dining, dancing, and entertainment under a night sky.

Services: The hotel's own ferry takes visitors back and forth to Hamilton. Laundry, babysitting.

Facilities: Large open-air, temperature-controlled swimming pool, scuba diving facilities.

✪ The Princess

76 Pitts Bay Rd., P.O. Box HM 837, Hamilton HM CX, Bermuda. ☎ **441/295-3000** or 800/
223-1818 in the U.S., or toll free 800/268-7176 in Canada. Fax 441/295-1914. 452 rms (all
with bath), 30 suites. A/C TV TEL. Bus No. 7 or 8. Rates (EP): Apr 2–Nov 25, $205–$295 single
or double; suites from $335; off-season, $145–$175 single or double; from $210 suites. MAP
$42 per person per day. AE, DC, MC, V.

On the edge of Hamilton Harbour, you'll find a regal pink "wedding cake" landmark. Often called the Hamilton Princess, it's been graced with countless visits from British aristocrats, Hollywood and European movie stars, and yachting enthusiasts since it opened, with international fanfare, in 1887. The hotel is named for Princess Louise, Queen Victoria's daughter, who stayed here shortly after its opening.

Today, this is the flagship of the Princess Hotel chain (with outstanding sports facilities) and undoubtedly the one hotel with the most history. It was initially designed as a wintertime palace for the very wealthy and boasted an all-wood construction to "guarantee against dampness." Before 1932, it had been reconstructed no fewer than four times. By World War II, the Princess's role as a deciphering center and inspection headquarters for each piece of mail transported from Europe to North America ensured its place in history (see "A Look at the Past" in Chapter 2).

The colonial core is flanked by modern wings, each of which is pierced with row upon row of balconied loggias. One of the hotel's more unusual salons is the Wedgwood-inspired Adam Lounge; originally built in 1927, it's the central and most formal salon of this hotel where prewar weekly balls were the social event of the colony. The property was designed around a concrete pier extending into the harbor, off of which lies a Japanese-style floating garden, complete with lily ponds, waterfalls, fountains, and trees. The botanical theme is repeated in the lobby, where a rivulet of water cascades past rock-climbing orchids near the huge windows.

In 1992 management renovated the well-decorated bedrooms and public salons, continuing a program of making a good property even better. Many of the guest rooms have private balconies; each room was designed "to create the feeling that you'd choose the same kind of bedroom if you owned a home here." Some 40% of the guests are repeat visitors.

Dining/Entertainment: The hotel has a wide array of bars and restaurants; for more information, refer to "City of Hamilton" in Chapter 6, "Dining," and Chapter 11, "Bermuda After Dark."

Services: Frequent ferryboat service (weather permitting) between the Hamilton Princess and the Southampton Princess, laundry, room service, babysitting.

Facilities: Heated freshwater swimming pool; unheated saltwater swimming pool; dive shop (independent concessionaire); guests can take the ferryboat (weather permitting) to the Southampton Princess for tennis, sailing, white-sand beaches, and golf. Moped rental available. The hotel's fitness center, one of the best on the island, is usually available to guests daily from 6am to 9pm. Featured are

Hamilton Accommodations & Dining

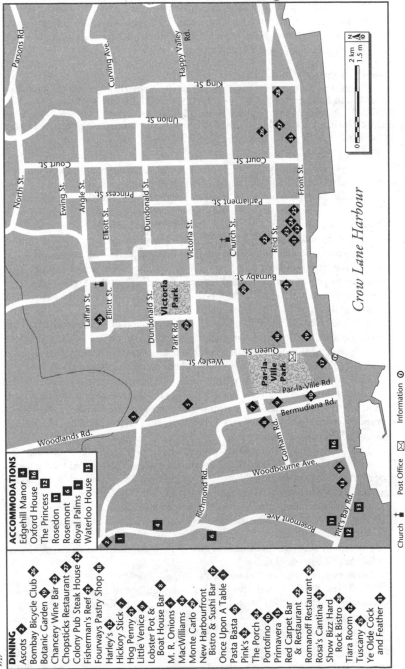

ACCOMMODATIONS
Edgehill Manor **4**
Oxford House **16**
The Princess **12**
Rosedon **11**
Rosemont **6**
Royal Palms **1**
Waterloo House **13**

DINING
Ascots **2**
Bombay Bicycle Club **26**
Botanic Garden **19**
Chancery Wine Bar **23**
Chopsticks Restaurant **27**
Colony Pub Steak House **41**
Fisherman's Reef **21**
Fourways Pastry Shop **18**
Harley's **42**
Hickory Stick **7**
Hog Penny **24**
Little Venice **9**
Lobster Pot &
Boat House Bar **8**
M. R. Onions **5**
MacWilliams **44**
Monte Carlo **29**
New Harbourfront
Bistro & Sushi Bar **47**
Once Upon A Table **3**
Pasta Basta **30**
Pink's **4**
The Porch **24**
Portofino **10**
Primavera **15**
Red Carpet Bar
& Restaurant **22**
Romanoff Restaurant **20**
Rosa's Cantina **33**
Show Bizz Hard
Rock Bistro **28**
Tiara Room **42**
Tuscany **45**
Ye Olde Cock
and Feather **31**

Church ✝   Post Office ⊠   Information ❶

9727

an exercise room, a massage area, saunas, showers, and advanced exercise equipment, including a Quinton Club Trac Treadmill, Stairmasters, Life Fitness Cycles, and a Badger/Magnum Nine Station Circuit Strength Machine. Water aerobics classes are held in one of the outdoor pools.

Sonesta Beach Hotel & Spa

South Shore Rd., Southampton Parish, P.O. Box HM 1070, Hamilton HM EX, Bermuda. ☎ **441/238-8122** or 800/766-3782 in the U.S. Fax 441/238-8463. 365 rms, 37 suites. A/C TV TEL. Bus No. 7. Rates (EP): Apr 1–Nov 15, $240–$450 single or double; suites from $620; off-season, $125–$250 single or double; from $310 suite. MAP supplement $55 per person per day. AE, DC, MC, V.

This long-established luxury resort, set on 25 acres of prime seafront property, was completely refurbished in 1994. It was built in the shape of a crescent, curving along the spine of a rocky peninsula whose jagged edges provide views of the Bermuda coastline. The only major hotel in Bermuda built directly on the beach, it boasts a trio of sandy swimming areas, ample lengths of oceanside walkways, and well-trimmed hedges of sea grape that separate the gardens from the limestone cliffs dropping the short distance to the Atlantic. The property is approached from a winding road that slopes down the hill from the road above it. A uniformed doorman greets visitors in front of a glass tunnel stretching over a flowering ravine and eventually opening into the tasteful art-deco inspired lobby. With its big windows, wood trim, and pastel shades, the lobby is like a 1920s interpretation of the view from a sailboat.

The hotel contains a world-renowned spa facility, and many clients check in on a weight-reduction and muscle-toning regime that is supervised by the staff.

The resort also incorporates a favorite beach on the island, Boat Bay, into its facilities. Shaped like a circle and flanked by limestone cliffs and sandy beaches, the bay was used long ago by gunpowder smugglers and later by rum-runners because of its well-camouflaged entrance. From the sea, the rocky coastline almost conceals the narrow inlet that supplies the bay's waters. With its encircling palm-covered cabañas and bars and its soft sandy bottom, the bay looks like a small corner of Polynesia transported onto the sands of Bermuda.

Each room has a private terrace, and offers a flowery kind of charm. Rates are based solely on the view. Reduced honeymoon packages and special family packages are available at discounted rates. A full children's program with professional counselors is also available from June 15 until Labor Day.

Dining/Entertainment: The hotel features three restaurants, including Lillian's, an elegant restaurant featuring a Northern Italian cuisine. The Boat Bay Club is a bistro-type eatery, and the Sea Grape Island Grill offers al fresco dining overlooking Boat Bay. MAP guests can dine in each of these restaurants as well as at Henry VIII. (See Chapter 6, "Dining.")

Services: Room service, laundry, babysitting.

Facilities: Beach, superlative spa facilities, outdoor swimming pool, indoor swimming pool, complete shop for snorkelers and scuba divers, children's playground, six tennis courts (illuminated for night play), and full-time tennis pro, who offers complimentary group lessons twice weekly.

✪ Southampton Princess

101 South Shore Rd., P.O. Box HM 1379, Hamilton HM FX, Bermuda. ☎ **441/238-8000** or 800/223-1818 in the U.S. or 800/268-7176 in Canada. Fax 441/238-8968. 600 rms, 37 suites. A/C TV TEL. Transportation: Ferry boats from Hamilton. Rates (MAP): Apr 2–Nov 25,

$319–$429 single; $369–$479 double; from $520 suite; off-season (EP), $145–$175 single or double; from $290 suite. AE, DC, MC, V.

The 100-acre resort is the biggest on the island and was built on top of a knoll between two views of the sea, at a point where Bermuda narrows to a spit of rock and sand. Since its erection, a team of landscape architects have turned the grounds into idyllic large-scale gardens. The hotel also has convention facilities, and many international companies hold annual get-togethers here.

Guests who never want to leave the shelter of the paneled public rooms enjoy a self-contained village of bars, restaurants, shops, and athletic facilities. These public rooms, scattered over three floors, are connected by baronial staircases. The Lobby Lounge, off the hotel lobby, contains floor-to-ceiling windows looking out over a garden area and the ocean beyond. It has skylights and an airy decor, including bamboo and wicker furnishings. What might be the most dramatic chandelier in Bermuda—a glass, brass, and wrought-iron Spanish-inspired piece especially designed for the space—illuminates three floors of festivities. The furnishings throughout the hotel are well-upholstered pieces, reflecting a kind of 18th-century English aura.

The guests rooms are arranged in wings that radiate more or less symmetrically from a central core. This design allows each of the luxurious bedrooms to incorporate a private veranda with a sweeping view of the water. Some rooms contain a minibar.

Some of the best parts of the resort are scattered throughout the gardens of the surrounding acreage. The beach and private cove lie within a five-minute walk. Although the terrace pool is ideal for a tropical drink in the sunlight, my preferred pool is a re-creation of a Polynesian waterfall, where streams of heated water spill off an artificial limestone cliff, while cascades of vines bloom above the waterjets of the swirling basin. Swimming is possible here even during colder weather because of the greenhouse constructed above. If you crave the salty waters of the sea, the hotel beach is sheltered in a jagged cove, flanked by cliffs and studded with rocky outcroppings lashed by the tides.

Dining/Entertainment: Meals are taken in one of the hotel's restaurants (see "Southampton Parish" in Chapter 6, "Dining"). Dining rooms include Windows on the Sound, a three-tiered palace that seems like a medley of London's Mayfair of the 1930s and New York's Rainbow Room. Through arched windows rising 20 feet are views of the islands of Great Sound. It's almost a nostalgic re-creation of the grand dining of an earlier era. Other choices include Wickets Brasserie, Newport Room, Rib Room, Whaler Inn, and Waterlot Inn.

Bar and restaurant facilities are also available on the beach, plus the main building is rich in entertainment facilities, covered separately in this guide. In addition, guests can also patronize the three restaurants at the resort's affiliated hotel, the Princess in Hamilton. In off-season, fewer restaurant choices are available with a diminished house count.

Services: A shuttle bus runs among the various hotel facilities; hotel ferryboats make runs along Little Sound into Hamilton. Also available are room service, laundry, babysitting, beauty salon, moped rental, massages. From June through Labor Day, an extensive activities program for children is offered.

Facilities: Private beach club; outdoor pool; indoor pool; par 3, 18-hole golf course; tennis; fitness center with spa facilities; private ferry to the Princess in Hamilton, weather permitting; water sports; moped rentals (available through independent concessionaires).

2 Small Hotels

More informal than the big luxury and first-class hotels are the places in the small-hotel category. Many of these establishments have their own dining rooms and bars, and some feature their own beaches or beach clubs. All of them offer pools and patios.

VERY EXPENSIVE

Harmony Club

South Shore Rd., P.O. Box PG 299, Paget PG BX, Bermuda. ☎ **441/236-3500** or 800/ 225-5843 in the U.S. and Canada. Fax 441/236-2624. 71 rms (all with bath). A/C TV TEL. Bus No. 7, 8, or 27. Rates (all-inclusive): Apr 15–Oct 15, $225 per person, based on double occupancy. Oct 16–Nov 28, $175 per person, based on double occupancy. No one under 18 admitted. Hotel grants 30% discount to clients who book 30 days or more in advance. AE, DC, MC, V. Closed Nov 29–Apr 14.

In 1987 the Forte hotel chain transformed a well-landscaped resort into the first all-inclusive, couples-only hideaway in Bermuda, but the "couples" can be in any known combination, including two friends who wish to travel together. It was originally called Harmony Club; and even earlier, in the 1830s, it had been known as Harmony Hall, the family estate of a Bermudian shipping merchant. It remained a private dwelling until the early 20th century. Its last renovation was in 1993.

The package includes all meals, drinks, and diversionary activities, giving participants the advantage of knowing exactly what their vacation will cost in advance. Visitors walk beneath a pink-and-white portico, leading them inside the reception area, where the daily activities are listed. Included in the prices are all taxes and gratuities; champagne, bathrobes, and toiletries; and dining and entertainment.

Each of the bedrooms is furnished with reproductions of Queen Anne furniture. Units are contained in a series of rambling pink-sided wings, which usually encircle formal gardens containing gazebos. No single rooms are available.

Dining/Entertainment: A full English tea is served every afternoon, free, and open-bar privileges, evening meals served by candlelight on fine china and crystal in the Garden Room, weekly cocktail parties, and daily entertainment. Harmony Club has a dine-around plan with the Belmont Hotel.

Services: Laundry, moped rental.

Facilities: Freshwater swimming pool; whirlpool; two tennis courts; Jacuzzis; two saunas; complimentary beach club privileges; unlimited use of a double-seat motorscooter (one per couple) during a week's stay; free greens fees at nearby Belmont golf course.

Pompano Beach Club

36 Pompano Beach Rd., Southampton SB 03, Bermuda. ☎ **441/234-0222** or 800/ 343-4155 in the U.S. or Canada. Fax 441/234-1694. 32 rms (all with bath), 20 suites. A/C TV TEL. Transportation: Hamilton ferry to Somerset. Rates (MAP): May 1–Nov 15, $335–$360 double; $345 suite. Nov 16–Apr 30, $220–$295 double; $230–$280 suite. Singles rented at $30 off the double rate. No credit cards.

On the southwest shore, the Pompano Beach Club was Bermuda's first fishing club when it opened in 1956. Today, it's also a great choice for golfers and one of the most delightful smaller hotels on the island, owned and operated by the Lamb family. Part of its allure stems from its setting on the side of a limestone hill, virtually surrounded by the Port Royal Golf Club. Years ago, it was cut in a stair-shaped series of terraces to accommodate the various buildings of this well-maintained property. Each of them is painted in a shade of rose called "Pompano pink."

From the terraced beach below the clubhouse, it's possible for water lovers to walk waist-deep along a clean sandy bottom for the length of 2½ football fields before finally reaching deep water. The 1993 renovated accommodations present this view to its best advantage and offer balconies or terraces from each of the hillside villas scattered over the landscaped property. Suites cost a bit less than the most expensive deluxe rooms. That's because these deluxe accommodations are larger, although they don't contain a division between the sleeping and the living areas. All units have minifridges, irons, and ironing boards. For guests who prefer to admire the sunlit ocean from the edge of a pool, the resort offers a crescent-shaped freshwater oasis with an adjacent bar, and a mosaic depiction of a pompano, the fish that made these waters famous. Other extras include a fireplace in one of the stone-trimmed lounges for colder evenings, and a moon gate.

Dining/Entertainment: Meals in the dining room, the Cedar Room, are international. The hotel maintains a dine-around plan with four other small Bermuda hotels. It's not a stuffy or formal place, and jackets and ties for men are required only three nights a week. Each dish is prepared by a team of five chefs. The hotel also has a British-style pub.

Services: Laundry, babysitting.

Facilities: Freshwater swimming pool; oceanside Jacuzzi; clay tennis court; easy access to the government-owned Port Royal Golf Course, designed by Robert Trent Jones, with a par of 71 (six of its holes lie immediately adjacent to the hotel); sunfish and windsurfer rentals.

The Reefs

56 South Shore Rd., Southampton SN 02, Bermuda. ☎ **441/238-0222** or 800/742-2008 in the U.S. or Canada. Fax 441/238-8372. 65 units (all with bath). A/C TEL. Bus No. 7. Rates (including MAP): Apr 15–Oct 10, $293–$355 single; $332–$402 double; off-season, $183–$305 single; $220–$290 double. No credit cards.

This lanai colony on Christian Bay is arranged along a low coral ridge. The uncrowded cluster of salmon-pink cottages faces a private beach of pink-flecked sand surrounded by palm trees and jutting rocks. On a ledge with an ocean view is a kidney shaped swimming pool. The Reefs offers lanais decorated with rattan furniture and island colors, all with private sun decks and ocean views. Bathrooms are small.

Dining/Entertainment: There is a choice of dining either in the plant-filled Terrace Dining Room or al fresco at Coconuts, the beach deck between palm trees. A Continental and North American cuisine is served. The main clubhouse has a beam-ceilinged nautical lounge offering entertainment seven nights a week in summer, ranging from calypso to pub-style sing-along favorites.

Services: Laundry, babysitting

Facilities: Beach, swimming pool, two all-weather tennis courts, fitness center.

Stonington Beach Hotel

South Shore Rd., P.O. Box HM 523, Hamilton, HM CX, Bermuda. ☎ **441/236-5416** or 800/447-7462 in the U.S. or Canada. For reservations and information, contact Prima Reservations Systems, 747 Third Ave., New York, NY 10017 (☎ **212/223-2848**). Fax 441/236-0371. 64 rms (all with bath). A/C TEL. Bus No. 7. Rates (MAP): Apr–Oct, $205–$245 single; $355–$395 double; Nov–Mar, $160–170 single; $220–$250 double. AE, DC, MC, V.

Overlooking South Shore in Paget Parish, this hotel is set in what used to be a grape arbor. The $6 million structure is operated by the Hotel of Hospitality and Culinary Institute of Bermuda, whose classrooms and headquarters lie at the top of a nearby knoll.

Some of the employees are students, supervised by professional international staff and trainers. Students are likely to be more helpful than some other battle-trained, jaded personnel in the hotel field, although if you're looking for mistakes you will no doubt find them.

A lamplit drive leads visitors through foliage up to the buff-colored facade. A stucco passageway follows a trail to an inner octagonal courtyard where a palm tree grows as a centerpiece. The reception area is high-ceilinged, its dark pine beams alternating with white plaster.

The accommodations are contained in four outlying buildings. Rooms are comfortably spacious, each with a wide balcony or patio, plus a view of the ocean. Furnished in fabrics of blue and yellow, they have ceiling fans, small refrigerators, and love seats that become extra folding beds. A complete refurbishing was done in 1994. The hotel's sandy beach is reached via steps cut through foliage and limestone.

Dining/Entertainment: A library bar with a fireplace is most inviting, as is the restaurant, the Norwood Room (see "Paget Parish" in Chapter 6, "Dining").

Services: Laundry, babysitting.

Facilities: Beach, freshwater swimming pool with terrace bar, two tennis courts, business center.

✪ Waterloo House

Pitts Bay Rd., P.O. Box HM 333, Hamilton HM BX, Bermuda. ☎ **441/295-4480** or 800/ 468-4100 in the U.S. Fax 441/295-2585. 22 rms (all with bath), 8 cottages. Bus No. 1, 2, 10, or 11. Rates (BP): Apr–Nov, $165–$255 single; $230–$340 double; $360–$400 cottage; Dec–Mar, $128–$195 single; $170–$260 double; $300 cottage. MAP $30 per person extra. AE, MC, V.

On the edge of Hamilton Harbour in Pembroke Parish is a remake and an extension of a private home circa 1910, lying on the outskirts of town center. The house was named to honor the defeat of Napoléon at Waterloo. Terraced gardens descend to the water in the style of the Italian Riviera. Behind salmon walls, the gardens are filled with palms and magnolias, poinsettias, and urns of ivy; a splashing fountain; and white iron garden furniture with fringed parasols. Guests can observe the British custom and take afternoon tea on the lawn at the water's edge. There are nooks for drinks and sunbaths. Shade trees stand on the fringe of an open-air, freshwater swimming pool. There are, as well, a private dock, a waterside barbecue area, and a terrace for rum-swizzle parties.

Inside, the drawing room is furnished with English antiques and decoratively tiled floors. The main dining room, overlooking the terrace and harbor, is dignified with Queen Anne chairs. On the lower terrace level is a bar lounge, with eclectic decorations, Moorish arches, English armchairs, and hand-woven pillows. The bedrooms vary in size and decorative treatment, each with its own flair, suggesting a country-house guest room.

EXPENSIVE

Newstead Hotel

27 Harbour Rd., P.O. Box PG 196, Paget PG BX, Bermuda. ☎ **441/236-6060** or 800/ 468-4111 in the U.S. Fax 441/236-7454. 48 rms (all with bath), 2 suites. A/C TEL. Transportation: Ferry from Hamilton. Rates (MAP): Apr 1–Jan 4, $216–$295 single; $256–$335 double; Jan 5–Mar 31, $160 single; $230 double. Suites $355–$375 year round. AE, MC, V.

On Harbour Road in Paget Parish, overlooking Hamilton Harbour, Newstead is owned by a local family. It is a Bermudian landmark, with a long history. The original guesthouse accommodated only 12 guests when it opened in 1923, but nowadays there is room for 107 guests. Part of the property, Lyndham, was the former home of Sir Richard and Lady Fairey. It was long ago expanded to include adjoining properties, forming a waterfront resort on a flowering hillside overlooking Hamilton Harbour. (From the estate, it's a 10-minute ferry ride to Hamilton.)

The ancestral home, painted in three shades of green, has become the hub of social activities. It is popular with the sailing set, and it's impossible to get in here during race week in Bermuda. The setting is traditional, with drawing rooms, a library, and lounges, furnished in part with English antiques, a true country-house flavor, and many informal touches.

On the extensive grounds are well-designed and furnished bungalows, with a view of either the harbor or the garden with its flowering hibiscus, coconut palms, and cut-flower beds. Accommodations are in either the main house or the garden bungalows.

Dining/Entertainment: The hotel restaurant is known simply as "The Dining Room." MAP guests can dine here every night or else avail themselves of a dine-around plan with two other cooperating hotels. At an outdoor terrace, guests can enjoy waterside barbecue buffets, rum-swizzle parties, calypso music, and dancing, according to the season. Newstead also operates Breccas, a casual dining spot overlooking Hamilton Harbour. Both Bermudian and international specialties are served here for lunch and dinner from June to early October, and evening entertainment is often provided.

Services: Laundry, babysitting, room service for breakfast only.

Facilities: Swimming pool (swimming is also possible from two private docks); sauna room; two clay tennis courts; privileges of the Coral Beach Tennis Club, which are extended to guests of Newstead; a nine-hole mashie golf course at Horizons, also available to guests.

Palmetto Hotel & Cottages

Harrington Sound Rd., P.O. Box FL 54, Flatts FL BX, Bermuda. ☎ **441/293-2323** or 800/982-0026 in the U.S. for reservations. Fax 441/293-8761. 42 units (all with bath). A/C TEL. Bus No. 10 or 11. Rates (MAP): Apr–Oct, $160–$200 single; $231–$271 double; off-season, $121–$148 single; $182–$234 double. AE, MC, V.

Palmetto Hotel & Cottages, in Flatts Village, Smith's Parish, was the ancestral home of the Bermudian Tucker family, whose best-known member is Teddy Tucker. He became famous in the 1950s for dredging up treasures from wrecked ships of the 17th century.

The walls of the hotel are pink, as are a cluster of cottages and outbuildings. The main building's reception area is paneled in Bermuda cedar.

Palmetto's location is on the waters of Harrington Sound, about 4½ miles east of Hamilton. A raised beach rests on the side of the sound, with access for both swimming and snorkeling to the sandy bottom of the bay.

The rooms are attractively furnished. In addition to 26 double rooms with bath in the hotel, there are 16 double units with bath in separate cottages, all with views of the water. The hotel also offers several special package plans.

Dining/Entertainment: Dinner can be taken on an à la carte basis or booked for your entire stay at the MAP rate. The Inlet Restaurant (see "Smith's Parish" in Chapter 6, "Dining") overlooks the moon gate, which frames a view of Harrington Sound. The Ha' Penny Pub is a darkly intimate hideaway with big windows behind the dark-grained bar. Afternoon tea is served here. In summer, barbecues are held on the terrace.

Services: Bus fare is provided to a South Shore beach that is five minutes away. There is also laundry service, as well as babysitting.

Facilities: Swimming pool that overlooks the water; swimming and snorkeling in bay; boat rentals.

White Sands Hotel & Cottages

55 White Sands Rd., Paget Parish PG BX Bermuda. ☎ **441/236-2023** or in the U.S. 800/548-0547. Fax 441/236-2486. 40 rms (all with bath). A/C TV TEL. Bus No. 7 or 8. Rates (MAP): Apr 1–Nov 15, $192.70–$227.50 single; $259.40–$317.40 double; Nov 16–Mar 31, $131.80–$166.60 single; $189.80–$224.60 double. AE, MC, V.

One of the lesser-known but eminently charming small hotels of Bermuda sits within a compound of salmon-colored buildings amid terraced gardens a short walk uphill from the semiprivate beach at Grape Bay. Originally built in 1953 by members of the Browne family (who visibly continue its management today), it has steadily expanded its size, the number of its facilities, and its loyal clientele. In fact, of all the hotels of Bermuda's South Shore this is the closest to the shops and restaurants of Hamilton, a 10-minute taxi or bus ride away.

Bedrooms contain wall-to-wall carpeting, large closets, small refrigerators, a radio, a coffeemaker, comfortable beds, and carefully coordinated color schemes of pink, green, or blue. Each is spacious, airy, and bright, and for the most part filled with conservatively modern furniture in light-grained woods. Especially noteworthy is a tower room (Room 222) whose five oversized windows provide an eagle's-nest view of the surrounding shoreline. Eight of the establishment's 40 bedrooms lie within a trio of two- and three-bedroom cottages. These are usually rented as complete units to extended groups of friends and family vacationing together.

Dining/Entertainment: A formal but relaxed dining room, The Captain's Table, outfitted in a colonial English motif; the Terrace Club poolside restaurant for breakfast and lunch; and an English-inspired pub, the Sandbar, open every night for food and drink.

Services: Room service 8–8:45am and 7–8:30pm; babysitters available with advance notice.

Facilities: A freeform swimming pool; a garden path leading to a wide, semiprivate beach, whose sands are finer than those of many other Bermuda beaches; easy access to nearby tennis, golf, and watersports facilities of other South Shore hotels; an on-site kiosk for the rental of mopeds.

MODERATE

Ⓢ Rosedon

Pitts Bay Rd., P.O. Box HM 290, Hamilton HM AX, Bermuda. ☎ **441/295-1640.** For information and reservations, contact Island Resorts Reservations, P.O. Box 4477, Lutherville, MD 21030; ☎ **410/628-1718** or 800/742-5008. Fax 441/295-5904. 42 rms (all with bath). TV TEL. Bus No. 7 or 8. Rates (BP): Apr–Nov, $156–$232 single; $166–$232 double; off-season, $110–$176 single; $120–$186 double. Extra person sharing room $32. MC, V.

Situated on the outskirts of Hamilton, in Pembroke Parish, this 1906 manor house is just across the lawn from the Princess Hotel and is surrounded by extensive gardens and lawns. Look for the loquat tree, a Bermuda trademark. Other shrubs include hibiscus, banana plants, and birds of paradise. Rosedon resembles a colonial-era plantation Great House, with a pristine white exterior and shutters painted a royal blue. It was once occupied by an English family, and was the first house in Bermuda with gas lights. The formal entry hall is dominated by an open staircase and a midway landing window. There are two antique-filled lounges. Guests can sit on a flagstone terrace under parasol tables around a large, temperature-controlled pool. The honor system prevails at Nigel's Bar.

Individually decorated bedrooms with private baths are rented out. The back modern veranda rooms—called lanai suites—open onto a pool, and there are, as well, air-conditioned colonial-style rooms in the main house; each unit has a private refrigerator. The Bermuda Plan rates include a full breakfast, room service, English afternoon tea, and tennis and beach use at Elbow Beach, with free round-trip taxi service (10 minutes).

3 Cottage Colonies

These cottage colonies are considered uniquely Bermudian. Each has a main clubhouse with a dining room, lounge, and bar, plus its own beach or pool. The cottage units are spread throughout landscaped grounds and offer privacy and sometimes luxury. Most have kitchenettes suitable for beverages and light snacks, but not for full-time cooking.

VERY EXPENSIVE

Ariel Sands Beach Club
34 South Shore Rd., Devonshire, P.O. Box HM 334, Hamilton HM BX, Bermuda. ☎ 441/236-1010 or 800/468-6610 in the U.S.; call collect from Canada. Fax 441/236-0087. 48 rms (all with bath). TEL. Bus No. 1. Rates (MAP): Apr–Oct, $154–$198 single; $268–$356 double; Nov–Mar, $122–$160 single; $204–$280 double. AE, MC, V.

This is one of the best cottage colonies in Bermuda, established in 1959. You'll reach it by going down a winding lane that leads through a park and eventually deposits you near a lime-green clubhouse with forest-green shutters.

The grounds are well landscaped, with flowering trees and coconut palms; each of the grounds offers a view of the ocean. One of the most original sculptures on the island is the stainless-steel statue of Ariel, who dances like a water sprite on the surf. The statue was made in Princeton, N.J., by Seward Johnson, Jr. The resort contains a series of public rooms, where in cold weather, a double-hearth fireplace throws light and heat into both a reception lounge and a conservatively attractive bar area designed in cardinal red to look like an English library. Those who want to explore Hamilton can take a public bus, which stops nearby. The 2$^1/_2$-mile ride takes about 15 minutes.

The often small accommodations have a private entrance and a simple but attractive decor of white walls, Bermudian flower paintings, and bentwood furniture. Most have private porches as well, although the least expensive rooms don't have sea views. Many of the settings, both private accommodations and public buildings, are based on themes from Shakespeare's *The Tempest*, including Miranda's Cabana, Sea Nymph, and Prospero. Each of them lies adjacent to other units, which can be connected to create units of up to eight rooms—ideal for large families or reunions of old friends.

Dining/Entertainment: An international cuisine is served, and in season a local calypso band often entertains.

Service: Laundry, room service during mealtimes, babysitting.

Facilities: Guests can swim in an oval freshwater pool, in a rectangular saltwater pool whose waters are replenished every day by rising tides, or at a sandy beach. The resort contains three tennis courts, two of which are lit for night games.

✪ Cambridge Beaches

30 Kings Point Rd., Sandys MA 02, Bermuda. ☎ **441/234-0331** or 800/468-7300 in the U.S., 800/463-5990 in Canada. Fax 441/234-3352. 59 units (all with bath), 16 suites. A/C MINIBAR TEL. Bus No. 7. Rates (MAP): Mar 1–Apr 9, $250–$340 single; $270–$370 double from $400 suite; Apr 10–Nov 15, $321–$429 single; $325–$450 double; from $485 suite; Nov 16–Feb 28, $209–$294 single; $230–$315 $220–$300 double; from $340 suite. No credit cards.

On a peninsula overlooking Mangrove Bay in Somerset, Cambridge Beaches has qualities no other cottage colony has, and for that reason it heads the list of desirables in its category. Its position is one of a kind, for it occupies the entire western tip of the island—25 acres of semitropical gardens, green lawns, and a choice of five palm-fringed private beaches. It also boasts a wealth of water sports programs, equipment, and facilities.

As the 1947 pioneer of Bermudian cottage colonies, Cambridge Beaches has at its center an old sea captain's house. The main lounges are tastefully furnished with some antiques; one lounge has a beamed pitched ceiling, chintz-covered sofas, and chairs placed around a fireplace. The prevailing flavor is that of a country estate.

Scattered throughout the gardens are well-furnished, pink-and-white units, some of which are nearly 300 years old and retain Bermudian architectural features. The restrained furnishings are color- and fabric-coordinated. All cottages, several of which were once private homes, have sun-and-breakfast terraces, mostly with unmarred views of the bay and gardens. Each unit also has a small refrigerator.

Transportation to Hamilton is provided by the hotel's ferry; from Hamilton you may take the Somerset bus.

Dining/Entertainment: Informal lounges for drinks include the Port O' Call Pub and the residents' piano bar. Calypso and other entertainment are often offered six nights a week. Dining is in the air-conditioned main room or else out on the terrace, where barbecues are sometimes held. The establishment has long been known for serving some of the finest food in Bermuda.

Services: Massage facilities, room service, laundry.

Facilities: The hotel has three all-weather tennis courts and a golf course, Port Royal, designed by Robert Trent Jones and only seven minutes away; the resort has its own putting green. Guests swim in a temperature-controlled pool or swim the many beaches. Cambridge Beaches has a full marina with Boston whalers and various kinds of sailboats. Water sports include windsurfing with instruction, canoeing, kayaking, snorkeling, and fishing with equipment available. Parasailing, sailing, and snorkeling trips, plus glass-bottom-boat excursions and fishing voyages, are also offered from the property. Adjacent to the colony are two bone fishing flats. The full-service spa features exercise equipment, a whirlpool, steam, a sauna, hair dressing, and some 50 types of skin, beauty, and relaxation treatments.

✪ Horizons and Cottages

South Shore Rd., P.O. Box PG 198, Paget PG BX, Bermuda. ☎ **441/236-0048** or 800/468-0022 in the U.S. Fax 441/236-1981. 50 units (all with bath). A/C TEL. Bus No. 7. Rates (MAP): Mar 15–Nov 30, $270–$400 single; $296–$650 double; off-season, $182–$280 single; $202–$375 double. No credit cards.

Horizons and Cottages has as its core a converted manor farm (ca. 1690), where much of the atmosphere of the past has been retained. A Relais & Châteaux member, it is set on a 25-acre estate with terraced gardens and lawns, atop a hill overlooking Coral Beach. The manor house has reception rooms, containing old

Bermudian architectural details. Throughout are some antiques from England and the continent; several drawing rooms have open fireplaces.

The complex consists of double accommodations in either the cottages or the main building. All are handsomely furnished—with Italian terra-cotta tile floors, scatter rugs, traditional tray ceilings, and ceiling fans—and all have separate dressing areas as well as private terraces overlooking the ocean. Some units are split-level. Minibars and TVs are provided on request.

Dining/Entertainment: The main dining room serves French *cuisine naturelle* that uses all fresh products, as guests sit on country chairs before an open fireplace. Lunch can be served on a terrace furnished with white garden furniture. In the evening, the terrace is transformed into an entertainment area, with informal dancing and often calypso music. Lunches and dinners, by reservation, can be exchanged at Newstead and Waterloo House.

Services: Laundry, room service, babysitting.

Facilities: It has its own nine-hole mashie golf course, 18-hole putting green, and tennis courts, as well as a heated freshwater swimming pool.

Lantana Colony Club

P.O. Box SB 90, Somerset Bridge SB BX, Bermuda. ☎ **441/234-0141** or 800/468-3733 in the U.S., 800/463-0036 in Canada. Fax 441/234-2562. 58 suites, 6 cottages. A/C MINIBAR TV TEL. Transportation: Hamilton ferry to Somerset Bridge. Rates (MAP): May–Oct, $255–$310 single suite; $300–$450 double suite; $470 cottage for 2; $700 two-bedroom cottage for 4. Nov–Mar, $200–$245 single suite; $255–$345 double suite; $380 cottage for 2; $580 two-bedroom cottage for 4. No credit cards. Closed Jan 5–Feb 15.

Established in the 1950s overlooking Great Sound, this complex is like a private club. Renovated in 1992, it caters to a quiet clientele interested in privacy and not seeking glitter or nightlife. A 25-minute ferry ride from Hamilton, it is spread over 23 acres of cultivated gardens, with both poolside and bay swimming, along with tennis courts.

Placed around the main building are clusters of Bermudian cottages and lanai suites. Accommodations are restrained and traditional in decor, with the emphasis on comfort; you'll even find an iron and hairdryer. One cottage has its own private swimming pool.

A popular rendezvous point is the clubhouse, which has a large fireplace.

Dining/Entertainment: The hotel's restaurant is open to the public (see "Sandys Parish" in Chapter 6, "Dining"). A superb dinner is served in the midst of much greenery and flowers. The chef prepares a continental cuisine, and the staff is well trained.

Services: Laundry, room service at breakfast only.

Facilities: Solarium, outdoor patio, freshwater pool, sundeck, two all-weather tennis courts, croquet lawn, putting green, small artificially created beach, and water sports from a private dock.

Pink Beach Club & Cottages

South Shore Rd., P.O. Box HM 1017, Hamilton HM DX, Bermuda. ☎ **441/293-1666** or 800/355-6161 in the U.S. Fax 441/293-8935. 81 units (all with bath). A/C TEL. Bus No. 1. Rates (MAP): Apr 15–Oct 31, $295–$360 single; $305–$370 double; off-season, $231–$251 single; $241–$261 double. MC, V. Closed Jan 5–Feb 28.

In Smith's Parish you'll find this colony of pink cottages surrounding two private South Shore beaches. The largest cottage colony on the island, it lies in an 18-acre garden setting, filled with bay grape trees and hibiscus bushes. The drawing room is decorated with mahogany wooden pieces.

A maid will come around to one of the little kitchenettes located just outside your door and prepare breakfast for you (just as you requested it the night before). The staff is one of the best on the island, and includes many who have been with Pink Beach since its inception in 1947.

The resort attracts a list of international habitués. Its cottages range from a studio (bed-sitting room, bath, and patio) to a full unit with living room and terrace.

Dining/Entertainment: The heart of the colony is the limestone clubhouse, painted pink, with its natural-wood dining room, where "backyard" vegetables and fresh seafood are served. Every table has a view of the ocean and the South Shore breakers. An international cuisine is served.

Services: Laundry, babysitting.

Facilities: A large saltwater pool, a sun terrace, and two tennis courts are found on landscaped grounds. Two championship golf courses lie about two minutes from the hotel.

St. George's Club

Rose Hill, P.O. Box GE 92, St George's GE, BX, Bermuda. ☎ **441/297-1200.** Fax 441/297-8003. 69 cottages. A/C TV TEL. Bus No. 6, 8, 10, or 11. Rates (EP): Year-round, $250 cottage for up to four; $450 cottage for up to six. AE, DC, MC, V.

This resort, on 18 acres atop Rose Hill, off York Street, in St. George's, features clusters of traditionally designed Bermudian one- and two-bedroom cottages. The complex functions primarily as a timeshare property, where units are rented to the public when the owners are not using them. The accommodations offer private balconies or patios, comfortable living and dining areas, fully equipped kitchens, and baths with sunken tubs and marble vanities. The units have views of the ocean, the pool, or the golf course.

Dining/Entertainment: An elegant restaurant, the Margaret Rose, is on the premises and is open to the public. Refer to the dining suggestions for St. George's in Chapter 6, "Dining." The Sir George Pub is also a popular rendezvous point.

Services: Laundry, babysitting.

Facilities: A convenience store, the Ample Hamper, may be found in the clubhouse. There are three freshwater swimming pools, one of which is heated, plus three all-weather tennis courts, one of which may be lit for night games. The beach club at Achilles Bay is connected by a short shuttle bus ride. Golfers receive preferential tee time at reduced rates on the adjacent 18-hole golf course, designed by Robert Trent Jones.

4 Housekeeping Units

Housekeeping apartments, Bermuda's efficiency units, vary from modest to superior. Most have kitchens or kitchenettes and minimal daily maid service. Housekeeping cottages all have fully equipped kitchens, are either on or convenient to a beach, and are air-conditioned. The cottages offer privacy and casual living.

EXPENSIVE

Fourways Inn

1 Middle Rd., P.O. Box PG 294, Paget PG BX, Bermuda. ☎ **441/236-6517** or 800/962-7654 in the U.S. Fax 441/236-5528. 5 rms (all with bath), 5 suites. A/C MINIBAR TV TEL. Bus No. 8. Rates (EP): Apr–Oct, $150 single; $220 double; $310 suite; Nov–Mar, $100 single; $140 double; $180 suite. MAP $40 per person extra. AE, MC, V.

Pink-sided, airy, and stylish, this cluster of Bermudian cottages was added to the garden of one of the best restaurants on the island, the Fourways Inn Restaurant (see Chapter 6, "Dining"). Its core is a former private home that dates from 1727. Each of five suites contains two accommodations, with a view of Hamilton Harbour or Great Sound, a patio, a private safe, a fully equipped kitchenette, conservatively comfortable furniture, a satellite-connected TV, and lots of extra touches. The cottages ring a communal swimming pool and a well-maintained garden. The beaches of the South Shore lie nearby. Children under 16 are not encouraged, and it wouldn't be their kind of place anyway.

Mermaid Beach Club

South Shore Rd., P.O. Box WK 250, Warwick WK BX, Bermuda. ☎ **441/236-5031.** Fax 441/236-8325. 76 units (all with bath, 44 with kitchens). A/C TEL. Bus No. 7. Rates (EP): Apr 15–Nov 1, $180–$212 single or double; $260–$370 apartments with kitchens. Off-season, $110–$130 single or double; $160–$270 apartments with kitchens. MAP $35 extra per person per day. AE, MC, V.

Set beside a curved shoreline that combines both rocky cliffs and sandy beachfront, this is a compound that consists of a series of two-story cement-sided buildings whose numbers and amenities have gradually increased since its establishment in the 1940s. On the premises is a beach and snack bar and a main bar outfitted in a nautical theme, a bike-rental shop, a restaurant (the Jolly Lobster), and a curved-sided swimming pool set on a terrace above the beach. All units have patios or balconies, and all but a handful overlook the sea. Those that don't overlook a garden. Bedrooms are simple and summery, with pastel colors and rattan furniture.

MODERATE

Angel's Grotto

P.O. Box HS 81, Smith's HS BX, Bermuda. ☎ **441/293-1986.** Fax 441/293-4164. 7 apts. (all with bath and kitchenettes). A/C TV TEL. Bus No. 3. Rates (EP): Apr 1–Oct 31, $105–$120 single or double. Off-season, $90–$110 single or double. AE, MC, V.

Set on 1¹/₂ acres of seafront land overlooking Harrington Sound, this complex of three white-sided buildings was originally built in the 1940s as a private house. Later, it functioned as a disco and nightclub, as is evident from its large seafront terrace, site of long-ago dance parties. Owned by Daisy Hart since 1981, it does not operate a restaurant or a bar, but instead provides well-equipped kitchens in each accommodation, a separate air-conditioned bedroom, and a combined pastel-colored living room/dining area. Those overlooking the water cost slightly more than those overlooking the land. The coastline adjacent to the hotel is too rocky for swimming, but a sandy beach lies within a 10-minute walk.

⑤ Astwood Cove

49 South Shore Rd., Warwick WK 07, Bermuda. ☎ **441/236-0984.** Fax 441/236-1164. 20 apts (all with bath). A/C TEL. Bus No. 7 from Hamilton. Rates (EP): Apr 1–Nov 15, $108–$118 single; $108–$138 double; Nov 16–Mar 31, $60–$80 single; $76–$90 double. No credit cards.

Nigel (Nicky) and Gabrielle (Gaby) Lewin own this homestead, built in 1720, on a dairy farm. The cove house has tradition. Three Astwood sisters, Maude, Ada, and Mary, willed the house with the stipulation that it always carry their name. The apartment resort enjoys a peaceful setting overlooking lightly wooded meadows and the South Shore, with such extra features as a sauna, a pool, and gas-fired barbecue stations.

Each of the 20 self-contained, air-conditioned rental units has a private bath with shower (no tubs), a telephone (no charge for local calls), a radio, ceiling fans, and a terrace or porch. Some of the units have sitting rooms, and all have kitchenettes, with English china. Guests prepare their own breakfast. An all-apartment building added in 1985 has a communal terrace and pavilion, with TV and an exercise machine. From here, the closest large beach, Long Bay, is a quarter of a mile away; however, Astwood's Beach and Mermaid Beach are only a three-minute stroll from the compound.

Longtail Cliffs

34 South Shore Rd., P.O. Box HM 836, Hamilton HM CX, Bermuda. ☎ **441/236-2864** or 800/637-4116 in the U.S., 800/267-7600 in Canada. Fax 441/236-5178. 13 units (all with bath). A/C TV TEL. Bus No. 7 from Hamilton. Rates (EP): Apr 1–Oct 31, $120 one-bedroom apartment for one or two, $255 two-bedroom apartment for three; $295 two-bedroom apartment for four; $40 per day for each additional person. Off-season, $90 one-bedroom apartment for one or two; $150 two-bedroom apartment for three; $170 two-bedroom apartment for four; $20 per day for each additional person. AE, MC, V.

You'll find this resort in a scenic spot in Warwick Parish. Bird-watchers will enjoy the dozens of longtails (a longtail is a form of seagull) that nest in the cliffs below. A swimming pool is set into the lawn, and a row of hedges signals the beginning of a steep drop-off toward the sea. Beachcombers can walk a short distance to one of the neighboring coves.

The facade from the road isn't dramatic, but once you're inside one of the rooms, especially those on the upper floor, you'll be rewarded with lots of space, cathedral-like ceilings, and comfortable accommodations. Each unit has a kitchen, where you can prepare your own breakfast or other meals; a radio and a wall safe; and a panoramic view of the sea. Twelve of the units contain two bedrooms and two baths. On the premises is a coin-operated laundry.

Marley Beach Cottages

South Shore Rd., P.O. Box PB 278, Warwick PG BX, Bermuda. ☎ **441/236-1143.** Fax 441/236-1984. 14 cottages. A/C TV. Bus No. 2 or 7. Rates (EP): Apr 1–Nov 15, $172–$256 single or double; $281–$320 cottage for four; off-season, $138–$205 single or double; $200 cottage for four. AE, MC, V.

These pink-walled cottages are set in a steep but beautifully landscaped plot of land, on the South Shore near Astwood Park, that was used for scenes in the movies *The Deep* and *Chapter Two*. More recently the scenery appeared in the film *Bermuda Grace*. A trio of narrow beaches lies at the bottom of the slope that leads to the sea, and a curved heated freshwater swimming pool and a whirlpool are on the premises. The airy cottages have their own sea-view patios and sense of spaciousness, as well as fully equipped kitchens and hibachis. Each cottage offers both a suite and a studio apartment, which can be rented as one unit or two, depending on your needs. Guests prepare their own meals or else dine out. These housekeeping cottages have been called complete "do-it-yourself" retreats, with groceries and drinks delivered daily.

Paraquet Guest Apartments

South Shore Rd., P.O. Box PG 173, Paget PG BX, Bermuda. ☎ **441/236-5842.** Fax 441/236-1665. 12 apartments (all with bath). A/C TV. Bus No. 7. Rates: (EP): Apr–Oct, $80 single without kitchen; $95 single with kitchen; $110 double without kitchen; $135 double with kitchen. Nov–Mar, $70 single without kitchen; $80 single with kitchen; $85 double without kitchen; $110 double with kitchen. No credit cards.

This buff-colored collection of Bermudian houses, attractively landscaped into a gentle knoll, is a five-minute walk from Elbow Beach. Built in the mid-1970s, the resort is owned by the Portuguese-born Correia family. Nine of the units have kitchenettes, and each has a private bath, maid service, and somewhat spartan but functional modern furniture. The focal point here is the restaurant and coffee shop (see Paraquet Restaurant in "Paget Parish" in Chapter 6, "Dining").

Ⓢ Pretty Penny
7 Cobb's Hill Rd., P.O. Box PG 137, Paget PB BX, Bermuda. ☎ **441/236-1194** or 800/ 637-4116 in the U.S. Fax 441/236-1662. 7 apartments. A/C TEL. Transportation: Hamilton ferry. Bus No. 8. Rates (EP): Apr–Nov, $125 single or double; off-season, $90 single or double. AE, MC, V.

The owner and manager of this home, located in an excellent neighborhood, is Bermudian Stephen Martin. You'll be welcomed into a bright and airy living room, his personal residence, for a weekly cocktail party. A fire usually burns in a stone hearth during cooler weather, but in summer Martin entertains on an outdoor terrace. A food market is within easy reach, so that guests can replenish their provisions, especially for breakfast. The ferryboat to Hamilton is just a two-minute walk from the front desk. A selection of beaches lies within a 10-minute walk of the premises, and there's a deck-ringed pool on the grounds.

Some of the names of the accommodations evoke a smile: Tuppence, Thruppence, Sixpence, Playpenny, and Sevenpence. Each is contained in its own hillside bungalow, with kitchenette and attractive furnishings; one unit contains a fireplace. Each of the units is suitable for at least two guests.

Rosemont
41 Rosemont Ave., P.O. Box HM 37, Hamilton HM AX, Bermuda. ☎ **441/292-1055** or **800/367-0040** in the U.S. Fax 441/295-3913. 34 units (all with bath), 3 suites. A/C TV TEL. Bus No. 7 or 8. Rates (EP): Apr–Oct, $126–$132 single or double; $240 suite; Nov–Mar, $94– $98 single or double; $225 suite. MC, V.

Rosemont is a cluster of gray-walled cottages, each with a large veranda, set on a flowered hillside a short distance from the Hamilton Princess Hotel. Cottages include two former homes built in the 1940s. The remainder of the complex consists of more modern structures built within the past 15 years or so. The harbor, with its passing ships, is visible from the raised terrace beside the small L-shaped swimming pool. The policy of the Rosemont is to "keep it quiet," so that the commercial travelers, families, and mature couples who stay here won't be disturbed; for that reason, the hotel usually doesn't accept college students or large groups. A grocery store is within a few minutes' walk, and the heart of the city lies only 10 minutes away. Elbow Beach, a 15-minute ride, provides saltwater swimming. Upon request, the hotel will arrange for a motor scooter.

Each of the well-furnished rooms has a kitchen, a radio/alarm clock, and a full bath, although units are often a little dark. It's possible to connect as many as three rooms together, which some families prefer to do. In addition to the regular rooms, the hotel offers three suites, with private entrances and luxurious furnishings. Rates do not include service and taxes. Laundry and babysitting can be arranged. There is no restaurant on the premises, as everybody cooks in.

Sandpiper Apartments
South Shore Rd., P.O. Box HM 685, Hamilton HM CX, Bermuda. ☎ **441/236-7093**. Fax 441/236-3898. 9 units (all with bath), 5 suites. A/C TV TEL Bus No. 7. Rates (EP): Mar 16– Nov 15, $115 single or double; $160 suite; off-season, $75 single or double; $120 suite. AE, MC, V.

Built in 1979 and frequently upgraded, this apartment complex is a suitable choice for a budget-conscious vacation and is within a short walk of several beaches. It is not for those seeking glamour, but you can relax in the outdoor whirlpool and swimming pool or lounge in the gardens. Nine of the units are studios suitable for single or double occupancy. The studios have bedrooms with two double beds, baths, and fully equipped kitchenettes. Five of the units have bedrooms with king-size or twin beds, kitchens, baths, and living and dining areas with two double pull-out sofa beds. All the apartments have radios, balconies, and daily maid service. The Sandpiper is only minutes away from restaurants and the supermarket.

Sky-Top Cottages

65 South Shore Rd., P.O. Box PG 227, Paget PG BX, Bermuda. ☎ **441/236-7984.** 11 units (all with bath). A/C MINIBAR TEL. Bus No. 7. Rates (EP): Mar 15–Nov 30, $81–$112.50 single; $90–$125 double; Dec 1–Mar 14, $67.50–$85.50 single; $75–$95 double. Extra person $25 in summer, $15 off-season. Weekly and monthly discounts off-season. MC, V.

Set on a hilltop above Paget's southern shoreline, opposite the Elbow Beach Hotel, this collection of cottages provides some of the most comfortably isolated accommodations in their price bracket. The units are contained in four cozy, English-style cottages, two of which, dating from early this century, were assembled into a single unit by the English-born wives of two local doctors, Marion Stubbs and Susan Harvey. Each cottage contains a conservative decor of furniture and carpeting, and each has a private bathroom as well as a small private terrace. Nine of the units contain fully equipped kitchenettes.

The units take their names from some of the flowers in the gardens, so you may find yourself staying in Morning Glory, Pink Corallita, or Allamanda. On all sides of the property, emerald-colored lawns encompass shrubs and trees whose sightlines stretch down to a view of the sea. Few social activities are planned, except for an occasional rainy-day party to cheer everybody up. Nevertheless, a kind of English-inspired camaraderie sometimes permeates the place. The sands of Elbow Beach are only a five-minute walk away, and Hamilton can be reached in about 10 minutes by cab, bus, or moped.

Surf Side Beach Club

South Shore Rd., P.O. Box WK 101, Warwick WK BX, Bermuda. ☎ **441/236-7100** or 800/553-9990 in the U.S. Fax 441/236-9765. 36 units. A/C TEL. Bus No. 2 or 7. Rates (EP): Apr–Oct, $175–$200 single or double; $250–$300 for up to four; off-season, $105–$125 single or double; $170–$200 up for four. Extra person in any unit $25. Extended stay off-season discounts granted. No credit cards.

The Surf Side Beach Club was terraced into a steeply sloping hillside that descends, after passing through gardens, to a crescent-shaped sweep of private beachfront. The property was purchased by Norway-born Erling D. Naess and his wife, Elisabeth, who designed it nearly a quarter of a century ago and who still maintain the varied array of flowering trees and panoramic walkways. The stonemasons added several quiet vantage points at various places in the gardens, from which visitors can see grouper and other fish swimming among the distant rocks of the shallow sea.

Accommodations include one-bedroom apartments near the terrace pool. Other lodgings are in hillside buildings. Each of the units is simple and sunny, furnished in bright colors with comfortable accessories; and each is self-contained, with a fully equipped kitchenette (English china, wine glasses, even salt and pepper shakers), a shower (no tubs), a radio, ceiling fans, and a private balcony or patio. Some of the accommodations have sitting rooms as well. There's a laundry on the premises.

5 Guesthouses

Guesthouses are usually comfortable old converted manor houses in garden settings. Some have pools and terraces. The smaller ones have fewer facilities and are much more casual with simple, often "lived-in" furniture. Most guesthouses serve only breakfast. Those taking fewer than 12 guests are usually small private homes; some have several housekeeping units, while others provide shared kitchen facilities for the preparation of snacks.

MODERATE

Edgehill Manor

Rosemont Ave., P.O. Box HM 1048, Hamilton HM EX, Bermuda. ☎ **441/295-7124.** Fax 441/295-3850. 9 rms (all with bath). A/C TV. Bus No. 7 or 8. Rates (CP): Mar 16–Nov 15, $95–$105 single; $105–$120 double; off-season, $65–$80 single; $80–$90 double. Children under 12 are charged $10 when staying in parents' room. No credit cards.

Directly outside the city limits, in a quiet residential area that is nevertheless convenient to restaurants and shopping in Hamilton, Edgehill Manor just might become your "little home in Bermuda." Painted green, it was built around the time of the American Civil War and still exudes an old-fashioned, homelike quality, attracting a rather middle-aged clientele. Your landlady is British-born Bridget Marshall, who still observes the custom of English tea in the afternoon, which she serves in a flowery nook. At least two units are equipped with kitchenettes, and all come with small balconies or patios. Each unit, however, has its own style. If you're interested, ask Ms. Marshall about her special honeymoon rates. Her continental breakfast, she is proud to say, is "all home baked."

Greenbank Guest House

17 Salt Kettle Rd., P.O. Box PG 201, Paget PG BX, Bermuda. ☎ **441/236-3615.** Fax 441/236-2427. 11 units (all with bath). A/C TEL. Transportation: Hamilton ferry. Rates (EP): Apr 1–Nov 14, $110–$120 single or double; Nov 15–Mar 31, $80–$100 single or double. AE, MC, V.

On the water's edge in Salt Kettle, this resort stands across the bay from Hamilton, which is reached by a 10-minute ferry ride. It's an old Bermuda home, hidden under pine and palm trees, with shady lawns and flower gardens. The oldest section is from the 1700s. The manager welcomes guests to an antiques-filled drawing room with its original floor, a fireplace, and a grand piano. The atmosphere is relaxed and personalized. Greenbank offers accommodations with private entrances, baths, and kitchens—either waterside cottages or garden view. There is daily maid service, but guests provide their own breakfast. Greenbank has a private dock for swimming, plus a boat rental and charter operation on the property where sailing, snorkeling, motorboats, and sailboats are offered.

⑤ Greene's Guest House

71 Middle Rd., P.O. Box SN 395, Southampton SN BX, Bermuda. ☎ **441/238-0834.** Fax 441/238-8980. 8 rms (all with bath). A/C TV TEL. Bus No. 7 or 8. Rates (CP): Year-round, $85 single; $100 double. No credit cards.

The outside of this place, which overlooks Great Sound, appears well maintained, clean, and unpretentious. A look on the inside reveals a pleasant and conservatively furnished environment that's more impressive than you might have initially supposed. The entryway is flanked by a pair of lions resting on stone columns. The dining room, which can be closed off from the adjacent kitchen by a curtain, is set with a full formal dinner service throughout the day. Wall-to-wall carpeting covers the floors of the entrance lobby as well as the spacious and well-furnished living room. Guests are free to use this room, as well as the sun-washed terraces in back. A swimming pool is in the back garden. The owners are Walter (Dickie) Greene and his wife, Jane.

Each of the bedrooms contains an ironing board and iron, a coffeemaker, a TV and radio, a telephone, a refrigerator, and air conditioning. Facing the sea there's a cozy bar, where guests use the honor system to record their drinks. Dinners can be prepared upon request. A public bus that stops at the front door runs into Hamilton. The beach and the Port Royal Golf Course are both about five minutes away.

Little Pomander Guest House

16 Pomander Rd., Paget P.O. Box HM 384, Hamilton HM BX, Bermuda. ☎ **441/236-7635.** Fax 441/236-8332. 6 rms (all with bath), 3 apartments with kitchens. A/C TV TEL. Bus No. 1, 7, 8. Rates: Apr 1–Oct 31, $115 single or double; $125–$150 apartments. Off-season, $80 single or double; $85–$110 apartments. Continental breakfast included with rental of rooms, not with rental of apartments. AE, MC, V.

Consisting of two pink-sided Bermuda houses separated from one another by another building not associated with the guesthouse, this establishment once functioned as the annex to what is now a privately operated tennis club across the street. (Known as the Pomander Tennis Club, it offers temporary memberships for $10, and free use of their tennis courts to guests of Little Pomander.) Little Pomander's main building is said to be one of the oldest houses on Bermuda, with foundations and a history going back to the 1630s. There's a grassy lawn stretching a short distance down to a rocky shoreline, and a view overlooking the cruise ships anchored in Hamilton's harbor. Bedrooms are tastefully decorated with floral prints and the kinds of curtains you might have expected in Austria, all installed by the owner's mother, Irene Trott, a decorator. Patricia Harvey is the owner. Full kitchenettes are part of each of the three apartments, but even the conventional bedrooms here are fitted with microwave ovens and small refrigerators.

Loughlands

79 South Shore Rd., Paget PG 03, Bermuda. ☎ **441/236-1253.** 25 rms (19 with bath). A/C. Bus Nos. 2 and 7 stop nearby. Rates (CP): Mar 15–Nov 14, $75 single without bath; $116 double with bath; off-season, $55 single without bath; $70 double with bath. No credit cards.

Loughlands is a stately, once-private residence built in 1920 as the home of the president of the Staten Island Savings Bank in New York, who bestowed his name, Lough, on the estate. It is now the largest guesthouse in Bermuda. Set on nine acres of landscaped grounds in the center of the island, it is plantation chalk-white, and its entry hall contains a large portrait of Queen Victoria. Loughlands was purchased in 1973 by Mary Pickles, who sold her large country house in Cornwall, England, and shipped many of her antiques to Bermuda. The bedrooms at Loughlands are handsomely decorated, some with high-post beds and antique chests. Rates include a continental breakfast, with such Bermudian touches as fresh citrus fruit or bananas and homemade preserves. On the grounds are a swimming pool and a tennis court; bus service to all parts of the island is available. Elbow Beach is just a short walk away.

ⓢ Oxford House

Woodbourne Ave., P.O. Box HN 374, Hamilton HM BX, Bermuda. ☎ **441/295-0503** or 800/548-7758 in the U.S. Fax 441/295-0250. 12 rms (all with bath). A/C TV TEL. Bus No.

1, 2, 10, or 11. Rates (BP): Mar 16–Nov 30, $118 single; $138 double; off-season, $93 single; $109 double. No credit cards.

Oxford House is one of the best and most centrally located guesthouses in Hamilton. Said to be the only property in Bermuda constructed specifically as a guesthouse, it lies on a side street leading into Front Street, near the Bermudiana Hotel. It was built in 1938 by a doctor and his French wife, who requested that some of the architectural features follow French designs.

The white- and cream-colored entrance portico is flanked by Doric columns, corner mullions, and urn-shaped balustrades. Inside, a curved stairwell sweeps upward to the spacious, well-furnished bedrooms, each of which is named after one of Bermuda's parishes. There's even an upstairs sitting room, bathed in sunlight. Each accommodation gives the feeling of a private home and contains a private bath, high ceilings, dressing areas, and a coffeemaker. Included in all rates is the Bermudian breakfast that features, in season, fresh-fruit salad made with oranges and grapefruit grown in the yard. The gracious overseer of the establishment is Welsh-born Ann Smith.

⑤ Royal Heights Guest House

Lighthouse Hill, P.O. Box SN 144, Southampton SN BX, Bermuda. ☎ 441/238-0043 or 800/247-2447 in the U.S. Fax 441/238-8445. 7 rms (all with bath). A/C TV. Bus No. 7 or 8. Rates (BP): Apr–Nov, $100 single, $125 double, $175 triple; off-season, $90 single, $100 double, $150 triple. Children under 12 $50 when staying in parents' room. MC, V.

Set at the top of a steeply inclined driveway near the summit of Lighthouse Hill, this guesthouse is convenient to the Southampton Princess Hotel and its assorted nightlife and restaurant facilities. This is a modern, turquoise-trimmed building, whose pair of wings embrace the front entryway. Terraced near the foundation, a swimming pool encompasses a view of the passing ships on Great Sound. Guests are welcome to congregate in the living room of the owners, Russel Richardson and his wife, Jean, who will suggest activities for you. Each of the very clean bedrooms has a balcony and comfortable furniture.

⑤ Royal Palms Hotel

24 Rosemont Ave., P.O. Box HM 499, Hamilton, HM CX, Bermuda. ☎ 441/292-1854 or 800/678-0783 in the U.S. or 800/799-0824 in Canada. Fax 441/292-1946. 12 rms (all with bath). A/C TV TEL. Bus No. 1, 2, 10 or 11. Rates (EP). Mar 16–Oct 31, $125–$135 single; $145–$155 double. Off-season, $99 single; $120 double. AE, MC, V.

In Pembroke Parish, a five-minute walk to Hamilton, the Royal Palms is family owned and managed, and is one of the most sought-after small hotels on the island, thanks to the care and restoration work of the brother-sister team, Richard Smith and Susan Weare. The exact date of the house is uncertain, but it's definitely a century old.

Residents nearby often walk by its garden to admire the marigolds and zinnias. The house is a fine example of Bermudian architecture, with coral-colored walls, white shutters, and a white roof, plus a wraparound front porch with rocking chairs and armchairs. Cozy public areas include the Ascots Restaurant, serving both European and Bermudian cuisine, along with a bar surrounded by a terrace, and a veranda overlooking a freshwater pool.

The guest rooms were converted from the living rooms, parlors, and bedrooms of what used to be a grand private house. Today, each of them is spacious, sunny, and comfortably furnished. Rich fabrics are used throughout, and most units have high ceilings and tall windows. Each accommodation is equipped with a tea kettle or coffeemaker, and many have small refrigerators. In the mews beside the hotel are four additional units, some with kitchen facilities.

INEXPENSIVE

Hill Crest Guest House

1 Nea's Alley, P.O. Box GE 96, St. George's GE BX, Bermuda. ☎ **441/297-1630.** Fax 441/297-1908. 10 rms (all with bath). A/C. Bus No. 1, 3, 6, 1C, or 11. Rates (EP): Year-round, $52 single; $75.40 double; $104.40 triple. No credit cards.

Hill Crest is a green-and-white, early-18th-century home, spread on the rise of a hill off Old Maid's Lane. With its wide verandas and its lawns (with a moon gate) and trees, it has a homelike look. The interior is pleasant and comfortable, filled with clutter and antiques. The small entry hall has Edwardian furnishings, and all the rather sparse but clean accommodations have private bathrooms and clock radios. A small honeymoon cottage is on the grounds. Hill Crest is about five minutes away from several restaurants, where you can go to eat breakfast; also to be found nearby are shops, golfing, the bus route, and all points of interest in the historic town of St. George's. Write to E. Trew Robinson at the address above for a reservation; the place has been in her family since World War I. By the way, in 1804 the Irish poet Thomas Moore roomed here for several weeks. He was quite taken with Nea Tucker next door and wrote her some romantic verse.

Salt Kettle House

10 Salt Kettle Rd., Paget PG 01, Bermuda. ☎ **441/236-0407.** Fax 441/236-8639. 8 units (all with bath, four with kitchenettes). A/C. Directions: Lies within a three-minute walk of the Salt Kettle Ferryboat depot. Rates (BP): Year-round, $42–$44 per person, single or double. Units with kitchenettes, $48 per person. No credit cards.

The main core of this guesthouse is a 200-year-old cottage which, over the years, was enlarged and embellished until it reached its present design of a sprawling and many-angled rambler. In the late 1970s, another cottage was custom-built on the lot's only remaining available space. Today, the compound is a cheerful architectural hodgepodge set on a narrow peninsula of land jutting into Hamilton's harbor. Views of the ships anchored in the harbor are almost always constant, and the Salt Kettle Ferry depot lies within a three-minute walk. There's a bar-lounge on the premises, and on-site management by the owner, Mrs. Hazel Lowe.

Dining 6

Wahoo steak, shark hash, mussel pie, fish chowder laced with rum and sherry peppers, Hoppin' John (black-eyed peas and rice), and the succulent spiny Bermuda lobster (called guinea-chick) await you in Bermuda. Trouble is, you'll have to search hard to find these offbeat dishes, since many hotels and a large number of restaurants serve typical international resort cookery. For a more detailed description of Bermudian cookery, refer to the "Bermudian Cuisine" section in Chapter 2, "Getting to Know Bermuda."

Bermudian food has improved in recent years, but dining out is still not the major draw to these islands. British dishes such as steak-and-kidney pie are common, as are American ones. Most of the meat has to be imported, so whenever possible it's best to stick to selections from the briny. The fish is generally excellent, especially Bermuda rockfish.

Sunday brunch is a Bermuda tradition. Hot and cold dishes are served buffet style at several restaurants, including my favorite for brunch, the Waterlot Inn in Southampton Parish (see below).

Most restaurants, at least the better ones, insist on a dress code, preferring men to wear a jacket and tie after 6pm. Note that all lunch and dinner prices quoted are per person.

Restaurants rated "very expensive" charge more than $50 per person, excluding drinks and service, the latter most often added at 15%. Restaurants judged "expensive" ask from $38 to $50 per person for dinner; "moderate," $25 to $38, and "inexpensive," any dinner for one for less than $25.

1 City of Hamilton

The location of Hamilton restaurants and pubs is shown on the map "Hamilton Accommodations and Dining," which appears in Chapter 3, "Accommodations" (page 81).

VERY EXPENSIVE

Romanoff Restaurant

34 Church St., just west of Burnaby. ☎ **441/295-0333.** Reservations required. Jackets and ties required for men. Bus No. 1, 2, 10, or 11. Appetizers $7.50–$18; main courses $33–$39; business lunch $17.75. AE, DC, MC, V. Mon–Fri noon–2:30pm and Mon–Sat 7–10pm. RUSSIAN/CONTINENTAL/FRENCH.

In an atmosphere evoking the style of Old Vienna, the cuisine of the Continent is dispensed. Wedgwood china, damask linen, brass lamps, and crystal accompany your repast in a burgundy-colored room with smoked-glass mirrors.

Appetizers include snails in garlic butter and smoked rainbow trout. The chef prepares crêpes filled with assorted seafood and also makes tempting kettles of soup, including the traditional Russian borscht, lobster bisque, and French onion soup. Dover sole is prepared in classic ways, but if you want something fresh from local waters, try either the broiled wahoo filet or the Bermuda lobster. Shashlik is served Georgian style (that is, flambéed with vodka), or you might prefer chicken Kiev or duckling á l'orange. However, the chef's pièce de résistance is his tournedos flambé Alexandra, which is beef tenderloin flamed with cognac and served with a sauce made at your table. Each night you can also select the chef's creation of the evening from a silver trolley. For dessert, try one of the marvelous soufflés or crêpes, or perhaps a zabaglione.

EXPENSIVE

Ascots

In the Royal Palms Hotel, 24 Rosemont Ave. ☎ **441/292-1854.** Reservations recommended. Bus No. 1, 2, 10, or 11. Lunch appetizers $5.75–$6.25; lunch main courses $9.75–$12.50; dinner appetizers $8.75–$13.75; dinner main courses $22.50–$28.50. AE, DC, MC, V. Daily noon–2:30pm and 6:30–10pm. Closed Sat lunch in winter. ITALIAN/FRENCH.

This restaurant is contained within a spacious house, originally built around 1870, that lies in a residential neighborhood at the end of a Bermuda country lane at the edge of Hamilton. Before-dinner drinks are served from a large bar crafted from Bermuda cedar and brass in a setting of antique porcelain, Queen Anne armchairs, and Welsh pine similar to that of a chintz-filled English country house.

In summertime, candle-lit tables are placed on the house's front porch and sometimes beneath a tent in the garden. Owner Claudio Vigilante, originally from San Remo, Italy, directs cuisine that might include pasta Claudio, prepared at your table by the owner himself using sun-dried tomatoes, black olives, capers, onions, garlic, and "a family secret." Other dishes are likely to include Thai-style beef salad, deep-fried Brie, grilled Bermuda snapper, Mediterranean chicken, lobster Royale, Bermuda fish cakes, chicken Royal Palm, or shrimp Ibiza. Dessert might include some of the best tiramisu on the island, or any of a wide array of sweet concoctions flambéed at tableside.

Monte Carlo

9 Victoria St. ☎ **441/295-5453.** Reservations recommended. Bus No. 1, 2, 10, or 11. Lunch appetizers $4–$9.75, lunch main courses $8.75–$12.50; dinner appetizers $4.25–$9.75, dinner main courses $18.50–$23. AE, MC, V. Mon–Fri noon–3pm; Mon–Sat 6–10:30pm. CONTINENTAL/ITALIAN.

This restaurant was established in 1991 behind Hamilton's city hall in a format which celebrates the cuisines of southern France and Italy. Seating is within one of two different dining rooms: booths and banquettes in the outer room are ringed with a local artist's impressions of the countryside around Monaco. Tables and chairs in the main dining room are focused around the warmth from a brick-sided fireplace. Menu items include bouillabaisse made with Atlantic seafish Marseilles-style; filets of tuna marinated in oil and herbs and grilled over charcoal; wahoo with a lobster sauce; rack of lamb with Provençal herbs; lamb chops *Côte d'Azur*; and veal scaloppine Riviera (i.e., sautéed with sun-dried tomatoes and peppers, and served with angel hair pasta). Desserts are wheeled with a flourish through the dining room on a trolley.

New Harbourfront Bistro & Sushi Bar

Front St. between Queen St. and Par-la-Ville Rd. ☎ **441/295-4207**. Reservations recommended. Bus No. 1, 2, 10, or 11. Lunch appetizers $4–$6; lunch main courses $7.50–$12; dinner appetizers $5.50–$12; dinner main courses $16–$25. AE, DC, MC, V. Mon–Sat 11:30am–6pm and 6:30–10pm. ITALIAN/SEAFOOD.

On the second floor of an old Hamilton building across from the ferry station in the center of town, this spacious restaurant was renovated with marine-blue and nautical accents. A balcony jutting out over the street has a limited number of tables popular in fine weather. Specialties include chateaubriand and young lamb with an apricot sauce, as well as poultry and veal dishes. Fresh swordfish in garlic-and-white-wine sauce is a standard, as are broiled veal chops with a mushroom sauce, vermicelli with lobster, and an array of other seafood dishes. The chef's specialty is called "The Bermuda Triangle," which is three different varieties of the best available fresh fish arranged on a platter. The fish can be either broiled or grilled and is served with three different sauces. Sushi selections are also available.

✪ Once Upon a Table

49 Serpentine Rd., west of City Hall. ☎ **441/295-8585**. Reservations required. Jackets required for men. Bus No. 1, 2, 10, or 11. Appetizers $6.50–$17.50; main courses $19.50–$39; fixed-price menu $46.50. AE, DC, MC, V. Dinner daily 6:30–9 or 9:30pm. Closed Jan. FRENCH.

I think I'd be drawn here just because of the charming name, but fortunately, it has a lot more going for it than that. If Bermuda ever had a belle-époque period, it can be found here in a restored and richly decorated 18th-century island home, furnished in part with antiques. An old island buggy in the front yard sets the tone of the place. Inside, you are shown to a table in one of the intimate rooms, with lace curtains at the windows.

Hospitable Bermudians operate this place and serve candle-lit dinners. You can order hot or cold hors d'oeuvres, such as baked French snails, or locally caught wahoo marinated with herbs and juniper berries. Soups include Bermuda fish chowder flavored with black rum and sherry peppers. You are given a main dish choice of fresh Bermuda fish—broiled, grilled, or pan-fried with banana, champagne, or lemon butter sauce. Rack of lamb coated with herbs and Dijon mustard must be ordered for two guests. Or you might select tournedos à la maison (beef tenderloin with pâté and a Madeira sauce). Dessert might include crêpes Alexandra or a homemade sorbet of the day. One section of the menu—called low cholesterol dishes—takes care of those who are paying careful attention to calories. You'll have a truly superb and memorable meal here.

Tiara Room

In the Princess, 76 Pitts Bay Rd. ☎ **441/295-3000**. Reservations required. Jackets and ties required for men. Bus No. 7 or 8. Appetizers $7–$11; main courses $15–$25. AE, DC, MC, V. Daily 6:30–9:30pm. CONTINENTAL.

The gourmet choice of the Hamilton Princess, this modernized restaurant focuses its decor around tiara-shaped chandeliers and a panoramic view of Hamilton Harbour. Dozens of flickering candles seem to set fire to the fine crystal and heavy silver. Flambé dishes are a specialty here, adding a touch of theatricality to the decor.

Bermuda Dining

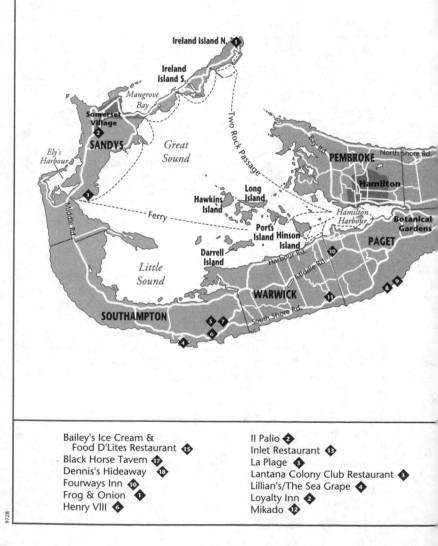

Atlantic Ocean

Ireland Island N. **1**

Ireland
Island S.

*Mangrove
Bay*

Somerset
Village **2**

SANDYS

*Ely's
Harbour*

*Great
Sound*

Middle Rd.

3

Ferry

Two Rock Passage

PEMBROKE   North Shore Rd.

Bay Rd.

Hamilton

Long
Island

Hawkins
Island

*Hamilton
Harbour*

Ports
Island   Hinson
Island

Botanical
Gardens

PAGET

Darrell
Island

Harbour Rd.

10

*Little
Sound*

Middle Rd.

8 **9**

WARWICK   **11**

South Shore Rd.

SOUTHAMPTON

5 **7**
6

4

Bailey's Ice Cream &
  Food D'Lites Restaurant **15**
Black Horse Tavern **17**
Dennis's Hideaway **18**
Fourways Inn **10**
Frog & Onion **1**
Henry VIII **6**

Il Palio **2**
Inlet Restaurant **13**
La Plage **3**
Lantana Colony Club Restaurant **3**
Lillian's/The Sea Grape **4**
Loyalty Inn **2**
Mikado **12**

9728

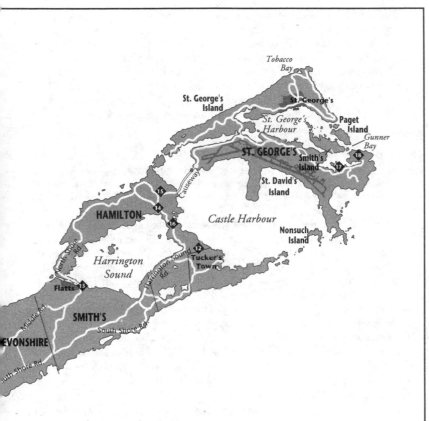

Tobacco Bay

St. George's Island

St. George's

St. George's Harbour

Paget Island

Gunner Bay

ST. GEORGE'S

Smith's Island

St. David's Island

Castle Harbour

Nonsuch Island

HAMILTON

North Shore Rd.

Harrington Sound

Tucker's Town

Harrington Sound Rd.

Flatts

Middle Rd.

SMITH'S

DEVONSHIRE

South Shore Rd.

South Shore Rd.

Atlantic Ocean

0 ___ 2 km / 1.5 m   N

Newport Room ◆5
Norwood Room ◆9
Ondine's ◆8
Paraquet Restaurant ◆8
Paw Paws ◆11
Plantation ◆16
Rib Room Steak House ◆5

Somerset Country Squire Tavern ◆2
Swizzle Inn ◆15
Tio Pepe ◆7
Tom Moore's Tavern ◆14
Waterlot Inn ◆5
Whaler Inn ◆5
Wickets Brasserie & Cricket Club ◆5

The cuisine is continental, and the menu often changes. For an appetizer, you might choose black and white angel hair pasta or escargots in brioche. Among the soup selections are chilled soup of the day and Bermuda fish soup. The chef prepares fish dishes and is said to search the eastern seaboard for unique aquatic catches. From this Atlantic bounty, try the scampi provençale or seafood casserole in saffron cream. Among the main poultry and meat dishes, you are likely to find roast Long Island duckling with a honey mustard sauce, or roast rack of lamb with herbs of Provence, and filet mignon with a béarnaise sauce.

MODERATE

Chancery Wine Bar

Chancery Lane between Reid and Front Streets. ☎ **441/295-5058.** Reservations recommended. Bus No. 1, 2, 10, or 11. Lunch appetizers $4–$12.75; lunch main courses $7.50–$19.50; dinner appetizers $4.50–$12.50; dinner main courses $16.50–$26.50. AE, MC, V. Mon–Fri noon–2:30pm; daily 6–10pm; bar daily 6pm–1am. CONTINENTAL.

Contained within a street-level building whose vaulted ceiling and thick stone walls date from the early 1900s, this cozy wine bar offers a candle-lit ambience very much like that of a European wine cellar. A trellis-covered courtyard in back contains a handful of tables for al fresco dining. Oenophiles appreciate the tasteful selection of vintages from around the world, more than 160 different wines. Despite its European antecedents, dress here is casual and the atmosphere relaxed. The menu is changed monthly. Therefore, you never know what you might get, perhaps an unusual soup, creamy rutabaga with caraway croûtons, or else a salmon, potato, and wild mushroom strudel, with Sevruga caviar, all served as appetizers. Main dishes are likely to include rack of veal chop stuffed with sun-dried tomatoes, or else medallions of pork, lamb, and beef tenderloin with a wild mushroom ratatouille, basil, and balsamic vinegar sauce.

Colony Pub Steak House

In the Princess, 76 Pitts Bay Rd. ☎ **441/295-3000.** Reservations recommended. Bus No. 7 or 8. Appetizers $3.75–$10.95; main courses $14.95–$29.95. AE, DC, MC, V. Daily 6:30–10pm. AMERICAN/STEAK.

Some dining critics consider this Bermuda's only true steak house, modeled after many counterparts in the U.S. The restaurant has its meat flown in fresh three times a week, and the portions are generous. Even if the goal of having "the best meat anywhere outside the U.S." isn't necessarily met, customers are generally satisfied. Start perhaps with the garlicky plate of escargots, then move on to a Caesar salad or else one made with beefsteak tomatoes and Bermuda onions. The most popular items on the menu are a 16-ounce New York strip sirloin and the 22-ounce lamb chops. The huge baked potatoes are flown in from Idaho. Those who aren't meat lovers will find a selection of fish and chicken, including the catch of the day. In the unlikely event you still have room for dessert, indulge in a chocolate brownie with cappuccino ice cream.

Fisherman's Reef

5 Burnaby Hill. ☎ **441/292-1609.** Reservations recommended. Bus No. 1, 2, 10, or 11. Appetizers $4.75–$12; main courses $18–$30; fixed-price lunch $14.95; "early bird" dinner (6–7:30pm) $18.95. AE, DC, MC, V. Mon–Fri noon–2:30pm; daily 6–10:30pm. SEAFOOD/BERMUDIAN.

Fisherman's Reef lies above the Hog Penny Pub in the heart of Hamilton and is a good choice for local seafood and typically Bermudian dishes. Its setting is predictably nautical, with a separate bar and cocktail lounge. You can order wa-hoo, one of Bermuda's most popular game fish, cut into steaks and topped with banana and bacon strips. Bermuda rockfish is also served. This is prepared in any of a half-dozen different ways. Although my favorite is grilled and served with a sauce of Black Seal rum, other diners prefer it either blackened in the Cajun style or served in the Mediterranean fashion with herbs and shrimp. Also, in season, Bermuda guinea chicks—that is, small lobsters—are broiled on the half shell. Ask the waiter about the daily catch—snapper, grouper, shark, or yellowtail—which can be pan-fried, broiled, or poached. Although most people come here for fish, the chef also prepares meat courses such as peppersteak flambé as well as a number of veal specials, including Oscar, marsala, and français. Banana fritters laced with black rum are a favorite dessert. Dress is informal.

Harley's

In The Princess, 76 Pitts Bay Rd., Hamilton. ☎ **441/295-3000.** Reservations recommended at dinner. Bus No. 7 or 8. Lunch appetizers $4–$5; lunch main courses $7–$14; dinner appetizers $7–$11; dinner main courses $9–$24. AE, DC, MC, V. High season (usually May–Oct) daily noon–4:30pm, Mon–Sat 6–10pm. Closed off-season (usually Nov–Apr). MEDITERRANEAN.

The popular Harley's is named after the bearded bon vivant who established the Prin- cess a century ago. In warm weather, tables are extended outside to the edge of the swimming pool, creating the effect of a flowering terrace on the Italian Riviera.

At lunch, you might want to dine on a thick sandwich, a fresh-tasting salad such as a Greek version of chicken with cashews and oranges, or one of the low-calorie and vegetarian selections. At dinner, this comfortable bistro features fresh pastas, a selection of pizzas, and a variety of Mediterranean-style main courses. Among the best liked are baked garlic shrimp and pan-fried lamb chops in a parmesan cheese crust. A dessert specialty is *torta con mele e gelato*, a flaky-crust apple pie pizza with vanilla ice cream and warm butterscotch cream.

Little Venice

Bermudiana Rd., between Par-la-Ville Road and Woodbourne Ave. ☎ **441/295-3503.** Reservations recommended. Bus No. 1, 2, 10, or 11. 2–course fixed-price lunch $13.75; lunch appetizers $6–$8.50; lunch main courses $13–$16; dinner appetizers $8.75–$9.50; dinner main courses $16–$28. AE, DC, MC, V. Mon–Fri 11:45am–2:30pm; daily 6:30–10:30pm. ITALIAN/CONTINENTAL.

This is one of the best-established and most visible Italian restaurants in Bermuda, a staple placed here as long ago as almost anyone can remember. The owner (originally from Capri) is proud of his specialties, one of which is *casseruola di pesce dello chef*. This consists of a medley of Bermuda-derived products, including lobster, shrimp, mussels, clams, and several kinds of fish cooked together with white wine, herbs, and tomatoes. Other choices include fish chowder, tournedos Rossini, several different veal dishes, and an array of pastas that include homemade ravioli stuffed with spinach and ricotta cheese. If you have room for dessert, you might try the zabaglione. Italian wines are featured, either in bottles or (less expensively) in carafes. An abbreviated menu is offered at lunchtime. Dress is "smart casual."

Ⓢ Lobster Pot & Boat House Bar

6 Bermudiana Rd. ☎ **441/292-6898.** Reservations recommended. Bus No. 1, 2, 10, or 11. Appetizers $4.75–$14; main courses $22–$25; fixed-price lunch $11.75; fixed-price dinner $25. AE, DC, MC, V. Mon–Sat 11:30am–5pm and 6–10:30pm. SEAFOOD.

Dating from 1973, this popular fish eatery located off Front Street specializes in local seafood cooked just right and with flair. Not surprisingly, the decor is nautical. Although the Bermuda fish chowder is laced with black rum and sherry peppers and is very good, you can get that elsewhere. A unique appetizer here is the curried Bermuda rockfish (delicately seasoned and rolled in a thin crêpe). Fresh oysters are available all year and are priced according to the season. I suggest the baked Bermuda fish for two—fresh fish that has been seasoned and stuffed. You can also try the lobster potpourri, the deep-fried tiger shrimp and scallops, or the wahoo steak (a game fish). Bermuda lobster (the so-called guinea chick) is available in season (that is, from mid-September until the end of March). The typical Bermuda banana fritter is a popular finish to a meal. Dress is casual.

MacWilliams

75 Pitts Bay Rd. ☎ 441/295-5759. Reservations not required. Bus No. 1, 2, 10, or 11. Appetizers $2.75–$3.25; main courses $9.50–$18. AE, MC, V. Daily 8am–10pm. INTERNATIONAL.

Set on the western waterfront road leading to the most congested part of Hamilton, this informal restaurant is sheathed in light-colored brick and neutral-colored paneling. This is a simple but worthwhile coffeeshop which does a thriving lunchtime business and is often patronized by clients of the relentlessly upscale Hamilton Princess, which lies nearby. It serves breakfast, lunch, and dinner, as well as coffee and snacks. Lunch includes an array of sandwiches, hamburgers, soups, and salads. The evening meal features such dishes as Bermuda fish dinners, fisher's platter, sirloin steak, liver with onions, spaghetti with meatballs, and barbecued ribs. Fish chowder is the most popular appetizer.

The Porch

93 Front St., between Burnaby and Parliament Sts. ☎ 441/292-4737. Reservations recommended. Bus No. 1, 2, 10, or 11. Lunch appetizers $3.95–$6.50; lunch main courses $7.75–$13.25; dinner appetizers $3.75–$7.25; dinner main courses $14.75–$21.50. AE, MC, V. INTERNATIONAL.

Lined with bricks and aged paneling, this warmly decorated restaurant lies within a century-old building which functioned for many years as a private apartment building and the island headquarters of American Express. As the restaurant's name implies, it boasts a porch with a prominent view over Hamilton's harbor, an English-style pub, and a wide outdoor terrace which tends to be abandoned in winter for cozier digs inside. (Navigate the stairs carefully as you climb up to this place from Front Street, and navigate them even more carefully coming down after having a drink or two.) Food is available throughout all parts of this establishment, even in the pub-style areas you might have thought would be reserved only for drinking.

The menu offers routine fare, with many veal and beef dishes predominating, including prime sirloin steak (10 ounces) or prime roast rib of beef with Yorkshire pudding. You can also order steak with shrimp and even wild boar in season, a throwback to the days of the early settlers on Bermuda. Lunches include sandwiches, salads, fresh fish, crab cakes, burgers, and oysters. You might want to drop in only for a drink. A pint of lager costs $4.50.

Primavera

69 Pitts Bay Rd. ☎ 441/295-2167. Reservations required. Bus No. 7 or 8. Lunch appetizers $3.75–$9; lunch main courses $16–$22; dinner appetizers $6.75–$12; dinner main courses $19–$25. AE, DC, MC, V. Tues–Fri 11:45am–2:30pm; daily 6:30–10:30pm. Closed Mon in winter. ITALIAN.

Primavera, in Hamilton West between Front Street and the Hamilton Princess, is a longtime staple on the dining scene and is often viewed as an alternative to the more traditional fare served in many of the island's restaurants. The cuisine is inspired by all the regions of Italy, including Sicily, Sardinia, and Rome. You might begin with a selection of either hot or cold antipasti, including a cold seafood salad or hot baked clams served in a marinara sauce. You can follow with a soup, perhaps minestrone, or a salad, most likely a Caesar. The array of pasta dishes features tortellini Primavera (the chef's surprise), or chicken cacciatore or sautéed veal with fresh vegetables. Top off your meal with an Italian espresso or a frothy cappuccino.

Red Carpet Bar and Restaurant
In the Armoury Building, 37 Reid St. ☎ **441/292-6195.** Reservations recommended. Bus No. 1, 2, 10, or 11. Lunch appetizers $3.50–$8; lunch main courses $6–$18; dinner appetizers $8–$11; dinner main courses $12–$26. AE, MC, V. Daily 11:30am–3pm and 6:30–10:30pm. ITALIAN/FRENCH.

The Red Carpet, in a 150-year-old building, serves many Italian dishes even though the atmosphere is evocative of an English pub. This place does a thriving lunch business thanks to the many offices in nearby buildings. Later, after work, its wood-trimmed bar is a popular place to relax with a beer amid a decor of dark-red carpeting, dim lights, and darkly stained trim. Lunches include sandwiches, cold platters, and a few hot dishes such as pan-fried fish, including Bermuda tuna and wahoo. Dinners feature a wider selection, including veal scaloppine, veal marsala, chicken cacciatore, filet mignon, and New York-strip sirloin. Many different pasta dishes are also featured.

Show Bizz Hard Rock Bistro
66 King St. at Reid St. ☎ **441/292-0676.** Reservations recommended. Bus No. 1, 2, 10, or 11. Lunch appetizers $3–$4; lunch main courses $8–$11; dinner appetizers $4–$7; dinner main courses $11–$18. AE, MC, V. Mon–Fri noon–2:30pm; Sun–Thurs 6–10pm, Fri–Sat 6–11pm. INTERNATIONAL.

Show Bizz is a small restaurant on the street level of a downtown office building. Inside, you'll find a black, white, and pink decor and the accessories you might expect in a jazzy pub in England. Photographs of the world's greatest entertainers, from the early days of the silent screen to world-class rock stars adorn the walls in a style inspired by *Planet Hollywood.* Don't limit your appreciation of this place just to its role as a restaurant. It's popular as an after-work bar with Hamilton's office workers, and after 10pm, the site transforms itself into a disco. Then, there's a two-drink minimum (you pay for the drinks in advance at the door) and the occasional appearance (usually on Friday or Saturday) of live rock bands.

Tuscany
Bermuda House, 95 Front St. ☎ **441/292-4507.** Reservations recommended. Bus No. 1, 2, 10, or 11. Lunch appetizers $5–$8; lunch pastas $8–$9; lunch main courses $12.75–$14.50; dinner appetizers $7–$8; dinner pastas $8–$10; dinner main courses $18–$21. AE, DC, MC, V. Mon–Fri 11:45am–2:30pm, daily 6:30–10:30pm. ITALIAN.

Established in 1994, this restaurant is on the second floor of a building overlooking Hamilton's Harbor. It contains a large mural commemorating the hills of Tuscany, a collection of copper artifacts similar to what you might find in a northern Italian farmhouse, and a narrow balcony with a half-dozen tables suspended above the pedestrian traffic of the harborfront walkway below.

Menu items include selections from throughout the Italian peninsula, including such pastas as ravioli with mushrooms, pasta fagiole, several kinds of risotto, scaloppines, grilled beefsteaks, and fish. Dishes deriving specifically from Tuscany include bruschetta Toscana (toasted garlic bread brushed with liver pâté), Tuscan-style codfish (with tomatoes, polenta, and black olives), and meats served with cooked spinach in the Florentine style. There's a choice of inexpensive Italian wines, and dessert might include a tiramisù. The staff derives mostly from Italy, is dressed in blues and blacks, and enhances the sense of Mediterranean flair.

INEXPENSIVE

Bombay Bicycle Club

In the Rago Furniture Building, 75 Reid St. ☎ **441/292-0048.** Reservations required. Bus No. 1, 2, 10, or 11. Appetizers $4.75–$7.50; main courses $13.95–$22; fixed-price lunch $11.95. AE, MC, V. Mon–Fri noon–2:30pm; Mon–Sat 6:30–11pm. INDIAN/CONTINENTAL.

Indian cuisine is expertly cooked and served in this third-floor upstairs hideaway where you can enjoy lunch or dinner in a relaxed atmosphere. For lunch, they offer "A Taste of India" buffet daily, and a variety of dishes ranging from mulligatawny soup to chicken, beef, lamb, and seafood served with a choice of sauces, in a spicy curry, or roasted in the tandoori oven. Indian vegetarian dishes and continental selections are also available. Dress is "smart casual."

Botanic Garden

In Trimingham's, 17 Front St., between Reid and Queen Streets. ☎ **441/295-1183.** Reservations not accepted. Bus No. 1, 2, 10, or 11. Soups and quiches $3.25; seafood salads $7.25–$8; sandwiches $3.50–$6; tea 65¢; pastries $1.75–$2.75. No credit cards. Mon–Sat 9:30am–4:30pm. INTERNATIONAL.

Housed on the third floor of the most famous department store in Hamilton, this place is filled with shoppers who know good value when they see it. This self-service place is informal and ideal for morning coffee or a British afternoon tea. The pastries, pies, and cakes are excellent, especially the banana bread and the gingerbread. An array of sandwiches is served as well. No heavy foods are served, since the cooking odors would permeate the items in the adjacent furniture department.

Chopsticks Restaurant

88 Reid St. ☎ **441/292-0791.** Reservations recommended. Bus No. 1, 2, 10, or 11. Appetizers $3.50–$6.95; main courses $10.50–$28. Daily noon–2:30pm and 6–11pm. CHINESE/THAI.

Although off the beaten track at the east end of Hamilton, Chopsticks offers some of Bermuda's best Chinese and Thai cuisine, including spicy soup, tangy pork ribs, and seafood. The chef specializes in Szechuan, Hunan, Thai, and Cantonese dishes, with an accent on fresh vegetables and delicate sauces. The fine food is served by a Bermudian staff.

Chicken dishes, including jade chicken with spears of broccoli and mushrooms and water chestnuts in a mild Peking wine sauce, are also a specialty. Peking duck is only served for two, and the staff must be informed 24 hours in advance. Seafood also figures heavily on the menu, as reflected by such dishes as shrimp in lobster sauce. Vegetarians will find a haven here, as there are many vegetable combinations made to be shared.

⑤ Hog Penny

5 Burnaby Hill. ☎ **441/292-2534.** Reservations recommended. Bus No. 1, 2, 10, or 11. Lunch appetizers $1.95–$5.25; lunch main courses $6.25–$16; dinner appetizers $4.95–$8.95; dinner main courses $14.95–$45; fixed-price dinner (5:30–7:30pm) $17.50. AE, DC, MC, V. Daily 11:30am–4pm and 5:30–10:30pm. ENGLISH/BERMUDIAN.

Bermuda's most famous pub, built and decorated in the British style with dark paneled rooms, offers draft beer and ale. Established in the early 1960s, this pub has fed and assuaged the thirst of hundreds of thousands of visitors ever since. Reservations are strongly advised, because the place is, to an increasing degree, mobbed. Old fishing and farm tools make up part of the decor, along with bentwood chairs and antique mirrors. At lunch you can order pub specials, including shepherd's pie and seafood crêpes, or a tuna salad. The kitchen prepares a number of passable curries, including chicken and lamb. Fish and chips and steak-and-kidney pie are the perennial favorites. Dinner is more elaborate, and the most expensive item on the menu is a whole lobster. You can always order a fresh fish of the day, perhaps Bermuda yellowfin tuna. The Angus beef is excellent, and you may want to precede your meals with Bermuda onion soup. There is nightly entertainment from 9:30pm to 1am; dress is casual.

M. R. Onions

Par-la-Ville Rd. ☎ **441/292-5012.** Reservations not required. Bus No. 1, 2, 10, or 11. Appetizers $3.95–$8.95; main courses $9.95–$22.95. Early bird 3-course dinner $13.95. AE, DC, MC, V. Mon–Fri noon–2:30pm; daily 5–10pm; bar daily 11:30am–1am. AMERICAN/BERMUDIAN.

The name of this popular restaurant and bar is a colloquialism. Bermudians are known as onions, and the "M. R." stands for "'em are," or "they are"; hence the name means "they are Bermudians." Designed like an Edwardian-era bar, it's done up with lots of brass, potted palms, leaf-green walls, and oak trim. Many caricatures of Bermudians hang on the walls, with a different portrait picked each month. If you go early, have a drink at the large rectangular bar that fills most of the establishment's front room. It's popular during happy hour (daily 5 to 7pm), when it is a favorite rendezvous for office workers in the neighborhood. Snacks are available in the bar until 10pm. Well-prepared meals are served in a rear dining room, with specialties including house onion soup and fresh fish that includes tuna, wahoo, rockfish, and mahi-mahi. Fish can be charbroiled, pan-fried, or served with amandine or spicy Cajun blackened style. Barbecued chicken, ribs, and steak are also served. You can also order an array of burgers, and beer by the pitcher or the glass. The dessert specialties are mud pie and cheesecake, or you can choose from the "sweet trolley." A bakery features onion bread. A nonsmoking dining room is available.

⑤ Pasta Basta

1 Elliott St. ☎ **441/295-9785.** Reservations not accepted. Bus No. 1, 2, 10, or 11. Salads $4.75; pastas $5.50 for half-portions, $9 for full portions. No credit cards. Mon–Fri 11:45am–11pm; Sat–Sun 5–11pm. PASTA.

This is the larger of two restaurants with the same pasta-and-salad format. (The other, Pasta Pasta, lies in St. George's, and has caused endless debate in Bermuda because of the slight difference in the spelling of its name.) Within a summery decor of tile-topped tables, blue-painted chairs, Tiffany-style lamps, and well-crafted oil paintings which showcase the foodstuffs of Italy, clients are presented a list of two kinds of salad (tossed and Caesar) and about a dozen different kinds of pasta. Served in full or half-portions, they include two kinds of lasagna (one of which is meatless), and a frequently changing array of fettuccine, spaghetti, and shell-shaped pasta with a choice of meat, seafood, and vegetarian sauces. On the day of my last visit, the daily special was shell-shaped pasta with sausage and onions in a pink sauce. Note that no wine, beer, or alcohol is served here, and local licensing laws do not allow you to bring your own drinks.

Portofino

Bermudiana Rd. ☎ **441/292-2375.** Reservations recommended. Bus No. 1, 2, 10, or 11. Appetizers $3.95–$8.95; main courses $8.25–$17.75; pizzas $9.95–$13.75. AE, MC, V. Mon-Fri noon–3pm; daily 6pm–midnight. Closed Dec. 25. ITALIAN.

The decor of this Italian trattoria evokes a warm and inviting place in northern Italy, complete with hanging lamps. It offers well-prepared and reasonably priced specialties, including three kinds of spaghetti and all the famous pastas, such as lasagna, ravioli, and cannelloni. A classic minestrone and 13 kinds of 9-inch pizza are offered. Standard and familiar Italian dishes include Venetian-style liver, veal parmigiana, chicken cacciatore, and beefsteak pizzaiola. The kitchen is noted for its ice cream desserts.

⑤ Rosa's Cantina

121 Front St. ☎ **441/295-1912.** Reservations required only on Fri and Sat. Bus No. 1, 2, 10, or 11. Appetizers $3.25–$7.50; main courses $13.95–$22.50. AE, MC, V. Daily noon–1am. TEX-MEX.

For your Tex-Mex fix, come to this place where you can fill up on such bounty as beef and chicken fajitas, zesty chili, nachos, tacos, and enchiladas, along with frozen margaritas to put the fire out. To the sound of the music of mariachi bands, you might begin with a hearty black bean soup, and then move on to *carne asado* (mesquite grilled rib eye steak), another chef's specialty. Texas ribs are featured as well. The restaurant is reasonable in price and serves the largest burritos on the island. The most desired seating is on the al fresco balcony.

Ye Old Cock and Feather

8 Front St. ☎ **441/295-2263.** Reservations not necessary. Bus No. 1, 2, 10, or 11. Lunch sandwiches, salads, and platters $5.75–$14.50; dinner appetizers $4–$11; dinner main courses $12.50–$18.75. AE, MC, V. Mon-Sat 11am–10:30pm, Sun noon–10:30pm. BRITISH/INTERNATIONAL.

Set within a centuries-old warehouse for whiskey, on Front Street between Burnaby Hill and Queen Street, this is one of the capital's most visible pubs and bars. According to its staff, the place appears in some of Hamilton's oldest photographs. Inside, there's a wide veranda overlooking the harbor, and a decor reminiscent of a warm-weather interpretation of a traditional British pub filled with suitably nautical artifacts. Lunches are simpler than dinners, and feature such dishes as salads, deep-fried cheese sandwiches, seafood combination platters, and beef pies. Dinners are more elaborate, with chicken Dijonnaise and oyster chowder. There's sometimes live evening entertainment in the bar area, and a crowd which can be congenially rowdy whenever the mood strikes.

2 Paget Parish

VERY EXPENSIVE

✪ Fourways Inn

1 Middle Rd. ☎ **441/236-6517.** Reservations in summer 1-2 days in advance. Bus No. 8. Lunch appetizers $5.50–$14; lunch main courses $16–$21; dinner appetizers $7.25–$19; dinner main courses $24–$52; Sunday brunch $27.50 per person. AE, MC, V. Daily 11:30am–2:30pm and 6:30–9:30pm. FRENCH/BERMUDIAN.

The Fourways Inn is considered by many to be the best restaurant in Bermuda. It has a mostly European staff and a certain kind of snobbish appeal. Once an

18th-century Georgian house built of coral stone and cedar, it has been converted into a dining room while maintaining the traditional Bermudian character and the old mahogany beams. Guests have a choice of dining inside or out, depending on the season. On most nights a pianist plays, and the atmosphere is relaxed. The old kitchen has been turned into the Peg Leg Bar with a whitewashed fireplace. Sunday brunch is an elaborate buffet.

An ambitious menu is featured at night. Try lobster salad with strips of avocado and cocktail sauce; baby rack of lamb (prepared either for one or two diners) sautéed with a mustard and herb sauce; escallop of veal with a citrus-flavored butter sauce; and a symphony of fresh fish and shellfish served with a red wine sauce. Desserts include five kinds of "instant soufflés," a favorite of which is called "dark and stormy" and includes chocolate, raisins, ginger beer, and dark rum. The wine cellar is among the finest on the island.

The Fourways Inn is a high-quality place, as reflected by its prices. Men should wear jackets and ties in the evening.

EXPENSIVE

Norwood Room

In the Stonington Beach Hotel, South Shore Rd., Paget. ☎ 441/236-5416 Reservations required. Jackets and ties required for men in the evening. Bus No. 7. Lunch appetizers $3.50–$6; lunch main courses $7–$18; fixed price dinner $45. AE, DC, MC, V. Daily noon–2pm and 7–8:30pm. CONTINENTAL.

The Norwood Room offers stately dining in a large sun-washed room, gracefully decorated in tones of blue and soft yellow. The room is laced with wood beams and a halo of arched windows looking out over the well-maintained foliage and the ocean. The restaurant is contained within a state-run hotel training institute. (see "Small Hotels" in Chapter 5, "Accommodations"). The service and attitude among the youthful employees are appealing, so don't avoid a visit here because of inexperienced staff. A pianist or harpist provides music in the evening.

Lunch is served in the dining room or on the patio, and at dinner there is a fixed-price menu. The last order is taken at 8:15pm.

Appetizers might include scallops in lobster sauce or a cold plate of marinated beef with onions, perhaps mushrooms stuffed with crabmeat or Bermuda fish chowder. Main courses sometimes feature fresh filets of Bermuda fish with prawns and mushrooms, and grilled sirloin with herb butter, the all-time favorite. The restaurant adjoins the Overplus Bar, where you may want to stop for a before-dinner drink.

MODERATE

Ondine's

In the Elbow Beach Hotel, A Wyndham Resort, 60 South Shore Rd., Paget. ☎ 441/236-3535. Reservations recommended. Bus No. 1, 2, or 7. Appetizers $6.50–$11.50; main courses $17.50–$28. AE, MC, V. Daily 6:30–9:30pm. INTERNATIONAL.

Decorated in tones of beige, green, and pink, this 200-seat restaurant is well known for its steak, fresh fish specials, and helpful service. Set on the ground floor of the Elbow Beach, a hotel recommended earlier in this guide, its large windows overlook the sea. Guests often begin at the salad bar before selecting such specialties as baked snails, Angus beef steaks, jumbo grilled scampi, or veal chops. There is also a wide array of desserts.

🌀 Family-Friendly Restaurants

M. R. Onions, in the city of Hamilton *(see p. 111)*. Taking its name from the colloquial name for Bermudians, this is one of the best family restaurants in the city of Hamilton. Kids go for the barbecue chicken, ribs, and steak. There's also an array of burgers.

Rosa's Cantina, in the city of Hamilton *(see p. 112)*. For Tex-Mex fare, this house of chili, burritos, fajitas, nachos, tacos, and enchiladas has no equal on the island. Children are given balloons to make the atmosphere most festive, and they're also offered coloring material and crayons when seated.

Wickets Brasserie & Cricket Club *(see page 118)*. Children's menus are available at this popular daytime eatery in the Southampton Princess Hotel. If you take your children there before 6:30pm, you can order dinner for them from the low-priced lunch menu which is still served that late in the day.

Pink's *(see page 129)*. Right in Hamilton, this place can serve the needs of the entire family weekdays until 4:30pm. Everything from breakfasts to well-stuffed sandwiches to picnic baskets can be purchased, as well as hot platters of inexpensively priced food.

INEXPENSIVE

Paraquet Restaurant

South Shore Rd., P.O. Box 173, Paget. ☎ **441/236-9742.** Reservations not required. Breakfast special (until 11am) $6.95; appetizers $2.75–$3.20; sandwiches $2.75–$8.45; main courses $10.65–$23.75. No credit cards. BERMUDIAN.

Set near a major traffic junction on the South Shore near the Elbow Beach Hotel, this unpretentious restaurant is the center of a recommended apartment cluster of the same name. From your table, you overlook a circular formal flower garden, which the Portuguese owners created. Although the lime-colored Formica, tiles, metal chairs, and plants are definitely coffee shop decor, some of the menu items are substantial restaurant fare. The chef specializes in home-style Bermudian fare. The establishment has one of the largest sandwich menus on the island, both hot and cold, as well as omelets, homemade soups (which always include a fish chowder of the day), and salads. You can order mixed platters, such as turkey breast and crabmeat, or such grilled dishes as T-bone steak, fried liver and onions, and roast half spring chicken.

3 Warwick Parish

Paw Paws

87 South Shore Rd., Warwick ☎ **441/236-7459.** Reservations recommended. Bus No. 7. Lunch appetizers $3.75–$6.50; lunch main courses $6.25–$13.50; dinner appetizers $4–$11.50; dinner main courses $14.75–$22.95. MC, V. Daily 9–11am, 11:30am–5pm, and 5:30–10pm. Closed Tues in winter. CONTINENTAL/BERMUDIAN.

About three miles west of Hamilton, the restaurant contains dozens of paintings and photographs of Bermuda landscapes, and murals showing the Bermuda forest underbrush. It features a Europeanized bistro menu with Bermudian specialties thrown in. In recent years they've risen above the middle bracket, family-trade image, offering a more ambitious cuisine that attracts the upmarket diner. Lunches feature club sandwiches, grilled chicken, salads, and the restaurant's trademark dish, a baked casserole with green paw paws (papaya), ground beef, and herbs, known as paw-paw montespan. In the evening the chef is likely to prepare such typical dishes as lobster ravioli in a cream-flavored basil sauce with strips of smoked salmon, or a seafood combo with scallops. Perhaps red snapper encased in puff pastry and served with a saffron-flavored cream sauce will appear on the menu. Other main courses include peppersteak in a cognac cream sauce and roast leg of lamb.

Under the same management, and immediately adjacent, are a pastry shop and an ice cream parlor.

4 Southampton Parish

VERY EXPENSIVE

✪ Newport Room

In the Southampton Princess, 101 South Shore Rd. ☎ **441/238-8000.** Reservations recommended. Jacket and ties required for men. Transportation: Ferry boats from Hamilton. Appetizers $7–$16; main courses $25–$30. AE, DC, MC, V. Daily 6:30–9:15pm (when the last orders are taken). Closed usually Jan–Feb. FRENCH.

There is no restaurant in Bermuda in which the decor is as sumptuously understated as it is in the Newport Room, and the French cuisine rates among the best in Bermuda as well. Everything about the place re-creates the expensive interior of a well-maintained yacht. A pair of exact miniature replicas of two of the winning sailing craft in the Newport to Bermuda race (reportedly costing $15,000 each) act as the illuminated centerpieces of a room that is entirely paneled in teak and rosewood, with appropriate nautical brass. Large illuminated paintings of the windblown regattas add a touch of color to an otherwise austere yet appealing room.

You'll be greeted at the entrance by a maître d'hôtel stationed beside a ship's compass. Settle into leather armchairs as you peruse the menu, which might include gourmet variations of *cuisine moderne,* such as duck breast with cinnamon and fig sauce. The menu changes frequently. A wide array of international wines, served in Irish crystal, complements each dinner.

EXPENSIVE

✪ Henry VIII

South Shore Rd. ☎ **441/238-1977.** Reservations required for dinner. Bus No. 7 or 8. Lunch appetizers $4–$7; lunch main courses $6–$12; dinner appetizers $5–$12; dinner main courses $20–$37; Sunday brunch $21.50 per person. AE, DC, MC, V. Mon–Sat noon–2:30pm; daily 6:30–10pm; Sun noon–3pm. ENGLISH/CONTINENTAL.

This pub restaurant, lying below Gibb's Hill Lighthouse between the Southampton Princess and the Sonesta Beach Hotel, has a contrived Tudor atmosphere, with oak furnishings, brass railing, ornaments, and period-style lighting fixtures. But don't let the hokey good Queen Bess atmosphere put you off. The food is worth a journey here. You might want to drop in at the split-level Oak Room Bar for some English beer on draft.

Hot pub lunches include steak-and-kidney pie, mussel pie, and plain old hamburgers. The Sunday brunch is popular. In the evening, the chef gets more elegant and turns out such whimsically named dishes as Court Jester (broiled seafood combination) and Steak Anne Boleyn (flavored with cognac and simmered in a madeira sauce). The chef also prepares an English mixed grill, peppersteak, and a chateaubriand. There is entertainment in the evenings.

Lillian's/The Sea Grape

In the Sonesta Beach Hotel & Spa, South Shore Rd. ☎ **441/238-8122.** Reservations recommended. Bus No. 7. Lillian's, appetizers $7–$12; main courses $18–$26; fixed-price menu $38. The Sea Grape, appetizers $4–$11; main courses $18–$22. AE, DC, MC, V. Lunch daily in the Sea Grape only, 11:30am–4pm. Dinner daily in both Lillian's and The Sea Grape 6–10pm. Closed, The Sea Grape only, Oct–Apr. ITALIAN/PACIFIC RIM.

Many visitors to Southampton Parish head for one of the Sonesta's restaurants, which include Lillian's (an art nouveau eatery specializing in the cuisine of North Italy), or The Sea Grape (an outdoor terrace adjacent to the sea). Which of the two they select is largely a function of the weather and their mood. Lillian's is the more glamorous of the two, with a pink and blue decor, an ambitious menu, and a formally correct staff. Menu items include selections of antipasto such as vegetable lasagna and house-smoked salmon, the latter served with roasted pepper risotto cakes, fennel, and aïoli. You might also begin with Tuscan-style white bean soup made with spinach and Italian sausage. Pizza is served and pasta can be ordered as either full or half courses. Main courses are likely to include baked wahoo with grilled polenta, roast Atlantic salmon with a fennel risotto, or else roasted rack of lamb with a vegetable lasagna.

The Sea Grape prides itself on a menu derived exclusively from the cultures of the Pacific Rim. For the most part, these include calorie- and cholesterol-conscious "clean" foods where sauces are served on the side, with recipes inspired by Californian, Korean, and Japanese cuisines. Appetizers range from spiced poached pineapple with coconut yogurt and candied ginger to grilled shrimp with a smoked bacon guacamole. A selection of soups is likely to include curried chicken soup with coconut and white rice. Main dishes are often grilled and served with fresh chutneys, salsas, and Yaki Soba noodles. Try, for example, sesame-crusted pork tenderloin or today's catch, priced according to market quotations.

✪ Waterlot Inn

In the Southampton Princess, Middle Rd., Southampton. ☎ **441/238-8000.** Reservations required. Jackets and ties required for men at dinner. Guests are transported from the hotel to this waterside inn in a shuttle. Appetizers $12–$17; main courses $24–$40; Sun brunch $30 adults, $17 children under 12. AE, DC, MC, V. Daily 6:30–9:15pm; Sun brunch 11:30am and 1pm (choice of seatings). MEDITERRANEAN.

Some 300 years ago, merchant sailors unloaded their cargoes directly into the basement of this historic inn and warehouse. Today the best way to approach it is still by water, and that's precisely what many Bermudians do, mooring their sailing craft in its sheltered cove. At one time the Darrell family owned this house and all the land stretching from Jew's Bay to the Atlantic on the other side of Bermuda. The land's most famous occupant, Claudia Darrell, ran one of the island's best-known eateries from the house until she died. Over the years the inn has attracted such patrons as Mark Twain, James Thurber, Eleanor Roosevelt, and Eugene O'Neill. After the landmark building was devastated by a gas explosion in 1976, the Southampton Princess had it renovated and today it's one of their gourmet restaurants.

Diners enjoy a drink in an upstairs bar, entertained by the resident classical pianist. After descending a colonial staircase with white balustrades, they can sit

Impressions

Had America ever suffered from land hunger . . . she would have seized Bermuda long ago. Wise, she took it not with soldiers, but with tourists, and today she controls it with dollars and an air base. There is nothing to be sorry about. The Bermudans stand on their tradition and their cash tills.

—Cecil Roberts, *And So to America* (1946)

in one of a trio of conservatively nautical dining rooms. Each is filled with captain's or Windsor chairs, oil paintings of old clipper ships, and lots of exposed wood. From the outdoor terrace, you can view the movement of pleasure craft in the bay. Main courses are likely to include poached chicken breast stuffed with foie gras and truffles, Riesling, cream, and seedless grapes; grilled rack of lamb with dried cherry chutney and mint; and the inevitable pan-fried Bermuda fish.

MODERATE

✪ Rib Room Steak House

In the Southampton Princess, 101 South Shore Rd. ☎ 441/238-8000. Reservations recommended. Transportation: Ferryboats from Hamilton. Four-course fixed-price menu $35. AE, DC, MC, V. Daily 6:30–9:15pm (when the last orders are taken). STEAKS/SEAFOOD.

The Rib Room Steak House sits atop the golf pro shop, near the tee-off point for the first hole. As you sit in the midst of panoramic windows and upholstered armchairs, you might start your evening with a Dark and Stormy (black rum with ginger beer). Follow that with a main course such as baby pork spareribs, several kinds of beef broiled over charcoal, or roast prime rib of beef with Yorkshire pudding. There is also a catch of the day or ten other choices, such as chicken with short ribs or broiled lamb chops. An extensive salad bar accompanies all dinners.

Tio Pepe

South Shore Rd., Horseshoe Bay, Southampton. ☎ 441/238-0572. Reservations recommended. Bus No. 7. Appetizers $9.75–$10; pizzas and pastas $8.50–$17; main courses $21–$23.50. AE, MC, V. Daily noon–10pm. ITALIAN.

Guests in this informal restaurant occupy either a wide garden-view terrace or one of three indoor dining rooms. Chianti bottles decorate the red and green (colors of Italy) interior, and are placed in strategic spots throughout. Catering to a Hamilton clientele who appreciate its nearness to the Southampton Princess Hotel and Horseshoe Bay Beach, the establishment serves pizzas, pastas, and the classic cuisines of Italy in generous portions with a bit of Mediterranean pizzazz. Don't be fooled by this establishment's Spanish-sounding name. Its cuisine is purely Italian, informal, and traditional.

Whaler Inn

In the Southampton Princess, 101 South Shore Rd. ☎ 441/238-8000. Reservations recommended. Transportation: Ferryboats from Hamilton. Fixed-price dinner $35. Daily 6:30–9:15. Closed Nov–Mar. SEAFOOD.

Famous for its seafood, this restaurant is perched at the top of a low cliff overlooking the rocks and pink sands that border the Atlantic near the Southampton Princess. Its landscaped terraces sprout with clusters of sea grape, Norfolk Island pine, and padded iron armchairs. From here you can view the sunsets that redden the lapping waves of one of the island's most secluded beaches. The interior's huge windows provide an airy setting where the panoramic view is the main decor.

Fixed-price items are chosen from a four-course table d'hôte menu with a wide selection of choices. To "bait your appetite," you can begin your repast with baked oysters Rockefeller, Bermuda fish chowder, or something as exotic as roasted pumpkin potato gnocchi served with roasted sunflower seeds. The chef's special main courses will be well-seasoned portions of whatever game fish the local fishers brought in that day, including yellowfin tuna, barracuda, shark, wahoo, or dolphin (the fish). Main courses not dependent on the whims of the tides or ocean currents include a kettle of seafood St. David's style, mussels marinière, and a deep-fried fisher's platter, along with the pan-fried local fish with almonds and bananas. You'll get a full array of Bermuda fish, either broiled or sautéed in butter. Your meal-topping treat could include banana fritters with black-rum sauce, or Armagnac ice cream with prunes. On Friday nights (usually from June through October), the restaurant features a popular Louisiana Cajun seafood festival, with indoor and outdoor dining, accompanied by a Dixieland band.

INEXPENSIVE

Wickets Brasserie & Cricket Club

In the Southampton Princess Hotel, 101 South Shore Rd. ☎ **441/238-8000.** Reservations not necessary. "Healthy start" breakfast buffet $12.50 per person; lunch appetizers $4–$6.75; lunch main courses $7–$11.75. AE, DC, MC, V. Daily 7–11am and noon–6:30pm. INTERNATIONAL.

Outfitted with all the memorabilia of a British-based cricket club, and painted in shades of soft greens, pinks, and whites, this brasserie and bistro features a health-conscious breakfast buffet with all the requisite low sodium and high fiber, and one of the longest and most comprehensive luncheon menus in Bermuda. The restaurant lies on the lower lobby level of Southampton Parish's most visible hotel, the Southampton Princess, and features a view over the hotel's swimming pool and the more distant ocean. Informal but traditional, it requests only that bathing suits be covered with a shirt. Since it remains open throughout the afternoon till 6:30pm, many Bermudians select it as the site of late lunches and—in many cases—early suppers.

Menu items include deli-style sandwiches, soups, chowders, pastas, salads, and such platters as grilled steaks, pork chops, and veal. Grilled grouper with citrus-butter sauce is probably the most popular fish served here. Children's menus are also available.

5 Sandys Parish

The following recommended eating places, of varied price and menu, are all located on Somerset Island.

EXPENSIVE

✪ Lantana Colony Club Restaurant

Somerset Bridge. ☎ **441/234-0141.** Reservations required. Jackets and ties required for men. Transportation: Hamilton ferry to Somerset Bridge. Fixed-price dinner $45, plus 15% service. No credit cards. Daily 7:30–9pm. Closed Jan 5–Feb 14. CONTINENTAL.

This is the elegant restaurant contained within this exclusive hotel. Guests sometimes prefer a drink near the fireplace of the huge salon before climbing the short flight of steps into the pastel-colored dining room. Ceiling trusses have been painted a pastel shade of spring green, and the neobaroque floral stencils were applied between garlands of Italian-style ornamentation. If you prefer a greenhouse effect, a second room has been glassed over with a solarium-style roof and surrounded with plants. A uniformed staff member will usher you to a table where a hibiscus has been placed at each place setting.

The frequently changing menu might include fresh salmon steak with dill sauce, prosciutto with melon, fish terrine, fish soup Lantana, grilled sirloin Delmonico style, breast of chicken with a whisky cream sauce, Bermuda fish meunière, veal Cordon Bleu, and grilled jumbo shrimp, any of which might be accompanied by grilled tomatoes Provençale. There is a large selection under each heading (appetizers, main courses, desserts, and so on). Live music is offered for dancing on certain nights of the week; call for information. Although most dinners are consumed in the hotel's main dining room, the venue moves to *La Plage* two nights a week (Wednesday and Friday) where the setting is open-air and less formal (see below). Regardless of the location, the food and prices are the same at dinner.

MODERATE

Il Palio

64 Main Rd. ☎ 441/234-1049. Reservations required. Bus No. 8. Appetizers $4.50–$11; main courses $13.50–$24. DC, MC, V. Tues–Sun 6–10pm. ITALIAN.

Named after the famous horse race in Siena, Italy, Il Palio lies in the center of Somerset in the west end of Bermuda, near several attractions that I'll cover later. If you arrive early, you can enjoy a drink in the bar downstairs before going upstairs to your well-set table. In a cozy, intimate decor, you might order fettuccine Alfredo, sautéed veal, pasta primavera, scaloppine, roast duckling with green peppercorn sauce, or steak Diana. A selection of 9-inch pizzas is also presented nightly.

La Plage

In the Lantana Colony Club, Somerset Bridge. ☎ 441/234-0141. Reservations recommended. Transportation: Hamilton ferry to Somerset Bridge. Lunch appetizers $2.50–$5; lunch main courses $12–$15; fixed-price dinner $45. No credit cards. Daily 12:30–2:30pm; Wed and Fri 7:30–9pm. INTERNATIONAL.

Walking toward this restaurant will give you a chance to admire the sculpture scattered throughout the gardens of the most exclusive hotel in Sandys Parish. In many ways, it's the perfect luncheon stopover during a tour of Bermuda's west end. The urn-shaped balustrades that separate the terrace from the cove, fresh flowers, and impeccable service are much like something you might find at the edge of a lake in northern Italy. A statue of an elfin girl experimenting with her mother's necklaces and lipstick stands guard beside the Roman-style pool where a stone cherub spurts water high into the air. A pier and a dock area a few steps away from the restaurant create the impression that a yacht might pull up at any moment. You'll be able to choose a table near the flowers of the sun deck, or one inside the pink-and-lemon summertime interior. You might begin with a Bermuda fish chowder, then follow with something from an array of offerings, which range from ordinary sandwiches (peanut butter and bacon) to elaborate fantasies such as salmon mousse, crêpes stuffed with beef and cheese, Bermuda mussel stew, and coquilles St. Jacques. Several salads are also offered, including a traditional chef's salad or one made with tropical fruit.

Loyalty Inn

Mangrove Bay, Somerset Village. ☎ **441/234-0125.** Reservations recommended. Bus No. 7 or 8, or ferry from Hamilton to Watford Bridge. Lunch appetizers $2.50–$4; lunch main courses $6.25–$15; dinner appetizers $3.50–$10.50; dinner main courses $25–$46; Sun brunch $23. AE, MC, V. Bar daily 11am–1am. Restaurant, Mon–Sat 11:30am–4pm; Sun noon–3pm; daily 6:30–10pm. INTERNATIONAL.

This 250-year-old converted home, which overlooks Mangrove Bay, is a white building that looks vaguely like a church. The bar, in the same building, is filled with captain's chairs and a mock fireplace. There's also an outdoor terrace. The restaurant with its decor of cedar paneling and small-paned windows attracts both visitors and locals. The menu of steak, chicken, sandwiches, and seafood is not elaborate, but the dishes are well prepared and the portions are generous. The fish chowder might be followed by either the fish plate or tasty scallops and a salad. In the evening, if you have the appetite, you can order a seafood dinner. The restaurant is about a five-minute walk east of the Watford Bridge ferry landing.

INEXPENSIVE

Frog & Onion

The Cooperage, Old Royal Navy Dockyard. ☎ **441/234-2900.** Reservations not necessary. Bus No. 7 or 8. Lunch sandwiches, salads, and platters $4.50–$9; dinner appetizers $5.25–$12; dinner main courses $9.25–$19.50. MC, V. Restaurant, daily 11am–4pm and 6–9:30pm. Bar, daily (with snacks) Mar–Nov 11am–1am, Dec–Feb noon–midnight. Closed Dec–Jan. BRITISH.

Set within what originally served during the 18th century as the cooperage (barrel-making factory) within the Royal Navy dockyards, this is about as quint-essential a British pub as anything else in Bermuda. It's facetious name derives from its Franco-Bermudian owners, French-born Jean-Paul Magnin (The Frog) and Bermuda-born Christopher West (The Onion). A pint of English lager costs $4.75, which you might enjoy within the shadows of the cooperage's enormous fireplace. Many clients remain to dine here. Lunches are simpler than dinners, and feature sandwiches, salads, lasagna, bangers and mash, and such bar pies as sweet lamb and curry; steak, turkey, and apricot; and vegetable and cheese. Evening meals include all the items available at lunchtime, as well as a wider range of liver, lamb, beef, and chicken dishes.

Somerset Country Squire Tavern

10 Mangrove Bay Rd., Sandys Parish. ☎ **441/234-0105.** Reservations recommended. Bus No. 7 or 8. Appetizers $5–$10; main courses $10–$25. AE, MC, V. June–Sept, daily 11:30am–4pm; off-season, daily 11:30am–3pm; year round Sun–Thurs, 6:30–9:30pm, Fri–Sat 6:30–10pm. Bar daily 11am–1am. BRITISH/SEAFOOD.

You pass through a moon gate arch to reach the raised terrace of this waterside restaurant, located in the center of the village. (This restaurant can be visited on a trip to the Old Royal Naval Dockyard on Ireland Island.) If you don't want to eat within the confines of the limestone blocks and hedges that ring the terrace, go to the interior dining room downstairs. The bill of fare ranges from British "pub grub" to fresh fish caught in local waters, or the traditional roast beef with York-shire pudding. Local Bermudian favorites include curried mussel pie and fresh Bermuda tuna or wahoo. Look for the specialties of the day, but count on char-broiled and barbecued meals. Most of the food is fairly routine, although the chef is especially proud of his Bermuda fish chowder, a tomato-based brew some locals cite as being the best in the west end. There is light entertainment three evenings a week, and barbecues from Sunday through Tuesday.

6 St. George's Parish

EXPENSIVE

Margaret Rose

St. George's Club, Rose Hill, St. George's. ☎ **441/297-1200.** Reservations required. Bus No. 8, 10, or 11. Appetizers $6.50–$18; main courses $23–$38. AE, DC, MC, V. Sat noon–3pm; Thurs–Tues 7–10pm. INTERNATIONAL.

Named after both Princess Margaret and Rose Hill (on which it sits), the fashionably decorated restaurant overlooks the harbor and the old part of town. Candlelight adds to the romantic ambience. You might begin with the award-winning Bermuda fish chowder or else enjoy an endive-and-rose-petal salad with a pine-nut-and-raspberry dressing. The wild-mushroom ravioli served in a thyme butter sauce is also an excellent appetizer. For your main selection, you might choose Bermuda fish Picasso (with a mosaic of fresh fruit and ginger), loin of lamb with an herb-and-garlic stuffing, or breast of Barbarie duckling, pink-roasted. Several pasta specialties are always featured, although certain dishes cited above may not always be available due to seasonal adjustments in the menu.

MODERATE

Carriage House

22 Water St., Somers Wharf. ☎ **441/297-1730.** Reservations recommended. Bus No. 3, 10, or 11. Lunch appetizers $4.25–$11; lunch main courses $6.50–$19.75; dinner appetizers $6–$12.50; dinner main courses $13–$45. Sunday buffet $23.50 per person. AE, DC, MC, V. Daily 11:30am–2:30pm and 6–9:30pm; Sun buffet brunch noon–2:15pm. BEEF/SEAFOOD.

Housed in an old waterfront storehouse in the same building as the Carriage Museum, the restored Carriage House specializes in beef as well as seafood. It keeps its 18th-century-warehouse look with two rows of bare brick arches, the effect softened by hanging baskets of greenery. After placing your order for dinner, you can help yourself to varied salads in the rear of the restaurant. Or you may want to enjoy a good selection of hot and cold hors d'oeuvres. The chef specializes in prime rib, the cost depending on the size of your steak which is always cut to order and served with a ramekin of creamed horseradish in the British tradition. English roast spring lamb is also a specialty. The most expensive item on the menu is lobster (see price above), but most other main courses are considerably cheaper. A different soup is offered every day. At lunch, a large selection of hamburgers is offered, along with sandwich platters, Bermuda fish chowder, pastas, soups, and oysters. A choice of excellent desserts is always available. Casual dress is accepted. When the place fills up, as on cruise ship days, service can be slow.

San Giorgio

Water St. ☎ **441/297-1307.** Reservations recommended. Bus No. 3, 10, or 11. Lunch appetizers $3.50–$8.50; lunch main courses $15–$19.50; dinner appetizers $4–$10.50; dinner main courses $15–$19.50; pizzas and pastas $10–$11. MC, V. Mon–Fri noon–2:30pm; Mon–Sat 6:30–9:45pm. ITALIAN.

To reach this little Italian restaurant next to the Tucker House Museum, guests climb a short flight of steps from a point opposite Somers Wharf. The 150-year-old building was originally a private house and later served as the local telephone exchange for St. George's. Today the place is an Italian bistro/trattoria deliberately informal, with red-and-white-checked tablecloths, a casual dress code, and a series of artifacts commemorating San Giorgio and his dragon. Most guests begin with a selection of antipasto. Several pasta dishes tempt diners, including tortellini and lasagna. For your main course, you can select from such dishes as breast of chicken sautéed with black-cherry-and-rum sauce. The chef also does hot shrimp salad and hot scallop salad. Fresh broiled wahoo with lemon butter sauce is regularly featured.

Wharf Tavern

Somers Wharf. ☎ 441/297-1515. Reservations recommended. Bus No. 3, 10, or 11. Appetizers $3–$7.50; main courses $8.50–$23; lunch sandwiches $5. MC, V. Daily 11am–11pm; bar daily 11am–1am. SEAFOOD.

Wharf Tavern, situated among the cluster of buildings that make up Somers Wharf, is a nautically minded, modern restaurant built on the ground floor of a building with a veranda. The building was converted from a 200-year-old warehouse. Only pedestrians are allowed nearby, which might account for the popularity of the porch and the window seats, and the darkly paneled bar area inside. Dinners could include curried mussels, Bermuda fish cakes with peas and rice, pan-fried or broiled rockfish, broiled wahoo, oysters on the half shell, steak-and-kidney pie, and a London-style mixed grill. All main courses are served with a salad and a "starch." Entertainment is presented on certain evenings beginning at 10pm. This is more likely to occur in summer than in winter. There's never any cover charge when entertainment is featured.

White Horse Tavern

King's Square. ☎ 441/297-1838. Reservations recommended for dinner. Bus No. 3, 10, or 11. Appetizers $4.50–$12; main courses $12–$20. MC, V. Lunch daily 11:30am–5pm; dinner daily 5:30–10pm. BERMUDIAN.

St. George's oldest tavern is a restaurant and cedar bar with a terrace jutting into St. George's Harbour. This white building with green shutters is one of the most popular taverns in all of Bermuda, and its location is so central you can't miss it. In fair weather (which is most of the time), guests prefer to sit on the terrace. The most frequently ordered item here is fish and chips, cooked in the manner of St. David's Island. The Bermuda fish chowder is also good. Or you can order mussel pie, codfish cakes, or grilled wahoo with tartar sauce. St. George's fish pot is the chef's specialty. At lunch, Tavern burgers, fresh salads, and open-faced sandwiches are served. Finish off with the White Horse chocolate cake. Dress is casual.

INEXPENSIVE

⑤ O'Malley's Pub on the Square

King's Square. ☎ 441/297-1522. Reservations not required. Bus No. 3, 10, or 11. Appetizers $3.50–$8.50; main courses $12.50–$25. AE, MC, V. Daily 8:30am–3am. AMERICAN/BERMUDIAN.

Here you'll find a two-level British pub, with a rustic atmosphere, in a building dating from 1785. On a good evening, the fun here has been compared to that of a prewar English music hall; the sing-alongs keep St. George's rocking. After a mug of beer at the downstairs pub level, guests can climb a spiral staircase to the upper-level tavern dining room, which has a veranda bar overlooking the square. Usually washed down with draft beer, the fish and chips is the most popular item; sandwiches are also available. Other good dishes include Bermuda fish chowder laced with rum and sherry peppers, pub-style chicken, and steak-and-kidney pie. Lunch begins at 11am, although simple foods on the lunch menu are served

St. George's Dining

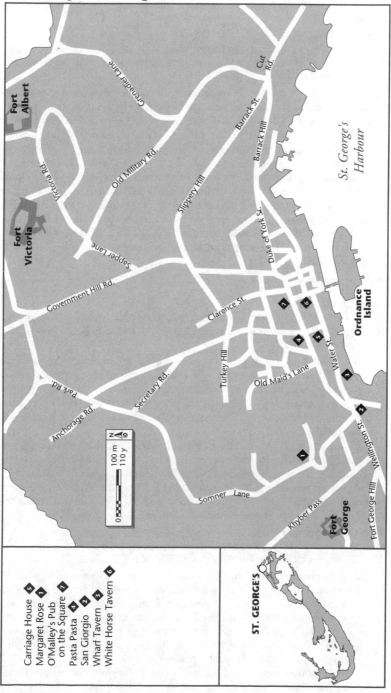

Carriage House **5**
Margaret Rose **1**
O'Malley's Pub
on the Square **7**
Pasta Pasta **4**
San Giorgio **2**
Wharf Tavern **3**
White Horse Tavern **6**

ST. GEORGE'S

9729

until 10pm. Dinner begins at 5:30pm and dinner main courses are served until 10pm.

⑤ Pasta Pasta

York Street, St. George's ☎ **441/297-2927.** Reservations not accepted. Bus No. 8, 10, or 11. Salads $4.50; pastas $5 for half-portions, $8.50 for full portions. No credit cards. Mon–Sat noon–10:30pm; Sun 5–10:30pm. PASTA.

This is the smaller and slightly less expensive of two Bermuda restaurants with the same owners and the same pasta-and-salad format. (Its twin, which is separately recommended in "Dining in Hamilton," has caused endless debate in Bermuda because of the slight difference in the spelling of its name.) Within a boldly colorful and summery decor which is well suited to the informality of pastas and salads, clients are presented a list of two kinds of salad (tossed and Caesar), and about a dozen different kinds of pastas. Served in full or half-portions, they include two versions of lasagna (one of which is meatless) and a frequently changing array of all shapes and sizes of pasta served with a choice of meat, seafood, and vegetarian sauces. Note in advance that no wine, beer, or alcohol is served here, and local licensing laws do not allow you to bring your own drinks. A goodly percentage of the pasta sold here is intended for take-out consumption. (All containers are microwavable.)

ST. DAVID'S ISLAND

Black Horse Tavern

34 Great Bay Rd., St. David's Island. ☎ **441/293-9742.** Reservations recommended. Bus No. 3. Appetizers $5–$8.75; main courses $13.25–$27. AE, MC, V. Tues–Sat 10am–1am; Sun noon–1am. INTERNATIONAL.

If you should land here, in a section of the island that Bermudians call "the country," you'll dine with the locals. The exterior looks like a dusty-rose-colored version of a private home, complete with green shutters and a rear glassed-in porch that looks over Smith's Sound. Over the years the tavern has been host to many celebrities, including Robert Stigwood, the Australian movie producer. Many of the guests show up in yachts.

You might begin your meal with curried conch stew, shark hash (made with minced puppy shark), fish chowder, or curried mussels. This could be followed by a sandwich, a burger, or perhaps a platter of fish and chips or chicken and chips. The chef also prepares a good sirloin steak and a chicken dinner. If your luck holds, the only Bermuda Triangle you'll ever encounter is a drink of that name made here with pineapple juice, orange juice, black rum, and Bermuda gold liqueur.

Dennis's Hideaway

Cashew City Rd. ☎ **441/297-0044.** Reservations required. Bus No. 3. Fixed–price dinners $25–$35. No credit cards. Dinner daily 7–10pm. SEAFOOD.

Dennis Lamb, a burly St. David's Islander, is one of the treasures of Bermuda. So is his quaint little eatery, located in the easternmost parish of St. George's. As you approach it, you're likely to see Dennis (part Irish, part Mohawk) working in his garden in front (he even grows the cabbage he uses in his coleslaw and the beets he pickles). He'll show you into his fisher's cottage by one of the island's little coves. Once inside, you'll feel you've left Bermuda and are visiting some little pocket-size country with a distinctive personality.

Descended from whalers and pilots—"wooden ships and iron men"—Dennis and his son will offer you a cuisine that has virtually disappeared in Bermuda's restaurants, one that is practiced only in private homes these days. For $35, he'll give you "the works," an array of dishes, including conch stew, dolphin (the fish), herb-flavored shark hash, shrimp, conch fritters—you name it (but please don't order the turtle, an endangered species). You may bring your own wine. If you don't want to eat so much, request the fish dinner for $25. The cottage is accessible by land or sea, and don't dress up.

(*Warning:* This Pa Kettle ambience is not for everyone, it must be pointed out. Reactions of readers have varied tremendously. Some repeat visitors give it high marks, claiming they've made at least 20 pilgrimages here during their annual visits to Bermuda. Some first-time visitors, however, claim that travel writers who send diners to this grubby place should be tarred and feathered. So go only if you're a bit adventurous!)

7 Hamilton Parish

EXPENSIVE

Mikado

In Marriott's Castle Harbour Resort, Paynters Town Rd., Tucker's Town. ☎ 441/293-2040. Reservations required. Bus No. 2 from St. George's. Appetizers $5.25–$7; main courses $25–$38; sushi $4.75–$6.25 per order (usually two pieces). AE, DC, MC, V. July–Sept, dinner only daily 6:30–9:30pm; off-season, dinner only Tues–Sun 6:30–9:30pm. JAPANESE.

Located on the lower level of the Marriott, which is also recommended in this guide, this is the only major Japanese restaurant on Bermuda, although some other places now serve sushi. You pass through lacquered gateways to reach a whimsically art deco version of a Japanese tea garden. A pond is traversed by a Japanese bridge. An experienced chef is assigned to each group of eight diners and prepares his cuisine, *teppan-yaki* style. Grills placed near each table permit diners to view whatever is cooking. Rare imported fish mixed with very fresh Bermuda fish, such as wahoo, are used for the sushi bar. All the traditional Japanese specialties, including tempura, along with an aromatic saké, are available. Dress is "smart casual."

✪ Plantation

46 Harrington Sound Rd., Bailey's Bay. ☎ 441/293-1188. Reservations recommended for dinner. Bus No. 1 and 3. Appetizers $5.50–$12.75; main courses $22–$32. AE, DC, MC, V. Lunch daily noon–2:30pm; dinner Mon–Sat 6:45–9:30pm; bar service from 10am. Closed mid–Dec to mid–Feb. BERMUDIAN.

The Plantation, a yellow colonial-style building with fireplaces and steep white roofs, stands at the site of Leamington Caves. The three rooms inside, with their carpeting, ceiling fans, and rattan furniture, have an inviting ambience. In fair weather, guests dine al fresco in the tropical garden shaded by a giant marquee. The bar with its Bermuda cedar base is ideal for a drink. Try such dishes as a crêpe filled with seafood and served with a light wine cheese sauce or a main course of charcoal-grilled fish with citrus butter or banana, raisin, and coconut. Some clients have found this a little too exotic, but the lamb with apple chutney and calvados sauce is generally a hit. Dress is "smart casual," and it's preferred that men wear a jacket.

Tom Moore's Tavern

Washington Lane, Bailey's Bay. ☎ 441/293-8020. Reservations required. Bus No. 1 or 3. Appetizers $5.50–$18; main dishes $24–$32. AE, MC, V. Dinner daily 7–9:30pm. Closed Jan 5–Feb 14. FRENCH/CONTINENTAL.

Bermuda's oldest eating house, built in 1652 and once a private home, is located on Walsingham Bay, near the Crystal Caves, in Hamilton Parish. It was visited in 1804 by the Irish romantic poet Thomas (Tom) Moore, who wrote some of his verses here; he made reference to a calabash tree that still stands, some 200 yards from the tavern.

The tavern is also the most famous dining room in Bermuda, having known many incarnations. In 1985 two Italians, Bologna-born Bruno Fiocca and his Venetian partner, Franco Bortoli, opened it for dinner and quickly established it as one of the most popular upmarket restaurants in Bermuda. Fortunately, they have maintained the old character of this landmark place, which has four fireplaces. The darkened cedar walls are a backdrop for the classical French and Italian cuisine served here.

Seafood is a specialty. A Bermuda-lobster tank is found outside during the season. The Bermuda fish from local waters is likely to be rockfish or yellowtail. If featured, try quails in puff pastry or duck with a raspberry-vinegar dressing. The setting, the English silver, German crystal, Luxembourg china, and the general ambience can help make a memorable visit. Men should wear a jacket.

INEXPENSIVE

Swizzle Inn

3 Blue Hole Hill, Bailey's Bay. ☎ **441/293-9300.** Reservations accepted for 5 or more only. Bus No. 3 or 11. Lunch appetizers $2.50–$6; lunch main courses $5.50–$12; dinner appetizers $4–$8; dinner main courses $8–$22. AE, MC, V. Daily 11am–1am. Closed Mon in Jan and Feb. BERMUDIAN/ENGLISH.

The home of the Bermuda rum swizzle lies west of the airport, near the Crystal Caves, and it is considered the oldest pub in Bermuda, dating back some 300 years. Thousands of business cards and graffiti cover the walls. The meaty Swizzleburger was voted best in Bermuda, and other pub favorites include fish & chips, conch fritters, and shepherd's pie. Bailey's Bay fish sandwich is a popular item at lunch, as are the onion rings. Dinner offers a wider menu variety appealing to several tastes and diets. Dining is available both inside and on the upper and lower patios. Also upstairs is a nonsmoking room along with a gift shop.

8 Smith's Parish

Inlet Restaurant

In the Palmetto Hotel, Harrington Sound Rd., at Flatts Village. ☎ **441/293-2323.** Reservations not required. Bus No. 10 or 11. Appetizers $5–$9.75; main courses $17–$28; lunch $14. AE, MC, V. Lunch daily noon–2:30pm; dinner daily 7–9:30pm; light snacks served in pub until 9:30pm. INTERNATIONAL.

In creating this restaurant, the owners added a slope-roofed modern addition onto what had been a paneled lounge lined with Bermuda cedar. You can select a seat near the big windows, which look over the moon gate, the swimming pool, and the harbor, or you can relax in the darker and more intimate recesses in the back.

A selection of sandwiches and burgers are available for lunch, and light snacks can be taken outside on the patio in fine weather. Dinners feature a more detailed menu and a wider selection of dishes. You might start with spinach or Caesar salad, or Bermuda fish chowder. Seafood courses include a casserole of shrimp and scallops, or perhaps fresh Bermuda fish, broiled or pan-fried. Meat dishes are likely to consist of grilled beef tenderloin, Bermuda chicken breast stuffed with pâté, and grilled medallions of pork in an apple brandy sauce.

9   Afternoon Tea & Sunday Brunch

AFTERNOON TEA

Bermuda still practices the British tradition of afternoon tea. (Ironically, in Britain itself, the tradition had been on the wane until it began to come back in the 1980s.) Many guests prefer to have afternoon tea at their hotels, which is a good opportunity to meet fellow guests. Others like to visit other hotels and have afternoon tea there. You should check first, however, as some hotels and resorts prefer to serve afternoon tea only to registered guests.

Among the previously recommended restaurants and cafés, the two most outstanding ones for a traditional afternoon tea are the **Botanic Garden** (see Section 1, "City of Hamilton," earlier in this chapter) and **Fourways Pastry Shop** (see Section 10, "Fast Food and Picnic Fare," below).

SUNDAY BRUNCH

Sunday brunch is a real tradition in Bermuda. A fortunate few visitors manage an invitation to a private Bermudian home for this meal. If their luck continues, they'll be served the traditional "Sabbath fare" of new potatoes with boiled salt cod, which is most often accompanied by slices of banana and avocado topped with an egg-enriched cream sauce. Many Bermudians also make a codfish dish flavored with tomatoes.

Nearly all hotels serve a traditional Sunday brunch. Many guests prefer to relax on Sunday morning and not leave their hotels; others like to visit one of the popular restaurants on the island featuring Sunday brunch, including the previously recommended **Henry VIII** or the **Loyalty Inn. The Carriage House** (see above) also serves one of the best and most well-attended brunches on the island. The most popular place in Bermuda for Sunday brunch? See below.

✪ Waterlot Inn

In the Southampton Princess, Middle Rd., Southampton. ☎ **441/238-8000.** Reservations required. Guests are transported from the hotel to this waterside inn in a shuttle. $30 adults, children under 12, $17. AE, DC, MC, V. Sun brunch two seatings: 11:30am and 1pm. SUNDAY BRUNCH.

This restaurant, recommended earlier in this chapter, is the most popular place on the island for Sunday brunch, attracting both visitors and Bermudians. It is imperative to reserve as far in advance as possible, because of the demand for tables. Brunch is buffet-style with all the classic dishes spread before you, including eggs Benedict, hot and cold meats, turkey platters, lamb dishes, and an array of seafood. There is also a station featuring a traditional Bermudian breakfast cuisine. Men might arrive in a smart blue blazer with tailored Bermuda shorts—it's all the fashion here.

10   Fast Food & Picnic Fare

FAST FOOD

Bailey's Ice Cream & Food D'Lites Restaurant

The corner of Wilkinson Ave. and Blue Hole Hill. ☎ 441/293-9333. Reservations not required. Bus No. 3 or 11. Ice cream $1.75 per scoop; sandwiches $2.50–$4.50 each. No credit cards. Mon–Sat 11am–6pm, Sun 11am–6pm. Closed Dec–Feb. ICE CREAM/SANDWICHES.

At Bailey's Bay, this place stands across from the also-recommended Swizzle Inn. For all-natural ice cream, there is no comparable spot in Bermuda—20 to 25 different flavors are made in the 40-quart ice-cream maker. The parlor is in a small Bermuda cottage, and there is a parking lot. You can eat your butterscotch crunch, almond delight, piña colada, or some other exotic ice cream flavor at one of the outdoor tables or take it away. A sandwich nook, which uses fresh-baked breads, is a popular attraction. Also featured are fresh-fruit ices, frozen yogurts, and natural juices.

Fourways Pastry Shop

In the Washington Mall, Reid St., at Queen St. ☎ **441/295-3263.** Reservations not accepted. Bus No. 1, 2, 10, or 11. Tea or coffee $1.25; sandwiches $3–$5; daily specials $6.75. AE, MC, V (for purchases of $25 or more). Mon–Sat 8am–4:30pm. PASTRIES/SANDWICHES.

This is one of Hamilton's most consistently popular lunchtime venues, serving hundreds of the capital's office workers every day. Although the establishment's most popular items include pastries, sandwiches, and endless cups of tea and coffee, they also offer at least three platters of the day which—when served with something to drink—comprise meals in themselves. Depending on what's available in the markets on any particular day, daily specials might include lasagna with a side salad; savory breast of chicken with greens; or platters of "deep-fried rice" with minced beef or pork.

PICNIC FARE & WHERE TO FIND IT

Those who have a penchant for picnics can indulge it while enjoying a bicycle ride through Sandys Parish. Start by going over Somerset Bridge, the smallest drawbridge in the world, and pedal along Somerset Road to Fort Scaur Park, where you can enjoy a panoramic view of Ely's Harbour.

There are many other desirable locations as well, including Spanish Point Park in Pembroke, a series of little coves and beaches. For here you don't need to go to the trouble of packing a picnic basket, since a lunch wagon rolls around (except in winter). Private picnicking is also available at one of the island's best beaches, Warwick Long Bay. There are restrooms at the western end if you'd like to wash up before you bite down.

Many kitchens of major hotels will prepare a picnic lunch for you, but you should make the request a day in advance. Or you can walk along Front Street in Hamilton, selecting sandwiches at the various cafés or a bottle of wine and some mineral water at a local shop. If it's a weekday, the best place to obtain supplies is the following.

The Hickory Stick

2 Church St. at Bermudiana Rd. ☎ **441/292-1781.** Reservations not accepted. Bus No. 1, 2, 10 or 11. Salads $2.75–$5.25; sandwiches $3.10–$6.50; hot takeaway platters $3–$5.25. No credit cards. DELI.

Set close to the rose-colored walls of the Princess Hotel in Hamilton, this might be one of the most popular delicatessens and take-out restaurants in the capital, serving a thousand clients a day, including many of the capital's office workers.

Although one section might remind visitors of a popular coffee shop (scones, donuts, and morning coffee provide doses of caffeine for the neighborhood residents), most clients prefer it for its overstuffed sandwiches and takeaway portions of food. Offerings include steaming portions of chicken parmesan, barbecued spare ribs, and fish cakes, although even more popular are the salads, sandwiches, and hot dogs, all of which employees will wrap as picnic food for open-air enthusiasts. Advance telephone orders are accepted, and often are a wise idea if you don't want to wait for your order to be prepared. Paper napkins and plastic knives, forks, and spoons are provided on request.

Pink's

55 Front St. ☎ **441/295-3524.** Reservations not accepted. Bus: No. 1,2, 10, or 11. Salads, sandwiches, and hot takeaway platters $3.25–$8. Breakfast croissant with coffee $2.75. Complete picnic boxes $14.50 per person. No credit cards. Mon-Fri 7:30–4:30pm; Sat 8:30–4:30pm. DELI.

Established in 1989 and named after Andrew Pink, its hardworking, English-born owner, this establishment has emerged as one of the capital's best-managed delis. Outfitted in a color scheme of (you guessed it) pink and teal blue, it serves hundreds of Hamilton's office workers every day in the form of non-fried (i.e., health-conscious) breakfasts (fresh-made croissants and scones), and flavorful lunches composed of well-stuffed sandwiches, the best and largest Caesar salads in Bermuda, and a rather unusual basil-pesto salad. Also available are an always changing series of hot platters such as beef pies and summer chicken (drenched in a sauce of sour cream, yogurt, thyme, and orange juice). One of the establishment's most appealing points is its wide second-floor veranda said to be the longest porch along Front Street, where canopies protect the outdoor tables from sun and rain.

7 What to See & Do

Bermuda is for fun and leisure. Even the major attractions are designed to be enjoyed without taxing anyone. Because of the island's small size, it's easy to get to know Bermuda parish by parish. After 20 miles or so, you'll run into the sea—so don't rush anywhere.

Even though a lot of people have been fitted into a tiny landmass, it doesn't look that way, mainly because houses have been built quite naturally into the landscape. There are no jarring billboards or neon signs to spoil the countryside, and because there are no car-rental companies, you'll encounter no traffic jams and no polluted air.

In Bermuda something is going on all the time. Sports are always a star attraction, especially golf and tennis. Sailing, horseback riding, and the pink-sand beaches are also potent lures. (See Chapter 9, "Beaches, Water Sports & Other Outdoor Activities.")

As for the sights, from the western tip of Somerset to the eastern end of St. George's, there is much to see in Bermuda, either by bike, ferry, bus, or taxi. You'll need plenty of time, though—the pace is slow. Cars can only travel 15 mph in Hamilton and St. George's, 20 mph outside the towns. This speed limit is rigidly enforced, and penalties for violation are severe.

Bermuda is divided into nine parishes (or counties): Sandys Parish (in the far western end of the island), Southampton Parish, Warwick Parish, Paget Parish (in which lies the greatest concentration of hotels), Pembroke Parish (seat of the government at Hamilton), Devonshire Parish, Smith's Parish, Hamilton Parish (not to be confused with the city of Hamilton), and St. George's Parish (at the far eastern extremity; also takes in the U.S. naval air base and the little island of St. David's).

In the early days these districts, which encompass about 21 square miles, were called "tribes." By the beginning of the 17th century the term "Tribe Road" was used to describe the boundaries between parishes. Pembroke, because it encloses the city of Hamilton, is the largest parish in population; St. George's has the most land area.

Many local guidebooks are fond of pointing out that "you can't get lost in Bermuda." Don't believe them! Along narrow, winding roads—originally designed for the horse and carriage—you *can* get lost, several times, especially if you're looking for an obscure guesthouse along some long-forgotten lane.

❓ Did You Know?

- More than 23,000 couples honeymoon here each year.
- Bermudians imported the idea of moon gates, large rings of stone used as garden ornaments from the Orient centuries ago. Walking through a moon gate is supposed to bring good luck.
- William Shakespeare's 1610 play, *The Tempest*, was inspired by the mysterious island.
- The British ship *Sea Venture*, headed for Virginia, was wrecked on Bermuda's reefs in July 1609.
- Somerset Bridge is the world's smallest drawbridge. Only 22 inches wide, the opening was built just big enough for a ship's mast to pass through.
- Bermuda has more golf courses per square mile than any other country in the world; there are eight of them on the island's approximate 21 square miles.
- The first game of tennis in the Western Hemisphere was played in Bermuda by Sir Brownlow Gray, the island's chief justice, in 1873.
- Shallow-water wreck diving is a popular island activity. More than 120 shipwrecks have been reported in the waters around Bermuda since the island was discovered.
- With Bermuda's springtime comes the blossoming of the Easter lilies, first brought to the island from Japan in the 18th century.
- The famous pink sand of Bermuda's beaches is actually millions of crushed tiny pink coral shells.
- Bermuda has no pollution and no illiteracy. And outdoor advertising and neon signs are banned.
- Bermuda's cruise-ship policy permits only four ships at a time in its harbors.
- Automobile rentals are banned in Bermuda. Only one person per household is permitted to own an automobile.
- Once believed to be extinct, the cahow bird was rediscovered in Bermuda, where today it nests in the late fall and winter months.

You won't stay lost for long, though. Bermuda is so narrow that if you keep going in either an easterly or westerly direction, you'll eventually come to a main road. At its broadest point Bermuda is only about 2 miles wide. The principal arteries are the North Shore Road, the Middle Road, and the South Shore Road, so you'll at least have some indication as to what part of the island you're in.

Sometimes it starts raining almost without warning. Never attempt to stay on your vehicle in drizzly or rainy weather. Pull off the road and wait. Skies usually clear rapidly and the road dries quickly, but it is easy to have an accident on Bermuda's slippery roads after a rain, especially if you're not accustomed to using a motor scooter.

Gasoline stations—called "petrol stations" here—appear fairly frequently in Bermuda. But once you "tank up," chances are you'll have plenty of energy to get you to your destination; for example, one tank of gas in a motorbike will take you from Somerset in the west to St. George's in the east.

In this chapter we'll go on a do-it-yourself tour, taking in Bermuda parish by parish. You could also take one of the walking tours described in Chapter 8.

SUGGESTED ITINERARIES

After you've landed in Bermuda, you may be eager to explore the island, especially if your time is short. Below is a suggested itinerary for the first five days. A week's visit will let you break up your sightseeing trips with time to relax, or enjoy the beach, or to go boating or engage in some of the other sports activities offered.

If You Have One Day

If you've only got one day to devote to sightseeing attractions, I suggest you spend it in the historic former capital of **St. George's.** It has everything from a ducking stool to narrow, alleyway-like streets with quaint names: Featherbed Alley, Duke of York Street, Petticoat Lane, Old Maids' Lane, Duke of Kent Street. You can spend a day exploring British-style pubs, seafood restaurants, shops (several major Hamilton stores have branches here), old forts, museums, and churches. You'll even see stocks and a pillory once used to humiliate wrongdoers.

If You Have Two Days

Day 1:   Spend Day 1 as above.
Day 2:   Devote this day to sightseeing and shopping in the city of **Hamilton.** Since it's likely that you'll be staying in one of the hotels in Paget or Warwick, a ferry from either parish will take you right into the city.

In Hamilton, you can always blend sights with shops, although for many visitors, the shops are more compelling. Try to time your visit to avoid the arrival of cruise ships. On those days, facilities in Hamilton can get cramped.

If You Have Three Days

Day 1–2:   Spend Days 1–2 as above.
Day 3:   For a third day of sightseeing, I suggest you take the ferry from Hamilton across Great Sound to **Somerset.** (Your cycle can be carried on the boat—you'll need it later.) You'll be let off at the western end of Somerset Island in Sandys Parish, where you'll find the smallest drawbridge in the world. It's easy to spend an hour walking around Somerset Village. Then head east until you reach a beach on Long Bay along the northern rim of the island. There are several places for lunch in Sandys Parish (see Chapter 6, "Dining"). The Somerset Country Squire

Impressions

[Many Britons in Bermuda, to their dislike,] find that while the colony is supposedly and unquestionably British—notionally, legally, officially—it is in very many senses dominated by the United States, is utterly dependent on the United States and can well be regarded, and not by cynics alone, as the only British colony which is more like an American colony, run by Bermudians, on Britain's behalf, for America's ultimate benefit.

—Simon Winchester, *The Sun Never Sets: Travels to the Remaining Outposts of the British Empire* (1985)

Tavern, a typical village inn, is one of the best. It's near the Watford Bridge ferry stop at the western end of the island.

After lunch you can go across Watford Bridge to Ireland Island, home of the Maritime Museum. On your way back to Somerset Bridge and the ferry back to Hamilton, you might take the turnoff to Fort Scaur. From Scaur Hill you'll have a commanding view of Ely's Harbour and a view over Great Sound. If you don't want to traverse Somerset again, the ferry at Watford Bridge will take you back to Hamilton.

If You Have Five Days

Days 1–3:   Spend Days 1–3 as above.
Day 4:   Make the most of this beach day, heading for Horseshoe Bay Beach in the morning. Spend most of your time there, exploring hidden coves in all directions. You can have lunch right on the beach at a concession. In the afternoon visit Gibbs Hill Lighthouse. After a rest at your hotel, sample some Bermudian nightlife.
Day 5:   To conclude your stay, head for Flatts Village, lying in the eastern sector of Smith's Parish. Explore the Bermuda Aquarium, Zoological Garden, and Natural History Museum, and consider an undersea walk offered by the Hartley family (see "Organized Tours," below). Have lunch at the Palmetto Hotel & Cottages, then visit Elbow Beach. Make sure you've purchased your duty-free liquor to take back with you. After having afternoon tea at one of the hotels, take in an island show that evening.

1 The Top Attractions

Although Bermuda is a small island, you really can't see much of it in a day or two. So, if you have more time, you may want to explore it methodically, parish by parish, as most visitors tend to do and as we shall do here, visiting the sights and attractions of each parish as we head from east to west. If your time is limited, however, you may want to consider only the highlights. They are:

- Walking tour of St. George's (covered in this chapter and in Chapter 8, "Walking Tours").
- Walking and shopping tour of city of Hamilton. Attractions are documented in this chapter and in Chapter 8, "Walking Tours". If you want to combine shopping and sightseeing, read also Chapter 10, "Shopping."
- Maritime Museum at the Royal Dockyard in the West End.
- Bermuda Aquarium, Zoological Garden, and Natural History Museum, along North Shore Road across Flatts Bridge.
- Crystal Caves, on Crystal Caves Road, a cave discovered in 1907.
- Leamington Caves, Harrington Sound Road, with its underground lakes.
- Verdmont, Verdmont Lane, in Smith's Parish. This 18th-century mansion stands on property once owned by the founder of South Carolina.
- Fort Hamilton, Happy Valley Road, a massive Victorian fortification overlooking the city of Hamilton and its harbor.
- Botanical Gardens, South Shore Road, a Shangri-La in the mid-Atlantic.
- Gibbs Hill Lighthouse, the oldest cast-iron lighthouse in the world.
- Horseshoe Bay Beach in Southampton, most photographed of the pink sandy beaches of Bermuda.
- Elbow Beach at Paget, Bermuda's top sun and swim stretch of sand.

2　St. George's Parish

Settled in 1612, the town of St. George's was once the capital of Bermuda, losing that position to Hamilton in 1815. The town was settled three years after Admiral Sir George Somers and his shipwrecked party of English sailors came ashore in 1609. The town was founded by Richard Moore, of the newly created Bermuda Company, and a band of 60 colonists. It was the second English settlement in the New World (Jamestown, Virginia, was the first). Named after England's patron saint, its coat-of-arms depicts St. George and the dragon. Sir George Somers died in Bermuda in 1610, and his heart was buried in the St. George's area (the rest of his body was taken home to England for burial).

Almost four centuries of history come alive here, and generations upon generations of sailors have set forth from its sheltered harbor. St. George's even played a role in the American Revolutionary War. Bermuda depended on the American colonies for food, and when war came, food ran dangerously short. Although a British colony, loyalties were divided, as many Bermudians had kinsmen living on the American mainland. A delegation headed by Col. Henry Tucker went to Philadelphia to petition the Continental Congress for food and supplies, for which the Bermudians were willing to trade salt. George Washington had a different idea, however. He needed gunpowder, and a number of kegs of it were stored at St. George's. Without the approval of the British/Bermudian governor, a deal was consummated that resulted in the gunpowder's being trundled aboard American warships waiting in the harbor of Tobacco Bay under cover of darkness. In return, the grateful colonies supplied Bermuda with food.

Today, St. George's still evokes a feeling of the past, and it's still actively inhabited. However, when cruise ships are in port, it is likely to be overrun with visitors. Many prefer to visit it at night and walk around and enjoy it then when they are not likely to be trampled underfoot. Of course, the major buildings will be closed, but you'll still get quite a feeling for the town.

IN TOWN

King's Square, also called Market Square or King's Parade, is the center of life in St. George's. The square contains the colorful Pub on the Square and White Horse Tavern, where you may want to stop for a drink after your tour. Also on the square you'll see a pillory and stock. Honeymooners like to have themselves photographed in them today, but they were used in deadly earnest in earlier times. Victims were sometimes placed in the pillory for a certain number of hours—sometimes with one ear nailed to the post! "Criminals" were burned on the hand or branded, fined in tobacco, nailed to the post, or declared "infamous." Often they had their ears cut off or were made to "stand in a sheet on the church porch."

Offenses for which Bermudians were punished in the early days offer an illuminating glimpse of the social life of the time. Along with such "usual" acts as treason, robbery, arson, murder, and "scandal," records of the assizes (courts) of the early 1600s include concealing finds of ambergris, exporting cedarwood, railing against the governor's authority, hiding tobacco, being "notorious cursers and swearers," leading an "uncivil life and calling her neighbor an old Bawd and the like," neglecting to receive Holy Communion, the acting of any stage play of any kind whatsoever, and playing at unlawful games such as dice, cards, and ninepins.

The street names in St. George's also evoke days of yore. **Petticoat Lane** (sometimes called Silk Alley) got its name when two recently emancipated slave girls were said to have paraded up and down the lane rustling their new and flamboyantly colored silk petticoats. **Barber's Lane** is also named for a former slave. It honors Joseph Hayne Rainey, a freedman from the Carolinas who fled to Bermuda aboard a blockade runner during the Civil War. He was a barber in Bermuda for the rest of the war. Upon its conclusion he returned to the United States and was elected to Congress, becoming the first black member of the House of Representatives during Reconstruction.

St. George's is about an hour's run east of Hamilton. To reach any of the attractions described below, take bus no. 1, 3, 8, 10, or 11 from Hamilton.

Visitors Service Bureau

King's Square. ☎ 441/297-1642. Free. Summer Mon–Sat 9am–1pm and 2–4:45pm; off-season Wed and Sat 9am–1pm and 2–4:45pm. Bus No. 1, 3, 8, 10, or 11 from Hamilton.

Here you can get a map and any information you might need before you set out to explore on your own. The bureau is opposite the Town Hall.

Town Hall

7 King's Square. ☎ 441/297-1532. Town Hall free; *Bermuda Journey* $3.50 adults, $2 children under 12. Town Hall Mon–Sat 10am–4pm. *Bermuda Journey*, Mon–Thurs 11:15am and 2:15pm, also Sat (May–Nov only) 12:15pm and 2:15pm. Bus No. 1, 3, 8, 10, or 11 from Hamilton.

Headed by a mayor, officers of the Corporation of St. George's meet in the Town Hall, which is near the Visitors Service Bureau. There are three aldermen and five common councillors. The Town Hall has a collection of Bermuda cedar furnishings, along with photographs of previous mayors. A half-hour multimedia, audiovisual presentation on the history, culture, and heritage of the colony, *Bermuda Journey* (produced by the people responsible for *The New York Experience*), is presented on the upper floor of the Town Hall several times a day.

Old State House

Princess St. ☎ 441/297-1260. Free. Wed 10am–4pm or by appointment; call Ray O'Leary at 441/292-2480. Bus No. 1, 3, 8, 10, or 11 from Hamilton.

Behind the Town Hall is Bermuda's oldest stone building, the Old State House, constructed with turtle oil and lime mortar in 1620. The Old State House, where meetings of the legislative council once took place, was eventually turned over to the Freemasons of St. George's. The government asked the annual rent of one peppercorn and insisted on the right to hold meetings here upon demand. The Masonic Lodge members, in a ceremony filled with pageantry, still turn over one peppercorn in rent to the Bermuda government every April. (Peppercorns were sometimes a form of payment in the old days. In the late 18th century, for example, two small islands off King's Square were sold for a peppercorn apiece. In 1782 Henry Tucker bought Ducking Stool Island, and in 1785 Nathaniel Butterfield bought Gallows Island; several years later Simon Fraser purchased both for 100 peppercorns and combined them into one, making what is today Ordnance Island.)

For those who have never witnessed the 45–minute spectacle of the annual rent payment, it begins around 11am with the gathering of the Bermuda Regiment on King's Square and the subsequent arrival of the premier, mayor, and other dignitaries, all amid the bellowing introductions of the town crier. As soon as all the principals have taken their places, a 17-gun salute is fired as the governor and his wife make a grand entrance in their open horse-drawn landau. His Excellency inspects a military guard of honor, while the Bermuda Regiment Band plays. The stage is, of course, now set for the center of attention: presentation of *a* pepper-corn, which sits on a silver plate atop a velvet cushion. Payment is made in a grand and formal manner, after which the Old State House is immediately used for a meeting of Her Majesty's Council.

Deliverance II

Ordnance Island. ☎ **441/297-1459.** $2.50 adults, 50¢ children under 12. Apr–Nov, Mon–Sat 10am–4pm; Dec–Mar, Wed and Sat 10am–4pm. Bus No. 1, 3, 8, 10, or 11 from Hamilton.

Across from St. George's town square and over a bridge is Ordnance Island, where visitors see a full-scale replica of *Deliverance I*, a pinnace (small sailing ship) con-structed in 1609 by the shipwrecked survivors of the *Sea Venture* to carry them on to Virginia.

A tape recording guides visitors through the ship. Alongside *Deliverance II* is the ducking stool, a replica of a horrible contraption used in 17th-century witch tri-als. Its use is demonstrated on Wednesday only.

St. Peter's Church

Duke of York St. ☎ **441/297-8359.** Free, but donations appreciated. Daily 10am–4:30pm (guide available Mon–Sat). Bus No. 1, 3, 8, 10, or 11 from Hamilton.

Back on King's Square, head east to the Duke of York Street, where St. Peter's Church, believed to be the oldest Anglican place of worship in the Western Hemi-sphere, is located. The original church on this spot, built by colonists in 1612 al-most entirely of cedar with a palmetto-leaf thatch roof, was almost destroyed by a hurricane in 1712. Some of the interior, including the original altar from 1615 (still in daily use) was salvaged, and the church was rebuilt in 1713. It has been restored many times since and provides excellent examples of architectural work of the 17th to the 20th centuries. The tower was added in 1814. On display in the vestry is a silver communion service given to the church by King William III in 1697. Before the Old State House was constructed, the colony held public meet-ings in the church. The first assize convened here in 1616, and the first meeting of Parliament was in 1620. Sunday and weekday services are conducted here.

Graveyard of St. Peter's

Entrance opposite Broad Alley. Bus No. 1, 3, 8, 10, or 11 from Hamilton.

Some of the tombstones in this graveyard are more than three centuries old; many tombs mark the graves of slaves. Here you'll also find the grave of Midshipman Richard Dale, an American, who was the last victim of the War of 1812. The churchyard also contains the tombs of Gov. Sir Richard Sharples and his aide, Capt. Hugh Sayers, who were murdered while walking the grounds of Government House in 1973.

Confederate Museum

King's Square. ☎ **441/297-1423.** Adults $4, free for children under 12. Apr–Oct, daily 9:30am–4:30pm; off-season, daily 10am–4pm. Closed public holidays. Bus No. 1, 3, 8, 10, or 11 from Hamilton.

This was once the Globe Hotel, headquarters of Maj. Norman Walker, the Confederate representative in Bermuda, and contains relics from the island's involvement in the American Civil War. St. George's was the port from which ships carrying arms and munitions ran the Union blockade. A replica of the Great Seal of the Confederacy is fitted to a Victorian press so that visitors can emboss copies as souvenirs.

Tucker House Museum

5 Water St. ☎ **441/297-0545.** $4 adults, free for children under 12 years. Apr–Oct, Mon–Sat 9:30–4:30pm; off-season, 10am–4pm. Closed public holidays. Bus No. 1, 3, 8, 10, or 11 from Hamilton.

This was the home of the well-known Tucker family of England, Bermuda, and Virginia. It displays a notable collection of Bermudian furniture, portraits, and silver. Also in the Tucker House is the Joseph Rainey Memorial Room, where this African American refugee (mentioned above) of the Civil War practiced barbering.

Carriage Museum

22 Water St. ☎ **441/297-1367.** Donation requested. Mon–Fri 10am–5pm. Closed public holidays. Bus No. 1, 3, 8, 10 or 11 from Hamilton.

Transportation in Bermuda was only by carriage until 1946, when the "automobile age" arrived. Many of these old conveyances have been preserved to delight present-day visitors to the island. The museum is in a renovated old Royal Engineers warehouse, located next to Somers Wharf.

Somers Garden

Duke of York St. ☎ **441/297-1532.** Free. Daily 8am–4pm. Bus No. 1, 3, 8, 10, or 11 from Hamilton.

The heart of Sir George Somers was buried here in 1610; a stone column perpetuates the memory of Bermuda's founder. The garden was opened in 1920 by the Prince of Wales (later King of England and subsequently Duke of Windsor).

Unfinished Cathedral

Blockade Alley. Bus No. 1, 3, 8, 10, or 11 from Hamilton.

After leaving Somers Garden, head up the steps to the North Gate, which opens onto Blockade Alley. The structure here is known as the "folly of St. George's." The plan was that this cathedral, begun in 1874, would replace St. Peter's. But the planners ran into money troubles, then a schism developed, and, as if that weren't enough, a storm swept over the island and caused considerable damage to the structure. Result: the Unfinished Cathedral.

St. George's Historical Society Museum

3 Featherbed Alley. ☎ **441/297-0423.** $2 adults, 50¢ children 16 and under. Tues–Thurs 10am–4pm. Bus No. 1, 3, 8, 10, or 11 from Hamilton.

Housed in a home built around 1700, this museum contains an original 18th-century Bermuda kitchen complete with utensils from that period. Exhibits include a 300-year-old Bible, a letter from George Washington, and Native American ax heads. (Some early settlers on St. David's Island were Native Americans, mainly Pequot.)

Featherbed Alley Printery

In Featherbed Alley. ☎ **441/297-0009.** Free. Mon–Sat 10am–4pm. Closed Wed–Thurs 11am–2pm and all holidays. Bus No. 1, 3, 8, 10, or 11 from Hamilton.

Here you'll find a working press—the kind invented by Gutenberg in the 1450s—that was in use for some 350 years. The alley gets its name because featherbeds were placed here for drunks to sleep on until they could sober up.

Old Rectory

At the head of Broad Alley, behind St. Peter's Church. ☎ **441/297-0879.** Free, but donations are appreciated. Wed 1–5pm. Bus No. 1, 3, 8, 10, or 11 from Hamilton.

Bermuda Attractions

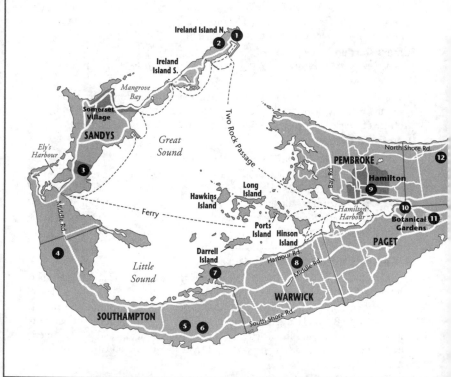

Atlantic Ocean

Ireland Island N. ①

②

Ireland Island S.

Mangrove Bay

Somerset Village

SANDYS

Ely's Harbour

③

Great Sound

Two Rock Passage

North Shore Rd.

PEMBROKE

Hamilton

⑫

Bay Rd.

Long Island

Hawkins Island

Ferry

Ports Island

Hinson Island

Hamilton Harbour

⑨

⑩

Botanical Gardens

⑪

PAGET

Middle Rd.

④

Darrell Island

⑦

Little Sound

Harbour Rd.

⑧

Middle Rd.

WARWICK

SOUTHAMPTON

⑤ ⑥

South Shore Rd.

DEVONSHIRE PARISH:
Palm Grove ⑬

HAMILTON PARISH:
Bermuda Aquarium, Museum
    & Zoo ⑮
Bermuda Perfumery ⑲
Crystal Caves ⑱
Leamington Caves ⑰

PAGET PARISH:
Botanical Gardens ⑪

Waterville (House) ⑩

**PEMBROKE PARISH
(Hamilton City):**
Bermuda Historical Society Museum ⑨
Bermuda National Gallery ⑨
Sessions House (Parliament Building) ⑨

ST. GEORGE'S PARISH:
Confederate Museum ⑳
Fort St. Catherine ㉒
Ocean View Golf Course ⑫

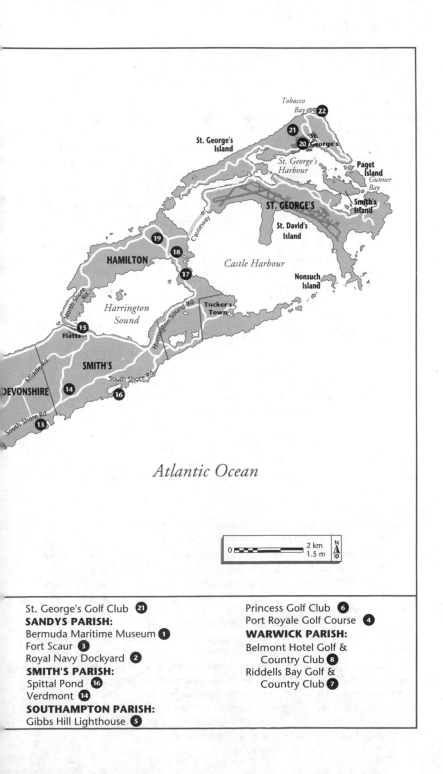

Atlantic Ocean

St. George's Golf Club **21**
SANDYS PARISH:
Bermuda Maritime Museum **1**
Fort Scaur **3**
Royal Navy Dockyard **2**
SMITH'S PARISH:
Spittal Pond **16**
Verdmont **14**
SOUTHAMPTON PARISH:
Gibbs Hill Lighthouse **5**

Princess Golf Club **6**
Port Royale Golf Course **4**
WARWICK PARISH:
Belmont Hotel Golf &
  Country Club **8**
Riddells Bay Golf &
  Country Club **7**

Built by a reformed pirate in 1705, this charming old Bermuda cottage was later inhabited by Parson Richardson, who was nicknamed the Little Bishop. Now a private home, it's administrated by the Bermuda National Trust.

Bridge House

1 Bridge St. ☎ **441/297-8211.** Free. Mon–Sat 10am–5pm. Mid–Jan to mid–Feb and Sat only, 10am–4pm. Bus No. 1, 3, 8, 10, or 11.

This long-established gallery, recently renovated, displays antiques and collectibles, old Bermudian items, original paintings, Bermuda-made crafts, as well as a studio that belonged to Jill Amos Raine, a well-known Bermuda watercolor artist. Owned by the National Trust, the house was constructed in the mid-17th century. It was home to several of the colony's governors. Perhaps its most colorful owner was Bridger Goodrich, a Loyalist from Virginia, whose privateers once blockaded Chesapeake Bay. So devoted was he to the king that he also sabotaged Bahamian vessels trading with the American colonies. The house is called Bridge because a bridge used to stand over a muddy creek (filled in now). (The Bridge House also operates Buckingham Arts and Crafts Centre, 2 King St. (☎ **441/297-8133**), also in St. George's. Everything in this gallery is also Bermuda made, the best of the works of local artists and craftspeople. It keeps the same hours as Bridge House.)

ON THE OUTSKIRTS OF TOWN

From its earliest days St. George's has been fortified, and although it never saw much military action, the reminders of those former days are interesting to explore. On the outskirts of the town, the forts are reached by Circular Drive.

Nearby, along the coast, is **Building Bay,** where the shipwrecked victims of the *Sea Venture* built their vessel, the *Deliverance,* in 1610.

Gates Fort

Cut Rd. No phone. Free. Daily 10am–4:30pm. Bus No. 1, 3, 8, 10, or 11.

Gates Fort was built by Sir Thomas Gates, one of the original band of settlers on the *Sea Venture.* The fort dates from 1609. Gates was governor-designate for the colony of Virginia.

Fort St. Catherine

Barry Rd. ☎ **441/297-1920.** $2.50 adults, free for children under 12. Daily 10am–4:30pm. Closed Christmas Day. Bus No. 1, 3, 8, 10, or 11 from Hamilton.

Towering above the beach where the shipwrecked crew of the *Sea Venture* came ashore in 1609 is Fort St. Catherine, first completed in 1614 and named for the patron saint of wheelwrights and carpenters. The fortifications were upgraded over the years. The last major reconstruction occurred from 1865 to 1878, so the fort's appearance today is largely the result of work done in the 19th century.

Now a museum, visitors begin their visits by seeing a series of dioramas, "Highlights in Bermuda's History." Museum figures are used to show various activities taking place in the Magazine of the fort, restored and refurnished as it was in the 1880s. Large Victorian muzzle-loading cannons can be seen on their original carriages. In the Keep, which served as the living quarters of the fort, you can see information on local and overseas regiments that served in Bermuda, a fine small-arms exhibit, a cooking-area display, and an exhibition of replicas of the crown jewels of England. A short audiovisual show on the St. George's defense systems and the forts of St. George's can be seen here.

3 Hamilton Parish

Around Harrington Sound, the sights differ greatly from those of St. George's—more action, less history. Public buses 1 or 3 from Hamilton get you here in about an hour. Hamilton Parish is bordered on the east by St. George's and on the southwest by Smith's Parish. The parish encloses **Harrington Sound,** a landlocked saltwater lake that is 1 1/2 miles at its widest and 2 1/8 miles long. It was named for John, first Lord Harrington of Rutland, England.

Some experts believe that way back in unrecorded time Harrington Sound was a cave that fell in. Its gateway to the ocean is through an inlet at Flatts Village. However, it is believed that there are underwater gateways as well. Several deep-sea fish have been caught in the sound.

For the best sightseeing view of the parish, visitors head for **Crawl Hill,** right before they come to Bailey's Bay. At this point, the highest place in Hamilton Parish, you can enjoy a view of the North Shore. Crawl is a corruption of the word *kraal,* where turtles were kept before slaughter. Shelly Bay, named for one of the passengers of the *Sea Venture,* is the longest beach along the North Shore.

The **Hamilton Parish Church,** reached by going down Trinity Church Road, stands on Church Bay and dates from 1623, when it was just a one-room structure. It has been much altered over three and a half centuries.

At Bailey's Bay, Tom Moore's Jungle consists of wild woods. The poet Tom Moore is said to have spent many hours writing poetry under a still-standing calabash tree. Since the jungle is held in private trust, permission has to be obtained to enter it. It's much easier to pay your respects to the Romantic poet by calling at the Tom Moore Tavern (see "Hamilton Parish" in Chapter 6, "Dining").

Bermuda Perfumery

212 North Shore Rd., Bailey's Bay. ☎ **441/293-0627.** Free. Apr–Oct, Mon–Sat 9am–5pm; Nov–Mar, Sun 9am–4:30pm. Closed Sun in winter. Bus No. 1 or 3.

Lili Perfumes are made here. Visitors are given guided tours showing the perfume-making process, including the old method of extracting scents from native flowers. Among the fragrances produced are passion flower, Bermuda Easter lily, and oleander jasmine. A small botanic garden with a seating area and walkways provides an attractive resting place. You can also visit the orchid house, with its more than 500 orchids, and the nature trail, which passes through a large area of the property that is planted with tropical flowers, shrubs, and trees. The perfumery has a gift shop, the Calabash.

✪ Bermuda Aquarium, Museum, & Zoo

North Shore Rd., Flatts Village. ☎ **441/293-2727.** $6 adults, $3 children ages 5–12, free for children under 5. Daily 9am–4:30pm. Closed Christmas Day. Bus: Take no. 10 or 11 from Hamilton, or no. 10 or 11 from St. George's. Directions: From Hamilton, follow Middle Rd. or North Shore Rd. east to Flatts Village; from St. George's, once over the causeway, follow North Shore Rd. or Harrington Sound Rd. west to Flatts Village.

Across Flatts Bridge, this complex is home to a wide collection of tropical marine fish, turtles, harbor seals, and other forms of sea life. In the museum you can see exhibits on the geological development of Bermuda, deep-sea exploration, and humpback whales. The complex also has a zoo with Galápagos tortoises, alligators, and monkeys, along with a collection of birds, including parrots and flamingos.

In the autumn of 1995, the complex plans to create a 140,000-gallon tank allowing visitors to enter an exhibit to experience a coral reef washed by ocean surge.

The tank will house a living coral reef, as well as reef and pelagic fish species. The tank will in fact hold the first living coral exhibit on this scale in the world, made possible by the Aquarium, Museum, and Zoo's success in the science of coral husbandry.

You can bring a picnic lunch or choose from one of several restaurants in Flatts Village. There is parking for cycles and cars across the street from the Aquarium.

✪ Crystal Caves

8 Crystal Caves Rd., off Wilkinson Ave., Bailey's Bay. ☎ 441/293-0640. $4 adults, $2 children ages 5–11. Free 4 and under. Feb–Mar and Nov–Dec Sun–Fri 10am–4pm; Apr–Oct daily 9:30am–4:30pm. Closed 2nd and 3rd weeks of Jan. Bus No. 1 or 3.

This cave is composed of translucent formations of stalagmites and stalactites, a setting including the crystal-clear Cahow Lake. Discovered in 1907, the cave is reached by a sloping path and a few steps. At the bottom, some 120 feet below the surface, is a floating causeway that follows the winding cavern, where hidden lights illuminate the interior. All tours through Crystal Caves are guided.

✪ Leamington Caves

46 Harrington Sound Rd., Bailey's Bay. ☎ 441/293-1188. $4 adults, $2 children ages 5–11, free for children under 5. Mon–Sat 9:30am–4pm. Closed Dec to mid-Feb. Bus No. 1 or 3.

This grotto, which is attached to the Plantation Club, has crystal formations and underground lakes. It was first discovered by a young boy, who noticed a small opening on the rocky hillside that he and his father were clearing for plowing in 1908. He slipped through the hole with a rope and candles and found a wonderland of natural cave splendors some 1.5 million years old. Guided tours take you along lighted walkways with handrails, through the high-vaulted, amber-tinted grotto.

Devil's Hole Aquarium

92 Harrington Sound Rd., ☎ 441/293-2072. $5 adults, $2 children 12 and under. Daily 10am–5pm. Bus No. 1 or 3.

The pool of this former cave is fed by the sea through half a mile of subterranean passages. A natural aquarium, it's stocked with some 400 individual fish, including moray eels, sharks, giant groupers, and massive green turtles. Visitors can tempt the pond's inhabitants with baited but hookless lines. It has been open to the public since 1834.

4 Smith's Parish

Smith's Parish, named for Sir Thomas Smith, a member of the Bermuda Company, faces the open sea on both its northern and southern borders. To the east is Harrington Sound, and to the west, bucolic Devonshire Parish.

The parish takes in **Flatts Village,** one of the most charming little parish towns of Bermuda, reached by bus 10 or 11 from Hamilton. This was a smugglers' port for about 200 years. The origin of the name is lost to history. Once it was the center of power for a coterie of successful "planter politicians" and landowners. Their government ranked in importance second only to that of St. George's, then the capital. People gathered at the rickety Flatts Bridge to "enjoy" such public entertainment as a hanging on the gallows. A so-called blasphemer in 1718 had his tongue bored through with a fire-hot poker. If the offense was serious enough, victims were drawn and quartered here. From Flatts Village you'll have good views of both the inlet and Harrington Sound.

For Spelunkers

Bermuda has one of the highest concentrations of limestone caves in the world. Most of this cave-making activity began during the Pleistocene Ice Age. As early as 1623, the adventurer Captain John Smith complained that he had encountered "vary strange, darke, cumbersome caves."

In Bermuda, nature's patient, relentless underground sculpting is a dream world for even the casual spelunker. Deep in the majestic silence of the earth's interior, you can roam in caverns of great stalactites and stalagmites of Gothic grandeur, and of delicacy and beauty.

This awesome underground has been the inspiration for creative achievements as diverse as Shakespeare's *The Tempest* and Henson Associates' "Fraggle Rock" muppets.

You can visit Crystal Caves or Leamington Caves, both reached along Harrington Sound Road *(see page 142 for more information)*.

At the top of McGall's Hill, which you can visit after seeing the Verdmont mansion (see below), is **St. Mark's Church.** A church built in 1746 once stood near the site of St. Mark's. When it became unsafe, a local family, the Trotts, donated land for the construction of St. Mark's, on which construction began in 1846, with the first services conducted on Easter Sunday in 1848. Work on the church continued, however, and subsequent additions—such as the chancel—were made until the closing years of the 19th century. St. Mark's Church was based on the same designs as the Old Devonshire Parish Church.

✪ Verdmont

6 Verdmont Lane, Collectors Hill, Smith's Parish. ☎ **441/236-7369.** $4 adults, children under 12 free. Apr–Oct Mon–Sat 9:30am–4:30pm; Nov–Mar Mon–Fri 10am–4pm. Closed one week in either Jan or Feb (dates vary). Bus No. 1 from Hamilton or St. George's.

This is an 18th-century mansion that holds a special significance to U.S. citizens interested in colonial and Revolutionary War history. It stands on property owned in the 17th century by William Sayle, who left Bermuda to found South Carolina on the American mainland and then became its first governor. The house was built before 1710 by John Dickinson, a prosperous ship owner who was also Speaker of the House of Assembly in Bermuda from 1707 to 1710. Verdmont passed to Mr. Dickinson's granddaughter, Elizabeth, who married the Hon. Thomas Smith, Collector of Customs. Their oldest daughter, Mary, married Judge John Green, a Loyalist who came to Bermuda in 1765 from Philadelphia. During and after the American Revolution, Green was judge of the Vice-Admiralty Court and had the final say on prizes brought in by privateers. Many American shipowners lost their vessels through his decisions. The house is now administered by the National Trust. It contains many antiques, china, and portraits, along with the finest cedar stair balustrade in Bermuda.

Spittal Pond

South Shore Rd. No phone. Free. Daily sunrise to sunset. Bus No. 1 or 3.

Follow the rather steep Knapton Hill Rd. west to South Shore Rd. turning at the sign for Spittal Pond, Bermuda's largest wildlife sanctuary. The most important of the National Trust's open spaces, it occupies 60 acres and contains about 25 species of waterfowl, which can be seen annually from November to May. Visitors are asked to keep to the scenic trails and footpaths provided. Bird-watchers, in particular, visit in January, when as many as 500 species of birds can be observed wintering on the pond.

Spittal Pond also shelters **Spanish Rock,** on a cliff facing the sea. It contains a cipher dating from 1543, probably carved by an Iberian mariner who may have been shipwrecked here.

5 Devonshire Parish

As you wander its narrow lanes, with some imagination you can picture yourself in the original Devon in England. The parish takes its name from the first Earl of Devonshire. It is a lush, hilly parish, rarely spoiled by commercial intrusions.

Along the North Shore Road is **Devonshire Dock,** long a seafarer's haven, near the border to Pembroke Parish. Fishers still bring in such catches as grouper and rockfish, so you can shop for dinner if you've been fortunate enough to get a nearby cottage with a kitchen. British soldiers in the War of 1812 came here to be entertained by local women.

At the **Arboretum** on Montpelier Road, you'll discover one of the most tranquil oases in Bermuda, an open space with a wide range of Bermudian plant and tree life, especially conifers, palms, and other subtropical trees. It was created by the Department of Agriculture, Fisheries, and Parks.

Along the South Shore Road, you can visit the **Edmund Gibbons Nature Reserve,** west of the junction with Collector's Hill. This portion of marshland, owned by the National Trust, provides living space for a number of birds and rare species of Bermuda flora. It's open daily at no charge. Visitors must keep out of the marshy area.

Nature Reserves

The National Trust in Bermuda has wisely protected the island's nature reserves. If you play by the rules—that is, don't disturb animal life or take plant life for a souvenir—you can explore many of these natural wonderlands, which form one of the most rewarding reasons to visit Bermuda, if you like to hike along nature trails.

The best of these is Spittal Pond in Smith's Parish *(see page 143),* along South Shore Rd., the island nation's largest nature reserve. Birders, especially during the months ranging from November through May, are drawn to the reserve to see herons, ducks, flamingos, terns, and many migratory fowl (the latter can't be seen after March).

This 60-acre untamed seaside park is always open to the public with no admission charge. The Department of Agriculture (call **441/236-4201** for information) offers guided tours of the refuge.

The island abounds with other places where nature has created and choreographed the show. Craggy formations shaped over the centuries out of limestone and coral dot the beaches along the southern coast, with towering cliffs forming a backdrop. The best of these is Natural Arches, one of the most photographed sights in Bermuda. Two limestone arches which took nature centuries to carve rise 35 feet above the beach. This natural attraction is signposted almost at the end of South Shore Road, directing you to Castle Harbour Beach.

Old Devonshire Church

Middle Rd. ☎ **441/236-3671.** Free. Daily 9am–5:30pm. Bus No. 2.

On Middle Road stands the Old Devonshire Parish Church, a house of worship said to have been built on the site in 1624, although the present foundation is from 1716. This is the major attraction of the parish. An explosion virtually destroyed the church on Easter in 1970, but it was reconstructed. Today the church is very tiny, looking almost more like a vicarage than a church. Some of the church relics survived the blast, including silver from 1590, said to be the oldest on the island. The church is built of limestone, with a high pitched roof constructed in the early English style. It was designed by Sir George Grove. The Old Devonshire Parish Church stands northwest of the "new" Devonshire Parish Church which dates from 1846.

Palm Grove

38 South Shore Rd. No phone. Free. Mon–Thurs (inclusive) 8:30am–5pm. Bus No. 1.

One of the delights of Devonshire Parish, this private estate lies 2¹/₂ miles east of Hamilton. It is famous for the pond that has a relief map of Bermuda in the middle of it. Each parish is an immaculately manicured grassy division. The site, which has some well-landscaped flower gardens, opens onto a view of the sea.

6 Pembroke Parish (City of Hamilton)

The city of Hamilton is not in Hamilton Parish but in Pembroke Parish, which is a peninsula that opens at its northern rim onto the vast Atlantic Ocean and on its southern side onto the beautiful Hamilton Harbour. Its western border edges Great Sound. The parish is named after the third Earl of Pembroke, who was a power in the Bermuda Company of 1616. Nearly one-fourth of Bermuda's population lives in Pembroke Parish, most of them in the capital of Hamilton.

The ideal way to see Hamilton, or the parish itself, for the first time is to sail in through Hamilton Harbour, past the offshore cays. You'll join fishers and the yachting set and cruise ships.

The Irish poet Tom Moore and the American humorist Mark Twain publicized the glories of Bermuda, but, for the British at least, the woman who put Bermuda on the tourist map was Princess Louise. The daughter of Queen Victoria, she spent several months in Bermuda in 1883. Her husband was the governor-general of Canada, so she traveled to Bermuda to escape the fierce cold up north. Although in the 20th century Bermuda was to play host to a string of royal visitors, including Queen Elizabeth II, Princess Louise was the first royal personage to set foot in the colony. And once she was here she turned up all over the island, visiting and chatting with its friendly people and winning their respect and admiration. Upon reaching Canada, she told reporters that she'd found the Shangri-La of tourist destinations.

In the early days there was only one hotel, the Hamilton Hotel on Church Street, which was destroyed by fire in 1955. The Hamilton Princess Hotel, still in existence and named in honor of Princess Louise, opened in 1884. Over the years it has had a colorful history, none more dramatic than when it was taken over by Allied agents in World War II.

If Princess Louise were to visit today, she would most likely be housed at **Government House,** which stands on North Shore Road and Langton Hill. Not open to the public, it is the residence of the governor of the island. The large grounds may be viewed on application to the governor's aide-de-camp. A Victorian residence, it has sheltered many notable guests, including Queen Elizabeth II and her husband, Prince Philip, as well as Prince Charles, Sir Winston Churchill, and President John F. Kennedy. The saddest moment for Government House was in 1973, when Gov. Sir Richard Sharples and his aide, Capt. Hugh Sayers, along with the governor's dog, Horsa, were assassinated while walking on the grounds. This tragedy led to a state of emergency in Bermuda.

While touring Pembroke Parish, visitors are fond of looking at **Black Watch Well** at the junction of North Shore Road and Black Watch Pass. Excavated by a detachment of the Black Watch Regiment, the well was ordered to be dug in 1894, when Bermudians suffered through a long drought.

CITY OF HAMILTON

Hamilton has been the capital of Bermuda since 1815. Once known as the "Show Window of the British Empire," both Mark Twain and Eugene O'Neill, who lived in places opening onto Hamilton Harbour, cited the beauty of the place. On little islands in the harbor, prisoners-of-war and victims of plague were held in prison or in quarantine, respectively.

A stroll along Front Street will take you by some of Hamilton's most elegant stores, but you'll want to branch off into the little alleyways to check the shops and boutiques to be found there. If you get tired of walking or shopping (or both), you can also go down to the docks and take one of the boats or catamarans waiting to show you the treasures of Little Sound and Great Sound.

On some days you may get to see locals buying their fresh fish—that is, that part of the catch not earmarked for restaurants—right from the fisherpeople who sell the "catch of the day" at Front Street docks. Although rockfish seems to turn up more often than any other fish, you'll also see snapper, grouper, and many other species. In the 1930s, seaplanes would land passengers right in Hamilton Harbour.

Most Bermudians consider the winter months too cold to wear Bermuda shorts, but come May, all the businesspeople along Front Street seem to don a pair. The British military introduced these shorts to Bermuda in the early part of the 20th century. By the 1920s and 1930s the garment had become very fashionable, although they were not worn to dinner parties or to church services. Originally worn with a white shirt, a tie, a jacket, and knee stockings, it was considered "daring" to wear the shorts five inches above the knee. And to go beyond that and wear Bermuda short-shorts could have gotten you ticketed by the police in the years after World War II. For some, Bermuda shorts, at least at summer cocktail parties, remain de rigueur.

Most people come to Hamilton to shop, but the city also contains a number of sightseeing attractions. Named for a former governor, Henry Hamilton, it was incorporated as a town in 1793. In 1815, because of its central location and its large, protected harbor, it was chosen as the island's new capital, replacing St. George's. Since Hamilton occupies only 182 acres of land in its entirety, it is most often explored on foot.

Today Hamilton is the hub of the island's economy, but long before it got such fancy labels as "showcase of the Atlantic," it was a modest outlet for the export of Bermuda cedar and fresh vegetables.

Hamilton boasts the largest number of eating and drinking establishments in Bermuda, especially on or near Front Street. These restaurants charge a wide range of prices, and there are many English-style pubs if you'd like to go on a pub crawl.

Although there is a huge conglomeration of bars, religion isn't neglected—there are 12 churches within the city limits, one or two of which merit a sightseeing visit.

Hamilton should be seen not only on land but also from the water, and there are frequent boating tours of the harbor and its coral reefs to enable you to do so. If you're visiting from other parishes, the ferry will let you off at the western end of Front Street, which is ideal if you'd like to pay a call to the **Visitors Service Bureau** and pick up a map. The location is near the Ferry Terminal. The staff here also provides information and helpful brochures. Hours are 9am to 4:45pm Monday through Saturday.

To return to the parishes of Paget, Warwick, and Sandys, ferries leave daily between 6:50am and 11:20pm. On Saturday and Sunday, there are fewer departures.

Opposite the Visitors Service Bureau stands the much-photographed **"Bird Cage,"** where it used to be possible to see a police officer directing traffic. Such a sight is now rare. For years visitors wondered if the traffic director was for real or placed there for tourist photographs.

Nearby is **Albouy's Point,** site of the Royal Bermuda Yacht Club, founded in 1844. The point, named after a 17th-century professor of "physick," is a public park overlooking Hamilton Harbour.

Bermuda Historical Society Museum

13 Queen St., Par-la-Ville Park. ☎ **441/295-2487.** Free. Mon–Sat 9:30am–12:30pm and 2–4:30pm. Bus No. 1, 2, 10, or 11.

After leaving the harbor, proceed up Queen Street to the Public Library and the Bermuda Historical Society Museum, which has a collection of old cedar furniture, antique silver, early Bermuda coins (hog money), and costumes, plus the sea chest and navigating lodestone of Sir George Somers, whose flagship, *Sea Venture,* was stranded on Bermuda's reefs in 1609. You will also find portraits of Sir George and Lady Somers as well as models of the ill-fated *Sea Venture,* along with models of *Patience* and *Deliverance.*

The museum lies in **Par-la-Ville Park** on Queen Street, which still dwells in the 19th century. It was designed by William Bennett Perot, Hamilton's first postmaster—from 1818 to 1862—and an eccentric one at that. As he delivered mail around the town, he is said to have placed letters in the crown of his top hat, so as to preserve his dignity.

Perot Post Office

Queen St., at the entrance to Par-la-Ville Park. ☎ **441/295-5151.** Free. Mon–Fri 9am–5pm. Bus No. 1, 2, 10, or 11.

Bermuda's first stamp was printed in this landmark building. Beloved by collectors from all over the world, the stamps, signed by Perot, are considered priceless. It is said that Perot and his friend, Heyl, who ran an apothecary shop, conceived the first postage stamp to protect the post office from cheaters. People used to stop off at the post office and leave letters but not enough pennies to send them. The postage stamps were printed in either black or carmine.

Philatelists can purchase Bermuda stamps of today in this same post office. For its 375th anniversary, Bermuda issued stamps honoring its 1609 discovery. One stamp portrays the admiral of the fleet, Sir George Somers, along with Sir Thomas Gates, the captain of the *Sea Venture.* Another depicts a building in the settlement of Jamestown, Virginia, which was on the verge of extinction when Sir George and the survivors of the Bermuda shipwreck finally arrived with supplies in late 1610. A third shows the *Sea Venture* stranded on the coral reefs of Bermuda. Yet another shows the entire fleet, originally bound for Jamestown, leaving Plymouth, England, on June 2, 1609.

Hamilton City Hall & Arts Centre

17 Church St. ☎ **441/292-1234.** Free. City Hall, Mon–Fri 9am–5pm; Bermuda Society of Arts, Mon–Sat 10am–4pm. Bus No. 1, 2, 10, or 11.

The City Hall, also home of the Bermuda Society of Arts, is an imposing white structure with a giant weather vane and wind clock to tell maritime-minded Bermudians which way the wind is blowing. Completed in 1960, the building is headquarters for Hamilton's municipal government. The theater on the first floor is the scene for stage, music, and dance productions throughout the year, and is also the main site of the Bermuda Festival. City Hall is also the venue for the **Bermuda National Gallery** (see below).

Also here, the Bermuda Society of Arts has since 1956 encouraged and provided a forum for contemporary artists, sculptors, and photographers of Bermuda. The gallery here contains ever-changing exhibitions, displaying the work of local artists as well as visiting artists. Although their goals are often shared, this society is a separate entity from the newer Bermuda National Gallery.

Bermuda National Gallery

City Hall, 17 Church St. ☎ **441/295-9428.** $3 adults; children under 16 admitted free. Mon–Sat 10am–4pm; Sun 12:30–4pm. Bus No. 1, 2, 10, or 11.

Located in the east wing of City Hall, the Bermuda National Gallery is the home of the Masterworks Bermudiana Collection, with artwork from artists such as Georgia O'Keefe, Winslow Homer, Charles Demuth, Albert Gleizes, Ogden Pleissner, and Jack Bush. The Masterworks Foundation was established in 1987 to return to the island works of art that depict Bermuda and to exhibit them.

The Bermuda National Gallery is also home to the Hereward T. Watlington collection, which includes paintings from the 15th to 19th centuries of artists such as Reynolds, Gainsborough, and de Hooch. The gallery also has displays of smaller paintings and watercolors collected by the Bermuda Archives and National Trust, as well as a room for changing exhibits.

While a National Gallery for Bermuda has been long overdue, Bermuda's humid climate and damaging sunlight made it necessary to build a gallery with proper climate control and lighting. As a result, the **Bermuda Fine Art Trust** was developed and incorporated by an Act of Parliament in 1982. In 1988, the Hon. Hereward T. Watlington bequeathed his collection of European paintings to the people of Bermuda on condition that they be housed in a European-standard climate-controlled environment. The Corporation of Hamilton offered the use of the East Exhibition Room of City Hall and gave a financial donation to begin construction of a proper facility.

Cathedral of the Most Holy Trinity

Church St. ☎ **441/292-4033.** Free. Daily 7:15am–5pm. Bus No. 1, 2, 10, or 11.

A short distance away, the Bermuda Cathedral on Church Street is the so-called mother church of the Anglican diocese. It was given status as a cathedral in 1894 and formally consecrated in 1911. A comprehensive restoration and enhancement program has just been carried out. Features of the building are a reredos, stained glass windows, and the carvings of the choir stalls.

Sessions House

21 Parliament St. ☎ **441/292-7408.** Free. Mon–Fri 9am–12:30pm and 2–5pm. Bus No. 1, 2, 10, or 11.

Built in 1819, this is an Italian Renaissance–style structure with a Jubilee Clock Tower, erected to commemorate the Golden Jubilee of Queen Victoria in 1887. The House of Assembly meets on the second floor, and visitors are allowed in the gallery (call **441/292-7408** to learn the time of meetings). On the lower level, the Chief Justice presides over the Supreme Court.

7 Paget Parish

Visitors flock to Paget for its South Shore beaches, the best on the chain of islands. Named after the fourth Lord Paget, the parish has a lot of historic homes and gardens, but most of them are not open to public view, except on special occasions. During the springtime College Weeks, the Elbow Beach Hotel is the center of most activities.

Most visitors who stay here in one of the section's many hotels use the ferry service, with landing docks at Salt Kettle, Hodson's, and Lower Ferry. It's also possible to "commute" by ferry to Warwick Parish or Sandys Parish to the west.

Paget Parish is the setting of **Chelston,** on Grape Bay Drive, the official residence of the U.S. consul-general (which is open only during the Garden Club of Bermuda's open-houses-and-gardens program in the spring). It stands on 14^{1}/$_{2}$ acres of landscaped grounds overlooking South Shore Rd.

✪ Botanical Gardens

Point Finger Rd., South Shore Rd. ☎ **441/236-4201.** Free. Daily, sunrise to sunset. Bus No. 1, 2, or 7. If you're on a bike or moped, turn left off Middle Rd. onto Tee St. At Berry Hill Rd., go right. About a mile farther on to the left is the signposted turnoff to the gardens on Point Finger Rd.

This 36-acre landscaped park is one of the major attractions of the island, with hundreds of flowers, shrubs, and trees all clearly identified; it is also riddled with pathways. Attractions include collections of hibiscus and subtropical fruit, an aviary, banyan trees, and even a garden for the blind. The property is maintained by the Department of Agriculture, Fisheries, and Parks. It's best to take one of the 90-minute walking tours that depart at 10:30am on Tuesday, Wednesday, and Friday, in season, from the Visitor Centre which also has a café selling sandwiches and salads (soup and chili in winter). From mid-November through March, tours are only on Tuesday and Friday. You can always visit on your own, however.

Waterville

5 The Lane (Harbour Rd.), corner of Pomander Rd. ☎ **441/236-6483.** Free. Mon–Fri 9am–5pm. Shop: Mon–Sat 10am–4pm. Bus No. 8 from Hamilton.

This is one of the oldest (built prior to 1735) houses in Bermuda, and was the home of seven generations of the prominent Trimingham family. It was from the cellar storage rooms of this house that James Harvey Trimingham started, in 1842, the business that was to become Trimingham Brothers, Ltd., one of Bermuda's finest Front Street shops. Waterville is now the headquarters of the Bermuda National Trust and houses its office, reception rooms, and shop, Trustworthy. Major renovations were carried out in 1811, and the house has been restored in this period's style. The two main rooms have also been furnished in this period, mainly with Trimingham family heirlooms specifically bequeathed for use in the house.

Waterville is just west of the Trimingham roundabout very near the city of Hamilton.

Paget Marsh

Middle Rd. ☎ **441/236-6483**. Free. Mon–Fri 9am–5pm by special arrangement. Bus No. 8 from Hamilton.

Paget Marsh is 18 acres of unspoiled woods and marshland, with vegetation and birdlife of ecological interest. It can be visited only when special arrangements are made with the National Trust (☎ **441/236-6483**).

Birdsey Studio

5 Stowe Hill, Paget. ☎ **441/236-6658**. Mon–Fri 10am–1am; Sat 9am to noon. Bus No. 8 from Hamilton.

One of Bermuda's best-known painters, Alfred Birdsey, came to Bermuda from his native England when he was seven years old. Around 1990, he radically changed his style, from the calendar-style art he now disdains, to bold, powerful canvasses with bright colors and forceful themes. Watercolors begin at $40 each; oils range from $100 to around $2,000.

8 Warwick Parish

Famed for its two golf courses, this western parish of Bermuda was named after the second Earl of Warwick, a shareholder in the Bermuda Company of 1610.

Warwick Long Bay, on South Shore Road, with public conveniences, is one of the finest beaches of Bermuda and forms the major attraction of the parish. In the vicinity, you can go inside **Christ Church,** across from the Belmont Hotel on Middle Road, daily from 9am to 4pm. Built in 1719, it is one of the oldest Scottish Presbyterian churches in the New World.

If you're in the parish on a Sunday morning, it seems that nearly everyone heads for Paw Paws Restaurant, a popular place serving local Bermudian food (see "Warwick Parish" in Chapter 6, "Dining").

9 Southampton Parish

This parish is a narrow strip of land opening at its northern rim onto Little Sound and on its southern shore onto the wide Atlantic Ocean. It is bordered by Warwick Parish in the east and Sandys Parish in the west. The U.S. Naval Air Station Annex is also here. If you see red flags hoisted in the area, take care. They're there to warn of aerial firing.

Known for its beaches, the parish was named after the third Earl of Southampton. **Horseshoe Bay** is one of Bermuda's most attractive public beaches, with changing rooms, a snackbar, and space for parking.

✪ Gibbs Hill Lighthouse

Gibbs Hill, Lighthouse Road between South Shore Rd. and Middle Rd. ☎ **441/238-0524**. $2, free for children under 5. Daily 9am–4:30pm. Bus No. 7 or 8 from Hamilton.

The main attraction of this parish is the Gibbs Hill Lighthouse, built in 1846. It is the oldest cast-iron lighthouse in the world. The panoramic view of the Bermuda islands and its sweeping shoreline from the outlook balcony at the top is worth the 185-step climb. The workings of the machinery are explained by the lighthouse keeper. In spring, visitors may spot migrating whales beyond the South Shore reefs. You can see a collection of shipwreck artifacts recovered by Teddy Tucker.

10   Sandys Parish

There are those who on arrival in Bermuda head directly for Sandys Parish and never leave until it's time to go home. For many, the far western tip of Bermuda is that special, with its rolling hills, lush countryside, and tranquil bays. The parish is actually made up of a group of islands, and was named in honor of Sir Edwin Sandys, one of the shareholders of the original Somers Island (Bermuda) Company, as well as a director of the Virginia Company and the East India Company.

Somerset Island, the largest of the Sandys group, where the village of Somerset lies, pays tribute to Sir George Somers of *Sea Venture* fame; Sandys Parish is often called Somerset. Somehow it has always stood apart from the rest of Bermuda. For example, during the U.S. Civil War, when most of the country sympathized with the Confederate cause, Sandys Parish stood firmly in the Union camp.

To explore this tip of the fishhook of Bermuda, it is best to take a ferry (fare of $3) plying the Great Sound, a 45-minute run from Hamilton to Waterford Bridge. Bikes can be taken aboard the ferry (motor-assisted cycles are assessed $3). Ferries also stop at Cavello Bay, Somerset, and the Royal Naval Dockyard. The **Visitors Service Bureau** is on Somerset Rd. near St. James' Church (☎ 441/234-1388). It's open Monday through Saturday from 10am to 4pm from May through November. After leaving Fort Scaur (see below), you can continue on the 17th-century **Somerset Bridge,** the world's smallest drawbridge. When open for marine traffic, the space between the spans is a mere 22 inches at road level. Much photographed, it is just big enough to allow the mast of a sailboat to pass through.

On Somerset Road is the **Scaur Lodge Property,** an open area that includes the site of Scaur Lodge, a Bermuda cottage that was severely damaged by a waterspout that moved up on land, turning into a tornado and driving across this neck of Somerset Island. This typical Bermuda steep-shoreline hillside is open daily at no charge.

Sandys Parish has areas of great natural beauty, including **Somerset Long Bay,** a public beach, which the Bermuda Audubon Society is developing into a nature preserve; and **Mangrove Bay,** a protected beach right in the heart of **Somerset Village.** You can take pictures from the public wharf. Try to walk around the old village; it's filled with typically Bermudian houses and contains some shops.

✪ Fort Scaur

Ely's Harbour, Somerset Rd. ☎ 441/234-0908. Free. Daily 9am–4:30pm. Closed Christmas. Bus No. 7 or 8 from Hamilton.

On the highest hill in Somerset, this fort was part of a ring of fortifications constructed in the 19th century, during the troubled relations between Britain and the United States. Built as a last-ditch defense line for the Old Royal Naval Dockyard, the fort was skillfully constructed to take advantage of the land contours in order to be well camouflaged from the sea. It has subterranean passages and a dry moat that stretches across the land from Ely's Harbour to Great Sound. Fort Scaur was opened to visitors in 1957 and has become one of Somerset's most popular tourist attractions. The fort offers views of Ely's Harbour and Great Sound, and points as far away as St. David's Lighthouse and Fort St. Catherine can be seen with the free telescope. Picnic tables, benches, and restrooms in the fort are provided. Surrounding it are 22 acres of parkland filled with interesting trails, picnic areas, a rocky shoreline for fishing, and a public dock for access from the sea.

Springfield Library and Gilbert Nature Reserve

Main Rd. ☎ **441/234-1980.** Free. Nature reserve sunrise to sunset. Library Mon and Wed 9am–1pm and 2–5pm; Sat 10am–1pm and 2–5pm. Bus No. 7 or 8 from Hamilton.

In the center of the island stands Springfield, an old plantation home restored by the National Trust that today houses Somerset Library, a branch of the Bermuda Public Library. The Gilbert Nature Reserve consists of five acres of unspoiled woodland and bears the name of the family who owned the property from the beginning of the 18th century until it was acquired by the Bermuda National Trust in conjunction with the Bermuda Audubon Society in 1973. No admission is charged for either the nature reserve, the home (the branch library), or the outbuildings (used as a nursery school).

St. James' Anglican Church

90 Somerset Rd. ☎ **441/234-2723.** Free. Daily 8am–6pm. Bus No. 7 or 8 from Hamilton.

This is considered one of the most beautiful churches in Bermuda. It was constructed on the site of a structure that was destroyed by a hurricane in 1780. The present church was built nine years later, with the unique feature of the altar facing west instead of the customary eastward position. That was the result of a new road that was cut through to the east side of the church because the ancient westside road was inadequate. The north and south aisles of the church were added in 1836, the entrance gate in 1872, and the spire and chancel in 1880. The church was struck by lightning in 1939, but was long ago restored.

11 Ireland Island

A multimillion-dollar cruise-ship dock and tourist village has grown up in this historic area, which was used by the British navy until 1951. The site also shelters the Bermuda Maritime Museum, the Neptune Theatre, the Crafts Market, and the Bermuda Arts Centre. Ferries from Hamilton stop at Ireland Island, in the extreme west end of Bermuda, once per hour from 7am to 6pm. The fare is $3 each way. A bus leaves Hamilton for the Royal Naval Dockyard every 15 minutes from 8am to 8pm Monday through Saturday. The journey takes one hour and costs $2.50 for adults, half price for children.

The **Royal Naval Dockyard** has been transformed into a park, with Victorian street lighting and a Terrace Pavilion and bandstand for concerts. Vendors can be found pushing carts filled with food, dry goods, and local crafts. A full-service marina with floating docks is in operation along with a marina clubhouse and showers.

On a historical note, when this dockyard, which had been on British Admiralty land, was sold in 1953 to the Bermudian government, it marked the end of British naval might in the western Atlantic.

✪ Bermuda Maritime Museum

Old Royal Navy Dockyard, Ireland Island. ☎ **441/234-1333.** $7.50 adults, $2 children under 18. Daily 10am–4:30pm. Closed Christmas. Transportation: Ferry from Hamilton. Bus No. 7 or 8.

In a large 19th-century fortress, built by convict labor, the museum continues to improve exhibits about Bermuda's nautical heritage. Its most famous exhibit is in the 1837 Shifting House, which was opened in 1979. It is devoted to various exhibits consisting of such artifacts as gold bars, pottery, jewelry, silver coins, and other items recovered from 16th- and 17th-century shipwrecks, including the *Sea Venture.* But most visitors come here to gaze at the Tucker Treasure.

A well-known local diver, Teddy Tucker, is credited with making the most significant marine find at that time when, in 1955, he discovered the wreck of the *San Antonio,* a Spanish vessel that went down off the coast of Bermuda in a violent storm in 1621. One of the great treasures of this find, the Pectoral Cross, was stolen before Queen Elizabeth II opened the museum in 1975. The priceless original cross was replaced by a fake. To this day, the original cross has never been recovered, and its mysterious disappearance is still the subject of much discussion.

The fortress's massive buildings of fitted stone, with their vaulted ceilings of English brick, are alone worth a visit. So are the 30-foot defensive ramparts; the underground tunnels, gunports, and magazines; and the water gate and pond for entry by boat from the sea. Exhibits in four exhibition halls illustrate the island's long, intimate connection with the sea—from Spanish exploration to 20th-century ocean liners, from overcanvassed racing dinghies to practical fishing boats, from shipbuilding and privateering to naval exploits. The Shifting House contains shipwreck exhibits, including some earthenware and pewter belonging to the English settlers aboard the *Sea Venture* wrecked in 1609.

As you enter the Parade Ground at the entrance to the museum, you'll notice a 10-foot-high figure of King Neptune. This is a figurehead from the HMS *Irresistible,* recovered when the ship was broken up in 1891 and now duplicated in Indiana limestone. The **Queen's Exhibition Hall** houses general maritime exhibits, including those on navigation, whaling, cable and wireless, and "Bermuda in Five Hours," this last a reference to the advertisements touting Pan American's early "flying boats." The building was constructed in 1850 for the storage of 4,860 barrels of gunpowder.

The **Forster Cooper Building** (from 1852) of the museum illustrates the history of the Royal Navy in Bermuda, including the Bromby Bottle Collection. This exhibit was opened in 1984 by Princess Margaret. The Boatloft houses part of the museum's boat collections, including the century-old fitted dinghy *Victory,* the 17-foot *Spirit of Bermuda,* and the *Rambler,* the only surviving Bermuda pilot gig. The original dockyard clock is a working exhibit on the upper floor, and chimes the quarters and the hours.

One of the most enjoyable ways to see the dockyard is on a guided walking tour, many of which are free. Tours change frequently, so it is best to check with the Visitor Service Centre at the dockyard to see what is available, if anything, at the time of your visit.

Bermuda's Luckiest Treasure Hunter

Edward Tucker is the most famous treasure retriever in the history of Bermuda. A local diver, he hit the jackpot in 1955 when he brought up a collection of gold bars and ornaments from the *San Antonio,* a Spanish vessel that had sunk in 1621. The treasure is on display at the Bermuda Maritime Museum on Ireland Island. The prize piece of the exhibition—a gold cross mounted with seven emeralds— was stolen only moments before Queen Elizabeth II arrived in 1975 for a royal opening. It was replaced with a replica.

Bermuda Craft Market

In the Cooperage Building, 4 Freeport Rd.☎ **441/234-3208.** Free. Daily 10am–5pm. Transportation: Ferry from Hamilton. Bus No. 7 or 8.

The market is the place to watch local artists at work and to buy their wares. Established in 1987, it offers works in Bermuda cedarwork, candles, clothing, dolls, fabrics, hand-painted items, jewelry, metal and gem sculpture, needlework, quilts, shell art, glass panels, and woven cane goods among other items.

Bermuda Arts Centre

4 Freeport Rd.☎ **441/234-2809.** Donation requested. Mon–Sat 10am–4:30pm; Sun noon–5pm. Transportation: By bus or ferry from Hamilton.

Art work by local artists is featured at this gallery. Original artwork and prints are for sale, and the artists presently in residence include a cedar sculptor, a watercolorist, and a jewelry maker. New exhibits are mounted frequently throughout the year.

12 Especially for Kids

Families with children will enjoy a wide variety of activities April through October when family fun can consist of water sports such as sailing, water skiing, snorkeling, or glass-bottom boat trips; tennis; visits to museums and caves; and a wide array of walking tours.

Most resort properties offer specific children's activities, and there are special family packages. Most of the larger properties will also provide babysitting services for minimal fees.

Here are some of the favorite activities for kids:

Bermuda Aquarium, Museum, & Zoo *(see page 141)* This provides a learning experience about the undersea world. Hand-held tape recorders are available for listening to the history of marine life while visiting live exhibits of Bermuda's native fish.

Bermuda Maritime Museum *(see page 152)* Entire families take equal delight in viewing the exhibits of Bermuda's nautical history in this authentic Victorian fortress museum.

Bermuda Railway Trail *(see page 167)* A nature walk for the whole family, this 21-mile trail can be walked in sections, as your energy and interest dictate. There are strolls overlooking the seashore or along quiet tree-lined alleyways.

Devil's Hole Aquarium *(see page 142)* The first established attraction in Bermuda—founded in 1834—this aquarium is located near Harrington Sound. Kids toss baited but hookless lines to feed fish and turtles in this natural marine environment.

Crystal Caves *(see page 142)* Two boys chasing a runaway ball in 1907 discovered this enormous cavern surrounded by an underground lake. Easy walkways take parents and children down into the caverns of the crystal caves located near Hamilton Parish.

Undersea Walk (see "Organized Tours," below) Explore the ocean floor with "helmet diving." Following a pre-dive educational lecture aboard the ship, children can walk along the ocean floor for face-to-face encounters with friendly native sea creatures.

Horseback Riding (see Chapter 9, "Beaches, Water Sports & Other Outdoor Activities") Spicelands Riding Center accepts riders over 21 years old, but the Lee Bow Riding center is well equipped for younger riders.

13   Special-Interest Sightseeing

FOR THE ARCHITECTURE LOVER

All of Bermuda holds special appeal for the architecture lover. Mark Twain wrote of the whiteness of Bermuda houses and roofs: "It is exactly the white of the icing of a cake, and has the same emphasized and scarcely perceptible polish. The white of marble is modest and retiring compared with it . . . clean-cut fanciful chimneys—too pure and white for this world—that will charm one's gaze by the hour."

For more details and lore, refer to "Bermuda Style" in Chapter 2, "Getting to Know Bermuda." The **town of St. George's**—being the oldest and most historic settlement—holds the most fascination for those interested in architecture (see Chapter 8, "Bermuda Walking Tours").

The **Old State House** is the oldest stone house in Bermuda, constructed in 1620. The governor at the time, Nathaniel Butler, believed that he was constructing the house in an Italianate style. He ordered workers to use a combination of turtle oil and lime as mortar. This set the style for subsequent buildings in Bermuda.

Many architects have wanted to finish the **Unfinished Cathedral** in St. George's, reached by going up Blockade Alley. Construction was launched in 1874, but a schism developed in the church and then there was no money to go ahead.

The **Old Rectory** in St. George's, now a private residence, dates from 1705 when it was built by a former pirate. Found on Broad Alley, it is distinguished by its Dutch doors, chimneys, shutters, and what is called a "welcoming arms" staircase.

From an architectural point of view, one of the most intriguing structures in St. George's is **St. Peter's Church,** standing on Duke of York Street. This is the oldest Anglican Church in the Western Hemisphere, dating from 1620. It was constructed to replace an even older structure from 1612 that had been badly assembled from posts and palmetto leaves. A storm did that church in in 1712. The present St. Peter's was rebuilt and enlarged in 1713. In 1833, the galleries on each side of the church were added. The section around the triple-tier pulpit is believed to be the oldest part of the structure, dating from the 1600s. The first governor of the island, Richard Moore, ordered construction of the dark red Bermuda cedar altar in 1615. It is the oldest surviving piece of woodwork from the colonial days.

Also in St. George's, **Tucker House,** on Water Street, was constructed of native limestone. The house is also interestingly furnished, mostly with pieces from the mid-1700s and early 1800s.

The other architectural monument of note in Bermuda is **Verdmont,** lying on Verdmont Lane in Smith's Parish. Dating from around 1710, it was once occupied by a wealthy shipowner. It has known many owners in its long history, including an American Loyalist, John Green, who fled from Philadelphia to Bermuda at the end of the War of American Independence. Built to resemble an English manor house, the house has a striking double roof and a quartet of large chimneys. Each room has its own fireplace. The sash windows are in a style once fashionable in certain English manor houses.

FOR THE LITERARY ENTHUSIAST

Bermuda has long been a haven for writers. It has figured in many works of literature, beginning with Shakespeare's play *The Tempest*. Shakespeare had not visited the island himself but was inspired by accounts he had read or heard of it.

The Irish poet Thomas Moore (1779–1852), who did visit Bermuda for several months in 1804, was moved by its beauty to write:

> *Oh! could you view the scenery dear*
> *That now beneath my window lies.*

Moore left more memories—literary and romantic—than any other writer ever to visit Bermuda. He once stayed at Hill Crest Guest House in St. George's (see Chapter 5, "Accommodations"). He soon became enamored of Nea Tucker, the teenage bride of one of the most prominent men in town. "Sweet Nea! Let us roam no more," he once wrote of his beloved.

It is said that the lovesick poet would gaze for hours upon Nea's veranda, hoping that she'd appear. A jealous Mr. Tucker one day could tolerate this no more and banished the poet from his property. St. George's honors this unrequited romance by naming the street down which Tom Moore was chased Nea's Alley.

One of the most popular restaurants in Bermuda is Tom Moore's Tavern (see Chapter 6, "Dining"). The restaurant was once the private home of Samuel Trott, who had built it in the 17th century. Unlike the jealous Tucker, descendants of Samuel Trott befriended Moore, and he was a frequent visitor to the house. In his writing, the bard immortalized the calabash tree on the Trott estate. He liked to sit under this tree and pen his verse.

Many famous writers were to visit Bermuda in the years to come, following in Moore's footsteps. There are no literary shrines, however, to any of them.

For Americans it was Mark Twain who helped make Bermuda a popular tourist destination. He published his impressions in the *Atlantic Monthly* in 1877–78

⭐ Frommer's Favorite Bermuda Experiences

Strolling Bermuda's Pink Sands. The pink sand beaches are reason enough to come to the island. Find your favorite cove (perhaps Whale Bay, Astwood Cove, or Jobson's Cove), and stroll aimlessly at dawn, at twilight, whenever your fancy dictates.

Cycling Across the Land. On a rented bicycle, or maybe a moped built for two, explore Bermuda from end to end. Start in St. George's in the East End and go all the way to the Royal Naval Dockyard in the West End.

Following the Deserted Railway Trail. As you follow this intermittent trail from one end of the island to the other, you'll see panoramic seascapes, exotic flora and fauna, and hear the soothing sounds of the island's bird life.

Touring by Horse and Buggy. No one has ever improved on this old-fashioned method of sightseeing and shopping along Hamilton's Front Street. Or, better yet, go on a two-hour shopping tour of Somerset Village in the West End.

Viewing Bermuda from Gibb's Hill Lighthouse. Climb the 185 steps of one of the oldest cast-iron lighthouses in the world for one of the Atlantic Ocean's greatest views. Springtime visitors may be lucky enough to see migrating whales beyond the shore reefs.

and in his first book, *The Innocents Abroad*. So enamored did he become of the island that, as he wrote many years later to a correspondent, he would fain choose it over heaven.

Following in Twain's footsteps, Eugene O'Neill came to the island in 1924, and returned several times, at least through 1927, living at Spithead in Warwick. While here, he worked on *The Great God Brown, Lazarus Laughed,* and *Strange Interlude*. O'Neill was convinced that cold weather adversely affected his writings. He also thought that Bermuda would "cure" him of alcoholism. His daughter, Oona, was born in Bermuda (she later married Charlie Chaplin). O'Neill and his family rented cottages on what is now Coral Beach Club property. Later, O'Neill bought the house Spithead, in Warwick. In 1927, however, his marriage ended, and O'Neill left his family—and Bermuda.

During the 1930s, several eminent writers made their way to Bermuda, with fountain pen and paper (or portable typewriter), in search of idyllic surroundings and perhaps a little inspiration: Sinclair Lewis, who, however, spent all his time cycling around "this gorgeous island"; Hervey Allen, who proved more prolific, penning *Anthony Adverse,* his prodigious best-selling novel, at Felicity Hall in Somerset; and James Ramsey Ullman, who wrote *The White Tower* on the island. Also among the literary visitors at this time was James Thurber, who during one of his several trips stayed long enough to finish *13 Clocks* at Lantana in Somerset.

Noel Coward came in 1956, with his longtime companion, Graham Payne, to escape "the monstrously unjust tax situation in England." He was not, he said, "really mad about the place," yet he purchased Spithead in Warwick, O'Neill's former home, and stayed some two years, working on *London Mornings,* his only ballet, and the musical *Sail Away.* The house is now in private hands.

Other names can be added to the list of famous authors who visited Bermuda through the years: Rudyard Kipling, C. S. Forester, Hugh Walpole, Edna Ferber, Anita Loos, John O'Hara, E. B. White, Philip Wylie.

Bermuda itself has produced several writers, who, although not as internationally prominent, have nevertheless gained some recognition. Among them are William S. Zuill, a former director of the Bermuda National Trust, who wrote *The Story of Bermuda and Her People,* an excellent historical account of the island. Other writers are Nellie Musson, Frank Manning, Eva Hodgson, and Dale Butler, all of whom have written of the lives of African-Bermudians.

14 Organized Tours

A major sightseeing attraction in Bermuda is a ride aboard one of the glass-bottom-boat Reef Roamer Cruises. The best of these is *Reefs and Wreck,* where passengers observe the wreck of the HMS *Vixen,* reef fish, and coral formations. Two-hour tours leave daily at 10am and 1:30pm, and cost $30 for adults.

The Bermuda Island Cruise offers a chance to see Bermuda in a day. The cruise highlight is a stop at the Historic Dockyard with time for shopping, sightseeing, and a visit to the Maritime Museum. A hot and cold buffet is served in St. George's, where more shopping and sightseeing is possible. Cruises leave daily at 10:30am, finishing at 4:30pm.

In the evening, the Pirate Party Night at Hawkins Island includes a buffet dinner, music from the Island Fever Band, and a Hot Spice Limbo show, with Gombey dancers and a complimentary bar. Adults pay $65 per person. Children under 18 must be accompanied by a parent. Departures are at 7pm on Tuesday,

Wednesday, Friday, and Saturday, returning at 10:30pm. On all these tours, children 7–12 go for half price (free 6 and under).

The cruises are operated by **Bermuda Island Cruises, Ltd.,** P.O. Box 2249 in Hamilton (☎ **441/292-8652**) and can be booked over the phone or at various hotel tour desks.

BDA Water Tours Ltd., P.O. Box 1572, Hamilton (☎ **441/295-3727**), offers two- and three-hour trips, most of which include the sea gardens; passengers board glass-bottom boats to view the wonders of coral reefs and fish. Also available are a variety of water trips, ranging from two-hour sea-garden tours to snorkeling and dinner cruises. You can call 24 hours a day for information.

To help find a solution for a threatening world problem, the **Bermuda Biological Station for Research, Inc.,** a U.S. nonprofit organization, has been given a grant to study the carbon cycle, as part of an understanding of climate change and the greenhouse effect by the U.S. National Science Foundation. Some $500,000 will be used every year for this research. The Bermuda Biological Station has the world's longest and most continuous data on the oceanographic absorption of human-released carbon dioxide, having tracked levels of it for more than 40 years over an area 13 miles southeast of Bermuda. The station also has kept extensive data on acid rain in the North American atmosphere.

Vacationers to Bermuda can learn firsthand what Bermuda-based scientists are studying at the station by taking a free hour-long guided tour of the station's grounds and laboratory in St. George's. Tour leaders explain what scientific studies are being conducted in Bermuda and how they relate to the overall world environment. Other topics discussed include the island's natural areas, including the coral reefs, protected by strict conservation laws, and how people have caused changes in the fragile ecological environment.

The special educational tours on Wednesday at 10am are conducted by scientists involved in the station's special projects and by specially trained volunteers. Visitors should assemble in the Biological Station's main building. Coffee and snacks are served, and participants are asked to give a donation for the refreshments.

For information on the tours, contact the Bermuda Biological Station for Research, Inc., 17 Biological Lane, Ferry Reach, St. George's (☎ **441/297-1880**).

Walking Tours 8

You can cover much of Bermuda on foot, especially the harbor city of Hamilton and the historic town of St. George's. Indeed, if you had the time you could walk—or, if you prefer, cycle—through all the parishes of the island, taking in the major attractions of each. But most visitors would rather devote their vacation time to less taxing pursuits, such as lying insouciantly on the beach or playing a leisurely game of golf.

If, however, you are among the hardy few and do not mind a little physical exertion if the reward promises to exceed the effort, then you should certainly consider taking one or perhaps all three of the walking tours suggested below. For the best way to familiarize yourself with a new place—city, town, or village—is by taking a stroll through it and experiencing its everyday activities close up.

WALKING TOUR 1
City of Hamilton

Start: The Visitors Service Bureau/Ferry Terminal.
End: Fort Hamilton.
Time: 2¹/₂ hours.
Best Time: Any sunny day.
Worst Time: When cruise ships are anchored in Hamilton Harbour.

Begin your tour along the harborfront at the:

1. **Visitors Service Bureau/Ferry Terminal.** (You might want to take an orientational ferry ride around the inner harbor; that way, you'll get an overview of Hamilton before concentrating on specific landmarks or monuments. Or you could take the ferry ride at the end of the tour.) Pick up some free maps and brochures of the island here.

From the bureau, you emerge onto Front Street again, the main street of Hamilton and its principal shopping artery. Before 1946, no automobiles were permitted on this street, but today its active traffic includes small automobiles (driven only by Bermuda residents), buses, mopeds, and bicycles. You'll also see horse-drawn carriages, which are the most romantic (although the most expensive) way to see Hamilton.

Observe the docks in back of the Ferry Terminal. Here is where you board ferries to the parishes of Warwick and Paget (for a description of their attractions, see Chapter 7, "What to See & Do"). You can also take a ferry across Great Sound, going to the West End (Somerset of Sandys).

Walk directly south of the Ferry Terminal toward the water, taking a short side street between the Visitors Service Bureau and the large Bank of Bermuda. You'll come to:

2. **Albouy's Point,** a small grassy park with benches and trees opening onto a panoramic vista of the boat- or ship-filled harbor. Nearby is the Royal Bermuda Yacht Club, an elite rendezvous of both the Bermudian and American yachting set—including lots of the rich and famous—since the 1930s. To use the word *royal* in its name, special permission had to come from Prince Albert, Queen Victoria's consort, in London. The club sponsors the widely televised Newport–Bermuda Yacht Race.

After taking in the view, walk directly north, crossing Point Pleasant Road, to the:

3. **Bank of Bermuda,** which can be visited Monday through Friday from 9:30am to 3pm. On the mezzanine is Bermuda's most extensive coin collection—at least one of every coin minted in the United Kingdom since the time of King James I (the early 17th century). Many Spanish coins used in colonial days are also on show. The most famous Bermudian money—also on exhibit—was called "hog money," the first coins ever minted on the island. In use since the early 1600s, the hog coin is stamped on one side with the ill-fated *Sea Venture* and on the other side with a wild hog, the main source of food, other than fish, for the early settlers. Look for an 1887 £5 piece depicting Queen Victoria, the issuance of which caused a protest in the British Empire. Critics claimed that the small crown made her appear foolish.

Upon leaving the bank, head east along Front Street to the point where it intersects with Queen Street. This is the site of the:

4. **"Birdcage,"** the most photographed sight in Bermuda. Here you'll sometimes, find a policeman (or perhaps a policewoman) directing traffic. If the "bobbie" is a man, he's likely to be attired in regulation Bermuda shorts. The traffic box, which was named after its designer, Michael "Dickey" Bird, stands at a little bit of Hamilton geography called Heyl's Corner, honoring an American southerner, J. B. Heyl, who operated an apothecary shop nearby in the 1800s.

Continue north along Queen Street until you reach:

5. **Par-la-Ville Park,** which was once a private garden belonging to the town house of William B. Perot, the first postmaster of Bermuda, who designed the gardens in the 19th century. He collected rare and exotic plants from all over the globe, including an Indian rubber tree which was seeded in 1847. Mark Twain wrote that he found the tree "disappointing" in that it didn't bear rubber overshoes and hot water bottles.

Also opening onto Queen Street at the entrance to the park is the:

6. **Bermuda Historical Society Museum,** 13 Queen Street, which is also the Bermuda Library. It's filled with curiosities, including cedar furniture, collections of antique silver and china, hog money, Confederate money, and other artifacts, including a 1775 letter from George Washington. The library has many rare books, including a 1624 edition of John Smith's *General Histoire of Virginia, New England and the Somers Isles.* If you'd like to rest and catch up on

Walking Tour—City of Hamilton

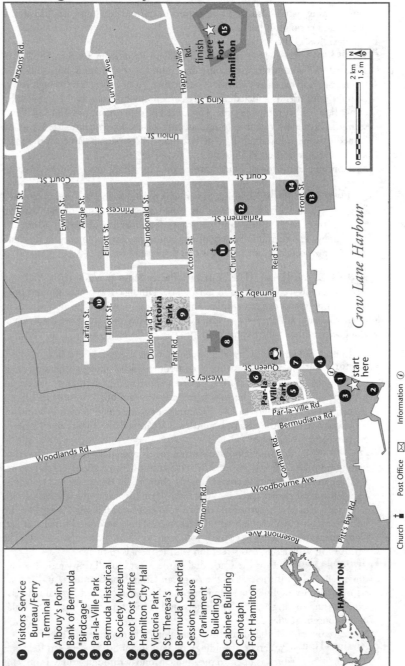

1. Visitors Service Bureau/Ferry Terminal
2. Albouy's Point
3. Bank of Bermuda
4. "Birdcage"
5. Par-la-Ville Park
6. Bermuda Historical Society Museum
7. Perot Post Office
8. Hamilton City Hall
9. Victoria Park
10. St. Theresa's
11. Bermuda Cathedral
12. Sessions House (Parliament Building)
13. Cabinet Building
14. Cenotaph
15. Fort Hamilton

Church ⊕   Post Office ⊠   Information ⓘ

HAMILTON

9731

your reading, you'll also find a selection of current local and English newspapers and periodicals here.

Next door is the:

7. Perot Post Office, which was run by William Perot from 1818 to 1862. It is said that he'd go down to collect the mail from the clipper ships, but would put it under his top hat so as to preserve his dignity. As he proceeded through town, he'd greet his friends and acquaintances by tipping his hat—and thereby delivering their mail at the same time. He started printing stamps in 1848. A Perot stamp is extremely valuable today, as only 11 are known to exist; some are owned by Queen Elizabeth II. The last time a Perot stamp came on the market, in 1986, it fetched $135,000.

Continue to the top of Queen Street, then turn right onto Church Street to reach:

8. Hamilton City Hall, 17 Church Street, which dates from 1960 and is crowned by a white tower. The bronze weather vane on top is a replica of the *Sea Venture*. Portraits of the queen and paintings of former island leaders adorn the main lobby. The Bermuda Society of Arts holds frequent exhibitions at this hall. The Benbow collection of stamps is also displayed here.

☕ TAKE A BREAK   The **Fourways Pastry Shop** at Washington Mall and Reid Street was recommended in Chapter 6, "Dining." It is on the ground floor of a shopping and office complex and serves the most irresistible pastries in town. You can also order ice cream, tartlets, quiches, and croissant sandwiches, along with espresso and cappuccino.

In back of Hamilton City Hall, opening onto Victoria Street, lies:

9. Victoria Park, a cool, refreshing oasis frequented by office workers on their lunch breaks. Containing a sunken garden and ornamental shrubbery, it also has a Victorian bandstand. The four-acre park was laid out in honor of Queen Victoria's Golden Jubilee in 1887. Outdoor concerts are held here in summer.

Cedar Avenue is the eastern boundary of Victoria Park. If you follow it north for two blocks, you reach:

10. St. Theresa's, a Roman Catholic cathedral that is open daily from 8am to 7pm. Dating from 1927, it was inspired by the Spanish Mission style of architecture. It is one of half a dozen Roman Catholic churches in Bermuda; its treasure is a gold and silver chalice given by Pope Paul VI on his visit to the island in 1986.

After a visit to the cathedral, retrace your steps south along Cedar Avenue until you return to Victoria Street. Cedar Avenue now becomes Burnaby Street. Continue south on this street until you come to Church Street where you cut left. A short walk along this street (on your left) leads to the:

11. Bermuda Cathedral, or the Cathedral of the Most Holy Trinity as it is sometimes called. This is the seat of the Anglican Church of Bermuda, and it towers over the city skyline. Its style is neo-Gothic, characterized by stained-glass windows and soaring arches. The lectern and pulpit duplicate those of St. Giles in Edinburgh, Scotland.

Leave the cathedral and continue east along Church Street to the:

12. Sessions House (Parliament Building), on Parliament Street, between Reid and Church Streets, which is open to the public Monday through Friday from 9am to 5pm. The Parliament of Bermuda is considered the third oldest in the world, after Iceland's and England's. You can see political action, Bermuda style, from the Visitors' Gallery. The speaker is attired in full wig and flowing black robes.

Continue to walk south along Parliament Street until you approach Front Street, where you should turn left to the:

13. Cabinet Building, between Court and Parliament Streets. The official opening of Parliament takes place here in late October or early November. In a plumed hat and full regalia, the governor makes his "Throne Speech." If you visit on a Wednesday, you'll see the Bermuda Senate in action. The building is open Monday through Friday from 9am to 5pm.

In front of the Cabinet Building is the:

14. Cenotaph, a memorial to Bermuda's dead in World War I (1914–18) and in World War II (1939–45). In 1920 the Prince of Wales laid the cornerstone. (Later, in 1936, as King Edward VIII he would abdicate to marry an American divorcée, Wallis Simpson, and later still, during World War II, now the Duke of Windsor, he would serve as governor of the Bahamas.) The landmark is a replica of the Cenotaph in London.

Continue east along Front Street until you reach King Street, then head north until you come to Happy Valley Road. Go right on this road until you see the entrance (on your right) to:

15. Fort Hamilton, an imposing old fortress on the eastern outskirts of Hamilton. The Duke of Wellington ordered its construction to protect Hamilton Harbour. Filled with underground passageways and complete with a moat and 18-ton guns, it was considered outdated even before it was completed. The fort never fired a shot, but it makes for interesting viewing nonetheless. Go if for no other reason than to enjoy the view of the city and harbor. In summer, try to time your visit for noon when the kilted Bermuda Isles Pipe Band performs a skirling ceremony on the green, accompanied by dancers and drummers. It's a fairly good walk to the fort, so wind down with some old-fashioned tea at the Fort Hamilton Tea Shoppe, where you can also order light refreshments.

WALKING TOUR 2
Historic St. George's Town

Start: King's Square.
End: Somers Wharf.
Time: 2 hours (not counting interior visits).
Best Time: Any sunny day except Sunday when much is closed.
Worst Time: When a cruise ship is anchored in harbor.

In the east end of the island, St. George's was the second English town to be established in the New World, after Jamestown in Virginia. For the history buff, it holds more interest than Hamilton. (For more detailed descriptions of its attractions, refer to "St. George's Parish," in Chapter 7, "What to See & Do.")

We'll begin the tour at:

1. King's Square, also known as Market Square and King's Parade, the very center of St. George's. Only some two centuries old, it's not as historic as St. George's itself. It was once a marshy part of the harbor—at least when the shipwrecked passengers and crew of *Sea Venture* first saw it. On the water's edge stands the Visitors Service Bureau, which you may want to visit to pick up additional information. Displayed on the square is a replica of the pillory and stocks that used to be used to punish criminals, and, in many cases, the innocent. You could be severely punished here for such alleged "crimes" as casting a spell over your neighbor's turkeys. Head south across the small bridge to:

2. **Ordnance Island,** jutting into St. George's Harbour. The British army once stored gunpowder and cannons here, but today the island contains *Deliverance II*, a replica of the vessel that carried the shipwrecked *Sea Venture* passengers on to Virginia. Alongside the vessel is a ducking stool, a contraption used in 17th-century witch trials. Retrace your steps across the bridge to King's Square. On the waterside stands the:

3. **White Horse Tavern,** a restaurant jutting out into St. George's Harbour. (For more details, refer to the section on St. George's, in Chapter 6, "Dining.") Consider the tavern for a luncheon stopover later. It was once the home of John Davenport, who came to Bermuda in 1815 to open a dry goods store. Davenport was considered a bit of a miser, and upon his death some £75,000 in gold and silver was discovered stashed away in his cellar. Across the square stands the:

4. **Town Hall,** near the Visitors Service Bureau. The hall is the meeting place of the Corporation governing St. George's. It contains antique cedar furnishings and a collection of photographs of previous Lord Mayors. *Bermuda Journey*, a multimedia audiovisual presentation, is shown here several times a day.

🌑 **TAKE A BREAK**   **O' Malley's Pub on the Square,** King's Square (recommended in Chapter 6, "Dining"). This British-style pub has a balcony overlooking the square. You can get a beer or a burger here, but many come mainly to watch the scene below.

From King's Square, head east along King Street, cutting north on Bridge Street. There you'll come to the:

5. **Bridge House Art Gallery,** 1 Bridge Street. Constructed shortly after 1700, this was once the home of several governors of Bermuda. Furnished with 18th- and 19th-century antiques, it is now home to an art gallery and souvenir shop. Return to King Street and continue east to:

6. **Old State House,** which actually opens onto Princess Street, at the top of King Street. This is the oldest stone building in Bermuda, dating from 1620, and was once the home of the Bermuda Parliament. It is the site of the ancient Peppercorn Ceremony, in which the Old State House pays the government "rent" of one peppercorn annually. (See "St. George's Parish," in Chapter 7, "What to See & Do," for details on this grand ceremony filled with pageantry.)

Continue your stroll down Princess Street until you come to the Duke of York Street, the entrance to:

7. **Somers Gardens.** The heart of Sir George Somers, the admiral of the *Sea Venture*, is buried here. The gardens, containing palms and other tropical plants, were opened in 1920 by the Prince of Wales.

Walk through Somers Gardens and up the steps to the North Gate onto Blockade Alley. If you look up the hill, you'll see what is known as "the folly of St. George's"—the:

8. **Unfinished Cathedral,** which was planned to replace St. Peter's (see below). Work began on the church in 1874, but eventually came to an end, as the church was beset by financial difficulties and a schism in the Anglican congregation.

Walking Tour—Historic St. George's Town

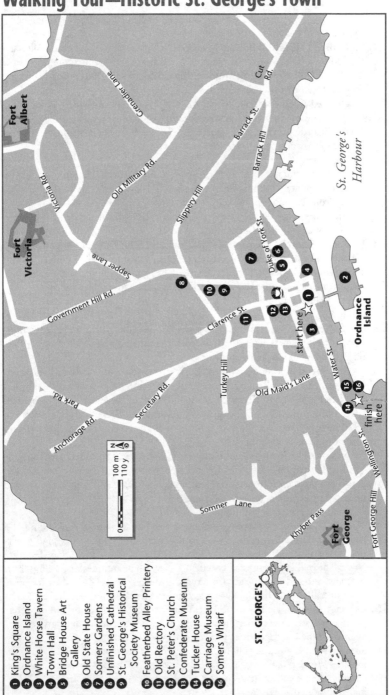

1. King's Square
2. Ordnance Island
3. White Horse Tavern
4. Town Hall
5. Bridge House Art Gallery
6. Old State House
7. Somers Gardens
8. Unfinished Cathedral
9. St. George's Historical Society Museum
10. Featherbed Alley Printery
11. Old Rectory
12. St. Peter's Church
13. Confederate Museum
14. Tucker House
15. Carriage Museum
16. Somers Wharf

ST. GEORGE'S

9732

After viewing the ruins, turn left onto the Duke of Kent Street, leading down to the:

9. St. George's Historical Society Museum, at the corner of Featherbed Alley and the Duke of Kent Street. An example of 18th-century architecture, the house contains a collection of Bermudian historical artifacts and cedar furniture. Around the corner on Featherbed Alley is the:

10. Featherbed Alley Printery, which has a working replica of the type of printing press invented by Johannes Gutenberg in Germany in the 1450s. Go up Featherbed Alley and straight onto Church Street. At the junction with Broad Lane, look to your right to see the:

11. Old Rectory, at the head of Broad Alley, behind St. Peter's Church. Now a private home, but administered by the National Trust, it was built in 1705 by a reformed pirate. If you'd like to go inside, it is open only on Wednesday and Friday from 10am to 4pm.

After seeing the Old Rectory, you can go through the back of the churchyard entrance, opposite Broad Alley, to reach:

12. St. Peter's Church. The church's main entrance is on Duke of York Street. This is believed to be the oldest Anglican place of worship in the Western Hemisphere. In the churchyard you'll see many headstones, some dating back three centuries. The assassinated governor, Sir Richard Sharples, was buried here. The present church was built in 1713, with a tower added in 1814. Across the street is the:

13. Confederate Museum. When it was the Globe Hotel, it was the headquarters of Major Norman Walker, the Confederate representative in Bermuda. It was once a hotbed of blockade-running.

As you continue along Duke of York Street, you reach Barber's Lane, honoring Joseph Hayne Rainey. A former slave from South Carolina, Rainey and his French wife fled to Bermuda at the outbreak of the Civil War. He became a barber in St. George's but eventually returned to South Carolina, where in 1870 he was elected to the U.S. House of Representatives—the first African American to serve in Congress.

Nearby is Petticoat Lane, also known as Silk Alley. The name dates from the 1834 emancipation, when two former slave women who'd always wanted silk petticoats like their former mistresses, finally got some and constantly paraded up and down the lane to show off their new finery.

Continue east until you reach:

14. Tucker House, opening onto Water Street. This was the former home of a prominent Bermudian family, whose members have included an island governor, a treasurer of the United States, and a captain in the Confederate Navy. The building houses an excellent collection of antiques, including silver, portraits, and cedar furniture. One room is devoted to relics of the previously mentioned Rainey. Diagonally across from the Tucker House is the:

15. Carriage Museum, 22 Water Street. Here are housed some of the more interesting carriages in use in Bermuda until 1946 when the automobile arrived. After visiting the Carriage Museum, you'll be at:

16. Somers Wharf, a multimillion-dollar waterfront restoration project, that now includes shops, restaurants, and taverns. It's the site of the Carriage House restaurant (in case you want to make a luncheon stopover), see Chapter 6, "Dining," for more details.

The Bermuda Railway Trail

One of the most unusual sightseeing adventures in Bermuda is following the Bermuda Railway Trail (or parts thereof), which stretches for 21 miles along an old train right-of-way across three of the interconnected islands that make up Bermuda. Opened in 1931, the Bermuda Railway was abandoned in 1948. Once the island's main source of transportation, the train gave way to the automobile.

Before setting out on this trek, arm yourself with a copy of the *Bermuda Railway Trail Guide*, obtainable at the Bermuda Department of Tourism in Hamilton or at the Visitors Service Bureau in Hamilton or St. George's. You're now ready to hit the trail of the old train system that was affectionately called "Rattle and Shake." (It is also considered the most costly rail line, per mile, ever constructed.) There are a variety of ways to explore the trail: horseback, bicycle, moped, or the ever-trusty feet.

Although the line covered 21 miles of the island between St. George's in the east and Somerset in the west, a three-mile stretch has been lost to roads in and around the capital city of Hamilton. For the most part, though, the trail winds along an automobile-free route, with some views of Bermuda not seen by the general public since the end of World War II.

As for some of the things you'll see en route, the trail cuts through the five-acre Springfield Library and Gilbert Nature Reserve (described on p. 152). You'll also see some of the rare Bermuda cedar, which nearly vanished in the blight that struck the island in the early 1940s. Along the trail, too, is much greenery and semitropical vegetation, such as the poinsettia, oleander, and hibiscus. Fort Scaur, the 1870s fortress in Sandys Parish, can also be seen and visited.

WALKING TOUR 3
Sandys Parish

Begin: Somerset Bridge.
End: Springfield Library and Gilbert Nature Reserve.
Time: 7 hours.
Best Time: Any sunny day.
Worst Time: When the weather's bad.

Sandys (pronounce it as if there were no *y*) is the far western parish of Bermuda, consisting of Somerset Island (the largest and southernmost), Watford, Boaz, and Ireland islands. When Bermudians cross over Somerset Bridge, they say they are "up the country."

Craggy coastlines, beaches, nature reserves, fisher's coves, old fortifications, winding lanes, and sleepy villages characterize the area. All the principal attractions lie along the main road from Somerset Bridge to the Royal Naval Dockyard, which is at the end of Ireland Island.

Although we are classifying this as a walking tour, because of the distances involved, you may want to rent a bicycle or moped to help you cover the longer stretches.

From the center of Hamilton, you can take a ferry to Somerset. Check the schedule, as some boats take 30 minutes to get there, while others take up to an hour. The longer trip gives you more time to take in the waters of Bermuda's Great Sound. You can take your cycle or moped aboard the ferry. You can also see the West End by public bus; refer to Chapter 7, "What to See & Do," for details on how to visit by bus.

To begin the tour, take the ferry from Hamilton to:

1. **Somerset Bridge,** linking Somerset Island with the rest of Bermuda. It was one of the first three bridges constructed in the 1600s, and is said to be the smallest drawbridge in the world—its opening is just wide enough to accommodate a sailboat mast. Near the bridge you can take a look at the old Somerset Post Office and see an 18th-century cottage known as Crossways.

After viewing this, walk up Somerset Road for some 75 yards to the entrance to the:

2. **Railway Trail,** which is confined to pedestrians, cyclists, and bikers. This trail follows the path of old "Rattle and Shake," the former Bermuda Railway line that once ran across the entire length of the island. Since it is unlikely that you'll walk the whole railway track (although some hearty visitors do just that), you may like to know that this particular section of the track, lying between Somerset Bridge and Sound View Road, is considered one of the most attractive on the island. Parts of the trail open onto the coast, affording panoramic vistas of the Great Sound.

The trail goes across the parkland of Fort Scaur, with its large moat. If you're there around noon, you might consider this as a picnic spot. If you've got all day for Somerset (highly recommended), you might also want to take time out for a swim before returning to your walking or cycling. Others prefer to take lunch at the Lantana Colony Club, one of the most exclusive cottage colonies on Bermuda (see Chapter 5, "Accommodations").

Follow the signposts to:

3. **Fort Scaur,** opening onto Somerset Road. The British, fearing an attack from the United States, constructed this fort on the highest hill in Somerset in the 1870s to protect Her Majesty's Royal Naval Dockyard. A huge dry moat was cut right across Somerset Island. Visitors wander at leisure around this fort, which proved unnecessary, since the feared U.S. invasion never materialized. If you stand on the ramparts, you'll be rewarded with a view of Great Sound. Through a free telescope, you can see such distant sights as St. David's Lighthouse and Fort St. Catherine in the East End of Bermuda. Filled with picnic areas, the fort stands on 22 acres of parkland. If you take the eastern moat all the way down to the Great Sound shore, you'll find ideal places for either swimming or fishing.

After exploring the fort grounds, resume your walk along the railway track and continue north for more than a mile until you come to Sound View Road. Go right here and stroll along this sleepy residential street containing some of the finest cottages in Bermuda. Continue around a wide arc, passing Tranquility Hill and Gwelly and Saltsea Lanes. When you come to Scott's Hill Road, take a right and go along for 85 yards or so to East Shore Road.

At the first junction, a little road branches off to the right. Take it. It's called Cavello Lane, and it will take you to:

Walking Tour–Sandys Parish

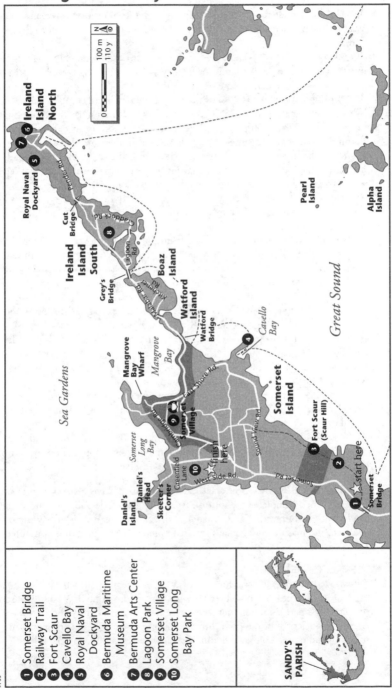

0 100 m
0 110 y

Ireland Island North

Royal Naval Dockyard

Ireland Island South

Cut Bridge

Penderra Rd.

Craddock Rd.

Lagoon Rd.

Grey's Bridge

Malabar Rd.

Kitchener Rd.

Boaz Island

Watford Island

Watford Bridge

Cavello Bay

Somerset Island

Fort Scaur (Scaur Hill)

Sound View Rd.

East Shore Rd.

Great Sound

Pearl Island

Alpha Island

Sea Gardens

Mangrove Bay Wharf

Mangrove Bay

Somerset Long Bay

Somerset Village

Mangrove Rd.

Daniel's Island

Daniel's Head

Skeeter's Corner

Greenfield Lane

West Side Rd.

finish here

Somerset Rd.

start here

Somerset Bridge

Ferry - - - -

① Somerset Bridge
② Railway Trail
③ Fort Scaur
④ Cavello Bay
⑤ Royal Naval Dockyard
⑥ Bermuda Maritime Museum
⑦ Bermuda Arts Center
⑧ Lagoon Park
⑨ Somerset Village
⑩ Somerset Long Bay Park

9733

SANDY'S PARISH

4. Cavello Bay, a sheltered cove and a stopping point for the ferry from Hamilton. Wait for the next ferry and take it (with your cycle or moped) to Watford Bridge and the:

5. Royal Naval Dockyard. You could spend an entire afternoon here, as there is much to see. On Ireland Island, the Dockyard is a sprawling complex spread across six acres. The major attraction here is the:

6. Bermuda Maritime Museum, at the heart of the Dockyard complex. Opened by Queen Elizabeth II in 1975, it allows visitors to cross a moat to explore the keep and the 30-foot-high defensive ramparts. There is an exhibition of Bermuda's old boats, documenting the island's rich maritime history.

Across the street from the Maritime Museum is the Old Cooperage Building, site of the Neptune Cinema. Adjacent to the cinema is the Craft Market, where you can go on a shopping expedition. Next door, call at the:

7. Bermuda Arts Center, which was opened in 1984 by Princess Margaret. It's a showcase of visual arts and crafts of the island and is a nonprofit organization staffed by volunteers.

It's a long walk to Somerset Village from the Dockyard, yet many view cycling or walking along its length one of the highlights of a trip to Bermuda. Some of the best beaches in Bermuda are found here, so if you get tired along the way, take time out for a refreshing dip in the ocean.

Leave by the south entrance to the Dockyard, walking down Pender Road for about half a mile. Cross Cockburn's Cut Bridge, heading for Ireland Island South. Go straight along Cockrange Road, which will take you to:

8. Lagoon Park. Enter the park as you cross over Grey's Bridge onto Ireland Island South. The park, which is crisscrossed by walking trails, has a lagoon populated with ducks and other wildfowl. There are places for picnics in this park, which is always open, charging no admission.

To continue, go across Grey's Bridge, entering Boaz Island, and walk or cycle along Malabar Road. On your right you'll see the calm waters of Mangrove Bay. You'll eventually arrive at:

9. Somerset Village, one of the most charming in Bermuda. One road goes through the village. Although you can do some serious shopping here, most of the stores are actually branches of larger stores in Hamilton.

☕ **TAKE A BREAK**   **Somerset Country Squire Tavern** (see Chapter 6, "Dining," for a complete description). At this English-style pub, you can order sandwiches or burgers, as well as such pub grub as steak-and-kidney pie or "bangers and mash" (sausages and mashed potatoes). The kitchen is also noted for its desserts.

Follow Cambridge Road west to:

10. Somerset Long Bay Park, which is always open. It often attracts families because of its good beach and shallow waters opening onto Long Bay. You can also picnic in the parkland. The nature reserve here is operated by the Bermuda Audubon Society, and the pond lures migrating birds in both spring and autumn, including the Louisiana heron, the snowy egret, and the purple gallinule.

Beaches, Water Sports & Other Outdoor Activities

Bermuda's climate is ideal for outdoor sports activities, the most popular of which among tourists are tennis and golf. If you're an enthusiast of either game, you'll find a fair number of tennis courts and professionally designed golf courses around the island where you may practice your swing, often with players of better than average ability. But if you should hesitate to pick up a racket or golf club because your game has been somewhat neglected of late, fear not: your Bermudian partner, on the court or on the links, will deem it quite improper to remark that your game is anything but superb; and if a word of friendly criticism is ever offered, be assured that it will be as gentle as the ocean breezes that sweep over the island.

1 Spectator Sports

The most often played spectator sports, in this tradition-bound British colony, are cricket, soccer, field hockey, and the not terribly genteel game of rugby. Boating, yachting, and sailing are also favorites, as there is a great deal of opportunity to participate in these water sports.

An overview of the country's sports-related options is given below. The Bermuda Department of Tourism can provide dates and venues for upcoming events.

CRICKET Its arcane rules have been memorized and are understood by far more Bermudians than you might have realized before your arrival. If you arrive in midsummer (the game's seasonal high point), you'll probably see several regional teams practicing on cricket fields throughout the island. Each match includes enough pageantry to remind participants of the game's imperial antecedents, and enough conviviality (picnics, socializing, and chitchat among the spectators) to provide sociological insights into Bermuda. The year's most important cricket event, the Cup Match Cricket Festival, occurs during late July or early August. Then, playoffs between Bermuda-based and visiting teams occur at the St. George's Cricket Club, Willington Slip Rd. (☎ 441/297-0374), and at the Somerset Cricket Club, Broome St. off Somerset Rd. (☎ 441/234-0327). Over the rest of the year, these organizations keep in close touch with the various cricket-related activities throughout the island.

FIELD HOCKEY   One of the great games of women's athletics involves opposing teams armed with curved wooden mallets. Each side—usually clad in knee socks and either shorts or kilts—tries to drive a small white ball into the opposing team's net. Bermuda has several different teams that play against one another on Sunday afternoons between October and April. In September, Bermuda welcomes massive throngs of field hockey enthusiasts from throughout the Atlantic basin. The venue is the Hockey Festival, held every year at the National Sports Club, Middle Road, Devonshire Parish (☎ **441/236-6994**). Admission is usually free.

GOLF   Enthusiasts claim that Bermuda offers some of the finest all-around golfing terrain in the world. Part of this derives from the climate, which supports lush driving ranges and putting greens. In addition, the ever-present golfing enthusiasts play at surprisingly high levels. Golf tournaments are held throughout the year, culminating in the annual, much publicized Bermuda Open in early October. Both amateurs and professionals are welcome to vie for one of the most sought after golfing prizes in the world.

HORSERACING   If you count yourself among the horse-loving set, check to see what events, if any, are taking place at the National Equestrian Club, Vesey Street in Devonshire (☎ **441/234-0485**). Beginning in September and lasting through Easter, harness races are staged about twice every month. One of the major equestrian events occurs in October, the FEI/Samsung Dressage Competition and Show-Jumping. More details are available from the Bermuda Equestrian Federation, P.O. Box DV-583, Devonshire DV BX (☎ **441/295-4434**). If you can't reach this organization on the phone (highly likely), ask at the tourist office or read the local press for news of events.

RUGBY   A blend of American-style football with European soccer, this rough 'n tumble game attracts many aficionados within Bermuda. Rugby players (devoid of protective padding) from several hotly competitive local teams seem to revel in this violent sport. The Easter Rugby Classic, attracting teams from throughout the British Commonwealth, is the final event in the island's rugby season, which runs between September and April. The locale for virtually every rugby game in Bermuda is within the National Sports Club, Middle Road, Devonshire Parish (☎ **441/236-6994**).

SOCCER   The fast-paced game of soccer is gaining increasing numbers of fans on both sides of the Atlantic. Bermudians view soccer as an important part of elementary education and therefore actively encourage this sport for children and teenagers. In early April, teams from countries around the Atlantic and Caribbean compete for the Diadora Youth Soccer Cup, with players in three different age divisions. Games are held on various fields and playing grounds throughout the island. More accessible to visitors at other times, however, are the many games between high school athletic teams, held regularly throughout the year.

YACHTING   Bermuda has never hesitated to draw upon its geographical position in the mid-Atlantic to lure the yachting crowd. The yacht-racing season runs every year from March to November, with most racing events taking place on weekends. Most yachting occurs within the relatively calm waters of Bermuda's Great Sound. Although watching these races from land can be confusing because of the shifting sightlines, the best land vantage points include Spanish Point, the islands northeast of Somerset, and Hamilton Harbour. Closer views are available from the decks of privately owned boats that anchor near the edge of the race course. Despite the confusion among newcomers when watching these carefully choreographed regattas, the sight of a fleet of racing craft with spinnakers and pennants aloft is always exciting.

In late June, Bermuda is the final destination in two of the most important annual races of the yachting world: the Annapolis–Bermuda Race and the even more prestigious Newport–Bermuda Race. Both provide enough visual distraction and maritime pageantry to keep even the most demanding maritime devotees enthralled. Participating yachts range from 30 to 100 feet in length, and their skippers are said to be among the most dedicated in the world.

Around Halloween, the autumn winds propel dozens of less exotic racing craft through the waters of the Great Sound. These compete in a series of one-on-one playoffs for the King Edward VII Gold Cup International Match Racing Tournament.

The island's yachting options are by no means limited to the above-mentioned handful of international competitions. Bermuda's sheltered bays and windswept open seas provide year-round enticement for anyone who has ever wanted to experience the thrill of a snapping jib and taut mainsail.

2 Beaches & Outdoor Activities

BEACHES

Bermuda is one of the world's leading beach resorts, its miles of pink-sand shoreline broken now and then by cliffs to form sheltered coves. Many stretches have shallow water for some distance out and sandy bottoms, making them safe for children and nonswimmers. Hotels and private clubs often have their own private beaches, but there is no shortage of public facilities in Bermuda, which are under the supervision of the Parks Division of the Department for Agriculture and Fisheries.

At most of the public beaches you'll find public restrooms and usually a place nearby for drinks or snacks. Although dozens of spots appropriate for sunbathing, swimming, and beachcombing will present themselves to you as you explore Bermuda, here is a listing of the island's most famous, arranged clockwise beginning with the south shore beaches closest to the city of Hamilton.

ELBOW BEACH   One of the most consistently popular beaches in Bermuda, Paget Parish's Elbow Beach incorporates almost a mile of (occasionally interrupted) pale pink sand and the swimming facilities of at least three hotels into its perimeter. There's usually a $3 fee imposed for visitors who are not residents of one of these hotels. The beach, because of the protective coral reefs that surround it, is usually considered one of the safest beaches on the island, and is the preferred venue for foreign college students vacationing on Bermuda during Easter break. The Elbow Beach Hotel/A Wyndham Resort (☎ 441/236-3535) offers umbrellas and beach chairs for rent; toilet facilities are available. Adjacent to the paid facilities lies the free public beach. Take bus no. 7 or 8 from Hamilton.

ASTWOOD COVE   Set within Warwick Parish, at the bottom of a steep and winding road that intersects with South Shore Road, this beach does not have any problem with overcrowding throughout most of the year because of its remote location. Astwood Park provides a lovely green backdrop to the beach itself. Take bus no. 7 or 8 from Southampton.

Ten Best Public Beaches

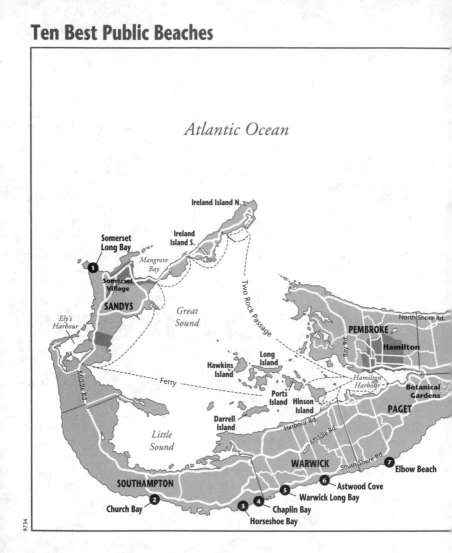

WARWICK LONG BAY Very different from the sheltered coves of nearby Chaplin and Horseshoe Bays (see below), this popular beach features a half-mile stretch of sand, one of the longest on the island. Against a backdrop of scrubland and low grasses, the beach lies on the southern side of South Shore Park, in Warwick Parish. Despite the frequent winds, the waves are surprisingly small because of an offshore reef. Jutting above the water less than 200 feet offshore is a jagged coral island that, because of its contoured shape, appears to be floating above the water's foam. There are restrooms at the beach's western end.

CHAPLIN BAY Straddling the boundary between Warwick and Southampton Parish, this small but secluded beach almost completely disappears during storms or particularly high tides. Geologists usually admire the open-air coral barrier that partially separates one half of the beach from the other. Chaplin Bay, like its more westerly (and more famous) neighbor, Horseshoe Bay (see below), lies at the southern extremity of South Shore Park. Take bus no. 7 or 8 from Hamilton.

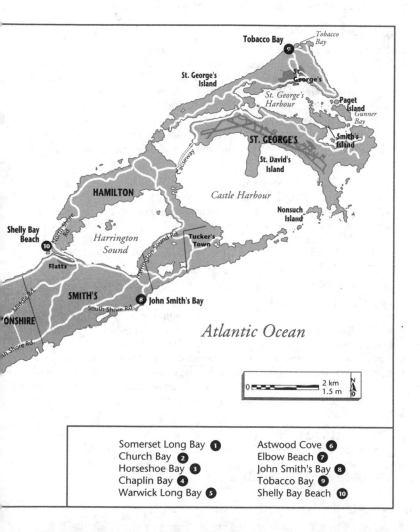

Somerset Long Bay ❶	Astwood Cove ❻
Church Bay ❷	Elbow Beach ❼
Horseshoe Bay ❸	John Smith's Bay ❽
Chaplin Bay ❹	Tobacco Bay ❾
Warwick Long Bay ❺	Shelly Bay Beach ❿

HORSESHOE BAY BEACH   Bermuda's most famous beach is the one at Horseshoe Bay, South Shore Road, Southampton Parish, where the Beach House (☎ 441/238-2651) contains lockers, changing rooms, toilets, and showers, as well as food, drink, and rental equipment for the beach or surf. You can also buy magazines, suntan lotion, and other sundries you may need. Take bus no. 7 or 8 from Hamilton.

CHURCH BAY   Although it lies along Bermuda's southwestern edge, at the point in Southampton Parish where the island hooks off to the northeast (and where the waves pound the shore mercilessly), this beach is sheltered by rows of offshore reefs. Marine life abounds within the relatively calm waters, much to the delight of snorkelers and swimmers. And if you're just planning to lounge in the sun, the beach offers unusually deep pink sands. Take bus no. 7 or 8 from Hamilton.

SOMERSET LONG BAY   Whenever offshore storms trouble the waters north-west of Bermuda, the water here is considered unsafe for swimming. Its bottom isn't always sandy or of a consistent depth, and many people consider the beach more suited to beachwalking than for actual swimming. Despite that, it's isolated enough from the bulk of Bermuda's population to appeal to anyone looking for seclusion. The undeveloped parkland of Sandys Parish shelters it from the rest of the island, and the beach's long length—about a quarter-mile of crescent-shaped sand—is unusual by Bermudian standards. You'll find restrooms, changing facili-ties, and panoramic sunsets. Reach it via Cambridge Road in Sandys Parish, or take bus no. 7 or 8 from Hamilton.

SHELLY BAY BEACH   Set on the north shore of Hamilton Parish within a cove whose encircling peninsula partially shelters it from the direct attack of the mid-Atlantic waves, this public beach offers abundant pink sand, changing rooms, a shop where you can buy souvenirs and film, a snack bar, and facilities where you can rent lounge chairs, beach towels, and snorkeling equipment. The Shelly Bay Beach House (☎ **441/293-1327**) is open daily from 10am to 7pm. Take bus no. 10 or 11 from Hamilton.

TOBACCO BAY BEACH   This is the most frequently visited beach on St. George's Island, and by far the most popular with day-trippers who visit the his-toric town of St. George's from their residence within more westerly Bermudian hotels. Visually, the beach probably resembles the broad open sands of Bermuda's southern shore more than anything else on the north side of the island. The beach's pale pink sand lies sheltered within a coral-sided cove a short walk west of both Fort St. Catherine and St. Catherine Beach (see below). Look for the area's Beach House, Naval Tanks Hill, St. George's (☎ **441/293-9711**), which offers equip-ment rentals, toilets, changing rooms, showers, and a snack bar. Take bus no. 10 or 11 from Hamilton.

JOHN SMITH'S BAY   This is the only public beach within Smith's Parish, and as such, tends to be popular with residents of Bermuda's eastern end. Long, flat, and richly scattered with pale pink sand, this beach usually has a lifeguard in warm weather. Toilet and changing facilities are on site. Take bus no. 1 from Hamilton.

BICYCLING

With a year-round average temperature of 70° F degrees, the weather in Bermuda is often ideal for bicycling unless you run into a rainy day, when you're liable to get splashed by a passing car. However, if conditions are balmy, you can have fun cycling, stay in shape, and take a hands-on approach to your sightseeing.

Push-bikes, the term Bermudians use to distinguish bicycles from mopeds, are a popular form of transport. Bicycles can be rented hourly, daily, or for the entire length of your Bermuda holiday. For information about cycle and scooter rentals, refer to "Getting Around" in Chapter 4. All the cycle liveries recommended also rent bicycles, and many hotels also make these available to their guests, with or without a fee. Fees in general are from $10 to $15 per day for the first day, and are then reduced to $5 per day for each day that follows. Both 3-speed and 10-speed pedal bikes are rented. It's always good to call one of these cycle liveries as far in advance as possible, since demand is great, especially from April through October.

Much of the island's terrain consists of flat stretches, although those hills provide what the government refers to as "challenges." Some of these climbs are steep with a push-bike, especially highways that run north and south along the island. The South Shore Road in Southampton and Warwick parishes often have bikers huffing and puffing.

Most roadways are well paved and maintained. The island's speed limit is 20 mph for all vehicles. One has to exercise caution when riding a bike or scooter on Bermuda's roads. In spite of the low speed limits, the roads are narrow and winding, and the traffic, especially during the day, tends to be heavy with Bermudians riding by in their cars. The operators of most cars and other vehicles are considerate of cyclists, but a car can approach suddenly without honking. The government discourages unnecessary blowing of horns. You might even be overtaken by fellow cyclists, as bicycle racing is one of the most popular sports in Bermuda.

In spite of all the tourist data extolling the glories of bicycle riding in Bermuda, the truth is that the roads are not suitable for beginning riders. You might reconsider before allowing a preteen to go cycling on the island. Some of the most interesting trails for cyclists are in Devonshire and Smith's parishes, and the sloping hills there will guarantee that you get your exercise for the day. But the landscapes make all that pushing worthwhile. Spittal Pond, a wildlife sanctuary, is best for cycling and has biking paths running along scenic shoreline cliffs. It is one of the most rewarding targets for the cyclist.

If you're a real demon on a bike, you can go further west and take the vigorous challenge by pumping up to Gibb's Hill Lighthouse, the oldest cast-iron lighthouse in the Western Hemisphere. The panoramic view from the foot of the lighthouse not only gives you a chance to catch your breath but makes the trip worth the effort.

If you'd like to go on a bicycle ride and a picnic, head for Sandys Parish. Start by going over Somerset Bridge, the smallest drawbridge in the world, then pedal along Somerset Road to Fort Scaur Park. Once there, enjoy a panoramic view of Ely's Harbour and then sample the goods in your picnic basket.

Only the hardiest cyclist traverses Bermuda in one day. The island is just 21 miles long and it is possible to bicycle across it in one day. But you'd better be a serious biker of great stamina. For most, it's far better to break up Bermuda into

Bird-Watching

There is a nucleus of bird-watching enthusiasts in Bermuda, but there are not many organized tours. Visiting bird-watchers are advised to make arrangements for tours with local enthusiasts.

Bird-watchers might contact David Wingate, Conservation Officer for the Bermuda government at **441/236-4201** or Eric Amos at **441/236-9056.** They occasionally—but not always—advise by phone of the island's best retreats, walkways, and hideaways. Before calling, pick up a copy of David Wingate's *Check List and Guide to the Birds of Bermuda* or Eric Amos's *A Guide to the Birds of Bermuda*, both of which titles are available at local bookstores.

You can also contact the Bermuda Audubon Society, P.O. Box 1328, Hamilton HM, Bermuda (☎ **441/293-7394**), for information about any organized field trips for birding in Bermuda.

a series of cycle trips, deciding on what interests you parish by parish and proceeding from there. To save cycling time, you can take your bike aboard various ferries, then begin cycling once you reach your desired destination. Bicycles are carried free on the ferries.

It is also possible to take your bike along the Bermuda Railway Trail (see p. 167). This is Bermuda's premier cycling route. The route is restricted to bicycle or pedestrian traffic.

The Railway Trail can be divided into seven sections, each with its own flavor and character. Visitors may choose a full day's start-to-finish cycle tour, or a detailed exploration of just one area of the trail.

The trail begins in Sandys Parish, the westernmost extremity of the island, where the Gilbert Nature Reserve and the Heydon Trust Estate give contrasting views of rural Bermuda. The first part of the trail ends at Somerset Bridge, the smallest drawbridge in the world.

The second section of the trail crosses from Sandys into Southampton Parish. A sense of 19th-century Bermudian life is felt here; Southampton includes much of Bermuda's 500 acres of arable land, as well as examples of traditional manor house architecture.

Entering Warwick Parish, the trail skirts Little Sound and then passes through an allspice forest. Approaching the island's central area, the west end's woodlands and fields become dotted with Bermuda's traditional old houses, some still accompanied by domed water tanks and old stone butteries. The trail then rises above Paget Marsh, a National Trust Nature Reserve, which includes Bermuda's oldest palmetto forest and a wide variety of bird life. The tour of Paget Parish ends with a ride through a 450-foot long railway tunnel, partially roofed with the thick roots of a rubber tree.

Picking up beyond Hamilton, Bermuda's capital city, the trail leads to Palmetto House, built in the shape of a cross and virtually unchanged since the 1700s.

After crossing a cricket pitch, or field, while moving from Devonshire into Hamilton Parish, the trail then edges the wild coastline along Bailey's Bay.

The final section of the trail is in the Parish of St. George's, where the windswept coast is rocky and rugged. The mariner's landmark of Sugarloaf Hill offers a panoramic seascape and view of St. George's.

FISHING

Bermuda is considered one of the world's finest fishing centers, especially when it comes to light tackle fishing. Blue marlin catches have increased dramatically, and Bermuda can also add bill-fishing to an already enviable reputation. Fishing is a year-round sport in Bermuda, but is best from May through November. No license is required.

Visitors to the island may obtain fishing information from the International Game Fish Association representative for Bermuda: Tom Smith (☎ 441/ 238-0112).

Bermuda Game Fishing Association, P.O. Box HM 1306, Hamilton HM FX, Bermuda, is an advisory body representing all the IGFA-affiliated clubs in Bermuda and caretaker for all local records and world records held locally.

DEEP-SEA FISHING

Wahoo, amberjack, blue marlin, white marlin, dolphin, tuna, and more can be found in these waters. In addition, Bermuda offers a wealth of equipment to help you get them.

Bermuda Sportsfishing

Creek View House, 8 Tulo Lane, Pembroke HM 02, Bermuda. ☎ **441/295-2370.** Daily 7am–10pm. Bus No. 1, 2, 10, or 11.

Bermuda Sportsfishing is run by the De Silva family, who have been in business for many years. They charge $600 for a half day of fishing and from $825 to $850 for a full day. If given enough notice, the family can compose groups of six, in which case the charge is, for example, only $100 per person for a half day with all equipment included in the price. Boats include a 50-foot all-wood vessel with two bathrooms, a kitchenette, three "fighting chairs," and space for up to 20 persons. There is also a 36-foot sportsfishing boat available.

REEF FISHING

Reef fishing is likely to turn up such catches as greater amberjack, almaco jack, great barracuda, little tunny, Bermuda chub, gray snapper, yellowtail snapper, and assorted bottom fish. Three major reef bands lie off Bermuda's shore. The closest one begins about ¹/₂ mile offshore, stretching for nearly 5 miles. The Challenger Bank is about 14 miles offshore, and Argus Bank is the most distant, at about 30 miles. Of course, the farther you go, the more likely you are to turn up big fish.

Several charter companies offer either half- or full-day charters. Arrangements can be made through Bermuda Sportsfishing (see "Deep-Sea Fishing," above).

SHORE FISHING

This type of fishing turns up such catches as bonefish, palometa (pompano), gray snapper, and great barracuda. Locals and most visitors prefer shore fishing at Spring Benny's Bay or West Whale Bay. Great Sound and St. George's Harbour are other promising grounds.

For most activities, directors at hotels will make arrangements for you. If they can't, go to **Mangrove Marina, Ltd.,** end of Cambridge Rd., Mangrove Bay, in Somerset (☎ **441/234-0914**). A rod, reel, and tackle can be rented there for $6 for 4 hours or $10 a day. A $20 deposit is required. You might also try **Four Winds Fishing Tackle, Ltd.,** 2 Woodlands Rd., in Pembroke (☎ **441/292-7466**). A rod, reel, and tackle rents there for $10 for 24 hours, requiring a $30 deposit.

GOLF

Since the first course was laid out in 1922, golf has been one of Bermuda's most popular sports. It can be played year-round, but early spring, winter, and fall offer the best seaside golf conditions. You must arrange your starting time at any of the eight courses in advance through the management of your guesthouse or hotel. Women's and men's clubs, either right- or left-handed, are available at each course, and most leading stores in Bermuda sell golf balls.

Tournaments are held throughout the year, with top players participating. For information, contact the **Bermuda Golf Association,** P.O. Box HM 433, Hamilton HM BX, Bermuda (☎ **441/238-1367**).

The Castle Harbour Hotel golf course is considered one of the most scenic courses on the island, while the Port Royal, designed by Robert Trent Jones, is a challenge to your golfing expertise. Two famous courses, the Mid Ocean Club at Tucker's Town and the Riddells Bay Golf and Country Club, are private, and introduction by a member is required before you can play there. Certain deluxe hotels can sometimes secure playing privileges at the Riddells Bay Golf and Country Club. One of the most photographed golf courses in Bermuda is at the

Southampton Princess Hotel, where rolling hills and flowering shrubs add to the players' enjoyment.

The golf courses listed below that are part of a hotel complex also allow nonguests to use their facilities. All of these golf courses have pros, and you can take lessons if you wish.

Belmont Hotel, Golf & Country Club

Between Harbour and Middle Rds., Warwick Parish. ☎ 441/236-1301. Daily 7am–5pm. Transportation: Ferry from Hamilton.

A Scotsman, Emmett Devereux, designed this 18-hole, par 70, 5,777-yard course in 1923, and its layout has long been a challenge to golfers. All golfing magazines write of its par-five 11th hole, with a severe dogleg left with a blind tee shot. It's sometimes difficult to finish uphill at number 18. Crystal caves under the turf sometimes cause the ball to roll unpredictably. In spite of these disadvantages, golf pros sometimes recommend the Belmont for beginning golfers. The first hole is said to be "confidence building." It is estimated that with a 9 or 10 handicap, golfers will shoot in the 70s at Belmont. But no one guarantees that. Most of the course is inland and there are few views of the Atlantic, as there are at many other courses in Bermuda. *Warning:* On weekends rounds of five hours or more are often typical. Greens fees are free for hotel guests, $53 for others. A full set of golf clubs rents for $25; gas golf carts rent for $34, handcarts $8. It can also be played as a 9-hole course.

Castle Harbour Golf Club

Tucker's Town, Hamilton Parish. ☎ 441/293-2040. Daily 7:30am–6pm. Bus No. 22. Exit off Harrington Sound Rd., follow Paynters Rd. to Castle Harbour resort entrance.

This 18-hole, par 71, 6,440-yard course is the only one in Bermuda requiring the use of a golf cart. Designed by architect Charles Banks, this resort championship course features challenging tee shots. The first tee by the clubhouse has often been compared to a "crow's nest" by golfing magazines. It gives you an immediate indication of what to expect with this course, a panorama of Castle Harbour's blue-green waters with the darker Atlantic in the distance. As you look down over the fairway, you'll think you're seeing the course from a helicopter. Winds sweeping in from the Atlantic make this course a constant challenge. Sometimes the greens are elevated, especially the 190-yard, par-three 13th hole, lying atop an embankment that rises about 100 feet. Golfers consider the 235-yard, par-three 18th hole as the hardest finishing hole on the island. That becomes even more evident if the Atlantic decides to send a wind out of the northwest. There are not as many sand traps as on other Bermuda courses. This is one of the costlier courses to play, but at least part of the money goes into maintaining the best-kept greens on the island. Greens fees are $85 for 9 or 18 holes. There are no caddies. A full set of clubs rents for $25; gas golf carts rent for $38 for 18 holes (mandatory use of golf carts); and shoe rental is $6.

Ocean View Golf Course

31 Parsons Lane, Devonshire. ☎ 441/295-6500. Daily 7:30am–6:30pm. Bus No. 2.

This course has 9 holes, par 35, 2,956 yards. Back in the 1950s, this was a club for African-Bermudians. Later, as other clubs started to admit black players, the course fell into disrepair. However, after spending some $3 million on it, the government has vastly improved the course, although old reputations live on. In the center of Bermuda in Devonshire Parish, it offers panoramic views of the ocean from many of its elevated tees. Golfers consider its terrain "unpredictable," and that combined with rambling hills make the course more challenging than it first appears. A few holes have as many as six tees. Winds from Great Sound might have more effect on your score than you think at first. The green on the 177-yard, par-three 5th hole has been cut into the coral hillside. Draped with semitropical vines, it gives golfers the eerie feeling of hitting the ball into a Bermudian cave. Traditionally, weekdays here have been the least crowded of any course in Bermuda. With improvements to the course, that condition might not always be true, however. Greens fees are $25 (for 9 holes or the course played for 18 holes). There are no caddies. A full set of clubs rents for $15; gas golf carts rent for $15 for 9 holes, $28 for 18 holes; handcart rental is $5 for 9 or 18 holes.

Port Royal Golf Course

Middle Rd., Southampton Parish. ☎ **441/234-0974.** Daily 7am–5pm. Bus No. 7 or 8.

This is an 18-hole, par 71, 6,565-yard public course. Jack Nicklaus might be found at the much-publicized 16th hole, a favorite for photo layouts in golf magazines. Both the 16th and also the 15th hole ring the craggy cliffs around Whale Bay. Sometimes winds from the Atlantic taunt golf balls hit from these holes. The 7th and 8th holes are, respectively, a dogleg par 5 and a windy par 3. Port Royal is so popular that some avid golfers have been known to reserve starting times a year in advance. Golf architect Robert Trent Jones designed the course along the oceanside terrain, and the course is owned and operated by the Bermuda government. Greens fees are $50 (reduced rates are available after 4pm). There are no caddies. A full set of clubs rents for $16, golf carts for $28, and handcarts for $7. The clubhouse, which overlooks the ocean and the 9th and 18th greens, boasts a bar and a restaurant serving breakfast and lunch.

Southampton Princess Golf Club

101 South Shore Rd., Hamilton. ☎ **441/238-0446.** Daily 7am–5pm. Bus No. 7 or 8.

On the grounds of one of the most luxurious hotels in Bermuda, this 18-hole, par 54, 2,684-yard course occupies not only the loftiest but one of the most scenic settings on the island. Elevated tees, strategically placed bunkers, and plenty of water hazards make this a challenge for golfers, who have been known to use every club in their bag when the wind blows in from the Atlantic. Against the backdrop of the Gibbs Hill Lighthouse, the 16th hole was designed in a cup ringed by flowering bushes. The vertical drop on holes one and two is almost 200 feet. Even experienced golfers like to "break in" on this course before taking on some of Bermuda's more challenging courses. Because of the hotel's irrigation system, we have found this course green when some other courses experienced "summer brown-outs." Greens fees for hotel guests are $29.50, $34.50 for visitors. There are no caddies. Rental of clubs is $13 per 18 holes and gas golf carts rent for $27 for hotel guests, $30 for visitors.

St. George's Golf Club

1 Park Rd., St. George's Parish. ☎ **441/297-8067.** Apr–Sept, Mon–Fri 8am–5:30pm; Sat–Sun, 7:30am–5:30pm. Off-season, Mon–Fri 8am–4:45pm, Sat–Sun 7:30am–4:45pm. Bus No. 6, 8, 10, or 11.

Redesigned by Robert Trent Jones Jr., this 18-hole, par 62, 4,043-yard course is the newest of the Bermuda government's golf courses. Lying on a headland at the northeastern tip of the island, it is within walking distance of St. George's. Links run along the hillsides, giving players panoramic vistas of the ocean. That also means that Atlantic wind velocity will have a big effect on your game. On some of the par-3s players need everything from a nine-iron to a driver to reach the green. Greens are the smallest on the island, some appearing no more than two dozen feet across. All that salt air makes greens slick. Traditionally, the course is not crowded at midweek. Greens fees for 9 or 18 holes are $35. There are no caddies. A full set of clubs rent for $16; gas golf carts go for $28, and handcarts for $5.

HORSEBACK RIDING

Spicelands Riding Centre

Middle Rd., Warwick Parish. ☎ 441/238-8212. Call daily 9am to 5pm the day before to make arrangements. Bus No. 7 or 8.

Here you'll find trail rides for $35 per person for 1 hour. The popular early morning ride, a 2-hour jaunt with a full breakfast following, costs $45 per person. From May to September, weekly evening rides costing $35 are offered.

Lee Bow Riding Stables

1 Tribe Rd., Devonshire Parish. ☎ 441/236-4181. Make reservations one day in advance; call daily 9am to 5pm. Bus No. 3.

Lee Bow is especially geared for children aged 6 to 18, although riders of all ages are accommodated, often in small groups of no more than four. Instruction is available. Lessons and trail rides are given for $25 per hour.

PARASAILING

Southampton Princess Hotel

101 South Shore Rd., Southampton Parish. ☎ 441/238-2332. Daily 8:30am–5pm. Transportation: Private hotel ferryboat from Hamilton.

From April to November, this hotel offers parasailing from a 40-foot catamaran. Rates are $50 per person for a single parachute. If you go only for the boat ride, the cost is $10 per person if space is available.

Marriott's Castle Harbour Resort

Paynters Town Rd., Hamilton Parish. ☎ 441/293-2543. Daily 8am–5pm (until 7pm July through September). Bus No. 2 from St. George's.

Parasailing here is from a Nordic Ascender, and up to six persons are taken out in a boat at a time. Single parachute rides cost $50 per person. If space is available, you can go along for just the boat ride for $15.

SAILING

Bermuda is one of the world's sailing capitals. Sail-yourself boats are available on a half-day (4-hour) or full-day (8-hour) basis.

Salt Kettle Boat Rentals

Ltd., Salt Kettle Rd., P.O. Box PG 201, Paget PG BX, Bermuda. ☎ 441/236-4863. Daily 9am–5pm. Bus No. 8.

Salt Kettle rents Sunfish, Daysailers, and motorboats. Sunfish are rented at $55 (4 hours) or $85 (8 hours), and a 17-foot O'Day Daysailer costs $85 (4 hours) or $135 (8 hours). Sailing instruction is also given.

Southside Scuba Water Sports

Grotto Bay Beach Hotel, 11 Blue Hole Hill, Hamilton Parish. ☎ 441/293-2915. Daily 9am–5pm. Bus No. 1, 3, 10, or 11.

Southside Scuba rents Sunfish for $50 (4 hours) or $95 (8 hours). A Broadsailer costs $20 per hour or $50 for 4 hours, and a kayak goes for $12 per hour. A wide range of other equipment is also available for rent, including Paddle Cats and Puffers.

Bermuda Caribbean Yacht Charter

2A Light House Rd., Southampton Parish. ☎ **441/238-8578.** Daily 9am–5pm. Bus No. 7 or 8.

Yachts for charter with a licensed skipper can be rented at a number of places, including Bermuda Caribbean Yacht Charter. The 52-foot ketch *Night Wind* operates from April to November and charges $320 for a half day, $500 for a full day for six passengers. Any additional person pays an extra $20 each.

SNORKELING

Marine biologists have always claimed that far more lies below the surface of the sea than usually appears above it. If you're a snorkeling enthusiast, a handful of Bermuda-based companies are ready, willing, and able to help you, or else you can be adventurous and do it on your own.

The best places to go snorkeling are at any of the public beaches (see Beaches, above). Many hotels are right on the beach and will either lend or rent fins, masks, and snorkels to you, plus advise you of the best sites in your neighborhood, so you don't have to cross the island.

You have a choice of going snorkeling on your own or else taking one of the cruises from an outfit recommended.

Die-hard snorkelers—some of whom visit Bermuda every year—as well as many snorkeling Bermudians, prefer Church Bay to all other spots for snorkeling. Church Bay lies on the south shore (continue west beyond Gibbs Hill Lighthouse), past the Southampton Princess Golf Course. This little cove, which seems to be waiting for a movie camera, is carved out of coral cliffs. Well protected and filled with snug little nooks in the coral, it also has the advantage of having the reefs fairly close to land. However, seas can be rough, as they can anywhere in Bermuda, so caution is always advised.

At the eastern end of the south shore, John Smith's Bay, lying to the east of Spittal Pond Nature Reserve and Watch Hill Park, is another preferred spot, especially if your hotel is in the east. Even more convenient, especially for snorkelers staying at St. George's, or else at a hotel near the airport, is Tobacco Bay, directly north of the St. George's Golf Course. Another good spot for snorkelers is West Whale Bay, although it is small. This bay lies along the south shore in the west end in Southampton. It is west of the Port Royal Golf Course. Yet another area preferred by many snorkelers is along the north shore of Devonshire, north of the Ocean View Golf Course.

Bermuda is known for the gin-clear purity of some of its waters, as well as for its vast array of coral reefs. Both inshore and offshore wrecks can be discovered, and this adds to the thrill of snorkeling.

If you don't like cold waters, the best snorkeling is possible from May through October, although snorkeling is a year-round pursuit. Wet suits are often worn in winter in waters with temperatures in the 60s.

The waters of the Atlantic can be rough at any time of the year, especially in winter. Therefore, winter snorkelers should head for the more sheltered waters of Castle Harbour and Harrington Sound, both large bodies of water lying in the east end of Bermuda. The reward for the snorkeler here is the bizarre coral formations, the underwater caves, the grottoes, and especially the schools of brilliantly hued fish.

If you don't go on a snorkeling cruise, it's better to rent a small boat (see "Sailing," above). Some of these boats have glass bottoms and rentals can be by the hour or else a morning or afternoon rental, or even a full day.

Some of the best snorkeling sites are only accessible from a boat; others can be reached by swimming, but it'd be a long swim. Of course, if you rent a boat, the rental company will give you advice. It seems that because of all the reefs around Bermuda, wrecked boats abound. If you're not familiar with Bermuda waters, it will be necessary to stay in the sounds, harbors, and bays, especially the already mentioned Castle Harbour and Harrington Sound. If you want to make trips to the reefs, it's better to take one of the recommended snorkeling cruises below.

Bermuda Water Sports

At the Grotto Bay Beach Hotel, Hamilton Parish. ☎ **441/293-2640.** May–Nov booking hours daily 9am–1pm and 6–9pm. Bus No. 1, 3, 10, or 11.

This center offers a glass-bottom snorkel cruise aboard a 60-foot motorized catamaran. Priced at around $35 for a $3^1/_2$ hour cruise, the experience includes free use of snorkeling equipment, and the expertise of a crew well-versed in the marine life of Bermuda's offshore reefs. There's a cash bar and a freshwater shower on board, as well as recorded music that imbues the event with something like a private party atmosphere.

Bermuda Water Tours

P.O. Box HM 1572, Hamilton Parish HMGX. ☎ **441/295-3727.** Booking hours 24 hour a day. Bus No. 1, 2, 10, or 11.

This outfit departs for snorkeling tours twice daily between April 1 and mid-November (weather permitting) from the docks near Hamilton Harbour's Ferryboat Terminal. Large glass-bottom boats, well equipped with a cash bar, showers, and an ample assortment of free snorkeling equipment, are used. On the return trip, complimentary rum swizzles and soft drinks are offered. A $3^1/_2$-hour tour costs $39.

Salt Kettle Boat Rentals

Salt Kettle, Paget Parish. ☎ **441/236-4863.** May 15–Oct 15 Mon–Fri 9:30am and 1:30pm and Sat 9:30am only. Call 9am–5pm Mon–Sat. Transportation: Ferryboat from Hamilton every 30 minutes.

Salt Kettle offers snorkeling cruises on a 35-foot cruiser (without a glass bottom) every Monday through Saturday. The $35, four-hour tour includes free use of snorkeling equipment. The boat stops above offshore reefs teeming with marine life, as well as at the sites of two underwater shipwrecks whose rusted hulks are eerily evocative of the many maritime disasters that so influenced the early history of Bermuda. Rum swizzles and soft drinks are included in the price.

TENNIS

Nearly all the big hotels, and many of the smaller ones, have courts, most of which are usually lit for night play. It's best to come to Bermuda with your own tennis clothing and sneakers since such an outfit may be required. Colored tennis togs, so popular in America, arrived in Bermuda some time ago—tennis outfits no longer have to be white.

Each of the facilities described below has a tennis pro on duty, and lessons can be arranged. In case you didn't come prepared, you can rent rackets and buy balls at each place.

Government Tennis Stadium

Cedar Ave., Pembroke Parish. ☎ **441/292-0105** for court reservations and to arrange lessons. Mon–Fri 8am–10pm, Sat–Sun 8am–7pm. Bus No. 1, 2, 10, or 11.

There are three clay and five Plexicushion courts. To play here costs $5 per adult and $3 per junior. An extra $5 is charged for lit play at night. Tennis attire is mandatory. Rackets rent for $4 per hour; balls cost $6 per can.

Port Royal Golf Course

Off Middle Rd., Southampton Parish. ☎ **441/234-0974**. Daily 8am–10pm. Bus No. 7 or 8.

The Port Royal Golf Course also has tennis facilities. The four Plexipave courts cost $8 in daytime; night play is $12 to cover the lights and court costs.

Elbow Beach Hotel/A Wyndham Resort Tennis Courts

60 South Shore Rd., Paget Parish. ☎ **441/236-3535**. Call for bookings daily 9am–5pm. Bus No. 1, 2, or 7.

At the Elbow Beach Hotel, there are five LayKold courts (one for lessons only). Hotel guests are charged $8 (others pay $12) to play here. Two of the courts are lit for night play, when hotel guests pay $12 and visitors are charged $15.

Southampton Princess

101 South Shore Rd., Southampton Parish. ☎ **441/238-1005**. Call daily 9am–5pm for arrangements. Bus No. 7 or 8.

This has Bermuda's largest tennis court layout, with 11 Plexipave courts, 3 of them lit for night play. Hotel guests pay $10 per hour and outsiders are charged $12 per hour; there is a $2 surcharge for lights at night. Rackets rent for $6 per hour, and balls cost $6 per can.

UNDERWATER SPORTS

Bermuda's waters are considered the clearest in the western Atlantic. Hence, they're ideal for scuba diving and snorkeling, as well as for helmet diving.

For snorkeling information, see above. Helmet diving enjoys great popularity in Bermuda. Underwater walkers, clad in helmets that are fed air through hoses connected to the surface, stroll along the sandy bottom in water to depths of 10 to 12 feet. These undersea walks are conducted among the coral reefs, with no lessons or swimming ability necessary. It's even possible to partake with contact lenses. These walks are viewed safe for anyone from 5 to 85 years of age, even non-swimmers. Participants can feed dozens of rainbow-hued fish which take food right from your fingers. They'll also be able to see sponges breathing and coral feeding.

For scuba divers, the "wonders of the deep" unfold as they float over barrel sponges and swoop through thickets of coral.

The waters around Bermuda (and this has been tested scientifically) are said to be the clearest in the Western Atlantic. Water temperatures average 62° F in spring and fall and 83° F in summer. Weather permitting, scuba schools function daily, and all dives are overseen by fully licensed scuba instructors.

Most dives are conducted from 40-foot dive boats, and a wide range of dive sites are covered. Night dives and certifications are offered as well.

Reefs, wreckage of boats and ships, a massive variety of marine life and coral formations, and underwater grottoes—all combine, along with that already clear water, to make Bermuda a choice spot for scuba divers. It's not as dramatic as the Cayman Islands, but may be more suited to novices who can learn the fundamentals and go diving in about 20 to 25 feet of water on the same day as their first lesson.

Die hard scuba fanatics dive all year; however, the best diving months are May through October. The sea is the most tranquil at that time and, as mentioned, the waters are often in the 80s. Oceanside dropoffs can go as deep as 65 feet in Bermuda.

In general, Bermuda reefs are still healthy, in spite of the talk about dwindling fish and dying coral formations. Sometimes, in addition to the rainbow-hued collection of schools of fish, you'll find yourself swimming with a barracuda.

All dive shops display a map of wreck sites, nearly 40 in all, the oldest of which go back 300 years. Actually, this mapped wreckage is only the best-known sites and those in the best condition. It is estimated that there are some 300 wreck sites off the coast of Bermuda. Dive depths to these sites vary between 25 and 85 feet. Inexperienced scuba divers may want to explore wreck sites off the western part of Bermuda, as these are sometimes found in shallow water, perhaps no more than 32 or so feet. Snorkelers sometimes frequent these shallow wreck sites as well.

Many of the hotels, as mentioned, have their own water sports equipment. If not, there are several independent establishments that rent equipment.

Note: Spearfishing is not allowed within one mile of any shore, and spearguns are not permitted in Bermuda.

Blue Water Divers Co. Ltd.

Somerset Bridge, Sandys Parish. ☎ **441/234-1034.** Daily 8am–6pm. Bus No. 6 or 7.

Bermuda's oldest and largest full-service scuba-diving operation offers introductory lessons and dives at $85 for a half-day experience. Daily one- and two-tank dive trips cost $60 and $75, respectively, with a $15 reduction if you have equipment. Snorkeling trips are $34 per half day. Full certification courses are available through PADI, NAUI, and SSI. All equipment is provided. Reservations are necessary.

Helmet Diving

The original undersea walk offered by Bronson Hartley can be arranged by writing or calling Mr. Hartley at 5 Northshore Rd., P.O. Box FL 281, Flatts FL BX, Bermuda (☎ **441/292-4434**). Anybody can take part in this adventure, featured twice in *Life* magazine. It's as simple as walking through a garden, and you won't even get your hair wet. A helmet is placed on your shoulders as you climb down the ladder of the boat to begin your guided walk. It is an ideal underwater experience for nonswimmers and those who must wear glasses. Safe and educational, the walk takes you to see the feeding of corals and breathing of sponges, as well as the feeding of sea anemones. The skipper and host, Mr. Hartley, personally conducts the tours. His ability to train fish in their natural habitat has been acclaimed in many publications. His 50-foot boat, *Carioca*, leaves Flatts Village daily at 10am and 2pm. The underwater wonderland walk costs $45 per adult or $30 for children under 12. Bus: No. 10 or 11.

South Side Scuba Water Sports

At Sonesta Beach Hotel & Spa, South Shore Rd., Southampton, and Grotto Beach Hotel, 11 Blue Hill Rd., Hamilton Parish (☎ **441/293-2915** for information about both locations). Call the day before, 7:30am–5:30pm. Bus No. 7 to Sonesta; no. 1, 3, 10, or 11 to Grotto Bay.

South Side Scuba is known for its daily two-tank wreck and reef dives, costing $65. A Resort Course lesson plus dive is $85. A single-tank dive goes for $50, and you can snorkel off the boat for $20. Deduct $10 if you have your own diving gear, except for Resort Courses; otherwise, the rates include all equipment. The company has two fully equipped, custom-built fiberglass dive boats, with the latest approved safety gear.

WATERSKIING

You can waterski in the protected waters of Hamilton Harbour, Great Sound, Castle Harbour, Mangrove Bay, Spanish Point, Ferry Reach, Ely's Harbour, Riddells Bay, and Harrington Sound. May through September is the best time for this sport. Bermuda law requires that waterskiers be taken out by a licensed skipper. Only a few boat operators participate in this sport, and charges fluctuate with fuel costs. Rates include the boat, skis, safety belts, and usually an instructor. Hotels and guesthouses can assist with arrangements.

Island Water Skiing

Grotto Bay Beach Hotel, Hamilton Parish. ☎ **441/293-2915.** Apr–Nov daily 8am–7:30pm, weather permitting. Closed Dec–Mar. Bus No. 1, 3, 10, or 11.

Up to three persons are taken out for skiing on board a Barefoot Nautique. You pay $40 for 15 minutes, $60 per half hour.

Bermuda Waterski Centre

Robinson's Marina, Somerset Bridge. ☎ **441/234-3354.** May–Oct daily 8am–7:30pm; periodically the rest of the year. Bus No. 6 or 7.

Up to five people can go waterskiing with a specially designed Ski Nautique. Lessons are available. The per-person charge is $50 for a half hour of skiing, $90 for one hour.

10 Shopping

Most of Bermuda's best shops are along Front Street in Hamilton. Here, where shopping is relaxed and casual, you'll come across many good buys. Among the choicest items are imports from Great Britain and Ireland, such as Shetland and cashmere sweaters, Harris tweed jackets, Scottish woolen goods and tartan kilts, and even fine china and crystal—many costing appreciably less than in their country of origin. Savvy shoppers from the United States will sometimes find that prices are at least 25% less than what they would be back home. But that's not always the case—in fact, some items appear overpriced, so you must be familiar with the Stateside prices, at least before committing yourself to serious purchases.

Other good buys are "Bermudiana"—products made in Bermuda or manufactured elsewhere exclusively for local stores. They include cedarwood gifts, carriage bells, coins commemorating the 375th anniversary of the island's settlement, flower plates by Spode, pewter tankards, handcrafted gold jewelry, traditional-line handbags with cedar or mahogany handles, miniature cottages in ceramic or limestone, shark's teeth polished and mounted in 14-karat gold, decorative kitchen items, Bermuda shorts (of course), silk scarves, and watches with Bermuda-map or longtail faces.

Liquor is also a good buy. You're allowed one quart duty free. But even with U.S. tax and duty, you can save between 35% and 50%, depending on the brand. Liqueurs offer the largest savings.

For other shopping ideas, see "Tips on Shopping" in Chapter 4, "Arriving in Bermuda."

1 The Shopping Scene

The best and widest choice of shopping is in Hamilton (see "Hamilton Shopping A to Z," below). Although the largest array of shops are on **Front Street,** you may want to explore the back streets as well, especially if you're an adventurous shopper.

The Emporium on Front Street, a restored building constructed around an atrium, contains a number of shops, including jewelry stores. **Windsor Place** on Queen Street is another particularly Bermudian shopping mall.

The "second city" of **St. George's** also has many shops, stores, and boutiques, including branches of famous Front Street stores. King's

Square, the center of St. George's, is filled with shops, with other major centers at **Somers Wharf** and on **Water Street.**

Don't overlook the shopping possibilities of the West End either. **Somerset Village** in Sandys Parish has many shops. But outshining them is the **Royal Naval Dockyard** area on Ireland Island. Here you can visit the Craft Market, Island Pottery, and the Bermuda Arts Centre, and you'll see local artisans at work.

STORE HOURS   Stores in Hamilton, St. George's, and Somerset are generally open Monday through Saturday from 9am to 5:30pm. When large liners are in port, stores often open in the evening or even on Sunday.

FINDING AN ADDRESS   Some Front Street stores post numbers on their buildings; *others do not.* Sometimes the number posted or used is the "historic" number of the building, having nothing to do with the modern number. But somehow it all works out: you can always ask for directions, as most Bermudians are willing to help. Outside of Hamilton, don't count on finding numbers on buildings at all, or even street names in some cases.

SALES TAX & DUTY   There is no sales tax in Bermuda. Bermuda is not a "duty-free" island. Depending on which country you're returning to, you may have to pay duty (see "Visitor Information, Entry Requirements & Money," in Chapter 3, "Before You Go").

"IN-BOND" (DUTY-FREE) SHOPPING   Goods such as liquor and cigarettes can be purchased at in-bond, or duty-free, prices—often at a savings of around 35%—and should be ordered several days in advance of your departure. You cannot consume these items in Bermuda; you pick them up at the airport at departure. They must be declared on your country's custom declarations. Liquor purchases should be made at one of the island stores, as the airport doesn't have an in-bond liquor store.

Note: Like many other nations, including several in the Caribbean, Bermuda falls under U.S. law regarding "Generalized System of Preferences" status. That means that items crafted at least 35% in Bermuda can be brought back duty free, regardless of how much you spent. If you've gone beyond your $400 allotment, make a separate list for goods made in Bermuda. That will make it easier for Customs and ultimately, for yourself.

2 Hamilton Shopping A to Z

ANTIQUES

Heritage House
2 Front St. West. ☎ **441/295-2615.**

The Heritage House sells nautical prints, English antiques, old maps, modern porcelain, and the largest collection of fine art on the island. There's also a collection of greeting cards designed by local artists and printed in Bermuda, plus top-of-the-line gifts. Look for their large collection of "Halcyon Days" pillboxes.

Pegasus
63 Pitts Bay Rd. (Front St. West). ☎ **441/295-2900.**

Pegasus has a wide range of antique prints, engravings, and magazine illustrations. You'll find no better anywhere in Bermuda. The inventory is varied, with old maps of many different regions of the world, and more than 1,000 literary, sporting, medical, and legal caricatures from *Vanity Fair.* These cost $20 to $200, depending on the subject. The hand-colored engravings of birds, fruits, and flowers are worth framing and sometimes cost as little as $40 each. Owner Robert Lee and his wife, Barbara, scour the print shops of the British Isles to stock this unusual store. Most prints range from the late 1700s to the late 1800s and are carefully grouped according to subject. The authenticity of whatever you buy is guaranteed in writing. They also offer ceramic house signs, costing $95 and up each, made at a small pottery in England. Each is unique, since the buyer chooses the design, after which the "house" and the house name or a number and street are hand-painted to his specifications. The shop also has a wide range of English greeting cards, many with botanical designs. All maps, lithographs, and engravings are duty free and will not affect your take-home quota. The shop is across the street from the Princess Hotel in Hamilton.

Timeless Antiques
26 Church St. ☎ 441/295-5008.

Terra-cotta tile steps lead you down to spacious display rooms where you can look over carved early English oak tables, chests, and chairs, clocks of all types and ages, icons, candelabra, pictures, what have you. The shop also provides expert clock repair and restoration services. Packing and shipping of larger items are arranged for you. The shop is opposite the bus terminal.

ART

Windjammer Gallery
Corner of Reid and King Sts. ☎ 441/292-7861.

Housed in a yellow cottage, this gallery exhibits paintings and bronze sculptures by local and international artists. It also has an extensive selection of cards, prints, and limited editions, including photographs and signed silk-screen prints. The gallery has the last private garden in Hamilton, adjacent to the gallery and used for the display of life-size sculpture. It also operates an additional gallery at 95 Front St. (☎ 441/292-5878).

ARTS & CRAFTS

Masterworks Foundation Gallery
Bermuda House Lane (97 Front St.). ☎ 441/295-5580.

Established in 1987 by a group of international philanthropists, this organization functions as a showcase for paintings by renowned European, Bermudian, and North American artists. Functioning to some degree as the country's most visible arts center, it sponsors frequent art exhibitions which have included works by Georgia O'Keefe (painted during the early 1930s in Bermuda), as well as seascapes by Winslow Homer and watercolors by local artist Ogden Pleissner. The organization also features guided art and architectural tours around the island (which are announced on a rotating basis), and functions as a headquarters and nerve center for other artistic endeavors and exhibitions throughout the year.

Ronnie Chameau Boutique
Trimingham's, 37 Front St. ☎ 441/292-1387.

Noted local artist Ronnie Chameau, known throughout the island for the charm of her handmade dolls, often creates the kind of art which might look its best around Christmastime. These doll-shaped ornaments are crafted from all natural

Hamilton Shops

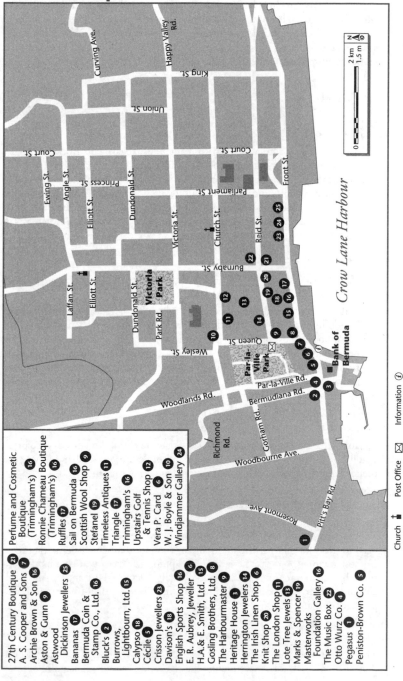

Crow Lane Harbour

27th Century Boutique **21**
A. S. Cooper and Sons **7**
Archie Brown & Son **16**
Aston & Gunn **9**
Astwood
Bananas **17**
Bermuda Coin &
  Stamp Co., Ltd. **16**
Bluck's **2**
Burrows,
  Lightbourn, Ltd. **15**
Calypso **5**
Cécile **5**
Crisson Jewellers **23**
Davison's **18**
Dickinson Jewellers **23**
English Sports Shop **16**
E. R. Aubrey, Jeweller **6**
H. A. & E. Smith, Ltd. **15**
Gosling Brothers, Ltd. **8**
The Harbourmaster **9**
Heritage House **3**
Herrington Jewelers **14**
The Irish Linen Shop **6**
Knit Shop **20**
The London Shop **11**
Lote Tree Jewels **13**
Marks & Spencer **19**
Masterworks
  Foundation Gallery **16**
The Music Box **22**
Otto Wurz Co. **4**
Pegasus **1**
Peniston-Brown Co. **5**

Perfume and Cosmetic
  Boutique
  (Trimingham's) **16**
Ronnie Chameau Boutique
  (Trimingham's) **16**
Ruffles **17**
Sail on Bermuda **16**
Scottish Wool Shop **9**
Stefanel **19**
Timeless Antiques **11**
Triangle **17**
Trimingham's **16**
Upstairs Golf
  & Tennis Shop **12**
Vera P. Card **6**
W. J. Boyle & Son **10**
Windjammer Gallery **24**

Church ✝   Post Office ⊠   Information ⓘ

9735

ingredients which include banana leaves, hazelnuts, and grapefruit leaves, each of which is gathered in her own and her friends' gardens throughout the island. Priced at under $20, each is individually boxed and gift-wrapped, and has a definite personality (and name, which the recipient can change) of its own. Ms. Chameau also fabricates historically authentic dolls, specializing in period costumes of the late 19th century.

BEACHWEAR

Calypso
45 Front St. ☎ **441/295-2112.**

Calypso sells casual, fun fashions, with many unusual garments from around the world, and carries the most comprehensive selection of swimwear in Bermuda. The assortment is complemented with Italian leather goods, espadrilles, hats, bags, and pareos. Italian ceramics and whimsical gift items are also sold. The store is also the exclusive island retailer of Louis Vuitton luggage and accessories. Branches are at both the Southampton and Hamilton Princess Hotels, the Sonesta Beach Hotel, The Coral Beach Club, and the Dockyard.

BOUTIQUES

Aston & Gunn
2 Reid St. ☎ **441/295-4866.**

Favored by office workers and investment bankers throughout the island, this shop sells the kind of career-oriented clothing worn by professionals throughout the island. Although most of the inventory is for men (with clothing imported from Germany and Holland), a smaller inventory is maintained for women as well. Representative designers include Ann Klein and J. McLaughlin. In addition to the predictable array of shirts, ties, jackets, and suits, the store is the exclusive island distributor of Calvin Klein undergarments.

Bananas
Front St. West, opposite the Bank of Bermuda. ☎ **441/295-8241.**

Bananas offers "Bermuda signature" items that are of good quality and colorful. You'll find T-shirts, jackets, beach bags, and beach umbrellas that will let your friends know where you've been. The store has several branches.

Davison's
27 and 73 Front St. ☎ **441/292-2083.**

Sportswear with a Bermudian flair is the specialty of this emporium of clothing, clothing accessories, and sporting equipment. It carries virtually anything you'd need to dress for and participate in any of the sports in which Bermuda excels. (Almost anything you select here would be appropriate to wear at your local country club after your return home.) Bags by Vera Bradley are also featured. Also available are culinary gift packages of Bermuda fish chowder, fish-based sauces, and packages of island herbs.

The London Shop
65 Washington Mall, Church St. ☎ **441/295-1279.**

The kind of store you might have expected in an upscale neighborhood of London, this store sells men's clothing by Pierre Cardin, as well as a handful of other prominent name designers. Suits range in price from $250 to $450, sports jackets begin at $135. There's also an inventory of dress clothes for teenage boys.

Ruffles
22 Queen St. (Windsor Place Mall). ☎ **441/295-9439.**

This shop specializes in the kind of clothing your daughter might wear to her first cotillion, or which her mother might wear to a formal ball or reception. Merchandise is updated with the seasons, with special emphasis on the Christmas holidays and the festivities which accompany it.

Stefanel
12 Reid St. ☎ **441/295-5698.**

This is the island's only outlet for the clothing designs of Carlo Stefanel, an increasingly well-known designer from Italy. Stocking merchandise for both men and women, the store sells tropical-weight men's suits crafted from cottons and linens, and handmade skirts (some of them knit) with contrasting jackets for women. There's a stylish array of accessories as well. No children's clothing is sold here.

Triangle
55 Front St. ☎ **441/292-1990.**

Catering to well-coiffed, well-tailored women who appreciate ease of garment-packing during travel, Diane Freis (pronounced "freeze") specializes in the kind of chic but simple women's clothing that is specifically engineered for its adaptability for travel. Garments are usually wrinkle-free and care-free, and most are designed in mosaic-inspired patterns of boldly contrasting colors and patterns. Inventory includes two-piece outfits, dresses, skirts, and evening jackets. Theoretically, none of the garments ever need ironing. Although pricey, these garments are said to cost less than comparable garments sold within North America.

27th Century Boutique
4 Burnaby St., between Front and Church Sts. ☎ **441/292-2628.**

Long known as a stylish and trend-setting boutique, it offers a selection of designer clothing, as well as silver costume jewelry and accessories. The store has a good collection of shoes—for both men and women—from Canada and London.

CASUAL WEAR & SUNGLASSES

Sail on Bermuda
Old Cellar, Front St. ☎ **441/295-0808.**

This shop offers everything in casual wear from bright bathing suits to accessories and children's wear. It also has the best T-shirts in Bermuda. A small addition, called Shades of Bermuda, has the finest collection of sunglasses on the island. The store also carries Sunny Caribbee products such as spices and hot sauces.

CHINA & GLASSWARE

A. S. Cooper & Sons
59 Front St. ☎ **441/295-3961.**

Bermuda's oldest and largest china and glassware store, family-owned since 1897, offers a broad range of fine bone china, earthenware, oven-to-table cookware, and jewelry. Among the famous names represented are Minton, Royal Doulton, Belleek, Aynsley, Wedgwood, and Royal Copenhagen. The Crystal Room contains

Orrefors, Waterford, Royal Brierley, and Kosta Boda among other selections. The Collector's Gallery is known for its limited editions of Bing & Grøndahl, Beswick, and Lladró. A perfume department has selections from the world's greatest perfumeries.

Bluck's
4 Front St. ☎ **441/295-5367.**

Established in 1844, Bluck's is well known for carrying some of the finest names in china and crystal, including Royal Worcester, Spode, Aynsley, Royal Doulton, and Herend porcelain from Hungary. The choice in crystal is equally impressive: Waterford, Baccarat, Daum, and of course, Lalique, exclusive with Bluck's. Upstairs, you'll find the Antiques Room filled with fine English furniture, antique Bermuda maps, and an array of old English silver. Bluck's has branch shops on Water Street in St. George's and in the Southampton Princess and Sonesta Beach hotels.

DEPARTMENT STORES

H. A. & E. Smith Ltd.
35 Front St. ☎ **441/295-2288.**

This store has been selling top-quality merchandise since 1889, at substantial savings over U.S. prices. Smith's comprehensive stock includes sweaters for men and women in cotton and in cashmere, lambswool, and Shetland, as well as British cosmetics and a collection from the top French *parfumeurs*. Smith's is noted for its selection of handbags, gloves, Liberty fabrics by the yard, and children's clothing. It also carries such merchandise as Fendi handbags from Italy, Burberrys rainwear from London, and Rosenthal china. A subsidiary, The Treasure Chest, across the street from the main store, carries a full line of French perfumes and gifts.

Trimingham's
37 Front St. ☎ **441/295-1183.**

Family-owned since 1842, Trimingham's specializes in fine European imports, often at considerable savings over U.S. prices. Spode, Aynsley, and Royal Worcester china are featured along with Waterford and Galway crystal. The cashmere, lambswool, and specialty knitwear collection is unrivaled in Bermuda, and Trimingham's own lines of men's and women's wear are known for their quality. French perfumes and European accessories are best buys here, as are fine jewelry, paintings, and gifts. Trimingham's Hamilton store is open daily. Branch shops are found throughout the island and at major hotels.

FASHIONS

Cécile
15 Front St. West. ☎ **441/295-1311.**

Cécile lies near the Visitors Service Bureau and the Ferry Terminal. It's well stocked and is a center for high fashion in Bermuda. Cécile's claims that a visit to the shop is like a visit to the fashion capitals of the world—from Germany, Mondi; from Hong Kong, Ciao and Ciaosport; from Israel, Gottex swimwear. Its sweater and accessory boutique is outstanding as well, with many hand-detailed and hand-embroidered styles. Cécile has branches at the Southampton Princess and Marriott's Castle Harbour.

Marks & Spencer
7 Reid St. ☎ **441/295-0031.**

This outlet, sometimes called "St. Michael," carries the reliable quality merchandise from Marks & Spencer in England. You'll find men's, women's, and children's fashions in everything from resortwear to sleepwear, including lingerie. There are also well-tailored dresses and suits, dress shirts, blazers, and British-tailored trousers, as well as swimwear, toiletries, and English sweets and biscuits.

FOOTWEAR

W. J. Boyle & Son
Queen and Church Sts. ☎ **441/295-1887.**

In business since 1884, this shop specializes in selling brand-name footwear made in England, Spain, Brazil, and the United States, including Clarks of England, Bally, and Enzo Angiolini. The store offers footwear for men, women, and children.

GIFTS

Vera P. Card
11 Front St. ☎ **441/295-1729.**

Vera P. Card is known for its offerings of "gifts from around the world." These include the island's largest collection of ship's clocks, mantel clocks, and table clocks. Famous-name watches include Nivada, Borel, and Rodania. The dinnerware collection features such famous names as Rosenthal, and the crystal department offers a wide assortment of Czech and Bohemian crystal, giftware, and chandeliers. Hummel and Lladró figurines are on sale, too. Look for Coalport English bone china, and for the "Bermuda Collection" of 14-karat jewelry. Other branches are found at 103 Front Street in Hamilton; 13 York Street and 7 Water Street in St. George's, and at the Sonesta Beach and Marriott Castle Harbour hotels.

JEWELRY

Astwood Dickinson Jewellers
83–85 Front St. ☎ **441/292-5805.**

Here you'll find a treasure trove of famous-name watches, including Patek Philippe, Cartier, Tiffany, Concord, Tissot, Omega, and Movado, plus designer jewelry, all at prices generally below U.S. retail. From its original Bermuda collection, you can select an 18-karat gold memento of the island, or else "The Island Watch" featuring flowers of the island. Other Astwood Dickinson shops are in the Walker Arcade and at the Sonesta Beach, Hamilton Princess, and Southampton Princess hotels.

Crisson Jewellers
55 and 71 Front St. ☎ **441/295-2351.**

Crisson is the exclusive agent in Bermuda for Rolex, Ebel, Raymond Weil, Cyma, and Gucci watches, as well as other well-known makers. It also carries an extensive selection of fine jewelry and gems.

E. R. Aubrey, Jeweler
19 Front St. West. ☎ **441/295-3826.**

Opposite the Ferry Terminal, this shop has a rich collection of gold chains, rings with precious and semiprecious stones, and charms, including the Bermuda longtail. The store also sells "Toggle" bracelets.

Herrington Jewellers
1 Washington Mall. ☎ **441/292-6527.**

This is one of the leading jewelry stores of Hamilton. It offers a good selection of gold and silver jewelry, and is the authorized dealer for Citizen watches. It also sells Timex watches and carries a vast selection of 14-karat gold chains, as well as rings made of precious and semiprecious stones. The Ana-Digi-Temp watch will even tell you the temperature.

Lote Tree Jewels
In the Walker Arcade. ☎ **441/292-8525.**

Don't expect the kinds of gemstones carried by conventional jewelers in this unusual jewelry store. Designs stress the traditions and workmanship of such countries as India and Afghanistan, and the Middle East. Inventory includes necklaces, chokers, rings, earrings, brooches, and a signature kind of ornament designed and distributed by the store's former owner, "Marybeads," crafted from 14K gold and freshwater pearls.

LEATHER ITEMS

The Harbourmaster
Washington Mall. ☎ **441/295-5333.**

This is your best bet for luggage and leather goods. Items in its leather collection, many often sold at prices 30% less than in the United States, include leather handbags from Italy, briefcases and luggage from Colombia, leather manicure sets, an extensive collection of wallets, and a large selection of nylon and canvas tote bags. The shop also sells a number of travel accessories, including luggage carts and many other items. A branch store is also located in Hamilton at the corner of Reid and Queen Streets (☎ **441/295-4210**), carrying essentially the same merchandise.

LINENS

The Irish Linen Shop
31 Front St. (corner of Queen St.). ☎ **441/295-4089.**

At Heyl's Corner, near the "Birdcage" police officer, this shop stocks not only table fabrics of pure linen from Ireland, but also a wide-ranging selection of other merchandise from Europe—everything from quilted placemats to men's shirts in French cotton from Souleiado of Provence. European linens purchased in Bermuda can often save you as much as 50% over American prices. The owners go over to Europe twice a year to bring back imports, including Madeira hand embroidery and Belgian lace. The shop has a branch on Cambridge Road, Mangrove Bay, in Somerset.

LIQUORS & LIQUEURS

Burrows, Lightbourn Ltd.
87 Front St. ☎ **441/295-0176.**

Burrows, Lightbourn Ltd., which is recommended for liquor purchases, has been in business since 1808. You can make your own combination-pack of liquors by asking for a "Select-a-Pac" consisting of any five fifths or two half gallons. Orders must be placed 24 hours prior to departure, except on Sunday, when 48 hours before departure is required. The store will deliver your liquor packages to the airport or else aboard ship. There are two stores in Hamilton, one in St. George's, one in Flatts Village, yet another in Paget, and one in Somerset. Of course, you can also buy liquor to drink while in Bermuda.

Gosling Brothers, Ltd.

At the corner of Front and Queen Sts. ☎ **441/295-1123.**

This large competitor of Burrows, Lightbourn has been selling liquor in Bermuda since 1806. Here's where you can buy Gosling's Black Seal dark rum, perhaps a bottle to sample on the island and another as an "in-bond" purchase to take back with you. The bottle you drink on the island is likely to cost 50% more than the "in-bond" bottle. If you want to purchase liquor to take home with you, you can make arrangements to have it sent to the airport, using your duty-free liquor allowance.

MUSIC

The Music Box

58 Reid St. ☎ **441/295-4839.**

By anyone's estimate, this is the largest and most complete record store in Bermuda, with an especially strong selection of music by local musicians whose live performances you might have heard in some of the island's hotels. Owned by Eddy de Mello, one of Bermuda's most influential music agents, this store stocks albums of the music we recommended earlier, as well as an impressive array of classical and popular music from other idioms. Especially visible are recordings by musical stars from the Bahamas and such Caribbean islands as Jamaica and Trinidad.

NEEDLEPOINT PATTERNS

Knit Shop

48 Reid St. ☎ **441/295-6722.**

The Knit Shop is the place to go if you knit, embroider, or sew. There is a good choice of needlepoint and cross-stitch patterns with Bermudian themes, all of which are also available in kits. It also carries craft supplies with kits for jewelry making and glass making.

PERFUMES

Peniston-Brown Co.

23 Front St. West. ☎ **441/295-0570.**

Opposite the Ferry Terminal, this shop carries almost all of the world's most popular perfumes, and you can learn something about the art of choosing and wearing perfume, from the shop's helpful "fragrance specialists." A branch of the store is found at 19 Queen Street in Hamilton. It's the Guerlain Shop (☎ 441/295-5535), and it's the exclusive agent for Guerlain products.

The Perfume and Cosmetic Boutique

In Trimingham's Department Store, 37 Front St. ☎ **441/295-1183.**

Set on the street level of Bermuda's largest department store, this is probably the island's most comprehensive emporium of every imaginable brand of perfume and cosmetics. Wander at will, but before your departure, an impulse purchase of merchandise by Estée Lauder, Clinique, Van Cleef & Arpels, Issey Miyake, Chanel, Boucheron, or Dior might be almost inevitable.

SILVER

Otto Wurz Co.

2 Vallis Building, 3–5 Front St. ☎ **441/295-1247.**

Otto Wurz lies at the western end of Front Street past the Ferry Terminal and the Bank of Bermuda between Par-la-Ville and Bermudiana Roads. It specializes in articles made of silver, including jewelry, charms, and bracelets. One section of the store is more "gifty" than the other, including a collection of pewter, cute wooden signs, and glassware which the store can engrave.

SPORTSWEAR

Upstairs Golf & Tennis Shop

26 Church St. ☎ **441/295-5161.**

Everything you'd need for success on the courts or on the links is sold in this amply stocked store. Among brands available for golfers are Ping, Callaway, Titleist, Lynx, and Spalding. Tennis enthusiasts will recognize brands by Dunlop, Slazenger, and many others. Also sold is rainwear from Scotland, suitable for Bermuda's rainy winters, for both men and women.

STAMPS & COINS

Bermuda Coin & Stamp Co. Ltd.

Walker Arcade, Front St. ☎ **441/295-5503.**

Philatelists and numismatists will enjoy this shop, where they can browse among a wide selection of stamps and coins, some of which are real treasures. Commemorative groupings are also offered.

WOOLEN GOODS

Archie Brown & Son

49 Front St. ☎ **441/295-2928.**

Archie Brown & Son, in business for more than half a century, features sweaters for men and women in cashmere, cotton, lambswool, and Shetland; for women, there are matching skirts. Colors range from neutral to spectacular.

English Sports Shop

95 Front St. ☎ **441/295-2672.**

This shop was established in 1918 and is credited with being one of the island's leading retailers of quality classic and British woolen items for men, women, and children. It has branch shops at the Hamilton Princess and Sonesta Beach hotels.

Scottish Wool Shop

7 Queen St. ☎ **441/295-0967.**

The Scottish Wool Shop carries a wide range of tartans for men, women, and children—all imported from Great Britain. It also has a wide selection of woolens and cottons made especially for this shop. Merchandise includes an array of women's accessories; children's toys; and Shetland, cashmere, lambswool, and cotton sweaters. The store will also take special orders on more than 500 tartan items.

3 Shops Around the Island

As you leave Hamilton and tour the island, you may want to continue your shopping expedition—especially for typical Bermudian items—at one of the following addresses.

For other shopping suggestions, consider the **Bermuda Craft Market** and the **Bermuda Arts Centre** (see "Ireland Island," in Chapter 7, "What to See & Do"). Those interested in Bermudian art might also want to pay a visit to the **Birdsey Studio** in Paget Parish (see "Paget Parish," in Chapter 7, "What to See & Do").

HAMILTON PARISH

Bermuda Glass-Blowing Studio and Showroom
16 Blue Hole Hill, Hamilton Parish. ☎ **441/293-2234.**

Bermuda's largest glass-blowing studio, and full-time employer of a half-dozen British-born artists and their assistants, is owned and operated by noted entrepreneur Gayle Cooke. Although part of the studio's output is for special commissions, most of its production is inspired by cutting-edge developments in the art glass world. Items on display in their showroom range in price from $10 to $1,000. The minimum commission is usually in excess of $500.

IRELAND ISLAND

Island Pottery
Royal Naval Dockyard, Ireland Island. ☎ **441/234-3361.**

At this popular attraction, visitors go inside a workshop occupied by Bermudian craftspeople. The spacious stone-built warehouse has a gift shop in one section and the workshop in the other. Artisans in traditional aprons toil over potter's wheels, turning out their wares. There's also a glassware artisan. Since the pottery is made in Bermuda, it is duty free.

Kathleen Kemsley Bell
Bermuda Arts Centre, 4 Freeport Rd., Ireland Island. ☎ **441/236-3366.**

A respected director of the Bermuda Arts Centre, Ms. Bell's studio creates historically accurate dolls, each crafted from papier-mâché and signed as an original work of art. Working from cramped premises within her family's garage, she has exported top-of-the-line dolls, known for their nuanced expressions, to buyers and collectors throughout Europe and North America. Prices begin at $350 each, and can go much, much higher. Ms. Bell prefers to work by pre-arranged commission only, and will carry her samples to whatever hotel a buyer specifies.

PAGET PARISH

Art House
80 South Shore Rd., Paget. ☎ **441/236-6746.**

The Art House specializes in original paintings and hand-signed lithographs by artist Joan Forbes. Ms. Forbes is a Bermuda-born artist who studied in Massachusetts and Canada before returning home to pursue a living creating watercolors and lithographs of Bermudian landscapes. Prices range from $10 to $50 for lithographs, and from $75 to $3,000 for original watercolors. She also sells an array of craft and gift items made on the island.

Mary Zuill Art Studio
10 Southlyn Lane, Paget West. ☎ 441/236-2439.

One of Bermuda's most enduring watercolorists, Ms. Zuill (who is in her 70s) maintains the British tradition in depictions of Bermuda landscapes and garden scenes. She'll work from photographs, and has been successfully commissioned to paint individual residences throughout the island. Paintings tend to range from $85 to $600, depending on their complexity. If visitors call for an appointment, they are welcome Tuesday through Friday from April through November only.

St. George's Parish

Bridge House Gallery
1 Bridge St., St. George's. ☎ 441/297-8211.

Set within one of the parish's oldest buildings, a two-story 18th-century home of some of the island's governors which is today maintained by Bermuda's National Trust, this well-stocked emporium is one of the richest shopping troves on the island's east end. It inventories a wide selection of antique and modern Bermudiana, including antique lace, Christmas ornaments, imported English porcelain, antique maps, old bottles, postcards, and unique mementos of Bermuda's unusual geography and history. One corner of the building is devoted to the studio and sales outlet of local artist Jill Amos Raine. The gallery is actually a sightseeing attraction and is treated as such (see "St. George's Parish" in "What to See & Do," Chapter 7).

Carole Holding Studios
Town Square, St. George's. ☎ 441/297-1833.

Respected watercolor artist Carole Holding is known for her skill in what might be Bermuda's most-loved art form, watercolor painting. Many of her works depict the peace and serenity of Bermuda's homes and gardens. A few of her works are commissions of individual island homes; more frequently, however, the subjects rely on her own inspiration. Although Ms. Holding's works are diffused in other gift shops throughout Bermuda, most of her inventory lies within her own shop on Town Square in St. George's.

Cow Polly
16 Water St., Somers Wharf, St. George's. ☎ 441/297-1514.

Named after a rather unpleasant-looking fish which abounds in Bermuda waters, this is an upscale gift shop which prides itself on its inventory of unusual objects imported from virtually everywhere. The theme is based on aquatic designs, often inspired by the forms of fish and by underwater mythology. Objects for sale include handpainted shirts, jackets, costume jewelry, and a good selection of the kind of necktie you wouldn't necessarily wear to a job interview.

Frangipani
Water St., St. George's. ☎ 441/297-1357.

This shop stresses color, a sense of fantasy, and a diverse inventory of unusual clothing and accessories for men and women. Merchandise includes costume jewelry, cotton sweaters, garments of handmade cottons and silks, and the kind of accessories you might not find elsewhere on the island.

Somer's Gift Shop

King's Square, St. George's. ☎ **441/297-1670.**

This gift shop in a historic old building offers a good selection of sterling silver jewelry and T-shirts. On Tuesday and Wednesday, it's also open in the evening from 7:30 to 10pm.

SOMERSET

The Old Market

Main Rd., Mangrove Bay, in the village of Somerset. ☎ **441/234-0744.**

The Old Market occupies premises dating from 1827, when it was built as a private home. This unusual boutique offers everything from old coins, brass, and crystal, to costume jewelry and casual clothes.

SOUTHAMPTON PARISH

Desmond Fountain Sculpture Gallery

In the mezzanine sculpture gallery of the Southampton Princess Hotel, 101 South Shore Rd., Southampton. ☎ **441/238-8840.**

As close to Bermuda's official sculptor as any other artist on the island, Desmond Fountain has created some of Bermuda's most visible public art. Much of his studio's output in recent years has been for privately commissioned works which appear within upscale private homes and gardens throughout Bermuda. Several life-size sculptures by him are found on the grounds of the Lantana Colony Club (see Chapter 5). One of the most charming is of a woman seated on a bench and reading a newspaper. Works begin at around $6,000 each.

Bermuda After Dark

The nightlife in Bermuda may not be the primary reason that visitors flock here. Yet there's a lot of it, although it seems to float from hotel to hotel. For this reason, it's hard to predict which pub or nightspot will have, say, the best steel-drum band or calypso music. Many of the local pubs feature sing-alongs at the piano bar, a popular form of entertainment in Bermuda. Most of the big hotels offer shows after dinner, with combos filling in between shows for couples who like to dance.

The tourist office and most hotels distribute free copies of such "what's happening" publications as *Preview Bermuda, Bermuda Weekly,* and *This Week in Bermuda.* A calendar of events also appears in *The Bermudian,* which sells for $4 at most newsstands.

You might also listen to the local TV station, which constantly broadcasts information for visitors, including not only cultural events but various other nightlife offerings around the island. Also, tune in to an AM radio station, 1160 (VSB), from 7am to 12:30pm daily; this broadcasts news of any cultural or entertainment events on the island. Discount tickets are almost never offered; students and senior citizens sometimes are granted discounts.

1 Cultural Entertainment

BERMUDA FESTIVAL

Bermuda's major cultural event is the ✪ **Bermuda Festival,** staged for a two-month period in January and February. Outstanding artists, including classical and jazz, perform on the island along with major theatrical entertainments. During the festival, performances are given every night but Sunday. Tickets for these events range in price from $18 to $40, and most of the performances are at City Hall Theater, City Hall, Church Street, Hamilton. For more information and reservations, write to: Bermuda Festival, P.O. Box 297, Hamilton HM AX, Bermuda (☎ **441/295-1291**).

MAJOR PERFORMING ARTS COMPANIES

The **Bermuda Philharmonic Society,** conducted by Graham Garton, presents four regular concerts during the season. In addition, special outdoor "Classical Pops" concerts are presented at the end of May in St. George's and the Royal Naval Dockyard. Concerts

The Hollywood Connection

Film buffs may be surprised to discover that Bermuda has an indirect link to *The Wizard of Oz*, the 1939 movie starring Judy Garland and a host of memorable, magical characters. It is Denslow's Island.

The privately owned island is named after W. W. Denslow, who created the original illustrations for the book on which the movie is based, *The Wonderful Wizard of Oz* (1900) by L. Frank Baum, and thus with his pen gave form to many of the characters depicted on the screen. Denslow lived in Bermuda at the turn of the century. The island, however, despite its famous association, is off-limits to visitors.

Several major films were shot in and around Bermuda. The most famous is *The Deep* (1977), starring Jacqueline Bisset, Nick Nolte, Robert Shaw, and Lou Gossett—a visually arresting movie about a lost treasure and drugs and, of course, scuba diving off the island's coast. For one of the scenes, a lighthouse near the Grotto Bay Beach Hotel was accommodatingly blown up.

The movie *Chapter Two* (1979), starring James Caan and Marsha Mason, was filmed partly in Bermuda. Based on the successful play by Neil Simon, it is the story of a playwright's bumpy romance soon after the death of his wife. The Bermuda scenes were shot at Marley Beach Cottage.

usually feature both the Bermuda Philharmonic orchestra and choir with guest soloists. Tickets and concert schedules may be obtained from the Harbourmaster, Washington Mall (☎ **441/295-5333**). Tickets generally range from $18 to $20, with seniors and students most often granted discounts, depending on the various performances.

Ask at the tourist office if the **Gombey Dancers** will be appearing at any time during your stay. This local dance troupe of highly talented men and women often performs in winter. This is the island's single most important cultural event with African influences, a tradition dating from the mid-1700s and once considered part of the "slave culture." On all holidays, you'll see the "gombeys" dancing through the streets of Hamilton in their colorful costumes.

In addition, the **Bermuda Civic Ballet** presents classical ballets at different venues on the island. Again, ask at the tourist office if any performances are scheduled at the time of your visit.

The **Gilbert & Sullivan Society of Bermuda** keeps alive the musical legacy of these English favorites, staging a production every year, most often in October. Sometimes this group will stage a popular Broadway musical. The events are highly advertised.

2 The Club & Music Scene

The Bermuda Follies

At the Palm Reef Hotel, 1 Harbour Rd., Hamilton Parish. ☎ **441/236-1000**. $25, including one free drink. Bus No. 7 or private hotel ferry. Closed Sunday and from late October to May.

Operated by a local entrepreneur and choreographer named Greg Thompson, this is a Las Vegas–style cabaret that has been presented at three or four different hotels since it began in the early 1980s. At press time, it was presented in the Palm

Reef Hotel, within a nightclub setting of small tables and clusters of chairs, although its venue could change during the lifetime of this edition. About a half-dozen entertainers, including a likable M.C., sing and dance, tell jokes, and disperse a series of Bermuda-based anecdotes that seem to go over well with the many cruise passengers who disembark *en masse* to see it. The costumes and glitter look like a hybrid between what dancers might wear in the Nevada desert and a banana plantation in Brazil, and everyone seems to have a good time. After the initial free drink, additional drinks cost around $6 each, plus tip. If you want dinner before the show begins, the cost is $50 per person. Reservations are recommended. Dinner begins at 8pm, the doors for nondiners open at 9:30pm. The show begins at 10pm Monday through Saturday, and lasts around 75 minutes.

Clay House Inn

77 North Shore Rd., Devonshire Parish. ☎ **441/292-3193** for reservations. Mon–Wed, $22.50 per person, including two drinks; Thurs–Sun, $10. Bus No. 10 or 11.

Although calypso and steel band music were born on islands farther to the south than Bermuda, this nightclub offers up those musical forms with panache. You're likely to be entertained in a folkloric celebration of island dances and both vocal and instrumental music—a carefully contrived package of Caribbean-style nostalgia. The folkloric shows are presented every Monday through Wednesday throughout the year. Other nights of the week, the Clay House Inn discards any notion of catering to a tourist audience and becomes a local hangout for jazz, reggae, and blues bands. From Monday through Wednesday, drinks are included in the entrance price. On other nights, drinks go for $4 each and are not included in the entrance price. Regardless of the venue, the music and/or show begins at 10:15pm, nightly, with no exact closing time.

The Club

Bermudiana Rd. ☎ **441/295-6693**. Nonmembers $15. Bus No. 1, 2, 10, or 11.

With its red velvet, mirrors, and brass, this club is sometimes favored by an older clientele of business and professional people in Bermuda. It's above the Little Venice restaurant, which has an understated mirrored entrance that reflects the two stone lions at its portals. Dress is "smart casual." There is dancing, and drinks cost extra. Complimentary admission is granted after you dine at the Little Venice, the New Harborfront, or La Trattoria restaurants. Open daily from 10pm to 3am.

Club 21

Royal Naval Dockyard. ☎ **441/234-2721**. Varies according to the jazz band performing.

If the night is right, this joint can be rocking. That's especially true when it's dedicated to jam sessions for local musicians and singers. You get hot jazz Tuesday through Saturday from 9pm to 2am and on Sunday from 8pm to 2am. Always call first to see that it's open. A pint of lager costs from $4.50.

The Gazebo Lounge

In the Princess, 76 Pitts Bay Rd., in Hamilton (the city). ☎ **441/295-3000**. $5 to $30, depending on the show. Bus No. 7 or 8.

The largest and most prestigious hotel chain in Bermuda prides itself on the array of talent that parades through the bar/lounges of each of its two hotels. The same type of entertainment is presented at the Neptune Club in the Southampton Princess (see below).

Depending on the venue, the season, and the availability of the artists themselves, some kind of entertainment is presented Monday through Saturday at each of the two properties. The schedule changes periodically, but music and comedy acts tend to begin around 9pm and continue, with breaks, up until around midnight.

Dinner/show packages are available, with dinner served in either of the hotel's dining rooms followed by a move into the bar-lounge just before the entertainment begins. Artists are likely to include singers, dancers, comedians, or dance troupes, all of whom work hard to keep their respective rooms alive. Also popular within both hotels are 90-minute plays presented by a local repertory company, whose schedules are adjusted seasonally.

Henry VIII

South Shore Rd., ☎ **441/238-1977**. $5. Bus No. 7 or 8.

This establishment, previously recommended as a restaurant (see Chapter 6), also functions as the premier comedy club of Bermuda. Live comedians are imported, usually from England, for performances Thursday through Tuesday from 9:30pm to 1am. Breaks in between long-running comedy monologues are sometimes interspersed with rowdy audience participation. The stage is visible from the pub and from one of the restaurant's three dining areas. Bottles of beer in the pub cost $4.50 each.

The Oasis Nightclub & Back Room Bar

In the Emporium Building, 69 Front St., Hamilton. ☎ **441/292-4978**. $15, including entrance to both the Oasis Club and the Back Room Bar. Bus No. 3, 7, or 11.

One of the leading nightlife venues on the island, the Oasis Club is reached by riding a glass-encased elevator to the second floor of a stylish commercial building in the center of Hamilton. It has been renovated into a New York warehouse style. Extensive work has improved the sound system and added lots of special effects lighting. TV monitors are widely used throughout the nightclub to provide background video effects. The extensive music repertoire includes the latest Top 40 dance music. The Back Room Bar still provides karaoke-style entertainment, but the emphasis is on live bands. Top North American club bands complement local bands playing a variety of rock and blues. The cover charge entitles a visitor to enter both establishments which are open daily from 9pm to 3am. Drink prices range from $4.95 to $5.60.

Neptune Club

The Southampton Princess, 101 South Shore Rd., in Southampton. ☎ **441/238-8000**. $5 to $30, depending on the show. Transportation: Ferryboat from Hamilton.

This newly renovated club offers both guests and nonresidents hours of entertainment with live shows and a dance club. One of the most popular entertainers on the island, Jimmy Keys, a comedian/impressionist/singer often performs at the club. On Sunday nights guests can also enjoy live local entertainment. After midnight the Neptune Club transforms itself into a dance club, and guests rock the night away with a disc jockey until 2:30am. The same shows and conditions apply to this club as to the Gazebo Lounge at the Hamilton Princess (see above).

3 The Bar Scene

Casey's

Queen Street, across from the Little Theater, Queen Street. ☎ **441/293-9549**. No cover. Bus No. 1, 2, 10, or 11.

Its aficionados claim it as their neighborhood bar. At least 90% of the clientele are Bermudians; the remainder are welcomed as newcomers. No food is served, but a pint of lager costs around $4.50, and the bar has the best jukebox on the island. The club is open Monday through Saturday from 10am to 10pm. Friday night is the most active. There is no live entertainment except for that jukebox.

Frog & Onion

The Cooperage, Old Royal Navy Dockyard, Ireland Island. ☎ **441/234-2900.** No cover. Bus No. 7 or 8.

Converted from an 18th-century cooperage, a barrel-making factory, this British-style pub lies within the Royal Navy Dockyards. (See Chapter 6 for its restaurant review.) Operated by a "frog" (a Frenchman) and an "onion" (a Bermudian), it is open daily March through November from 11am to 1am and Tuesday through Monday from December through February from noon to midnight. A pint of lager costs $4.75, and you can enjoy bar snacks throughout the afternoon and evening.

Hog Penny

5 Burnaby Hill, in Hamilton (city). ☎ **441/292-2534.** No cover. Bus No. 1, 2, 10, or 11.

With a name that Clint Eastwood might have invented for one of his California bars, this is the best-known pub in Bermuda (see Chapter 6 for its recommendation as a dining choice). There is nightly entertainment from 9:30pm to 1am, and dress is very casual, often quite casual. In between drinks and the music, you can order such pub grub as "bangers and mash" or even steak-and-kidney pie. The place is dark and smoky but seems to always be full. A pint of lager costs $4.50.

Hubie's

Angle St. at Court St. in Hamilton (the city). ☎ **441/293-9287.** No cover. Bus No. 1, 2, 10, or 11.

Well known as a neighborhood bar, this drinking and social outlet is the territory of Hubie Brown, who has been known to play the drums at infrequent intervals during the weekend jazz sessions. These are presented only on Friday and Saturday nights from 7 to 10pm, and the only price the aficionados pay is the cost of a drink. The rest of the week, every day from 10am to 10pm, the site functions solely as a bar—no food, no music, just the neighbors getting together over drinks. Beer costs $2.50 during normal hours; $3.25 after the music begins.

Loyalty Inn

Mangrove Bay, Somerset Village. ☎ **441/234-0124.** No cover. Bus No. 7 or 8, or ferry from Hamilton to Watford Bridge.

If you're out in the West End at night, this 250-year-old home overlooking Mangrove Bay has one of the most frequented bars in the area. (For a dining review, see Chapter 6.) Find a captain's chair and enjoy a pint of lager for $4.50 or else take your drink outside on the terrace in fair weather. The bar is open daily from 11am to 1am.

O'Malley's Pub on the Square

King's Square, St. George's. ☎ **441/297-1522.** No cover. Bus No. 3, 10, or 11.

Out in the East End centered at St. George's, this pub takes its inspiration from England. Both drinkers and diners (see Chapter 6 for its dining review) occupy two floors in a building from the late 18th century. Sing-alongs are not uncommon here where a mug of beer costs from $4.50. If you get hungry, you can order some fish and chips in the true pub tradition.

Show Bizz Hard Rock Bistro

66 King St. at Reid St. in Hamilton (city). ☎ **441/292-0676.** Cover $9, including two drinks. Bus No. 1, 2, 10 or 11.

Recommended previously as a restaurant, this popular place might also be your nighttime venue. After 10pm, the club becomes a hot disco. Sometimes action goes on into the early hours, depending on the crowd. You'll pay for drinks at the door (a two-drink minimum). Occasionally, especially on Friday and Saturday, live rock bands are presented.

Swizzle Inn

3 Blue Hole Hill, Bailey's Bay, in Hamilton Parish. ☎ **441/293-9300.** No cover. Bus No. 3 or 11.

The home of the Bermuda rum swizzle, this bar and dining choice lies west of the airport near the Crystal Caves and the Bermuda Perfume Factory. See Chapter 6 for details on its dining possibilities. The Swizzleburger can be ordered throughout the day, as can fish and chips. Sports aficionados are usually found playing a game of darts. In the old days you might run into Ted Kennedy here, although his present wife steers him to more sedate places. The jukebox plays both soft and hard rock. The tradition here is to tack your business card to any place you can find a spot, even the ceiling. A pint of lager costs from $4.50. The inn is open daily from 11am to 1am. It is closed, however, on Mondays in January and February.

Wharf Tavern

Somers Wharf, St. George's. ☎ **441/297-1515.** No cover. Bus No. 3, 10, or 11.

For swizzling glasses of tropical rum punch and for talk of sailing the high seas, this is the preferred spot in St. George's in the East End. In a converted warehouse from two centuries ago, you can enter the darkly paneled bar area inside where a pint of lager costs from $4.50. The tavern is also a dining choice (see Chapter 6 for food recommendations). But it's also possible to come here just to drink, as many do. The bar is open daily from 11am to 1am.

Ye Old Cock and Feather

8 Front St. in Hamilton (city). ☎ **441/295-2263.** No cover. Bus No. 1, 2, 10, or 11.

In a converted warehouse, between Burnaby Hill and Queen Street, this is one of the most enduring pubs and restaurants in Bermuda (see Chapter 6 for a dining review). Considered at times the busiest watering hole along Front Street, it is both like a jazzy English pub or perhaps something you'd find along the Florida Keys. The most desired place to eat is the balcony upstairs overlooking the harbor. But these tables go quickly. From April through November, live entertainment is presented in the bar. A pint of lager costs $4.50.

Index

Accommodations, 34–35, 70–100
  at-a-glance, 78–79
  cottage colonies, 34, 61, 89–92
  guesthouses, 34, 61, 97–100
  Hamilton, 81
  honeymoon resorts, 5–6, 39–40
  housekeeping units, 34, 61, 92–96
  resort hotels, 34, 61, 71–83
  small hotels, 34, 84–89
  tips on, 61
Air Travel, 46–49
  arriving in Bermuda, 53–54
  for disabled travelers, 44
  money–saving tips, 47–49
Albouy's Point, 147, 160
Alcohol, 28, 66
Annual events, festivals, and fairs, 37–39
Arboretum, 55, 144
Architecture, 22, 155
Area code, 63
Art museums
  Bermuda National Gallery, 148
Astwood Cove, 1, 173
Astwood Park, 1, 156, 173

Babysitting, 45
Bailey's Bay, 7, 9, 141, 178
Bank of Bermuda, 63, 160
Banks, 63–64
Barber's Lane Alley, 4, 135
Bar scene, 205–206
Beaches, 1–2, 8, 9, 10, 61, 130, 131, 132, 141, 144, 150, 156, 173–76, 183
  Astwood Cove, 1, 156, 173
  Chaplin Bay, 2, 174
  Church Bay, 2, 175

Elbow Beach, 1, 9, 133, 173
  Horseshoe Bay Beach, 2, 9, 10, 133, 175
  John Smith's Bay, 176, 183
  Shelly Bay Beach, 2, 141, 176
  Somerset Long Bay, 2, 10, 132, 151, 176
  Tobacco Bay Beach, 2, 176
  Warwick Long Bay, 1, 174
Belmont Hotel, Golf & Country Club, 180
Bermuda Aquarium, Museum & Zoo, 55, 133, 141–42, 154
Bermuda Arts Centre, 152, 154, 170, 189
Bermuda Audubon Society, 13, 151, 170, 177
Bermuda Biological Station, 38, 158
Bermuda Cathedral. See Cathedral of the Most Holy Trinity
Bermuda Civic Ballet, 203
Bermuda College Weeks, 9, 37, 149
Bermuda Craft Market, 154, 189
Bermuda Festival, 9, 14, 37, 202
Bermuda Glass Blowing Studio, 55
Bermuda Historical Society Museum, 147, 160–62
Bermuda Library, 160–62
Bermuda Maritime Museum, 5, 9, 39, 133, 152–53, 154, 157, 170
Bermuda National Gallery, 148
Bermuda National Trust, 13, 143, 149, 152, 166
Bermuda Perfumery, 55, 141

Bermuda Philharmonic Society, 202–203
Bermuda Public Library, 147, 152
Bermuda Railway Trail, 3, 9, 56, 154, 156, 167, 168, 178
Bermuda shorts, 15, 146
Bermuda Triangle, 18
Bicycling, 3, 55, 58–60, 130, 151, 156, 176–78
"Bird Cage," 147, 160
Birdsey, Alfred, 22, 150
Birdsey Studio, 150
Bird-watching, 11, 13, 143, 177. See also nature reserves
Black Watch Well, 146
Blockade Alley, 4, 137, 155, 164
Boat rentals, 59
Boaz Island, 8, 10, 56, 167, 170
Bookstores, 57, 64
Botanical Gardens, 10, 12, 39, 133, 149
Bridge House, 140
Bridge House Art Gallery, 140, 164
Business hours, 64
Bus travel
  for senior citizens, 58
  within Bermuda, 57–58, 130

Cabinet Building, 163
Carriage Museum, 137, 166
Cars and driving
  rentals, 64, 131
  safety tips, 57, 65
Castle Harbour, 8, 11, 59, 180, 183, 184, 187
Castle Harbour Golf Club, 179, 180
Castle Islands Nature Reserve, 59
Cathedral of the Most Holy Trinity, 148, 162
Cavello Bay, 151, 170

Caves
    Crystal Caves, 9, 55, 133, 142, 143, 154, 207
    Leamington Caves, 6, 9, 55, 133, 142, 143
Cenotaph, 163
Chaplin Bay, 2, 174
Chelston, 149
Children
    and bus travel, 58
    and cruise ships, 50, 52
    restaurants, 114
    sights and attractions for, 154
    travel tips for, 45
Christ Church, 150
Church Bay, 2, 141, 175, 183
Churches and Cathedrals
    Cathedral of the Most Holy Trinity, 148, 162
    Christ Church, 150
    Hamilton Parish Church, 141
    Old Devonshire Parish Church, 10, 55, 143, 145
    St. James' Anglican Church, 152
    St. Mark's Church, 143
    St. Peter's Church, 11, 17, 136, 137, 155, 166
    St. Teresa's Cathedral, 162
    Unfinished Cathedral, 4, 137, 155, 164–65
Climate, 9, 11, 36–37, 64
Club scene, 203–205
Comedy clubs, 205
Confederate Museum, 136, 166
Consulates, 65
Cricket, 39, 171–72
Cruise ships, 49–52, 131
Crystal Caves, 9, 55, 133, 142, 143, 154, 207
Cuisine, 25–26
Currency exchange, 33, 34, 64
Customs, 31–32, 54, 64

Dance, 24, 37, 157, 203
Deliverance II, 136
Denslow's Island, 203
Dentists, 64–65
Devil's Hole Aquarium, 142

Devonshire Dock, 144
Devonshire Parish, 10–11, 55, 130, 144–45, 177, 178, 180
Dining customs, 26–27
Disabled travelers, tips for, 43–44
Dive sites, 2–3. See also Underwater Sports
Doctors, 41, 65
Documents required for entry, 30–31
Drugstores, 65

Edmund Gibbons Nature Reserve, 144
Elbow Beach, 1, 9, 133, 173
Electricity, 65
Ely's Harbour, 59, 133, 151, 177, 187
Embassies, 65
Emergencies, 65
Entertainment and nightlife, 202–207
Eyeglasses, 65–66

Families, tips for. See also Children
Fast Facts, 63–69
Fauna, 13–14
Ferries, 57, 60, 130, 132, 147, 149, 152, 159–60, 168
Festivals. See Annual events, festivals, and fairs
Field Hockey, 172
Fishing, 13–14, 38,
    deep-sea, 178–79
    reef, 179
    shore, 179
Flatts Village, 11, 55, 60, 133, 142
Flora, 11–12
Forster Cooper Building, 153
Fort Hamilton, 9, 55, 133, 163
Fort St. Catherine, 9, 140, 151, 168, 176
Fort Scaur, 133, 151, 167, 168
Fort Scaur Park, 177

Gardens. See Parks and Gardens
Gasoline, 66, 131
Gates Fort, 140

Gibbs Hill Lighthouse, 4, 133, 150, 156, 177, 181
Gilbert Nature Reserve, 152, 167, 178
Golf, 3, 4, 10, 13, 37, 39, 53, 130, 131, 150, 172, 179–82
    Belmont Hotel, Golf & Country Club, 180
    Castle Harbour Golf Club, 179, 180
    Mid Ocean Club, 179
    Ocean View Golf Course, 180–81, 183
    Port Royal Golf Course, 3, 179, 181, 183, 185
    Riddell's Bay Golf Course, 4, 179
    St. George's Golf Club, 181–82, 183
    Southampton Princess Golf Club, 181, 183
Gombey Dancers, 24, 157, 203
Government House, 145–46
Great Sound, 3, 4, 8, 56, 60, 132, 133, 145, 146, 151, 168, 172, 173, 179, 181
Green, John, 5, 21, 143, 155

Hamilton, 8, 9, 10, 11, 15, 19, 26, 38, 50, 53, 54, 55, 56, 58, 130, 132, 133, 134, 135, 151, 152, 167, 170, 178, 189
    accommodations, 81
    restaurants, 6, 7, 81, 101–12
    shopping, 189–99
    sights and attractions, 145–49
    walking tour, 159–63
Hamilton City Hall & Arts Centre, 148, 162, 202
Hamilton Harbour, 10, 50, 51, 55, 145, 146, 147, 172, 184
Hamilton Parish, 2, 11, 13, 55, 130, 141, 145, 176, 178
    restaurants, 6, 7, 125–26
    shopping, 199
    sights and attractions, 141–42
Hamilton Parish Church, 141

Harrington Sound, 8, 11, 55, 141, 142, 143, 183, 184, 187
Hawkins Island, 3, 157
Helmet diving, 133, 154, 185, 186
Historical museums
  Bermuda Historical Society Museum, 147, 160–62
  Bermuda Maritime Museum, 5, 9, 39, 133, 152–53, 154, 157, 170
  Carriage Museum, 137, 166
  Confederate Museum, 136, 166
  St. George's Historical Society Museum, 137, 166
History, 5, 17–21
Holidays, 37
Home exchanges, 41
Honeymoon resorts, 5–6, 39–40
Horse-drawn carriages, 57, 60–61, 137, 156, 166
Horseback riding, 3, 45, 53, 130, 154, 182
Horse racing, 172
Horseshoe Bay, 2, 10, 56, 150, 174
Horseshoe Bay Beach, 2, 9, 10, 133, 175
Hospitals, 66
Hurricane season, 37

Information sources. *See* Tourist information
Insurance, 42–43
Ireland Island, 5, 8, 9, 10, 56, 58, 133, 167, 170, 189
  shopping, 199
  sights and attractions, 152–54

John Smith's Bay, 176, 183

King's Square, 4, 58, 134–35, 136, 163–64

Lagoon Park, 170
Leamington Caves, 6, 9, 55, 133, 142, 143
Libraries, 147, 152, 160–62, 167
Literary figures, 156–57
Little Sound, 4, 146, 178

Mail, 66
Mangrove Bay, 3, 56, 59, 151, 170, 187, 206
Maps, 57, 67
Medicines, 42
Mid Ocean Club, 179
Money, 33–36
Moore, Richard, 17, 134, 155
Moore, Thomas, 4, 6, 141, 145, 156
Mopeds, 55, 57, 58–60, 131, 151, 176
Museums. *See* Art museums, historical museums
Music, 24–25, 203–206
  balladeer tradition, 24
  calypso, 25, 204
  classical, 37, 202–203
  gombey music, 24
  jazz, 37, 202, 204, 206
  reggae, 25, 204

Nature reserves, 150, 151, 170, 183
  Castle Islands Nature Reserve, 59
  Edmund Gibbons Nature Reserve, 144
  Gilbert Nature Reserve, 152, 167, 178
  Paget Marsh, 13, 150, 178
  Spittal Pond Nature Reserve, 13, 55, 143–44, 177, 183
Nea's Alley, 4, 156
Newspapers/magazines, 67

Ocean View Golf Course, 180–81, 183
Old Devonshire Parish Church, 10, 55, 143, 145
Old Rectory, 137–40, 155, 166
Old State House, 38, 135–36, 155, 164
Ordnance Island, 135, 164

Package tours, 52–53
Paget Marsh, 13, 150, 178
Paget Parish, 1, 10, 12, 56, 60, 130, 132, 133, 147, 173
  restaurants, 7, 112–14
  shopping, 99–100
  sights and attractions, 149–50

Palm Grove, 145
Parasailing, 182
Parishes, 11, 130
Parks and Gardens, 144, 145, 183
  Arboretum, 55, 144
  Astwood Park, 1, 156, 173
  Botanical Gardens, 10, 12, 39, 133, 149
  Fort Scaur Park, 177
  Lagoon Park, 170
  Par-la-Ville Park, 55, 147, 160
  Somerset Long Bay Park, 170
  Somers Garden, 4, 137, 164
  South Shore Park, 1, 2, 3
  Victoria Park, 55, 162
Par-la-Ville Park, 55, 147, 160
Passports, 30–31
Pembroke Parish, 10, 11, 14, 15, 55, 130, 144
  sights and attractions, 145–49
Perot, William Bennett, 4, 147, 160, 162
Perot Post Office, 147–48, 162
Pets, 67
Petticoat Lane, 4, 132, 134–35, 166
Photographic needs, 67
Police, 67
Port Royal Golf Course, 3, 179, 181, 183, 185
Post offices, 67

Queen's View, 4

Rainey, Joseph Hayne, 4, 135, 137, 166
Restaurants, 6–7, 26, 81, 101–29
  afternoon tea, 14, 26, 127, 133, 163
  brunch, 27, 127
  for children, 114
  fast food, 27, 56, 127–28
  Hamilton, 6, 7, 81, 101–12
  Hamilton Parish, 6, 7, 125–26
  Paget Parish, 7, 112–14
  picnic fare, 128–29
  pubs, 26, 132, 146, 206

St. David's Island, 7,
124–25
St. George's Parish,
121–25
Sandys Parish, 7, 118–20
Smith's Parish, 126
Southampton Parish, 6,
7, 115–18
tips on, 62
Warwick Parish, 114–15
Restrooms, 67
Riddell's Bay Golf Course, 4,
179
Royal Naval Dockyard, 5, 9,
39, 50, 54, 56, 58, 133,
151, 152, 156, 167, 168,
170, 189, 202
Rugby, 37–38, 39, 172

Safety, 68
Sailing, 3, 154, 172, 182–83.
See also Yachting
St. David's Island, 2, 5, 8, 11,
27, 56, 58, 130, 137
restaurants, 7, 124–25
St. David's Lighthouse, 4, 5,
56, 151, 168
St. George's Golf Club,
181–82, 183
St. George's Harbour, 8, 11,
16, 19, 49, 51, 164, 179
St. George's Historical
Society Museum, 137, 166
St. George's Island, 2, 5, 8,
11, 176
St. George's Parish, 11, 20,
21, 25, 38, 58, 130, 131,
141, 142, 156, 157, 178
restaurants, 121–25
shopping, 133, 200–201
sights and attractions,
134–40
St. George's Town, 4, 9, 11,
17, 26, 54, 55, 58, 130,
155, 132, 178, 189, 202
walking tour, 163–67
St. James' Anglican Church,
152
St. Mark's Church, 143
St. Peter's Church, 11, 17,
136, 137, 155, 166
St. Peter's graveyard, 136
St. Teresa's Cathedral, 162
Sandys Parish, 2, 4, 10, 25,
56, 130, 132, 147, 149,
151, 176, 177, 189
restaurants, 7, 118–20

sights and attractions,
151–52
walking tour, 167–70
Scuba diving. *See* Underwater
sports
Senior citizen travelers, tips
for, 44
Sessions House (Parliament
Building), 8, 149, 162
Sharples, Richard, 17, 20,
136, 146, 166
Shelly Bay Beach, 2, 141, 176
Shipwrecks, 2–3, 9, 10, 16,
18, 19, 131, 183, 186
Shopping, 54, 55, 180–201
antiques, 63, 189–90
art, 63, 154, 190,
199–200, 201
arts & crafts, 54, 63, 154,
190–92, 199
beachwear, 192
boutiques, 192–93, 201
casual wear, 193
china & glassware, 55,
193–94, 199
department stores, 194
duty-free, 189
fashions, 194–95
footwear, 195
gifts, 195, 200
Hamilton, 189–99
Hamilton Parish, 199
Ireland Island, 199
jewelry, 154, 195–96,
201
leather items, 196
linens, 196
liquors & liqueurs,
196–97
music, 197
needlepoint patterns, 197
Paget Parish, 199–200
perfumes, 63, 197–98
pottery, 63, 189, 199
St. George's Parish, 133,
200–201
silver, 63, 198
Somerset, 201
Southampton Parish, 201
sportswear, 198
stamps & coins, 198
sunglasses, 193
tips on, 62–63
woolen goods, 198–99
Sightseeing, 4–5, 9, 130–54
for children, 165
organized tours, 157–58

special-interest, 155–57
itineraries, 132–33
walking tours, 159–70
Silk Alley, 4, 134–35, 166
Single travelers, tips for,
44–45, 52, 53
Smith's Parish, 2, 11, 13,
130, 133, 141, 144, 155,
176, 177
restaurants, 126
sights and attractions, 9,
142–44
Snorkeling, 2, 3, 45, 154,
175, 183–84, 185, 186
Soccer, 172
Somers, George, 17, 26, 134,
137, 147, 151
Somers Garden, 4, 137,
164
Somerset Bridge, 4, 56, 58,
59, 131, 132, 133, 151,
167, 168, 178
Somerset Island, 4, 8, 10, 56,
132, 151, 167, 168
Somerset Long Bay, 2, 10,
132, 151, 176
Somerset Long Bay Park,
170
Somerset Parish, 4, 38, 130,
131, 151, 157, 172
Somerset Village, 10, 53, 54,
56, 59, 60, 132, 151, 168,
170, 189
shopping, 201
Southampton Parish, 2, 10,
56, 130, 173, 174, 175,
177
restaurants, 6, 7,
115–18
shopping, 201
sights and attractions,
150
Southampton Princess Golf
Club, 181, 183
South Shore Park, 1, 2, 3
Spanish Point, 4, 172, 187
Spa vacations, 40–41
Spelunking, 143. *See also*
Caves
Sports
recreational, 156, 173–76
spectator, 37–39, 171–73
underwater, 2–3, 45, 53,
131, 133, 154, 175,
183–87
Springfield Library, 152, 167
Swimming. *See* Beaches

Taxes, 68, 189
Taxis, 54, 57, 58, 130
Telephone numbers
  for disabled travelers, 44
  emergency, 65
  transit information, 69
  weather information, 69
Telegrams/Telexes/Faxes, 68
Telephones, 68
Temperatures, average
  monthly, 36
Tennis, 37, 39, 53, 130, 131,
  172, 184–85
Theaters, 202
Time, 69
Tipping, 69
Tobacco Bay, 134, 183
Tobacco Bay Beach, 2, 176
Tourist information, 29
Tours, organized, 157–58
  by boat, 147, 157–58
  for disabled travelers, 43
  for senior citizens, 44
  for singles, 45
Town Hall, 135, 164

Transportation
  from the airport, 54
  within Bermuda, 36,
    57–61
Traveler's checks, 33
Traveling
  for disabled travelers,
    43–44
Tucker, Edward, 153
Tucker House Museum, 21,
  137, 155, 166
Tucker's Town, 11, 54, 55,
  59, 179
Twain, Mark, 6, 11, 49, 145,
  146, 156, 160

Undersea Walk, 133, 154
Underwater Sports, 2–3, 45,
  53, 131, 133, 154, 175,
  183–87
Unfinished Cathedral, 4,
  137, 155, 164–65

Verdmont, 5, 9, 55, 133,
  143, 155

Victoria Park, 55, 162

Warwick Long Bay, 1, 2, 4,
  9, 10, 56, 174
Warwick Parish, 1, 2, 10, 56,
  60, 130, 132, 147, 149,
  150, 157, 173, 174, 177,
  178
  restaurants, 114–15
Waterskiing, 154, 187
Waterville, 149–50
Watford Island, 8, 56, 167
Weddings, 39–40, 53
White Horse Tavern, 164

Yachting, 38, 39, 130,
  172–73, 172. *See also*
  Sailing

Zoos and aquariums
  Bermuda Aquarium,
    Museum & Zoo, 55,
    133, 141–42, 154
  Devil's Hole Aquarium,
    142

Now Save Money on All Your Travels by Joining

Frommer's
T R A V E L   B O O K   C L U B

The Advantages of Membership:

1. Your choice of any **TWO FREE BOOKS.**

2. Your own subscription to the **TRIPS & TRAVEL** quarterly newsletter, where you'll discover the best buys in travel, the hottest vacation spots, the latest travel trends, world-class events and festivals, and much more.

3. A **30% DISCOUNT** on any additional books you order through the club.

4. **DOMESTIC TRIP-ROUTING KITS** (available for a small additional fee). We'll send you a detailed map highlighting the most direct or scenic route to your destination, anywhere in North America.

Here's all you have to do to join:

Send in your annual membership fee of $25.00 ($35.00 Canada/Foreign) with your name, address, and selections on the form below. Or call 815/734-1104 to use your credit card.

Send all orders to:

FROMMER'S TRAVEL BOOK CLUB
P.O. Box 473 • Mt. Morris, IL 61054-0473 • ☎ 815/734-1104

YES! I want to take advantage of this opportunity to join Frommer's Travel Book Club.

[ ] My check for $25.00 ($35.00 for Canadian or foreign orders) is enclosed.
   All orders must be prepaid in U.S. funds only. Please make checks payable to Frommer's Travel Book Club.

[ ] Please charge my credit card: [ ] Visa or [ ] Mastercard

   Credit card number: _____

   Expiration date: ___ / ___ / ___

   Signature: _____

   Or call 815/734-1104 to use your credit card by phone.

Name: _____

Address: _____

City: _____ State: _____ Zip code: _____

Phone number (in case we have a question regarding your order): _____

Please indicate your choices for TWO FREE books (*see following pages*):

   Book 1 - Code: _____ Title: _____

   Book 2 - Code: _____ Title: _____

For information on ordering additional titles, see your first issue of the *Trips & Travel* newsletter.

Allow 4–6 weeks for delivery for all items. Prices of books, membership fee, and publication dates are subject to change without notice. All orders are subject to acceptance and availability.

AC1

The following Frommer's guides are available from your favorite bookstore, or you can use the order form on the preceding page to request them as part of your membership in Frommer's Travel Book Club.

FROMMER'S COMPLETE TRAVEL GUIDES

(Comprehensive guides to sightseeing, dining and accommodations, with selections in all price ranges—from deluxe to budget)

Acapulco/Ixtapa/Taxco, 2nd Ed.	C157	Jamaica/Barbados, 2nd Ed.	C149
Alaska '94-'95	C131	Japan '94-'95	C144
Arizona '95	C166	Maui, 1st Ed.	C153
Australia '94-'95	C147	Nepal, 3rd Ed. (avail. 11/95)	C184
Austria, 6th Ed.	C162	New England '95	C165
Bahamas '96 (avail. 8/95)	C172	New Mexico, 3rd Ed.	C167
Belgium/Holland/Luxembourg,		New York State, 4th Ed.	C133
4th Ed.	C170	Northwest, 5th Ed.	C140
Bermuda '96 (avail. 8/95)	C174	Portugal '94-'95	C141
California '95	C164	Puerto Rico '95-'96	C151
Canada '94-'95	C145	Puerto Vallarta/Manzanillo/	
Caribbean '96 (avail. 9/95)	C173	Guadalajara, 2nd Ed.	C135
Carolinas/Georgia, 2nd Ed.	C128	Scandinavia, 16th Ed.	C169
Colorado '96 (avail. 11/95)	C179	Scotland '94-'95	C146
Costa Rica, 1st Ed.	C161	South Pacific '94-'95	C138
Cruises '95-'96	C150	Spain, 16th Ed.	C163
Delaware/Maryland '94-'95	C136	Switzerland, 7th Ed.	
England '96 (avail. 10/95)	C180	(avail. 9/95)	C177
Florida '96 (avail. 9/95)	C181	Thailand, 2nd Ed.	C154
France '96 (avail. 11/95)	C182	U.S.A., 4th Ed.	C156
Germany '96 (avail. 9/95)	C176	Virgin Islands, 3rd Ed.	
Honolulu/Waikiki/Oahu, 4th Ed.		(avail. 8/95)	C175
(avail. 10/95)	C178	Virginia '94-'95	C142
Ireland, 1st Ed.	C168	Yucatán '95-'96	C155
Italy '96 (avail. 11/95)	C183		

FROMMER'S $-A-DAY GUIDES

(Dream Vacations at Down-to-Earth Prices)

Australia on $45 '95-'96	D122	Ireland on $45 '94-'95	D118
Berlin from $50, 3rd Ed.		Israel on $45, 15th Ed.	D130
(avail. 10/95)	D137	London from $55 '96	
Caribbean from $60, 1st Ed.		(avail. 11/95)	D136
(avail. 9/95)	D133	Madrid on $50 '94-'95	D119
Costa Rica/Guatemala/Belize		Mexico from $35 '96	
on $35, 3rd Ed.	D126	(avail. 10/95)	D135
Eastern Europe on $30, 5th Ed.	D129	New York on $70 '94-'95	D121
England from $50 '96		New Zealand from $45, 6th Ed.	D132
(avail. 11/95)	D138	Paris on $45 '94-'95	D117
Europe from $50 '96		South America on $40, 16th Ed.	D123
(avail. 10/95)	D139	Washington, D.C. on $50	
Greece from $45, 6th Ed.	D131	'94-'95	D120
Hawaii from $60 '96 (avail. 9/95)	D134		

FROMMER'S COMPLETE CITY GUIDES

(Comprehensive guides to sightseeing, dining, and accommodations in all price ranges)

Amsterdam, 8th Ed.	S176	Minneapolis/St. Paul, 4th Ed.	S159
Athens, 10th Ed.	S174	Montréal/Québec City '95	S166
Atlanta & the Summer Olympic		Nashville/Memphis, 1st Ed.	S141
Games '96 (avail. 11/95)	S181	New Orleans '96 (avail. 10/95)	S182
Atlantic City/Cape May, 5th Ed.	S130	New York City '96 (avail. 11/95)	S183
Bangkok, 2nd Ed.	S147	Paris '96 (avail. 9/95)	S180
Barcelona '93–'94	S115	Philadelphia, 8th Ed.	S167
Berlin, 3rd Ed.	S162	Prague, 1st Ed.	S143
Boston '95	S160	Rome, 10th Ed.	S168
Budapest, 1st Ed.	S139	St. Louis/Kansas City, 2nd Ed.	S127
Chicago '95	S169	San Antonio/Austin, 1st Ed.	S177
Denver/Boulder/Colorado Springs,		San Diego '95	S158
3rd Ed.	S154	San Francisco '96 (avail. 10/95)	S184
Disney World/Orlando '96 (avail. 9/95)	S178	Santa Fe/Taos/Albuquerque '95	S172
Dublin, 2nd Ed.	S157	Seattle/Portland '94–'95	S137
Hong Kong '94–'95	S140	Sydney, 4th Ed.	S171
Las Vegas '95	S163	Tampa/St. Petersburg, 3rd Ed.	S146
London '96 (avail. 9/95)	S179	Tokyo '94–'95	S144
Los Angeles '95	S164	Toronto, 3rd Ed.	S173
Madrid/Costa del Sol, 2nd Ed.	S165	Vancouver/Victoria '94–'95	S142
Mexico City, 1st Ed.	S175	Washington, D.C. '95	S153
Miami '95–'96	S149		

FROMMER'S FAMILY GUIDES

(Guides to family-friendly hotels, restaurants, activities, and attractions)

California with Kids	F105	San Francisco with Kids	F104
Los Angeles with Kids	F103	Washington, D.C. with Kids	F102
New York City with Kids	F101		

FROMMER'S WALKING TOURS

(Memorable strolls through colorful and historic neighborhoods, accompanied by detailed directions and maps)

Berlin	W100	Paris, 2nd Ed.	W112
Chicago	W107	San Francisco, 2nd Ed.	W115
England's Favorite Cities	W108	Spain's Favorite Cities (avail. 9/95)	W116
London, 2nd Ed.	W111	Tokyo	W109
Montréal/Québec City	W106	Venice	W110
New York, 2nd Ed.	W113	Washington, D.C., 2nd Ed.	W114

FROMMER'S AMERICA ON WHEELS

(Guides for travelers who are exploring the U.S.A. by car, featuring a brand-new rating system for accommodations and full-color road maps)

Arizona/New Mexico	A100	Florida	A102
California/Nevada	A101	Mid-Atlantic	A103

FROMMER'S SPECIAL-INTEREST TITLES

Arthur Frommer's Branson!	P107	Frommer's Where to Stay U.S.A.,	
Arthur Frommer's New World		11th Ed.	P102
of Travel (avail. 11/95)	P112	National Park Guide, 29th Ed.	P106
Frommer's Caribbean Hideaways		USA Today Golf Tournament Guide	P113
(avail. 9/95)	P110	USA Today Minor League	
Frommer's America's 100 Best-Loved		Baseball Book	P111
State Parks	P109		

FROMMER'S BEST BEACH VACATIONS
(The top places to sun, stroll, shop, stay, play, party, and swim—with each beach rated for beauty, swimming, sand, and amenities)

California (avail. 10/95)	G100	Hawaii (avail. 10/95)	G102
Florida (avail. 10/95)	G101		

FROMMER'S BED & BREAKFAST GUIDES
(Selective guides with four-color photos and full descriptions of the best inns in each region)

California	B100	Hawaii	B105
Caribbean	B101	Pacific Northwest	B106
East Coast	B102	Rockies	B107
Eastern United States	B103	Southwest	B108
Great American Cities	B104		

FROMMER'S IRREVERENT GUIDES
(Wickedly honest guides for sophisticated travelers and those who want to be)

Chicago (avail. 11/95)	I100	New Orleans (avail. 11/95)	I103
London (avail. 11/95)	I101	San Francisco (avail. 11/95)	I104
Manhattan (avail. 11/95)	I102	Virgin Islands (avail. 11/95)	I105

FROMMER'S DRIVING TOURS
(Four-color photos and detailed maps outlining spectacular scenic driving routes)

Australia	Y100	Italy	Y108
Austria	Y101	Mexico	Y109
Britain	Y102	Scandinavia	Y110
Canada	Y103	Scotland	Y111
Florida	Y104	Spain	Y112
France	Y105	Switzerland	Y113
Germany	Y106	U.S.A.	Y114
Ireland	Y107		

FROMMER'S BORN TO SHOP
(The ultimate travel guides for discriminating shoppers—from cut-rate to couture)

Hong Kong (avail. 11/95)	Z100	London (avail. 11/95)	Z101